TEACHING
ECONOMICS
& BUSINESS

EDITED BY
STEVE HODKINSON
& MARTIN JEPHCOTE

EBEA

Economics & Business
Education Association

ACC NO : 029955-3
TITLE : TEACHING
BUSINESS

DDC(1) : 330.0T

D0519532

Heinemann Educational Publishers
Halley Court, Jordan Hill, Oxford OX2 8EJ
a division of Reed Education & Professional Publishing Ltd

MELBOURNE AUCKLAND FLORENCE
PRAGUE MADRID ATHENS SINGAPORE
TOKYO SAO PAULO CHICAGO
PORTSMOUTH NH MEXICO IBADAN GABORONE
JOHANNESBURG KAMPALA NAIROBI

Southampton City College Library

Bookseller: B M B C

Requisition No: B k 0 1 2 0

Class No: 330 . 0 7

Date: 10 . 7 . 96

Accession No: 2 9 9 5 5

© Steve Hodkinson and Martin Jephcote, 1996

First published 1996

99 98 97 96
10 9 8 7 6 5 4 3 2 1

British Library Cataloguing in Publication Data
A catalogue record for this book is available from the British Library

ISBN 0 435 33098 5

Designed by Aricot Vert Design
Typeset by Books Unlimited (Nottm) NG19 7QZ
Printed and bound in Great Britain by Clays Ltd, St Ives plc

Acknowledgements
The publisher would like to thank the following for permission to reproduce
copyright material:
Adamantine Press, London for the figure from *Paradigms in Progress* (© Hazel
Henderson 1991) by Hazel Henderson on p. 267; Butterworth-Heinemann for the
figure on p. 346; Further Education Funding Council for the figures on p. 363 and p.
362; HMSO for the figures on pp. 86-8, 180 and 358 and the data in page 94. Crown
copyright reproduced with the permission of the Controller of HMSO; Institute for
Fiscal Studies for the table on p. 91 and the information on pp. 94-5; Leeds
Development Education Council for the figures on pp. 252, 257 and 259; Monopolies
and Mergers Commission for the report on Carlsberg and Allied-Lyons on pp. 86-8;
National Advisory Council for Education and Training for the figure from *National
Targets from Education and Training*: 'Developing Skills for a Successful Future' on
p. 33; National Association of Advisors and Inspectors of Business and Economics
Education for the figure from *Inspection of Business Studies and Economics in
Schools* on p. 366; National Council For Vocational Qualifications for the figure on p.
32; Northern Ireland Curriculum Council for the adapted worksheet on pp. 164-8;
Nuffield Foundation for the figures from *Nuffield Economics and Business Project*:
Student Book & Teachers' Resources on pp. 144 and 146; Office for Standards in
Education for the figure on p. 358; Oxford University Press for Worksheet A,
reproduced with permission from *Business Studies* by David Butler (1989) on p. 166;
Pizza Hut for the logo on p. 336; Routledge, London for the figure from *LOGO
Mathematics in the Classroom* by Hoyles, C. and Sutherland, R. (1989) on p. 187;
The Guardian on pp. 85-6, 92 and 93; ©Times Newspapers Limited for the articles
on pp. 89-90 and 105; *Wales on Sunday*, Western Mail & Echo Ltd., Cardiff for their
kind permission to reproduce the figure on p. 102; Whitbread for the logo on p. 336.

The publisher have made every effort to trace copyright holders. However, if any
material has been incorrectly acknowledged, we would be pleased to correct this at
the earliest opportunity.

Contents

Contributors

Editors

Steve Hodkinson – Professor of Teacher Education, School of Education, Brunel University. Steve Hodkinson has been actively involved in the promotion and development of economics and business education, as Assistant and Deputy Director to the 'Economics 14–16' Project (1980–4), manager of the 'Economic Awareness Teacher Training' (EcATT) programme at the University of Manchester (1986–95) and as Chair of the Economics Association/EBEA (1989–92).

Martin Jephcote – Lecturer in Education, School of Education, University of Wales Cardiff. Martin Jephcote was a member of the EcATT team at the University of London, Institute of Education (1987–90) and Project Officer for the 'Economic Awareness as a Curriculum Entitlement in Wales' project, at the Department of Education, University College of Swansea, 1990–3. He is an active supporter of the Economics Association/EBEA and was Chair of Publishing and Marketing (1990–3).

List of contributors

Alison Atkinson: Senior Lecturer in Education, School of Education, University of Brighton

Stephen Barnes: Co-Director of Nuffield Economics and Business Project, University of Sussex

Keith Brumfitt: Co-ordinator of Secondary Education, School of Education, University of Brighton

Ian Chambers: Adviser, Business and Careers Education, Tameside Local Education Authority

Paul Clarke: Senior Lecturer in Education, Worcester College of Higher Education

Peter Davies: Senior Lecturer in Economics, Staffordshire University

Neil Denby: Head of Economics and Business, Economic Awareness Co-ordinator, Fartown High School, Huddersfield

Dave Dickson: Senior Lecturer, Faculty of Education, University of the West of England, Bristol

Richard Dunnill: Senior Lecturer in Education, Canterbury Christ Church College

Alan Hamlin: Reader in Economics, University of Southampton

Alma Harris: Staff Tutor in Education, Open University

Sue Hatt: Senior Lecturer in Economics, University of the West of England, Bristol

Nick Heard: Principal Officer, Northern Ireland Council for the Curriculum, Examinations and Assessment (CCEA)

Kieron James: Head of Economics and Business at a comprehensive school in the north east of England

Denis Lawton: Professor of Education, University of London, Institute of Education

Chris Leonard: Education Adviser, Dorset Education Business Partnership

David Lines: Co-Director of Nuffield Economics and Business Project, University of London, Institute of Education

Martyn Lucas: A course coordinator for GNVQ at a comprehensive school in the north west of England

Susannah Nakarada: Assistant Head of Careers at a comprehensive school in the west of England

Colin Parsons: Education Consultant, Surrey County Council, OfSTED Registered Inspector of Schools

Susan Squires: General Adviser, Economics and Business Education, Sefton Local Education Authority

Heather Stretch: Careers and Compact Co-ordinator, Gwendraeth Valley Comprehensive School, Drefach, Lannelli, Dyfed

Linda Thomas: Professor of Education, School of Education, Brunel University

Jenny Wales: Co-Director of Nuffield Economics and Business Project, University of London, Institute of Education

Nancy Wall: Co-Director of Nuffield Economics and Business Project, and Research Fellow, University of Sussex

Ken Webster: Consultant, Economics and Environmental Education

Nigel West: Leeds Development Education Centre

Keith Wood: Lecturer in Education, University of London, Institute of Education

Preface

Teaching Economics and Business is an expression of the wider responsibility of the EBEA as a subject Association and builds on *Teaching Economics*. It is a new book with a new approach, comprising four parts, each introduced by the Editors with the intentions of providing an overall context and raising some important questions which the reader may wish to consider. It is a compilation and does not attempt to capture all recent developments or to give those included equal emphasis. It represents what people working in the field saw as important to report. Overall, the book conveys the sense of change witnessed over the last ten years and records the responses made by the professional community of economics and business educators. In five or ten years' time it will be interesting to look back and assess the impact of these changes. No doubt there will be other interesting challenges ahead. The four parts are:

- *Economics and business in a changing curriculum.* This part places economics and business education in the broader social, economic and political contexts which influence and determine curricula.

- *Teaching and learning.* This part begins by considering the changing nature of economics and business education at A level and introduces a number of other issues which impact on the teaching and learning process, including gender issues, differentiation, information technology and assessing diverse evidence.

- *The whole curriculum.* This part gives recognition to the work that has been achieved in trying to establish economics education as a curriculum entitlement for all.

- *Teacher development.* This part looks at supporting teachers throughout their careers, from the early days of a beginning teacher through to the role of a team leader. The final chapter provides some insight into the inspection process and suggests how economics and business teachers might prepare themselves.

Acknowledgements

We are grateful to all contributors who have given so generously of their time and who openly share their experience and knowledge.

We acknowledge and appreciate the role of Sue Walton and her colleagues at Heinemann Educational for their continuing commitment to economics and business education and to the work of the EBEA.

We are grateful, too, for the help provided by the following in advising on the content of the book: Susan Squires, Brian Atkinson, Geoff Hale, Linda Thomas, Keith Wood, Keith Brumfitt and Jenny Wales, and to Robert Wilson who compiled the index.

Steve Hodkinson
Martin Jephcote

PART 1

ECONOMICS AND BUSINESS
IN A CHANGING CURRICULUM

1 A changing curriculum: discussion

Steve Hodkinson and Martin Jephcote

The introductory chapters in previous editions of *Teaching Economics* (Lee, 1967, 1975; Atkinson, 1985) were characterized by attention to epistemological and psychological bases for the teaching of economics. The first section in this book represents a departure from that tradition, a departure largely prompted by two developments of the 1980s and 1990s.

First, as teachers we all find ourselves seeking to handle the implications of working in an education system in which control over the purpose and content of what we teach in schools and colleges has been increasingly taken out of the hands of the professional community of educators and into the political arena of parliament, government departments of education, training and employment and government appointed agencies. Purpose and content are increasingly centrally rather than locally determined and teachers responsive agents rather than professional initiators.

Second, as teachers we have been drawn not only into the search for a direct causal link between education (and training) and the relative failures of the economy in past decades, but also into the search for a national solution through education and training to the demands imposed by the need to create a modern internationally competitive economy.

Denis Lawton and Martin Jephcote (Chapters 2 and 3) take us to the heart of these two issues, providing the context through which the specific economics and business education contribution of Colin Parsons (Chapter 4) can be understood and interpreted, and the backcloth to our own decisions as curriculum managers in schools and colleges.

Denis Lawton uses the example of the emergence of a National Curriculum for schools in England to question the principles which underpin that curriculum. He provides a critique of its outcomes to date in a range of areas including economics/business and social science. However, despite his powerful rationale to justify an education in economy (of which business is part) for all young people, he is less than optimistic that this can be obtained through a curriculum in which the mode of delivery (subjects) is only passingly related to its supposed aims (Lawton, p. 8) and in which pressures to 'slim it down' lead to the delineation of those subjects outside of the social, political and economic contexts in which they are to be found.

Martin Jephcote broadens the scope of the discussion to include that of the

3

'needs of the economy'. He rehearses international evidence and theories which link relative failure in education and economy. This is not a new issue for teachers of economics and business. It was present at the outset of the Economics Association's move in the early 1970s to establish economics education in the 14–16 curriculum and which led to the Economics Education 14–16 Project (Parsons, p. 42). It may also be that the recent decline in numbers of students opting for A level economics (Parsons, p. 43) and specialist university economics courses is partly related to a perception that the current teaching of economics is insufficiently related to students' need to understand their relationship with the demands of the economic system. The search for a response to this perception partly led to the establishment of the Economics 16–19 Project in the early 1990s (Parsons, p. 53) and the development of new courses (Wall *et al.*, Chapter 10; Linda Thomas, Chapter 6; Dave Dickson, Chapter 8). Time will tell as to whether the current upsurge in the study of business by students of all ages (Parsons, p. 43–4) will experience a similar reversal of fortune.

Martin Jephcote's contribution also provides the necessary backcloth to and critique of movements and events that are seeing a rapid change in the skills requirements of teachers of economics and business as they find themselves at the sharp end of developments in competence-based vocational qualifications. This is introduced briefly by Colin Parsons in Chapter 4 and some of its implications for 16–19 education and teacher education are developed in later sections of the book (Thomas, Chapter 6; Atkinson, Chapter 14; Wood, Chapter 22; Brumfitt, Chapter 23). The chapters in this first section raise genuine dilemmas for teachers of economics and business and for their students who must make life choices and learn in a context of rapid change. Resolving such decisions involves taking a stance in response to at least three questions:

- What principles should underpin our curriculum in economics and business education and who should determine them?

- Is a competence based approach compatible with the development of the critical awareness and understanding of economics and business we have long sought to achieve?

- What is our responsibility to the education of all students as opposed to those who choose to opt for our subjects?

Whilst the chapters themselves can do little more than encourage critical reflection of such questions, our responses as teachers and members of a subject association will have an important impact on educational output in the years to come. The rapid development of business GNVQ, the almost certain equally rapid development of business as part of the new Key Stage 4 vocational initiative, and the current joint status of economics and business as major optional subjects at GCSE and A level, place teachers of economics and business studies in an almost unique position. Our role in advising head teachers and college principals on the elements that should comprise a coherent economics and business curriculum, and in advising students on their choice of routes (A level or GNVQ, or A level and GNVQ) and on choice of subject (economics or business, or economics and business, or other subjects), will help to shape entry into higher education and into employment. That such decisions will have major long-term implications was brought forcibly to our attention recently, for example, when a civil servant in the Department for Education and Employment (DFEE) asked of us: 'If we fail to persuade students to opt for A level economics where will the next generation of economists come from?'

References

Atkinson, G.B.J. (1985). *Teaching Economics*, 3rd edn, Oxford, Heinemann Educational.

Lee, N. (ed.) (1967). *Teaching Economics*, Oxford, Economics Association.

Lee, N. (ed.) (1975). *Teaching Economics*, 2nd edn, Oxford, Heinemann Educational.

2 The changing context: the National Curriculum

Denis Lawton

Introduction

I am not an economist, nor a teacher of economics. But I feel strongly about the place of economics and business in the school curriculum – or rather about the place that economics ought to have in the education of *all* young people.

My special field in education is curriculum studies, which includes theories about curriculum planning and design as well as studies of the politics and control of the curriculum. For the past twenty years or so there has been plenty to write about. Sometimes I find it useful to divide my subject into three levels: first, keeping a more or less straightforward 'surface' narrative of curricular events; second, trying to explain those events in terms of 'deeper' structural, social and ideological pressures; and third, discussing changes in education and curriculum theory both as a cause of some events and as the result of others. In this chapter I want to start by discussing some aspects of curriculum theory, then move on to the most important curriculum event in recent years, the 1988 National Curriculum, and finally to suggest possible future developments.

Curriculum theories

Let me start with a little curriculum theory. When the National Curriculum was introduced in 1988 it was criticized for a number of reasons. Some curriculum theorists tended to focus on the lack of explanations for its design: Kenneth Baker's National Curriculum was simply a list of subjects unsupported by any theory – only common sense. It was also pointed out that the list of subjects was almost identical to the subjects demanded in the 1904 Secondary Regulations. That would not have mattered had there been some justification for such a list – then or now. Others complained that a list of subjects (whether justified or not) was – in 1988 – a strange way of designing a curriculum. That particular attack was based on two curriculum ideas. The first was that subjects *may* be a useful way of 'delivering' the curriculum, but a stage in the curriculum design process had been missed out. Before deciding on a list of subjects, a plan should have specified more general aims or purposes. The second criticism was that a list-of-subjects approach will tend to leave out many areas which any serious analysis would show to be important – one of those areas would certainly be economics.

Perhaps there was a list of general aims or purposes in the background to the 1988 curriculum. A list of aims had been contained in the DES publication *Better Schools* (1985), and had occasionally been used as part of the rhetoric to explain the need for a national curriculum. The guiding statement (revived in the Education [Schools] Act 1992) was that schools should be responsible for the intellectual, cultural, social, moral and spiritual development of pupils; it was supported by a set of general principles or aims:

- to help pupils develop lively, enquiring minds and the ability to question and argue rationally – and to apply themselves to tasks and physical skills;

- to help pupils acquire understanding, knowledge and skills relevant to adult life, and employment in a fast-changing world;

- to help pupils use language and number effectively;

- to help pupils develop personal moral values, respect for religious values, and tolerance – of other races, religions and ways of life;

- to help pupils understand the world in which they live, and the interdependence of individuals, groups and nations;

- to help pupils to appreciate human achievement and aspirations.

Although John White and colleagues (1981) had been critical, from a philosophical view, of an earlier version of the *Better Schools* principles, the real curriculum problem was that it was impossible to find any justification of the ten subjects in terms of those principles (or any reason for omitting other subjects). The problem is not so much with that list of principles as with the fact that no attempt had been made to relate those general aims to the list of subjects prescribed for the National Curriculum, or to justify the chosen subjects in terms of the guiding principles.

Cultural analysis

There are many possible ways of designing and justifying a curriculum, whether it is a national curriculum or a school-based plan. I will not review all the possibilities here, but will concentrate on one which will at least serve the purpose of indicating why the National Curriculum list of ten foundation subjects simply will not do. It will also emerge from the discussion why any sensible curriculum plan in the 1980s (and 1990s) should have included economics.

I want to begin by defining curriculum as 'a selection from the culture of a society'. The definition is, for most people, uncontroversial (although there is a problem if you refuse to accept the existence of 'society'!). The definition should be uncontroversial provided that 'culture' is used in the sociological/anthropological sense of 'the sum total of the knowledge, attitudes and habitual behaviour patterns shared and transmitted by the members of a particular society' (Linton, 1940).

All societies have the problem of passing on their way of life to the next generation. In simple societies culture is transmitted by members of the family or by means of other 'face to face' relations. In complex societies, the division of labour and the extent of social mobility make it impossible for everything to be transmitted informally, and the task is partly entrusted to schools. The task of education is to make available to the next generation what we regard as the most worthwhile aspects of our culture. Schools have limited time and resources, so the curriculum has to be planned to ensure that the best selection from culture is made.

It is at this stage that controversy may begin. Whilst the definition of curriculum as selection from culture is uncontroversial (what else could it be?), the process of selection is likely to give rise to some argument. Those responsible for making the selection have a duty to demonstrate that it is neither arbitrary nor idiosyncratic – it should be open to rational enquiry and justification. A curriculum cannot be value-free, but those designing a curriculum should be able to explain why certain aspects of culture are given priority over others – for example, why poetry rather than bingo. One way is to develop a process and set of principles based on traditional cultural heritage – 'cultural analysis'. But it is important to avoid such a traditional approach being merely backward-looking and static.

The process of cultural analysis involves four kinds of questions:

- What kind of society already exists?

- In what ways is the society developing?

- How do its members appear to want it to develop?

- What kinds of values and principles will be involved in deciding on this 'development', as well as on the educational means of achieving it?

To facilitate this kind of analysis three kinds of classification are needed: first, deciding on the major parameters – the cultural invariants or human universals; second, outlining a method of analysis moving from cultural invariants to cultural variables; third, a means of classifying the educationally desirable knowledge and experiences.

Cultural invariants/human universals

Some way of subdividing culture is necessary because there is no self-evident classification which would be superior to all others. Bruner (1965) anticipated similar questions when he began writing about curriculum. He asked (1971): 'What is human about human beings? How did they get that way? How can they be made more so?' His answer, in the context of 'Man – A Course of Study', was a set of five *humanizing forces* which should be central to the curriculum: tool-making; language; social organization; prolonged childhood; the urge to explain. This has some similarity with the list I shall propose, except that from an anthropological point of view Bruner's five headings are too limited, unless 'social organization' is stretched to include almost everything.

In terms of the task in hand, we need a list that is short enough to be manageable, but long enough to facilitate important distinctions. I have elsewhere (Lawton, 1989) suggested using the language of conventional anthropological studies and dividing human universals into the following nine categories:

- a socio-political system
- a communication system
- a rationality system
- a technology system
- a morality system
- a belief system
- an aesthetic system
- a maturation system
- an economic system

I suggest that all societies possess all nine of those systems – in other words they are human universals or cultural invariants. But the expression and organization of the universals varies enormously from one culture to another, and over time within some cultures.

From human universals to cultural variants: from culture to curriculum

For each of the nine systems I shall begin, first, by defining or describing the human universal; second, relating that cultural feature to England at this time; third, the educational and cultural problems or issues associated with that system will be briefly mentioned; and finally I will comment, where appropriate, on the 1988 or 1995 versions of the National Curriculum.

In the course of this discussion, certain values will become clear: democratic values, particularly concerned with developing a curriculum for all, with as much equality of access as can be achieved in an unequal society; educational values which accept that complete equality of achievement is neither possible nor desirable and that some kinds of differentiation are necessary within a curriculum – a common curriculum is not a uniform curriculum; and values relating to the quality of life which will give priority to certain kinds of knowledge and experiences. Some of those values may be open to challenge.

The socio-political system

All societies have some kind of social structure – a system of defining relationships within a society. Kinship, status, role, duty and obligation are the key concepts. In some societies the social structure is simple, stable and taken for granted; in others it is complex, changing and open to question. The socio-political system tends to be closely related to economic and technological factors: when western European societies were largely agricultural, the dominant political factor was possession of land; but as trade and industry developed, land ownership became less important than the ownership of the means of production.

10

It is difficult to summarize the English social and political system. We can say that England is a densely populated, urban industrial society in which social class is still a dominant factor influencing education and other life chances. It is not a pure system of social class because there are such feudal vestiges as the House of Lords, the monarchy and other titles which are still influential and distort the class structure in a variety of ways. Whole books have been written on aspects of this subject: for example, David Marquand (1988), *The Unprincipled Society*, or Anthony Sampson (1992), *The Essential Anatomy of Britain: Democracy in Crisis*. Such books tend to stress the fact that although we have survived the loss of Empire, we face other kinds of constitutional and social crises.

In modern societies the young grow up in a social world that they do not understand and are given little help to make them less confused. A good curriculum would equip the young with an understanding of such concepts as 'social class', 'social structure', 'social mobility'; it would also equip the young with an understanding of our complex political system. This would not simply include knowledge about government institutions, but an understanding of the values and the value conflicts inherent in our system. At the moment many young people leave school completely ignorant of the political structure and with a very hazy notion of their own social system.

In England there has been a long debate about 'education for citizenship' and whether young people acquire social and political understanding more effectively by direct or indirect methods – by traditional history and geography or by specific programmes. This major problem remains unsolved in the National Curriculum, despite the efforts of the National Curriculum Council (NCC) (see below).

The communication system

One of the most significant differences between humans and other animals is the ability to communicate. Communication is by no means absent in other animals, but even the most sophisticated animal systems are crude compared with human communication – especially the ability to communicate by means of language. In those societies where language is entirely spoken, children can learn to develop the communication skills they need informally, simply by interaction with parents and others. In pre-literate societies age, experience and 'memory' are more valued. Communication consists of more than language: signs, symbols and signalling systems have to be learned by each generation.

In societies like England where written language has developed, two important changes occur. First, writing has to be consciously acquired, probably in school; second, those who acquire writing have an advantage over the 'illiterate'. The invention of print intensifies such differences: printed texts make specialized knowledge available, but only for the educated.

In England language has always been recognized as an important part of the school curriculum, but there have been constant disputes about exactly what should be taught and what teaching methods should be used. Reports from Newbolt (1921) to Kingman (DES, 1988) and Cox (1991) have all discussed the teaching of English. Oral language has often been neglected, and many schools have not yet developed an adequate policy for language across the curriculum. The teaching of specialist forms of English such as the language of science and the language of social science have yet to receive the attention they deserve. Similarly, many schools lack programmes dealing with non-linguistic communication.

The national curriculum debate about English included arguments about traditional English and also about whether film and television studies should be included: in the latest version (January 1995) of National Curriculum English, teachers are encouraged to expose pupils to a wide range of media – of 'high quality'. But the debate is by no means over: many teachers of English are dissatisfied with some aspects of the curriculum, and still regard the assessment procedures as invalid.

The rationality system

All societies are rational in the sense of having rules about what is reasonable and what is acceptable as an explanation. The kinds of explanation will differ from time to time and from place to place: in sixteenth century Europe it was still regarded as rational to explain some events in terms of witchcraft; in some societies it still is. Levi-Strauss (1966) classified societies as 'hot' societies characterized by scientific thinking and 'cold' (primitive) societies which are 'time-suppressing' and rely on myth rather than science and history to explain their world.

England was an early example of a society which developed the 'hot', scientific version of rationality: it was associated with the Protestant Reformation in the sixteenth and seventeenth centuries questioning traditional authority and attempting to explain the universe scientifically. Newtonian science provided rules to explain the physical universe; the economics of Adam Smith, and the utilitarian philosophy of Bentham and Mill attempted similar explanations of human behaviour.

In England scientific knowledge and rationality have become dominant but not total. The school curriculum includes science but many children learn the subject without understanding scientific method and reasoning. And pupils are rarely taught to distinguish scientific reasoning from other ways of thinking in poetry, for example, or even in the social sciences. There is a danger that the dominant form of rationality is seen as the only form of rationality. Critics have alleged that some economists have mistakenly tried to take over the methods of the physical sciences rather than concentrate on the essential human qualities of *homo economicus.*

The National Curriculum gives priority to science by including it as a core subject and by encouraging 'double science' in the secondary curriculum; but not all problems have been solved – there is a shortage of good science teachers; science is seen by many as a boring subject and the link with technology is unclear. Rational understanding of the methods of social sciences is often absent: greater efforts are made to develop understanding of the physical world than the social, political or economic.

The technology system

Many writers (including Bruner) have referred to human beings as tool-using and tool-making animals. Recent studies of chimpanzees and other primates show that they too use and make tools of a simple kind, but hardly on a scale deserving the word 'technology'. The process of learning to use tools is always an important feature of human cultures. The system of technology will range from the simple, where every member of society can master the whole of the technology, to the very complex where no one individual can understand all of it. Specialization is an economic advantage but aggravates the problem of differential access to knowledge. Society may become divided into those who master computerized information retrieval and those who lack the skills even to find out.

In England, despite being in the forefront of the industrial revolution, there are particular cultural features which have caused technology to receive low priority – the 'gentleman ideal' which has devalued practical knowledge. This feature of English culture has been discussed in detail by Barnett (1986) and Weiner (1981).

One of the problems facing curriculum planners is deciding what *all* young people need to know, and what can be left for more specialist studies. In the past the English education service has not produced sufficient numbers of workers with middle-range technical skills; it has also produced an elite of managers and bureaucrats whose understanding of technology is limited. Various attempts have been made to achieve a better balance for all levels of ability: for example, the Technical and Vocational Education Initiative (TVEI) which, with some success, channelled millions of pounds from the Department of Employment into schools and colleges. TVEI funded teacher involvement in curriculum development and emphasized new subject areas (such as business studies and information technology). Unfortunately, the National Curriculum was framed quite differently – as we shall see below.

The National Curriculum technology has been extremely difficult to get right, and will probably have to change again soon. At the same time the government has created the National Council for Vocational Qualifications (NCVQ) responsible for coordinating standards for National Vocational Qualifications (NVQ); and in 1992 an attempt to bridge the gap between academic and vocational studies was made in the form of General National Vocational Qualifications (GNVQ). In December 1993, Dearing proposed vocational and occupational options for the 14–16 age group whilst making some other 'entitlement' subjects optional (see below). It is easy to point to this aspect of culture as an example of cultural lag and curriculum inertia; it is more difficult to put it right, but more careful cultural analysis would help.

The morality system

Human beings are naturally moral, in the sense that all societies have some code of behaviour and make distinctions between right and wrong. What is regarded as appropriate in one society may be different from the rules operating in another place or time. In some societies the moral code is unitary and taken for granted; in others, there is value pluralism and the problem of transmitting morality to the young becomes more difficult.

England is now an example of moral pluralism with a largely secular morality. Since the Reformation the idea of a single moral system has been weakened: Christianity split into a number of denominations and sects, and the notion of religious and moral authority was questioned. By the late nineteenth century a mixture of utilitarian and Christian principles provided a basis for moral thinking, but the two were sometimes contradictory. In the twentieth century, especially after the Second World War, immigration from non-Christian societies added to the pluralism. It is now difficult to regard England as a Christian society despite the continued requirement of compulsory religious education and a corporate act of worship in all maintained schools.

The absence of teaching about the moral system is a serious gap in many schools. Dearden (1968) recommended that schools should teach elementary ethics and the development of moral autonomy. Some schools use programmes based on Button (1981,1982) or adaptations of *Lifeline* materials (McPhail *et al.*, 1972). But the problem is often ignored.

This issue was generally played down in discussions of the National Curriculum. One Secretary of State, John Patten, showed real concern about the problem, but tended to preach at teachers rather than try to solve a curriculum problem. He antagonized teachers and failed to make a significant contribution. The National Curriculum Council (NCC) did produce a discussion document, *Spiritual and Moral Development* (April 1993), which I will discuss briefly since it does have some relevance to economics and business. It is a very brief paper – only ten pages – but even so it manages to confuse the issues. This is partly because questions of spiritual development and moral development are combined when it would have been better to keep them separate. (In my terms, the moral system should be distinguished from the belief system.) Schools were exhorted to develop a policy on moral and spiritual development (and urged not to try to assess them!). Unfortunately too much seemed to be expected of compulsory religious education and a corporate act of worship. Much more work on this topic is needed, not least to cope with various minority groups.

The belief system

Every society has a dominant belief system. In some it will be religious,

14

perhaps based on divine revelation. In others, beliefs may be derived from creation myths. In the West, religious beliefs have tended to become weaker, but have not disappeared. Societies are referred to as 'secularized', where 'man is the measure of all things' and scientific explanations occupy a dominant position. There are close connections between the belief system, the morality system and the rationality system.

One of the problems for England is that there is a lack of consensus about the belief system. Some studies have shown that there is an underlying set of beliefs which are shared by the majority of the population – a complex mixture of religious, political (democratic) and scientific beliefs and values – but there is also a good deal of confusion, especially among the young.

In a secular society it is still important that someone should have responsibility for mapping out the conceptual territory and related experiences desirable for transmitting a belief system. Durkheim long ago pointed out the problem of a society unsure of its own belief system – *anomie*; he feared that the lack of 'social solidarity' might destroy modern western societies.

This is another problem unsolved by the National Curriculum – although an attempt was made (see below) to include personal and social skills as cross-curricular elements. But what is lacking is not just 'skills' but much more fundamental understanding of the basic values that hold society together. The problem will not be solved by enforcing rules about corporate worship nor by improving religious education syllabuses.

The aesthetic system

All human beings have aesthetic drives and needs. Every society produces some kind of art, even those close to subsistence level. If a society makes cooking pots they will probably decorate them, and criteria of excellence will develop: some decorations will be judged to be superior to others.

Perhaps the best insight into the English aesthetic system is contained in *The Englishness of English Art* (1964) by Nikolaus Pevsner. In our history art was originally closely connected with religion, and when it was separated art was cut off from the everyday life of the majority. A number of problems emerge for a society when this happens, especially where the value system is pluralistic. At a time of rapid social and technological change criteria of excellence become blurred. Problems of the aesthetic system are related to other problems and contradictions within the social structure.

There are a number of problems in England: the separation of 'art' from 'popular art', the difficulty in a plural and rapidly changing society of defining what counts as art, and the standards of various art forms. Other countries, including France, have made more successful efforts to include aspects of 'cultural heritage' in the curriculum, but many teachers in England seem uneasy about that approach. The Gulbenkian Report (1982), *The Arts in Schools*, contains a useful review of some of the problems.

The National Curriculum discussion of art and music made some progress, but the post-Dearing version (DFE, 1995) makes both subjects, as well as history and geography, completely optional after age 14. This is a pity because in National Curriculum art and music pupils are introduced to aesthetic principles and invited to make comparisons between western and non-western cultures. It is surely a mistake to abandon these aspects of an entitlement curriculum at age 14. This is one of several unresolved value conflicts.

The maturation system

Bruner specified our long childhood as one of the 'humanizing forces'. Every society has a set of customs and conventions concerned with growing up. Anthropologists have written extensively on the variety of child-rearing practices which exist. Growth, maturity and ageing are treated differently in various societies, but there are always important customs to be observed. In some developed industrial societies, the problems of transition may be great, partly because there are no clear stages and no clear rules to be applied. With the growth of industrialization and urbanization, state agencies, including schools, have taken over some of the functions of the family.

In England there is a lack of consensus about appropriate standards of behaviour either for very young children or for adolescents: many adults appear to believe that the pendulum has swung too far in the direction of 'permissiveness' and have called for a return to traditional customs and 'Victorian' values (Anderson, 1988).

It is part of the function of education to sort out as much of the confusion as possible and to develop 'healthy' maturation. It can no longer be assumed that boys and girls will learn about child-rearing within their own families, and it has been suggested that child-rearing should be incorporated into the school curriculum – for boys as well as girls.

The opportunity of putting right this deficiency by the National Curriculum was missed: health education and sex education are also very inadequately dealt with.

The economic system

Every society has some means of dealing with the problem of scarce resources, their distribution and exchange, ranging from the very simple to the extremely complex.

Most adults in England have only a very hazy idea about their own economic system and how it works. Many attempts have been made to characterize this aspect of England in the 1990s: for example, the paper by Finegold and Soskice (1988) showing the danger of England being trapped in a low-cost, low-skill equilibrium; or more generally, Will Hutton (1995), *The State We're In*; and Hampden-Turner and Trompenaars (1994), *The Seven Cultures of Capitalism*.

The major educational problem is to define what all young people need to know about their economic system, and then to find time to make this knowledge available to all pupils, in a way that avoids accusations of distortion, bias and even indoctrination. This is difficult because what needs to be learned includes questions of attitudes as well as knowledge. Begging the question of curriculum organization – that is, whether it would be preferable to retain Economics/Business Studies as a separate 'subject' or to integrate this aspect of social science with social and political dimensions – it would be important to include the following key concepts and ideas. I would not myself wish to make a great deal of the distinction between Economics and Business Studies: business is often deliberately more practical in its intent, but I would not wish Economics to be presented as a set of abstract, theoretical ideas remote from the world of reality. One of the problems of English secondary education is that we are too ready to make unnecessary distinctions between 'academic' and 'vocational': very often the academic would benefit from more 'real life' whereas 'vocational' subjects can and should be taught in a way that ensures they are not merely vocational preparation but general education too. Perhaps the key element is that both should be taught in a critical and creative way – involving what might be as well as what is. Economics and Business exemplify that point extremely well.

What should be included in a curriculum for all? It seems to me, as an outsider, that the most fundamental set of concepts is that of *choice* in conditions of *scarcity*. We are quickly into the worlds of *supply* and *demand* and eventually *price* and the notions of *market*, *cost*, and *opportunity cost*. As a lapsed sociologist I would not want to wait too long before introducing the related concepts of *division-of-labour* and *specialization*. It would also be important to make links with political understanding by means of discussing different kinds of *enterprise*, *public* and *private*, and the *mixed economy*. It would also be essential to include an outline of *public expenditure* and *revenue*, including *taxation policies*; and, of course, how all this influences other aspects of real life such as *unemployment*. By the end of secondary education, young people should have a general appreciation of *banking*, and such aspects of 'the City' as *stocks and shares*, the *Stock Exchange*, and the market internationally as well as nationally. Finally, the notion of national *wealth*, *exports* and *imports*, and the *balance of payments* should be included.

A tall order? Yes, but no more ambitious than the principle, now generally accepted, that everyone needs to understand the basics of science and technology. So why not social science? I will avoid the temptation of discussing how to teach all those fascinating topics: I seem to recall that twenty years ago the name of Bruner was invoked to silence potential critics. And why not? Much has changed, but the assumption that it is possible to teach complex ideas to all young people in some intellectually honest form is still valid.

The National Curriculum was unfortunately framed without including a social science dimension, and the opportunity of including economic understanding in the curriculum for all pupils was missed (see below).

The 1988 National Curriculum

By the early 1980s there were many reasons for recommending a review of the curriculum, and in 1988 there was an opportunity to plan and design a national curriculum which would not only have established national guidelines, but also have brought the curriculum up to date in a variety of ways. Ideally, a national curriculum in 1988 would have gone beyond a 'reform' based on ten subjects. It might have been unrealistic to think in terms of a full-blooded cultural analysis approach, but one real possibility would have been to have reformed the curriculum by extending the availability of the HMI Entitlement model. During the late 1970s and early 80s, the Inspectorate had developed a curriculum model based not on subjects but on 'areas of knowledge and experience' (DES, 1983). This model had been used by volunteered schools and LEAs to improve their own school-based planning and implementation. This was proving to be very effective, until the HMI model was marginalized, or virtually ignored, by the Baker proposals in 1987/88.

It may seem strange that the opportunity for real curriculum reform was missed because in many respects Baker was a modernizer – that is, he saw that many aspects of the education system were lagging behind the needs of an industrial democratic society, and genuinely wanted to bring the curriculum up to date. Before becoming Secretary of State for Education, Baker had become Chairman of the Hansard Society in 1975, and had been sympathetic to those who wished to introduce political understanding into the curriculum. Similarly, as Minister of State for Industry and Information Technology he had perceived the need to include technology and information technology in the school curriculum. Yet when in 1987 he had the opportunity to bring about a complete rethinking of the curriculum, he simply reverted to the 1904 list of subjects, merely adding technology instead of Latin. Why?

I have suggested elsewhere (Lawton, 1992, 1994) that the answer lies partly in the ideological value conflicts within the Conservative Party. I have tried to show that a minority of conservatives were Privatizers, wishing to abolish compulsory schooling and leave education (including the curriculum) to market forces; there was also a larger group of Minimalists who admitted the need for a national education service, but wanted to keep it cheap: they would have concentrated on a narrow, core curriculum, emphasizing the basic skills necessary for employment. (Margaret Thatcher seemed usually to give her support to this group.) A third group, the Pluralists (including Kenneth Baker), wanted a good general education for all which would include differentiation between types of pupil. Bearing these three ideologies in mind, it is interesting to read the different views of education and curriculum contained in the various memoirs and autobiographies that have appeared since 1988. There was certainly a clash between Baker and Thatcher (see Lawton, 1994) and according to Nigel Lawson (1992) Baker occasionally received a 'hand-bagging' for his stubbornness. Her preference for a narrow, basic core curriculum was clear:

'The national curriculum – the most important centralising measure – soon ran into difficulties. I never envisaged that we would end up with the bureaucracy and the thicket of prescriptive measures which eventually emerged. I wanted the DES to concentrate on establishing a basic syllabus for English, mathematics and science with simple tests to show what pupils knew.'
(Margaret Thatcher, *The Downing Street Years,* HarperCollins, 1993, p. 593)

It is clear that Kenneth Baker had to fight for his version of a broad curriculum, however imperfect we may consider it to be. We might speculate that he would have had very little chance with an even broader curriculum which tried to modernize education in other respects and include aspects of political, social and economic culture.

Events in the period 1988–1995

Given that the 1987/88 discussions of the National Curriculum produced a very imperfect design plan (ten foundation subjects plus religious education), it was not surprising that the statutory body set up by the 1988 Act to keep the curriculum under review – the National Curriculum Council – should attempt to put right some of the defects by filling some of the gaps (see the Bibliography).

Almost as soon as it was set up in 1988, the NCC began to argue that the National Curriculum was not intended to be the whole curriculum: individual schools would have the responsibility for school-based curriculum design and for converting the National Curriculum into the whole curriculum; the NCC started planning how the ten-subject National Curriculum might be complemented by cross-curricular work of various kinds. In 1989, NCC produced *The Whole Curriculum* (Curriculum Guidance 3). The NCC theory which was being developed was couched in a new metalanguage. There was a general term – cross-curricular *elements* – which were intended to 'integrate the curriculum'. The elements were of three kinds: *dimensions, skills and themes. Dimensions* were rather ambitious – aiming to promote personal and social development across the whole curriculum, involving all teachers. The dimensions were particularly concerned with equal opportunities and multicultural education. Cross-curricular *skills* were of six kinds (although at the time the six were only referred to as examples):

Communication skills	Problem-solving
Numeracy	Personal and social skills
Study skills	Information technology

Finally, there were to be five cross-curricular *themes*:

Economic and industrial understanding (EIU)	Health education
Careers education	Education for citizenship
	Environmental education

This was an ambitious programme which might have worked, given a sensible implementation programme for the National Curriculum as a whole. Even so, cross-curricular elements would always have had to struggle for time and resources, since they were designated as 'non-statutory guidance', whereas the foundation subjects were a legal requirement for all maintained schools. The cross-curricular theory was, however, in accord with the way that some more enlightened schools were preparing to tackle the problem of the whole curriculum, and some pioneering work had taken place during the 1970s and 80s with Her Majesty's Inspectorate (HMI) and a small number of Local Education Authorities (LEAs) (DES, 1983).

Unfortunately, cross-curricular elements began to be pushed further and further into the background. It was never completely clear how all the elements would be integrated: the NCC gave some guidance on 'permeation' but was always anxious not to appear to be too directive. The separate booklets for the themes were, despite some criticisms, generally helpful. The documents on *Economic and Industrial Understanding, Health Education, Careers Education and Guidance, Education for Citizenship* and *Environmental Education* all appeared at intervals in 1990. But by that time it was quite clear that the problem of an overcrowded curriculum was pre-eminent: the requirements of the ten foundation subjects alone were thought to need more than the total time available. In addition, the fact that assessment results were being used to distinguish between schools and converted into league tables intensified the tendency for schools to give high priority to the statutory requirements rather than non-statutory guidance.

It soon became clear that cross-curricular elements were also a low *political* priority. There was no official statement to that effect, but it was generally known that the education secretaries who followed Baker felt that the top priority was to get the foundation subjects on stream and assessed according to the published timetable. One of the education secretaries ordered NCC – informally – to stop any further work on cross-curricular elements.

Whatever the reasons may have been, it has been shown by Geoff Whitty and his colleagues that the take-up by schools of the five cross-curricular themes has been poor, and that the themes receiving most attention were *Careers* (which already existed in most schools before the National Curriculum) and *Health Education* (which could most easily be integrated with subject work). *EIU, Citizenship* and *Environmental Education* fared much less well. (Whitty *et al.*, 1994). It might have been expected that EIU would have received greater priority than it did, because in 1992 the NCC published another set of documents for Key Stages 3 and 4 (funded by the Department of Trade and Industry) dealing with the interface of EIU and English, Maths, Science, Design and Technology, IT, History, Geography and Modern Foreign Languages. These booklets attempted to persuade subject teachers that little or no extra time would be needed for this kind of EIU, but the battle was really already lost: the main complaint of teachers in 1992/93 was the impossibility of implementing the foundation subjects as required by the Statutory Orders.

In 1993 the question of overload, combined with teacher dissatisfaction with the tests (especially in English), resulted in the boycott of all assessment for Summer 1993. Sir Ron Dearing, a non-educationist but allegedly a good listener, was brought in as Chair of the School Curriculum and Assessment Authority (SCAA) which had replaced NCC and SEAC in 1993. His commonsense solution was to prune both the amount of curriculum content and the assessment that was legally required. During the period of the review he was lobbied by a number of representatives of pressure groups interested in one or more cross-curricular themes. But he was clearly more concerned with reducing the load than in broader questions of curriculum design and coverage. The official SCAA position was to reiterate the doctrine that the National Curriculum was not the whole curriculum, and that responsibility for the whole curriculum, and therefore for cross-curricular themes, rested with individual schools. Cross-curricular themes received hardly a mention in either the Interim or Final Reports of the Dearing Review (July and December, 1993). Another missed opportunity!

The future

The next few years will not be very favourable for education for Economic and Industrial Understanding – the post-Dearing National Curriculum has to be put into operation. But within the five years of stability promised, there will be opportunities for schools to be thinking not only about the National Curriculum but about the whole curriculum. There are also problems connected with changes in Initial Teacher Training which may delay progress.

Within the existing structure there is some scope for action. The 1988 Education Act requires schools to provide a balanced and broadly-based curriculum. Parents may be stimulated by discussions of Citizens' Charters and Rights to look for broader developments in the school curriculum.

There are other kinds of possible pressures. The OfSTED inspection framework (1994) requires inspectors to report on the evaluation of 'the quality, breadth and balance of the curriculum, its planning and organization, in terms of its capacity to meet the needs of all pupils ...'. Surely this must include EIU? There are also signs that some schemes of education and training at 16–19 will include Economics and Business Education of some kind. Finally, we should not give up hope that SCAA under new management will – in time – come back to some guidance to schools on this issue.

All that is, however, tinkering with the problem – making the best of a very unsatisfactory National Curriculum. I would much prefer a more radical solution: a vision of lifelong education in a 'learning society'. In such a vision, for example, that of the National Commission on Education (1993) or Ranson (1994), a social science orientation would be central to the whole educational process. A vision of society and education of this kind would necessarily see the active citizen as much more than a consumer in a society dominated by market forces.

References

Anderson, D. (1988). *Full Circle?* London, Social Affairs Unit.

Barnett, C. (1986). *The Audit of War*. London, Macmillan.

Bruner, J. (1965). *The Process of Education*. Cambridge, Mass, Harvard University Press.

Bruner, J. (1971). *The Relevance of Education*. London, George Allen & Unwin.

Button, L. (1981; 1982). *Group Tutoring for the Form Teacher. 1: Lower Secondary School; 2: Upper Secondary School*. London, Hodder & Stoughton Educational.

Cox, B. (1991). *Cox on Cox: An English Curriculum for the 1990s*. London, Hodder & Stoughton Educational.

Dearden, R.F. (1968). *Philosophy of Primary School Education*. London, Routledge & Kegan Paul.

Dearing, Sir R. (July 1993). *The National Curriculum and its Assessment: Interim Report*. London, School Curriculum and Assessment Authority.

Dearing, Sir R. (December 1993). *The National Curriculum and its Assessment: Final Report*. London, School Curriculum and Assessment Authority.

Department of Education and Science (DES) (1983). *Curriculum 11–16: Towards a Statement of Entitlement (Curricular Re-appraisal in Action)*. London, HMSO.

Department of Education and Science (DES) (1985). *Better Schools*. London, HMSO.

Department of Education and Science (1988). *Report of the Committee of Inquiry into the Teaching of English Language (Kingman Report)*. London, HMSO.

Department for Education (DFE) (January 1995). *The National Curriculum*. London, HMSO.

Finegold, D. and Soskice, D. (1988). 'The failure of training in Britain', *Oxford Review of Economic Policy*, vol. 4, no. 3, pp. 21–53.

Gulbenkian Foundation (1982). *The Arts in Schools*. London, Calouste Gulbenkian Foundation.

Hampden-Turner, C. and Trompenaars, A. (1994). *The Seven Cultures of Capitalism*. Piatkus.

Hutton, W. (1995). *The State We're In*. London, Cape.

Lawson, N. (1992). *View from No.11: Memoirs of a Tory Radical.* London, Bantam.

Lawton, D.(1989). *Education, Culture and the National Curriculum.* London, Hodder & Stoughton.

Lawton, D. (1992). *Education and Politics in the 1990s: Conflict or Consensus?.* London, Falmer Press.

Lawton, D. (1994). *The Tory Mind on Education 1979–1994.* London, Falmer Press.

Levi-Strauss, C. (1966). *The Savage Mind.* London, Heinemann.

Linton, R. (ed.) (1940). *Acculturation.* New York, Appleton–Century–Crofts.

McPhail, P., Ungoed-Thomas, J.R. and Chapman, H. (1972). *Moral Education in the Secondary School.* Harlow, Longman.

Marquand, D. (1988). *The Unprincipled Society.* London, Fontana.

National Commission on Education (1993). *Learning to Succeed.* London, William Heinemann.

National Curriculum Council (1989). *The Whole Curriculum* (NCC Curriculum Guidance 3). London, NCC

National Curriculum Council (April 1993). *Spiritual and Moral Development.* London, NCC.

Newbolt Report (1921). *The Teaching of English in England.* London, Board of Education.

Office for Standards in Education (1994). *Framework for the Inspection of Schools: Revised May 1994.* London, OfSTED.

Pevsner, N. (1964). *The Englishness of English Art.* London, Peregrine Books.

Ranson, S. (1994). *Towards the Learning Society.* London, Cassell.

Sampson, A. (1992). *The Essential Anatomy of Britain: Democracy in Crisis.* London, Hodder & Stoughton.

Thatcher, M. (1993). *The Downing Street Years.* London, HarperCollins.

Weiner, M.J. (1981). *English Culture and the Decline of the Industrial Spirit 1850–1980.* Cambridge, Cambridge University Press.

White, J. *et al.* (1981). *No Minister: A Critique of the DES Paper 'The School Curriculum'.* London, Institute of Education, University of London, Bedford Way Paper 4.

Whitty, G., Rowe, G. and Aggleton, P. (1994). 'Subjects and themes in the secondary school curriculum', *Research Papers in Education,* vol. 9, no. 2, pp. 159–81.

Bibliography of National Curriculum Council publications

(1989). *The Whole Curriculum* (NCC Curriculum Guidance 3).

(1990). *Health Education.*

(1990). *Careers Education and Guidance.*

(1990). *Economic and Industrial Understanding.*

(1990). *Education for Citizenship.*

(1990). *Environmental Education.*

(1992). *Economic and Industrial Understanding: English.*

(1992). *Economic and Industrial Understanding: Mathematics.*

(1992). *Economic and Industrial Understanding: Science.*

(1992). *Economic and Industrial Understanding: Design and Technology.*

(1992). *Economic and Industrial Understanding: Information Technology.*

(1992). *Economic and Industrial Understanding: History.*

(1992). *Economic and Industrial Understanding: Geography.*

(1992). *Economic and Industrial Understanding: Modern Foreign Languages.*

(April 1993). *Spiritual and Moral Development.*

3 Vocational education and training: problems and policy

Martin Jephcote

Introduction

This chapter looks at the background to vocational education and training (VET) in the UK, examines the shortcomings of pre-existing systems and recent policy responses, and makes a brief assessment of the capability of National Vocational Qualifications (NVQs) and General National Vocational Qualifications (GNVQs) to provide a solution. In the space constraints of this chapter it is not possible to give a full account of each of these areas. Instead, an overview is provided from which implications for the future of teaching economics and business can be identified.

In Britain there is a divide between, on the one hand, 'education', and on the other, 'training'. The division is reflected by differences in attitudes and status attached to each, the separation of an 'academic' curriculum from a 'vocational' and for students differences in labour market destinations and their economic futures. In recent years there has been wide agreement among politicians, educationalists and employers about the need for 'education and training' to be more responsive to the needs of industry and this is apparent both in government rhetoric and in policy. As the 1994 White Paper (*Competitiveness: Helping Business to Win*, Cm 2563) stated:

'Hard working people with high skills, and the knowldege and understanding to use them to the full, are the lifeblood of a modern internationally competitive economy. While we are second to none in securing results from those in our society who choose the most academic options we need to raise further the attainment of those, whatever their age, who choose vocational education and training.' (p. 30)

There is no doubt that government has succeeded in raising the profile of vocational education if not its status. It has developed a new system with two significant features. First, it has established a coherent framework for qualifications with complementary progression routes for NVQs and GNVQs and traditional academic qualifications. Second, unlike traditional qualifications, NVQs and GNVQs are based on a competency model of assessment in which learners have to meet specified performance criteria and from which it is possible to set national standards.

It is in the context of GNVQs that the implications for economics and business must be set. GNVQs were introduced to increase participation rates in post-16 education, to remove the academic–vocational divide and to promote parity of esteem. The success of 'Business', at least as measured in numbers of students on GNVQ Business courses, underlines its vocational relevance. Business is, therefore, firmly established within the framework for education and training and contributing to meeting the government's National Targets for Education and Training. For many teachers this will be unproblematic, but others will wonder whether they have crossed the divide and, if so, with what consequences. To consider the wider significance of the possible impact of GNVQs, readers are referred to the contributions of Parsons (Chapter 4) and Leonard (Chapter 16).

The context

For more than 100 years the UK economy has been in a state of prolonged economic decline relative to many of its major European and worldwide economic competitors. This is a fact which is not in dispute. However, the causes of this relative decline and, in turn, suggestions as to what the UK needs to do to halt it, are the subject of debate. Space does not permit a detailed account of the UK's economic history; we might, in any case, think that our present concerns need to be forward-looking rather than backward-looking. We do, however, need to be aware of the legacy of the past which, arguably, has left UK teachers and students, employers, employees and policy-makers with dominant values and attitudes towards industry, work, enterprise and, indeed, about the purpose and nature of VET. It is argued, for example, that Britain suffers owing to the prevalence of an 'anti-industrial culture' (Ahier, 1991) and from the 'persistent characteristics of British society' (Mathieson and Bernbaum, 1991), including a lack of enthusiasm and preparation for the worlds of industry and commerce.

Shortcomings

In recent years the alleged shortcomings of the UK's system of education and training, and particularly its VET provision, have been targeted as both a contributory cause of the UK's continued relative economic decline and as a means to improving the UK's economic performance. Some commentators have noted the deliberate attempt at making education responsible so that the focus of discussion is no longer on the 'economic problem' but is on the 'educational problem' (Finn, 1985). In effect, poor education and low standards of achievement are blamed as the cause of economic decline. Keep and Mayhew (1988) considered this very point, necessitated by the fact that much of current VET policy is based on the assumption that such a relationship exists. Their conclusion was that current research in this area is unidimensional and failed to offer an overall understanding of what is a complex area. However, what we know is that during the 1980s the government played on these fears – the apparent failure of education and training – and, by an appeal to popular sentiment, was able to shift public opinion and policy so that the needs of industry have been made a primary goal of education (Apple, 1989).

There is of course not a single problem; rather, it may be be viewed as a composite of factors.

Finegold and Soskice (1988), for example, asserted that the UK has the worst-educated workforce and poorest record of vocational training among industrial and economic competitors, and is caught in a 'low-skills equilibrium'; and Corrigan (1991) suggested that low levels of training and skill are responsible for low levels of productivity. Low levels of investment in capital (Daly, 1985) leaves UK workers with less-efficient machinery with which to produce, and this is compounded by the failure in the UK to train new labour within the workplace (Jarvis and Prais, 1988). Keep and Mayhew (1988) added to the blame the 'distinctive heritage' of craft apprenticeships, and in particular the way in which individual craft workers's skills could be utilized were 'circumscribed' in the workplace by job demarcation, poor industrial relations and an authoritarian management structure which undervalued training, relying instead on authoritarian structures.

Many attempts to link poor economic performance to inappropriate VET and, in turn, answers to the UK's VET problem, have been based on international comparisons. There is now a substantial body of literature which compares UK VET with other countries – for a review see, for example, Keep (1993), *Missing Presumed Skilled: Training Policy in the UK*. In short, if we take countries who outperform the UK economically, then can we identify features of their education and training arrangements which could account for this? This was an idea to which the National Commission on Education's *Learning to Succeed* was very attracted (1993, pp. 2–4; also 1995). The Commission drew on the work of the NIESR (Green and Steadman, 1993) to show a 'substantial gap in performance' of 16- and 18-year-olds compared with Germany, France and Japan, and in VET pinpointed inadequate training as an explanation of why UK manufacturing productivitiy rates were 20 per cent lower than in France and Germany. And in the same vein Cooke and Morgan (1991) identified Germany as having better vocational training – that is, the provision of technical skills and knowledge, and the promotion of generic skills such as the ability to work in teams, social skills and problem-solving abilities.

Perhaps what we need to question, or remind ourselves of, at this stage is the possible dangers of driving VET policy on the belief that there is a link with economic failure. Even if it is the case, we should consider wider social issues and policies and the need to improve the overall quality of life and not simply measurable improvements in the standard of living. Recent European Commission White Papers (1994a, b) have noted that, other things being equal, it is those countries such as Germany and Japan who have the highest levels of general education and training and who are least affected by problems of competiveness and employment. However, the Commission does not see education and training as the sole solution to economic and associated social

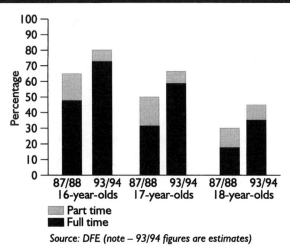

Source: DFE (note – 93/94 figures are estimates)

Figure 3.1 Participation in education by 16–18 year olds in England

problems. The White Papers convey a greater sense, than I think is apparent in the UK, of blending economic and social policy – as they state, these go 'hand-in-hand'.

Drawing from recent literature, the current shortcomings of the UK's system of VET, as compared with our major economic competitors, can be summarized as:

- the low quality of pre-16 education;

- the non-vocationalization of pre-16 school and 16–19 school education;

- low post-16 staying-on rates in academic or vocational education and training (although there has in recent years been a remarkable increase, as illustrated in Figure 3.1);

- a failure to respond to the 'skills challenge' of the future based on likely future working patterns and technologies.

So why is it that the UK is in this position? Again, the explanations are complex and controversial, but for simplicity they may be paraphrased as the following:

- VET has until recent years not been on the political agenda. Rather, political debate has focused on the pre-16 curriculum – comprehensive education and more recently the National Curriculum, opting out and so on;

- there has been a 'provider-led' market in which VET provision has been led by a disparate array of examining boards and institutes;

- the state structure and competition between departments for control of VET has hampered the move to a coherent system;

- there is a second-class image associated with technical and work-related subjects;

- financial pressures and economic uncertainty lead to lack of investment in VET;

- low levels of education and training of managers are translated into a general lack of concern for training of the workforce;

- there has been a failure to assign responsibility for VET. Government see it as an industrial problem, while industry see it as a problem for the government.

The government's response to these problems has been to try to influence the school and college curriculum and, increasingly, through a variety of measures, to take control. However, even though we have had 15 years of continuous Conservative Party control, this period is marked with a degree of internal political conflict and in education it is marked by contradictions and tensions between different government departments. It is suggested that, overall, this period has been dominated by the emergence of the 'New Right' with its emphasis on liberal tradition. It is the dominance of the 'New Right' and its concern with 'tradition' that explains why, during the 1980s, attempts to vocationalize the pre-16 school curriculum failed. Chitty (1990) suggested that the desire for direct influence over the curriculum was more important than its precise content. In the longer-term, the prized goal was that of securing a National Curriculum in which the government has dictated the content of the curriculum and in which the acquisition of subject-based knowledge has been made a priority over and above the acquisition of vocational skills.

More importantly, one has to realize that in the original conception of the National Curriculum there was virtually no room for any type of vocational preparation, providing a weak foundation on which to build in post-16 education. Vocational preparation together with the preparation of young people for the wider challenges and responsibilities of life outside and after school was left to the discretion of individual schools. The reality was that many schools gave these matters a higher priority than the prescribed National Curriculum seemingly permitted. Whether or not this was necessarily a bad thing – that is, whether all vocational preparation is best left to post-16 – is a moot point. But for the sake of completeness I should state that the government's review of the National Curriculum (Dearing, 1993a, b) has identified the need for more vocational preparation in the 14–16 age range. But whether this will be viewed by colleges and employers as a useful preparation is yet to be seen. By offering a programme of study from 14 to 19, schools might provide a more coherent programme in which learning experiences are continuous and progressive. Schools are, however, unlikely to be able to match the more extensive and specialist resources of colleges nor the teams of specialist educators and trainers. The likelihood is that schools will attempt to exploit the opportunity to keep students in the school system to benefit from the increased income this generates.

Responses: towards a coherent framework for qualifications

It is not possible to recall here the detail of the developments that took place in the 1980s and which led Guy (1991) to call it '... the decade of initiatives and initials in education and training'. (We may recall, for example, the TVEI and the Certificate of Pre-Vocational Education – CPVE.) Raggatt and Unwin (1991) show this period to be one of massive change and increasing intervention in the country's VET infrastructure. Initially, much of this change came about through the actions of teachers and educationalists; it gave rise to the benefits of diversity of provision together with the drawbacks associated with *ad hoc* development. Government and its agencies sought to consolidate these changes and, as a result, the degree of teacher control and diversity of provision have given way through increased intervention.

In post-16 education the prime concern of government, at least through the Department for Education, has been with the maintenance of academic standards as represented in the A level qualification. The status of A levels, considered to be the 'gold standard' remains largely unchallenged and protected, and continues to be regarded as the traditional entry route into university and the professions. What is apparent is that the main response to the shortcomings in the UK's system of VET came not from the Department for Education but from the Department of Employment and a number of its quangos. According to Wolf (1995, p. 127), Employment Department officials saw themselves as 'shock-troops or change agents in the cause of better education and training', believing a competency-based system to be more effective – that is, more suited to promoting economic recovery. Indeed, it was the Secretary of State for Employment who had overall responsibility for vocational education and training strategy in Great Britain and was responsible for training policy in England – the Secretaries of State for Scotland and Wales were responsible for training policy in Scotland and Wales respectively. The tasks of overseeing, setting up and servicing a new system were to fall respectively to the Department of Employment's Training, Enterprise and Education Division (TEED; formerly the MSC), the National Council for Vocational Qualifications (NCVQ), and the regional network of Training and Enterprise Councils (TECs). This is a clear indication of the mistrust, at the time, of educationalists and the Department for Education to secure better VET provision. The merger of the two departments in June 1995 into the Department for Education and Employment (DFEE) might well signal a change in attitude but is likely to be more an exercise in reducing overlap and expenditure.

The government (Department of Employment, 1994a) proposed a training strategy that was:

'... *capable of responding flexibly and coherently to changes in customer expectations, new markets and opportunities arising from new technologies ... this flexible approach ... is a prerequisite of both business and individual success*' (p. 4) and they went on to add:

'It is an approach founded upon many parties working in partnership towards agreed goals rather than upon legislation' (p. 4).

The infrastructure on which the strategy is based comprises:

- compulsory school education for all, based on the National Curriculum;

- reorganized further education, including the incorporation of colleges and a funding mechanism designed to ensure that colleges are more responsive to the needs of students and employers;

- a national framework of qualifications, including NVQs based on national standards set by employers and GNVQs;

- a network of regional Training and Enterprise Councils (TECs) (employer-led agencies which develop training strategies to meet the skill requirements of their communities) and a network of national Industry Training Organizations (ITOs – employer-led bodies which act as a focal point for training in their sector, by monitoring skill needs, setting standards and encouraging training).

The strategy is based on four priorities: investing in the skills needed for business creation and growth, and for individual success; maintaining the skills and providing support to the unemployed and disadvantaged to enable them to compete for employment and contribute more effectively to the economy; encouraging and enabling young people to gain skills and enterprising attitudes needed for the workforce and to realize their potential throughout working life; and, making the market for vocational education and training work better, responding to the changing needs of employers and individuals.

In post-16 VET there has been a gradual move to a competency-based system of training and accreditation and with it an attempt to raise the status of vocational education and training. Originally, the new system was conceived as the means of providing a coherent national framework of work-based training and accreditation. This is known as the National Vocational Qualification (NVQ). An NVQ is a statement of competence relevant to an occupation and indicates that a person is competent to perform a range of work-related activities and possesses underpinning skills, knowledge and understanding required for performance in employment. As Jessup (1991) stated, the statements of competence were derived:

'... not from an analysis of education and training programmes or the preconceptions of educators and trainers, but from a fresh analysis of present-day employment requirements' (p 18).

The NVQ has now been extended to include a college-based programme – the General National Vocational Qualification (GNVQ) – and replaces many existing vocational qualifications. It is intended to provide a broad-based vocational education combining basic skills and a body of underpinnning

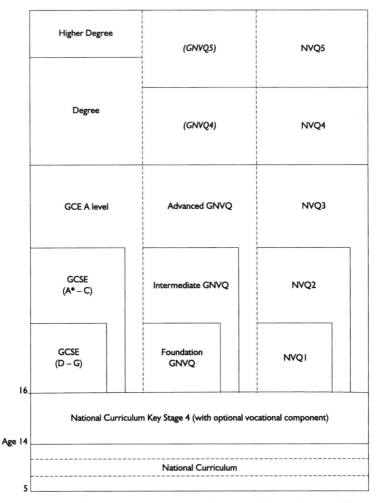

Figure 3.2 Framework for post-16 education (GNVQ Briefing, June 1995)

knowledge in a specific vocational area together with core skills – application of number, communication and information technology. It is suggested (NCVQ, 1995) that the attainment of both vocational and core skills provides a foundation from which students can progress either to further and higher education, or into employment and further training. At level 3 (advanced) the GNVQ provides, for the vocationally inclined student, an alternative to the academic A level in what has optimistically been dubbed the 'vocational A level'. Together with the 'traditional' system of assessment, the UK now has what may be regarded as a coherent framework of qualifications at post-16. The framework (taken from the GNVQ Briefing, June 1995, p. 27) is set out in Figure 3.2 and shows the opportunities for people to combine different types of qualifications or to move between pathways and from one level to the next. In addition, there is an emerging 'vocational pathway' at Key Stage 4 enabling students to gain a Part One GNVQ (an intermediate level will span GCSE grades A–C and

National Targets for Education and Training

"Developing skills for a successful future"

Aim

To improve the UK's international competitiveness by raising standards and attainment levels in education and training to world class levels through ensuring that:

1. All employers invest in employee development to achieve business success.

2. All individuals have access to education and training opportunities, leading to recognised qualifications, which meet their needs and aspirations.

3. All education and training develops self-reliance, flexibility and breadth, in particular through fostering competence in core skills.

Targets for 2000

Foundation learning

1. By age 19, 85% of young people to achieve 5 GCSEs at grade C or above, and Intermediate GNVQ or an NVQ level 2.

2. 75% of young people to achieve level 2 competence in communication, numeracy and IT by age 19; and 35% to achieve level 3 competence in these core skills by age 21.

3. By age 21, 60% of young people to achieve 2 GCE A levels, an Advanced GNVQ or an NVQ level 3.

Lifetime learning

1. 60% of the workforce to be qualified to NVQ level 3, Advanced GNVQ or 2 GCE A level standard.

2. 30% of the workforce to have a vocational, professional management or academic qualification at NVQ level 4 or above.

3. 70% of all organisations employing 200 or more employees, and 35% of those employing 50 or more, to be recognised as Investors in People.

Figure 3.3 National Targets for Education and Training

a foundation level grades D–G) both as a qualification in its own right and as a credit towards a full GNVQ at post-16. It should be noted that Business is among the three subjects to be piloted in the period 1995–97.

At the heart of the new system is the replacement of what might be described as a 'provider-led' approach with a 'client-led' approach. Providers were an amalgam of colleges, teachers, examining bodies and other professionals who exerted control over the curriculum. The newer 'client-led' approach sets out to meet the combined needs of the learner, of industry and of society which are now defined, not by the learner, but by the government and employers through the NCVQ. Funding, particularly in further education, is linked to the attainment of externally set targets, including recruitment and retention, and to the achievement of the National Targets for Education and Training (NTETs), set out in Figure 3.3.

Whether or not these targets can be met remains to be seen. Important questions have to be asked about the quality of the education and training which takes place and whether or not students are properly equipped for their present and future roles as workers. Do they possess the knowledge, skills and abilities required now, together with the ability and aptitude for continuous learning? In this respect we are reminded by the report of a EUROTECNET conference (Evans, 1993) – *Industrial Change in Europe* – which stated that 50 per cent of the workforce in the EU will not be in traditional employment by the year 2000, and in that period 70 per cent of the technology currently used by the workforce will no longer exist. Yet, 80 per cent of the workforce in the year 2000 is already in employment and only 20 per cent will join the workforce as newcomers or returners.

An implication of these statistics is that we will have to find new and complementary structures of training and education, based on new and innovative partnerships between trainers and employers. As the Department of Employment (1994b, p. 77) stated, lifetime learning means more than some adults receiving training for their immediate job, and there is a need to encourage more and broader training. Overall, we are being urged to consider a move towards the development of a learning society and a new learning culture. This need is made more urgent as the worldwide knowledge revolution continues to transform the way in which work is done and the way in which people live, placing a 'high premium' on the development of education and training (National Commission on Education, 1995). But as Ranson (1994) questioned, we will have to see whether the policy and principles of the marketplace together with the concentration of power in the hands of central government will lead to its realization or frustration. Clearly, the UK has set its hopes on the achievement of the targets and the ability of the new system of education and training to deliver.

The importance of the success of the new system should not, however, be understated. Raggatt (1991, p. 61) suggested that the introduction of the competency-based system might well be the last chance for the UK to develop a credible and high-quality system of VET capable of producing highly skilled, versatile and flexible workers necessary for effective economic competition. With regard to NVQs he noted evidence of three problems.

First there is the narrowness of approach. NVQs are occupationally specific to single sectors or single industries and tend to be geared towards short-term training rather than to future skill needs. Some industries require workers who are flexible and multi-skilled, but the narrowness of NVQs may fail to meet this need and may also leave workers lacking occupational mobility. Clearly, a balance has to be struck between the advantages which specialization gives rise to and the drawbacks of over-specialization in a rapidly changing industrial and commercial world.

Second, given the pace of technological and economic change, workers must take on board the concept of 'lifelong learning'. There is, therefore, a need to instill in workers a sense of the nature of the changing world and the need for them to be open to change, to retrain and adapt to new working environments.

Third, NVQs lack breadth. They concentrate on how to do a job rather than understanding the processes, and nor do they provide an adequate general education. The significance of this fact becomes clear when one realizes that in the UK those who enter VET – at work or at college – are generally of a lower academic ability than their peers in VET in many other European countries (Prais, 1993). The argument is, of course, that overall standards, personal qualities and adaptability (lifelong learning) would improve if the British system gave more emphasis to general education.

Turning to the GNVQ, the value and integrity of the new system, the training and the qualification it offers, has already been doubted. A variety of evidence gathered by or on behalf of the media not only suggested some corruption in the system but also seriously challenged the credibility of the course content. Notable in their discontent were the findings of a Channel Four Television (1993) enquiry which concluded that:

'... far from becoming world leaders in education and training as is sometimes claimed, Britain is in danger of falling even further behind ... some of the changes threaten a disaster of epic proportions' (p. 4).

Comparisons were made, for example, with the Dutch, French and German systems and the standards attained. In two respects it was suggested that the NVQ/GNVQ system does not match the German. First, it was claimed that at a given age and in a given occupational group or industrial sector what is required of students in the UK is at a lower level than in Germany. Second, it was claimed that the NVQ/GNVQ courses are too concerned with what students can do and not enough with what students need to know and understand.

Given the newness of the system and the sea change it signifies, we should not be surprised that the new system has attracted the attention of the media and active researchers; it provides an easy target for both. NCVQ (1993) responded comprehensively to each of the criticisms raised in the Channel Four Television 'Dispatches' programme, and pointed out a number of false assertions, lack of evidence and lack of representation, and pointed too to the substantial press coverage which the programme and its findings received. Reports from OfSTED (1994) and the FEFC (1994) for England have much to commend GNVQs for, but both reports identified a number of issues yet to be resolved. OfSTED (p. 39) called for improvements in the unit specifications (which in the case of Business and other phase-one pilot subjects was dealt with in June 1995) and for more rigorous assessment procedures to provide consistent national standards. The FEFC (p. 29) called for, amongst other things, a clarification of the knowledge and understanding required in units, especially the mandatory core skills, and for a tightening of the external testing regime.

In his interim report of the review of 16–19 qualifications, Dearing (1995) noted the need to consider greater opportunities to combine vocational and A level courses and for the need for all forms of education and training to be rigorously assessed. At a different level, Thomas (Chapter 6), drawing on the work of Barnett (1994), provides a formidable challenge to the competency-led model on which NVQs and GNVQs are based. She warns of the strength of the operational competence ideology and the dangers of its insidious nature which needs constantly to be challenged since 'at their most persuasive they represent a denial of the independence of mind which should characterize human learning'.

The government claims to be committed to the promotion of vocational education and training. The new Minister for Education (Gillian Shepard) has stated clearly her view that the priority is to ensure that GNVQs are widely respected. In a newspaper article (*Sunday Express*, 28 August 1994) she stated:

'Our competitors recognise that there are other aptitudes and abilities that are critical to success as a nation and important for the fulfillment of the individual – so must we ... We have not been as successful in establishing a rigorous and high quality challenge to young people – of all abilities – with more practical, vocational talents and interests. Compared with countries such as Germany, we have not succeeded in establishing vocational routes which are as well respected as more purely academic routes.'

Conclusion

At face value GNVQ Business offers a bright future for teachers, students and the economy. The uncertainties in the 14–19 school and college curriculum caused at the time of the introduction of the National Curriculum have been removed and once more Business is well placed. Students have a clearer progression route in which they can take up opportunties at work or pursue further and higher education; opportunities have been broadened and are no longer the preserve of the academically inclined. For the economy the hope is that the GNVQ together with NVQs and traditional qualifications will provide a trained, educated and flexible workforce able to respond to the changing needs of industry.

There can be few who do not agree that industry needs to be better served and that education and training have a role to play in bringing about economic recovery and increased competitiveness. However, those involved in education – the professional community of teachers and other interested parties – are charged with greater responsibilities. Schools and colleges have a broader function than preparing people for work. Education, and perhaps training too, have a role to play in securing the principles of a democratic society; this is less well reflected in government rhetoric, policy and funding. Further, we have to guard against the continuing advance of the competence-based model and define its limitations. Extending the model to include A levels and degrees is not the answer, but this key difference in approach remains at the source of the education and training divide. Paradoxically, the new system is likely to widen rather than close the divide, emphasizing the narrowness of vocational qualifications.

References

Ahier, J. (1991). 'Explaining economic decline and teaching children about industry', in: Moore, R., and Ozga, J. (eds), *Curriculum Policy*, Oxford, Pergamon Press.

Apple, M. W. (1989). 'Critical introduction: ideology and the state in educational policy', in: Dale, R. (ed.), *Modern Educational Thought*, Milton Keynes, Open University Press.

Barnett, R. (1994). *The Limits of Competence*, Philadelphia, Oxford University Press.

Channel Four Television (1993). 'All our futures: Britain's education revolution'.

Chitty, C. (1990). 'Central control of the school curriculum, 1944–1987', in Moon, B. (ed.), *New Curriculum – National Curriculum*, Milton Keynes, Open University Press.

Cooke, P., and Morgan, K. (1991). *Industry, Training and Technology Transfer*. Cardiff, Regional Industrial Research.

Corrigan, P. *et al.* (1991). *The Cultural Development of Labour*, Basingstoke, Macmillan.

Daly, A. *et al.* (1985). 'Productivity, machinery and skills', *National Institute Economic Review*, vol. 111, 48–61.

Dearing, R. (1993a). *The National Curriculum and its Assessment: An Interim Report*, York and London, National Curriculum Council and School Examinations and Assessment Council.

Dearing, R. (1993b). *The National Curriculum and its Assessment: Final Report*, York and London, National Curriculum Council and School Examinations and Assessment Council.

Dearing, R. (1995). *Review of 16–19 Qualifications: Summary of the Interim Report*, London, HMSO.

Department of Employment (1994a). *Training in Britain: A Guide*, London, HMSO.

Department of Employment (1994b). *Labour Market and Skill Trends 1995/96*, Skills and Enterprise Network 231.

European Commission White Paper (1994a). *European Social Policy, A Way Forward*, Luxembourg, Com (94) 333.

European Commission White Paper (1994b). *Growth, Competitiveness, Employment: The Challenges and Ways Forward into the 21st Century*, Luxembourg.

Evans, A. (1993). *Industrial Change in Europe*, Synthesis Report of a EUROTECNET Conference, Birmingham, UK, 1993.

FEFC (1994). *General National Vocational Qualifications in the Further Education Sector in England*, National Survey Report.

Finn, D. (1985). 'The MSC and the Youth Training Scheme: a permanent bridge to work?', in: Dale, R. (ed.), *Education, Training and Employment*, Oxford, Pergamon Press.

Finegold. D., and Soskice, D. (1988). 'The failure of British training: analysis and prescription', *Oxford Review of Economic Policy*, vol 4, no 3, 21–53.

Green, A. and Steadman, H. (1993). *Educational Provision, Educational Attainment and the Needs of Industry: a Review*, London, NIESR.

Guy, R. (1991). 'Serving the needs of industry', in: Raggat, P. and Unwin, L. (eds), *Change and Intervention: Vocational Education and Training*, London, Falmer Press.

Jarvis, V., and Prais, S.J. (1988). *Two Nations of Shopkeepers: Training for Retailing in France and Britain*, NIESR.

Jessup, G. (1991). *Outcomes: NVQs and the Emerging Model of Education and Training*, London, Falmer Press.

Keep, E. (1993). 'Missing Presumed Skilled: Training Policy in the UK', in: Edwards, R. et al. (eds), *Adult Learners, Education and Training*, London, Routledge, pp 91–111.

Keep, E., and Mayhew, K. (1988). 'The assessment: education, training and economic performance', *Oxford Review of Economic Policy*, vol 4, no 3, pp i–xv.

Mathieson, M., and Bernbaum, G. (1991). 'The British disease: a British tradition?', in: Moore, R. and Ozga, J. (eds), *Curriculum Policy*, Oxford, Pergamon Press.

National Advisory Council for Education and Training (July 1985). *Report on Progress Towards the National Targets*.

National Commission on Education (1993). *Learning to Succeed*, London, William Heinemann.

National Commission on Education (1995). *Learning to Succeed, the Way Ahead*, London, NCE.

NCVQ (1993). *A Statement on 'All our Futures'*, NCVQ.

NCVQ (June 1995). *GNVQ Briefing: Information on the Form, Development and Implementation of GNVQs*, NCVQ.

39

OfSTED (1993). *Quality and Standards of GNVQs; GNVQs in Schools 1993/94*, London, HMSO.

Prais, S. (1993). *Economic Performance and Education: The Nature of Britain's Deficiencies*, NIESR, Discussion Paper 52.

Raggatt, P. (1991). 'Quality assurance and NVQs', in: Raggat, P. and Unwin, L. (eds), *Change and Intervention: Vocational Education and Training*, London, Falmer Press.

Raggat, P. and Unwin, L. (1991). 'A collection of pipers', in: Raggat, P. and Unwin, L. (eds), *Change and Intervention: Vocational Education and Training*, London, Falmer Press.

Ranson, S. (1994). *Towards the Learning Society*, London, Cassell.

Wolf, A. (1995). *Competence-Based Assessment*, Buckingham, Open University Press.

White Paper (1994). *Competitiveness: Helping Business to Win*, Cm 2563, London, HMSO.

4 Economics and business in the curriculum: their changing roles

Colin Parsons

Background

Economics and business education is present in the school curriculum in three forms:

- *The whole curriculum* – in which economic awareness is an integral part of primary and secondary education both as an identified cross-curricular theme, 'Economic and Industrial Understanding', and as part of a pupil's entitlement to broad and balanced provision.

- *The pre-16 formal curriculum* – in which Economics and Business Studies may be offered as options for GCSE and as an integral part of other courses.

- *The post-16 curriculum* – in which Economics and Business Studies feature as significant choices in a range of examination contexts particularly at A level and GNVQ.

The foundations for the development of economics and business education today were laid in the early years after the Second World War. Before then economics was mainly confined to the Oxford and Cambridge Scholarship Examination, under its more usual guise of Political Economy, or as part of the Higher School Certificate as a syllabus for the university entrance examination. Even so, economics was slow to become an accepted subject for university entrance; but its popularity grew as an A level social science subject in the 1950s and 60s and, subsequently, at O level, often as a sixth-form option. Indeed, in the early 1950s very few schools taught economics at all and, where it was taught, it was often in the hands of non-specialists.

In 1954, 2800 pupils chose O level Economics and there were 2500 entries at A level. This soon increased and, by 1961, there were over 6000 A level entries and nearly 7000 at O level. The peak of O level entry reached over 43 000 in 1981 and there were over 42 000 at A level, making it the fifth most popular choice. There were over 100 000 candidates in CSE Economics in 1976 when it was the eighth most popular subject. The decline in numbers taking economics at 14–16 coincided with the curriculum constraints imposed by the National Curriculum and the narrowing of option choices. By 1991 there were just over 24 000 candidates, but this fell steadily so that by 1993 there were 16 700 and 14 000 in 1994. Now only 2.5 per cent of the total year-group entry take economics. At A level there were over 46 000 candidates in 1989, but this fell to 37 000 in 1993 and to just under 30 000 in 1995. There is also some concern about the failure of economics to appeal to girls. Nearly twice as many boys as girls opt for the subject at A level and there is nearly the same imbalance at GCSE. Whether or not this is a reflection of a perception of the subject as a male domain, or whether it reflects the style of teaching and assessment, is unclear. Certainly there is no current evidence that teachers promote such an imbalance.

It was not until the mid-1960s that business studies was first considered, initially as a joint development between Marlborough College and participating state secondary schools. This initiative became the new A level Business Studies course examined by Cambridge for the first time in 1974. The course was led by a curriculum team which also undertook teacher training to maintain a supply of suitably qualified graduate teachers whose approach to the subject was significantly unconstrained by conversion from economics teaching. Once the subject became an accepted part of the curriculum and increasingly acceptable for university entrance in its own right, many teachers switched successfully between the two subjects. Although different, both subjects appeared to owe much to common foundations in analysis, understanding and decision-making.

The expansion of the candidate entry in business studies at GCSE coincided with the transition to the GCSE examination in 1987 when there were approximately 20 000 entries. By 1990 this had reached nearly 60 000 and nearly 100 000 in 1993. In 1994 there were 107 000 entries which indicated considerable confidence in the subject despite the National Curriculum pressures upon it (see Figure 4.1). However, National Curriculum constraints mean that the entry has fallen so that numbers taking the subject have now stabilized at about 17 per cent of the year-group. Indications are that there is a gender balance in the entries whereas economics is significantly preferred by boys. Whereas numbers in A level Economics have fallen away, there has been a growth in A level Business Studies from 10 000 in 1989 to 21 000 in 1992 and 29 000 in 1995 (Figure 4.2). With a small peak in 1991, aggregate numbers for the two subjects at A level have been consistently about 56 000 over the last five years, with a significant shift in the balance towards business studies, the so-called 'entrepreneurial route'. Evidence suggests that GNVQs are having a significant impact on post-16 education and, for many students, are an alternative to A levels (Figure 4.3). Business GNVQ is far and away the most popular subject with about 43 per cent of awarded GNVQs.

Economic awareness

From its inception, economics was seldom taught below Year 10 of secondary schools, although it sometimes had a place in the core curriculum especially as part of a social science provision. The first major impetus for the development of broad curricular approaches to the subject was announced with the Economics Association's 14–16 Project. This major curriculum initiative was

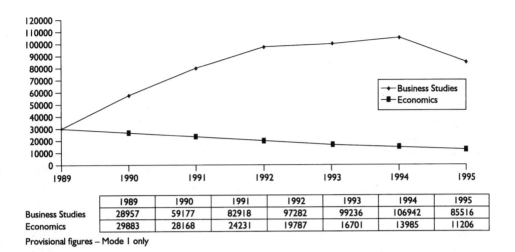

	1989	1990	1991	1992	1993	1994	1995
Business Studies	28957	59177	82918	97282	99236	106942	85516
Economics	29883	28168	24231	19787	16701	13985	11206

Provisional figures – Mode I only

Figure 4.1 Number of candidates examined in Business Studies and Economics at GCSE level 1989–95

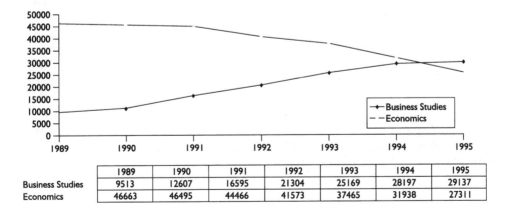

	1989	1990	1991	1992	1993	1994	1995
Business Studies	9513	12607	16595	21304	25169	28197	29137
Economics	46663	46495	44466	41573	37465	31938	27311

Figure 4.2 Number of candidates examined in Business Studies and Economics at A level 1989–95

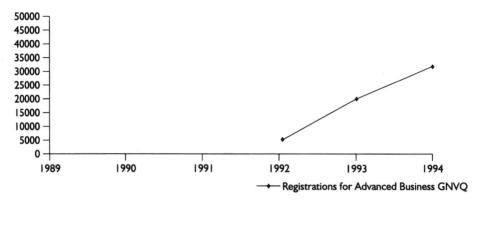

	1992	1993	1994
Registrations for Advanced Business GNVQ	3000	17419	32057

Figure 4.3 Number of registrations for Advanced Business GNVQ 1992–94

initially supported by the Esmée Fairbairn Trust at Hull University (Phase 1, 1976–78) and then progressed to the development at Manchester University (Phase 2, 1980–83) of materials for use in schools, and finally into a stage of publication and dissemination (1984–86). The broad rationale for this approach was underlined in the report *Curriculum 11–16* by Her Majesty's Inspectors of schools (DES, 1977):

'If some people think that schools are not appropriate places for instructing young people in economic competence, then two questions arise: Where else can this task be undertaken methodically for all citizens? In an industrial democracy, can we leave this task to mere chance, probably depriving vast numbers of people of an understanding of the very processes and issues which affect their lives as citizens and workers?' (p. 53).

Also in 1977, the Economics Association produced a report entitled *The Contribution of Economics to General Education*. This set out the case for the inclusion of an economics component in general education, with guidance on the objectives to be sought and the appropriate content to be included:

'If education is to prepare school leavers fully for their future roles in society, provision must be made in the curriculum for all pupils to have an opportunity to develop a basic level of competence in economics and to acquire at least the socially necessary standard of economic literacy' (§ 38).

In its document *A Framework for the School Curriculum* (1980), the Department of Education and Science highlighted that:

44

'... pupils need to be given a better understanding of the economic base of our society and the importance to Britain of the wealth creating process' (§ 33).

The purpose of the Economics Education 14–16 Project was to help teachers to develop courses in economic understanding for all pupils in the 14–16 range as an essential part of their general education. It promoted curriculum development by teachers and established a range of exemplar materials to promote further ideas and good practice. It also established a network of teacher support through professional development in close conjunction with local authorities.

Whereas the initiative was closely in line with contemporary thinking, it was not intended to produce young entrepreneurs or to inculcate young people into the ways of the economy. Rather it sought to address a range of issues to encourage pupils to think for themselves and develop questioning attitudes. To this end, its exemplar materials (Longman, 1984) set challenging questions like 'Why are things considered as a necessity in one country looked upon as luxuries in another?' or 'Why can producers create and maintain markets whilst remaining independent of consumer preferences?'. The intention was to encourage teachers to develop their own materials and to use the project as an initiator of ideas. It certainly did much to challenge the assertion that, since powers of deduction and abstract reasoning do not develop much before the age of 16, economics teaching before this age must be largely descriptive (Edwards *et al.*, 1954, pp. 167–70).

The development of the 14–16 Project spawned a number of other initiatives. In particular was the growth of interest in 'economic awareness' for pupils below the age of 14. Linton (1985), for example, addressed the issue from a particularly primary perspective and identified four aims:

- To create an awareness, through situational involvement, of an expanding spiral of basic economic concepts, including needs satisfaction (consumption); resources, scarcity, work (production and distribution); specialization, interdependence, cooperation (exchange).

- To enable pupils to appreciate an ever-widening range of adult problems, whenever possible, in real, as distinct from theoretical, terms, and so promote and enrich social maturation.

- To encourage and assist pupils in making simple judgements and to inculcate habits of systematic investigation.

- To achieve economic literacy and numeracy.

The Economics Association established its own Primary Working Party which sought to influence developments in schools. As reported in the Association's Journal (1991):

'We would argue that business and economics education can be developed as a continuum in schools from 5–18 starting with the foundation of

economic awareness in the primary years. We seek to generate an interest in the business world, not in the supposed spirit of the enterprise culture, but encouraging questioning approaches. We will start with contexts which are familiar to very young children – perhaps the world of shopping or toys – and use this as a vehicle for enquiry. We will analyse their spending decisions with five or six year olds in order to consider the reasons behind them. Why did they choose apples instead of sweets? How far was price or supposed value for money a factor in their choice? What is 'value for money' anyway? Who is affected by the decision they make and how? Whereas the model is simple and the context limited, even very young children become aware that they have many wants but only limited means to satisfy those wants. When they make a choice, they forsake alternate choices and these choices have implications for others. They will begin to develop an understanding of what it means to be underprivileged and this is how their experience is broadened into further contexts' (p. 174).

Going on to reflect on pupils at Key Stage 2, the working party stated:

'Primary school children should be able to make some 'value for money' judgements, to appreciate the implications of choices and explore issues concerning gender stereotyping, equal opportunities and issues relevant to the developing world. The aim must be to encourage them to make value judgements based on sound evidence, effective reasoning and tolerance' (p. 174).

Economic and Industrial Understanding (EIU) has no monopoly of this approach but it makes a significant contribution alongside other cross-curricular themes.

Economics and business education in the 14–16 curriculum

The growth of economics in the 14–16 curriculum during the 1960s and 70s was based initially on the improvement of courses and then on the development of appropriate textbooks which gave encouragement to the view that there was a place for analytical as well as descriptive approaches to learning in the area of social studies. However, the whole rationale of GCE and CSE economics was still to present pupils with a range of concepts and analytical diagrams to try to help them make sense of simplified versions of quite complex theory. There were a number of interesting teaching and learning developments through this period, although these were slow to be reflected in the examination structure.

With the curriculum development associated with GCSE in the mid-1980s there was an increase in the use of project work and of responses to original articles and data in both learning and assessment. This made it a more dynamic curriculum experience and one which offered more effective opportunities for pupils to develop critical objectivity whilst, at the same time, encouraging their individual interests. However, it was still seen as a relatively turgid subject and one which appealed to boys more than girls. Current changes introduced by the School Curriculum Assessment Authority (SCAA) following new criteria in economics limit the coursework component of assessment to 20 per cent and have promoted a range of newly constructed syllabuses. Whether or not these will be reflected in a reversal of the decline in its popularity remains to be seen.

The curriculum from which business studies emerged in the early 1980s often addressed the needs of pupils, mainly girls, of middle to lower ability. The traditional menu of typewriting, commerce and office practice was attractive to many schools who saw the package as offering a vocational direction for a significant group. The changing nature of employment and the increasing recognition of the rights of all pupils to have a broad and balanced education challenged that position. Change was slow at first but, by the mid-1980s, many schools had begun to adopt a business curriculum which reflected this right and included some of the content of traditional commerce with analytical approaches taken from economics.

The new information technologies often became an integral part of the course in schools and it was often necessary for business studies teachers to be at the forefront of IT development. However, much of the content of these business studies courses was still essentially descriptive, despite attempts to introduce analytical skills through teaching and learning processes. Some of the innovative approaches of BTEC courses were reflected in the new approach to O level/CSE Business Studies and, subsequently, GCSE. In particular, this strongly influenced a double option course in Business and Information Studies (BIS) where examination by case study represented a major breakthrough, especially since it became the norm for the content of the case study to be presented to pupils in advance. This confirmed that the skills to be examined were essentially those practised in business, where consideration of a variety of alternative strategies was considered good practice. This was a hard lesson for examination groups to accept, but it was very much in line with what teachers considered good practice and promoted effective teaching. In this respect, the double-option/double-certification BIS course was a vital formative influence. It was also significant that the BIS team were able to support the curriculum with extensive national backup, based on local groups, and in-service courses for teachers.

It is interesting to note that curriculum development appeared to be bringing economics and business studies more closely together at a time when their similarities were more important than their differences. In November 1990 an HMI statement on Business and Economics Education 5–16 commented:

'Economic and business education cannot be easily separated. An understanding of everyday problems ultimately requires both an

understanding of economic principles and the detail of particular business organisation and structure' (§ 1).

However, distinctions were being made in the eyes of parents and curriculum planners as well as subject specialists. Business studies was increasingly seen as offering an interesting and well-resourced curriculum which was attractive to employers. Brech (1994) stated his view of the philosophical difference:

'Economics and business cover the same ground. Indeed in many respects they are identical. But they approach the common ground from exactly the opposite ends. Economics starts with individual concepts, such as the theory of demand, price formation, price elasticity, income elasticity, and integrates them into a total system. Business, on the other hand, starts with the total system – the operation of a company – and works down to the individual concepts such as price formation, price and income elasticity and the demand function' (p. 172).

By the end of the 1980s, however, it was clear that the position of both business studies and economics at GCSE was being seriously questioned. Many schools had reacted to the National Curriculum by focusing the curriculum in Years 10 and 11 on the ten National Curriculum subjects plus RE. Economics had often been dropped altogether and the number of option groups offering business studies had fallen to one or two – often in schools where the majority of a year-group had followed the subject. When Technology was introduced as a National Curriculum subject in 1990, the inclusion of elements of business education was viewed very positively by many in the field. Blowers (1991), for example, stated:

'The introduction of technology ... represents a welcome extension of business education experiences to a wider age group of pupils than we have seen before in primary and secondary schools' (p. 95).

However, it was clear that, despite notable exceptions, business education was not delivered as specified in the programmes of study and this was regarded as a blessing by many traditional teachers of design technology. HM Inspectorate (DFE, 1992) noted that:

'Technology lessons were visited in this and parallel surveys, but little movement was found towards introducing business and economic dimensions' (§ 57).

Many examination boards reacted to the National Curriculum by producing integrated syllabuses combining elements of business education with technology. This often challenged organization in schools and forced unlikely marriages between departments. Despite this, Economics and Business Studies departments usually survived and some interesting and valuable curriculum links were established in design technology, home economics and business education.

In December 1992 the Department for Education and Science announced further proposed changes for Technology within the National Curriculum. These proposals continued to identify a clear role for business education at Key Stages 3 and 4, but also implied a rejection of EIU at Key Stages 1 and 2 and a significant reduction in the importance of cross-curricular themes. Whereas the main reasons for including economic and business elements in programmes of study at Key Stages 3 and 4 were to provide an important element of the vocational content of full and short courses, the decision to play down the role of EIU was a serious blow. Cullimore (1993) pointed out that:

'... members should get involved in Design and Technology because, if they do not, then it is likely that business and economics will disappear in a rigorous form from the vocational curriculum which looks likely to develop at Key Stage 4. ... In previous times business education has been seen as a major provider of pre-vocational education. This may well slip away if technology takes the mantle. It is essential therefore to ensure that within the new vocational subjects (short courses and full GCSEs) there is a significant input from business and economics' (p. 96).

Davies (1994), in a survey of 600 schools in north-west England and Clwyd, recognized that the high profile of business studies at Key Stage 4 was vulnerable to curriculum pressure. However, he noted that the arguments for a reduced statutory curriculum core:

'... offer substantial encouragement for economics and business studies in Key Stage 4. The 40% of schools not offering business studies or economics at GCSE should be challenged by the report's endorsement of the desirability of making the subjects available as options. The allocation of 40% of curriculum time to options (sic) returns Key Stage 4 to a position when business studies was rapidly expanding. The encouragement of a vocational pathway promotes an area of the curriculum where business studies has always been prominent. Free standing short courses may provide opportunities for GCSE economics and business studies to gain footholds in the curriculum in schools where senior management would be less than keen on a full GCSE course. Above all, a 14–19 framework for curriculum planning suits a subject area which has never achieved a profile in the pre-14 curriculum' (p. 42).

The present rationale of business education is that young people should have access to experiences which will enable them to understand and participate in the business world. The key feature of new GCSE criteria for business studies introduced in 1994 is an emphasis on *understanding* of the business world so that candidates are expected to know *why* things occur as well as what is likely to happen. At Key Stage 4, such a range of experiences is likely to include three elements according to the EBEA Business Education KS4 Working Group (1995, p. 32):

- knowledge of practice and skills relating to the individual in their role as producer, consumer and citizen (including problem-solving, decision-making, enterprising and teamwork skills);

49

- critical understanding of the features and dynamics of different types of organization, including profit-making, charitable and public services, large and small, from different perspectives (economic, social, financial, legal and technological);

- the use of information technology to analyse and communicate as well as being a decision-making tool.

At Key Stage 4 the most likely implication is the development of GNVQs and vocational GCSEs. Business education should be as broad-based as possible so that more tightly focused choices can be made at 16. Decisions will have to be made in all schools as to whether modern foreign languages and design and technology will be delivered as full courses, and there will be pressure to offer them within combined courses, possibly with business studies. These may be welcomed from a curriculum development point of view, but they have considerable resource and timetabling implications and represent entirely new areas of knowledge so far as most teachers are concerned. As the KS4 Working Group stated:

'The model of Business Studies which is recommended in a Key Stage 4 vocational curriculum is one which develops a broad education encompassing both business decision making skills and economics. Any Business Studies examination course GCSE, GNVQ or other vocational qualification has to balance rigour with relevance otherwise it will lose credibility' (p. 33).

Post-16 economics and business studies

When the first edition of *Teaching Economics* was published in 1967, all examination boards had a similar structure for A level Economics, with two essay papers of up to 3 hours. By the time of the second edition, most had added a multiple-choice paper and this was followed by the introduction of data response questions. Together this package was thought to address the balance between synthesis and analysis and to require detailed understanding of aspects of the syllabus but precluding concentration on a limited number of areas. Similar developments in the Scottish Higher Grade structure also reflected this thinking. AS levels were introduced to allow students to choose subject areas other than those from which their A levels were taken. In practice AS has not promoted the development of economic understanding across the sixth form. Some schools and colleges have used AS courses simply as a one-year stepping stone to A level in the same subject or made dual A and AS entries to cover weaker candidates against A level failure. Macfarlane (1993) stated the problem succinctly:

'The new (AS) courses have tended to reinforce rather than counteract the specialist approach. A survey in 1990 showed that, for every student who was using an AS course to provide a contrast to an A-level programme, three were doing so to complement it' (p. 27).

50

In March 1994 the Secretary of State asked SCAA to review the take-up of AS levels as a means of extending choice and breadth in the curriculum. SCAA's proposals include greater publicity and increased dissemination of good practice. Whether or not a change occurs in thinking by curriculum planners in schools remains to be seen.

The growth of A level Business Studies switched the emphasis from theoretical analysis and model-building in economics towards a broad understanding of the world of business, including problem-solving and decision-making, often including the opportunity to apply business IT. Traditional A level Economics studied how resources are used to produce and distribute goods and services involving individuals, households, firms and the government in decision-making. A level Business Studies stressed the importance of marketing, production, finance, accounting and business psychology and set these against the economic environment. From the outset, it placed an emphasis on case studies, business games and simulations, industrial and commercial visits, individual projects and research tasks. The flavour it offered was new and sometimes innovatory and, although it appeared similar to economics in many respects, it was significantly different in others.

Five recent developments in post-16 economics and business education appear to be particularly significant:

- the introduction of new subject cores for GCE A levels which has precipitated important changes in A and AS level syllabuses;

- the modularization of A level syllabuses;

- the Nuffield Economics and Business Project;

- the EBEA 16–19 curriculum project in economics;

- the development of GNVQ in schools and colleges.

The number of changes in economics syllabuses prompted by the new SCAA regulations varies between examination boards. For some, only little change has occurred either in content or methods of assessment. For others there has been much more significant change, with increased emphasis on skills and application – for example, a move towards a core-plus-options model with a multiple-choice and essay test of the core and stimulus data to test the options. As Vidler (1995) notes, less importance is being attached overall to mastering economic theory and, in particular, there is:

- less emphasis on some traditional areas of content, such as Keynesian 45-degree line approaches;

- greater examination of the strengths and weaknesses of the market economy;

- reduced assessment weightings for knowledge and understanding, with most marks now being awarded for achievement of higher-order skills;

- greater focus on the application of economics to contemporary issues.

The content of A/AS courses approved by SCAA has been christened the 'new economics'. Perhaps the most straightforward view of what students will learn within it is provided by the Economics 16–19 Project *Newsletter* (EBEA, 1994a). This asserts that the 'new economics':

- helps students to appreciate the power of the discipline's mainstream paradigm;

- expects students to develop their theoretical knowledge, skills and understanding;

- encourages students to approach the learning of economics holistically;

- challenges students to become actively involved in the learning process.

GCE examining boards are developing links with GNVQ and it seems likely that joint courses at A and AS level will be delivered through GNVQ units. Some AS courses concentrate on aspects of knowledge in the core, as a subset of the A level syllabus, and assessment may be by modular or traditional methods. Several boards now offer modular syllabuses at A level in both Economics and Business Studies. These allow candidates to complete assessment requirements in parts, usually corresponding to school terms, or as a whole, and some permit an individual project or special study as part of the course. In all courses in economics the emphasis seems to be on the application of economic concepts, principles and theories, and candidates are encouraged to use their understanding of economics in the context of contemporary economic issues.

Modular approaches in business studies are an accepted feature, but these are to be developed to accommodate AS certification as well as the new SCAA business core, and there will be an opportunity for candidates to repeat modules in order to improve marks and to take up to four years for the course. Modules in economics have been designed to meet the SCAA core requirements and include traditional essay and data response questions, but some boards also include the use of case studies in assessment. At least one board has produced a combined modular A level in Business Studies and Economics which will include the two subject cores.

New A/AS syllabuses

ECONOMICS
14 new syllabuses:
10 A level (of which 3 are modular)
4 AS level (of which 2 are modular)

BUSINESS STUDIES
16 new syllabuses:
11 A level (of which 7 are modular)
5 AS level (of which 4 are modular)

JOINT COURSES – BS/E

JOINT COURSES – GCE/GNVQ

The Nuffield Project syllabus is based on a core-plus-options approach and allows for four outcomes from a single syllabus: A level Economics; A level Business; A level Economics and Business; or AS level Economics and Business. Assessment is by means of a strategy and stimulus paper testing the core and a stimulus paper to test the options, as well as a portfolio in which the student demonstrates the skills of investigation. Nuffield intends to offer an integrated application of ideas through both teaching strategies and assessment so that classroom materials, books and examinations provide an environment in which concepts and ideas are put to work. A prime objective of the Nuffield development is that students are involved in activity-based work which leads them to an understanding of abstract concepts which can be applied over and over again in a variety of contexts to reinforce understanding. This involves a wide range of individual research, original resources and extensive use of computers as well as textbooks which specifically support the scheme. This approach already appears to have enhanced the general level of student motivation in some schools and allowed smaller sixth forms the opportunity to offer both economics and business studies at A level. There is an extensive network of support groups which provide a focus for teacher liaison as well as activity days for students and joint INSET for teachers.

The EBEA Economics 16–19 Project represents one of the most significant UK curriculum developments in economics education. It aimed to influence the content of the subject in schools and the way in which it would be taught. Over a period of three years more than 200 academics, educationalists, industrialists and teachers worked collaboratively to produce materials and share views which would support teachers in the delivery of the new economics, whatever examination syllabus they chose. This involved an extensive and rigorous review of the traditional content of A level Economics, of which it is fairly critical, and research into the effectiveness of a number of teaching strategies. For example, the Project attempted to create learning environments in which students could gain active experience of economics by involvement in problem-solving and active enquiry so that the skills and concepts developed could be applied to unfamiliar contexts. They also developed the concept of 'economic thoughtfulness' (see Chapter 6) to provide a coherent approach to learning. The Project has also had a significant input into SCAA, NCVQ and the GCE examination boards. The Project operated through six regional groups, based on EBEA branches, and each focused on the key issues of content and process.

The formal work of the Project was brought to a conclusion in July 1994 when the EBEA began the dissemination phase. It produced two key texts: *Teaching and Learning the New Economics* (EBEA, 1994b) which considers what the 'new economics' is all about and what are the most effective teaching strategies; and *Core Economics* (EBEA, 1995) which addresses key theory through the context of curriculum issues and problems and includes a number of tasks and investigations to help students to develop skills of analysis, application, data handling and communication. This is more of a workbook than a

53

traditional textbook and contains a range of case studies. Workshops continue to support teachers in coming to terms with the new economics, including changes in content, information technology applications, new assessment objectives and the increasing emphasis on skills and application together with implications for teaching and learning.

GNVQs are vocational qualifications covering broad areas. They are designed to develop a range of skills along with a sound basis of underpinning knowledge and understanding and an appreciation of how to apply relevant knowledge in a work context. Students are assessed through regular external tests and continuous assessment of work done during the course. They are currently available at Foundation, Intermediate and Advanced levels and are being piloted at 14–16 in Health & Social Care and Manufacturing. The pilot is a two-year course consisting of three vocational units and three core skill units, broadly equivalent to two GCSEs (D–G Foundation, A*–C for Intermediate), occupying 20 per cent of curriculum time at Key Stage 4. Whilst it seems that the focus of activity in GNVQs has shifted towards developments at Foundation level and vocational programmes in schools at Key Stage 4, the grading criteria for existing GNVQs have been revised to include a fourth theme, Quality of Outcomes, to add to Planning, Information Seeking and Handling, and Evaluation.

In 1993/94 over 80 000 students registered for GNVQs at over 2500 centres. In 1993/94, 1236 Advanced GNVQs were awarded and 85 per cent of those students applying for higher education places received offers. The growth in popularity of GNVQs coincides with the blurring of differences between traditional A level courses in schools and vocational certification in colleges. The government's intention is that GNVQs will be given parity of esteem with A levels. In 1993 the Education Secretary announced that Advanced GNVQs would be known as 'vocational A levels'. In order to ensure rigour in GNVQ courses, a need highlighted by OfSTED in its national report *GNVQs in Schools 1993/94*, the National Council has a plan of action to improve the external testing regime and accreditation procedures for schools and colleges. OfSTED felt that, whilst an Advanced GNVQ was broadly equivalent to two GCE A level passes, significant aspects of the new courses needed to be improved as a matter of urgency to ensure quality and rigour, including better course design, improved quality control for centres, and tougher external checks on standards. Business is by far the most popular course offered for GNVQ at Intermediate and Advanced levels and commands 43 per cent of awarded GNVQs.

Conclusion

So what can be concluded from this brief sketch of our subject area? What does the future hold?

Traditional schools continue to provide a menu of economics, often holding onto GCSE courses because they have a glowing success rate and find that they lay a sound foundation for A level. More significantly in numerical terms are schools that offer only business studies (in one of several forms) at GCSE and then provide a menu of choice at A level. Thirdly are schools and colleges that offer business-related GNVQ courses at post-16 level, often alongside A levels in economics and business studies. In the case of further education colleges this full range of choices is increasingly placed alongside higher-order courses and those that specifically address local occupational demands, often supported financially by employers.

The future of subject provision is uncertain in Years 10 and 11 where economics is in decline, business studies is settling down following its flirtation with design and technology, and vocational preparation courses are under serious consideration. The opportunities presented by changes in the National Curriculum are real and must be seen as encouraging. Post-16 provision is buoyant and will remain so, both within courses themselves but also in terms of the rationalization of academic and vocational routes. This writer's crystal ball suggests the following scenario for economics and business:

- GCSE Economics will continue to offer realistic preparation for A level and remain popular in schools where expertise continues to be available. It is unlikely to be seen as a growing opportunity.

- GCSE Business Studies has faced its nadir and survived to offer realistic opportunities alongside Design and Technology and within a slimmed down National Curriculum. It is likely that curriculum designers and planners will see the opportunities which the subject provides for pupils of all abilities and respond by offering appropriate resource levels. For many, this will reverse a trend within their school.

- Vocational foundation courses in Years 10 and 11 are in their infancy but it is likely that many schools will introduce them as a preparation for a GNVQ route – but without creating a cohort of second-class students. Much depends on the successful development of the courses themselves by a range of validating agencies.

- A level Economics has responded very effectively to new curriculum requirements by SCAA. There is every possibility that its popularity will grow again, certainly in the school and sixth-form college sector, where teachers already value the opportunities offered by a skills-based curriculum. It is important to communicate this view to curriculum decision-makers.

- A level Business Studies, having grown significantly in popularity, has established a clear training need amongst teachers so that the vast majority of those trained in the field can now offer more than one subject. This ensures at least a continuing provision in schools and colleges.

- Both economics and business studies are likely to join with other A level subjects in offering an increasingly modular provision so that more interesting combinations of subject are available as choices. It is important that these are on offer to students and are not just prescribed by teachers.

In line with this development is the exciting joint subject venture of Nuffield – which raises a wider range of potential curriculum developments, including pre-16.

- It is essential that there be an immediate rationalization of the differences between academic and vocational routes post-16 so that schools and colleges can offer a menu of courses which are attractive to students without having to select a chosen route at an early stage. Universities can contribute significantly by raising, in practice, their recognition of GNVQ.

- It is still important to keep cross-curricular provision on the school agenda, despite any apparent playing down of its importance by curriculum agencies. EIU is still a very important element in pupils' entitlement and there is extensive evidence to demonstrate the contribution it can make to general and subject-specific education.

Finally, teachers will do well to remember the importance of the skills and outcomes they want to deliver through the subjects and to ensure that these are at the forefront of curriculum planning. In many respects they are more important than the content of the subjects which is so often a vehicle for that delivery – although content is undeniably important in the effective delivery of examination syllabuses.

References

Blowers, S. (1991). *Business Education and the National Curriculum*, in: Whitehead, D. and Dyer, D. (eds), *New Developments in Economics and Business Education*, London, Routledge & Kegan Paul.

Brech, R. (1994). 'The challenge and rewards of experiential learning', *Economics and Business Education*, vol. 2, part 4, no. 8, pp. 172–3.

Cullimore, D. (1993). 'Business and economics education and the proposals for technology', *Economics and Business Education*, vol. 1, part 1, no. 2, pp. 95–7.

Davies, P. (1994), 'Pressures and opportunities in Key Stage 4', *Economics and Business Education Journal*, vol. 2, part 1, no. 5, pp. 38–42.

DES (1977). *Curriculum 11–16: Working Papers by HM Inspectorate – A Contribution to the Current Debate*, London, HMSO.

DES (1980). *A Framework for the School Curriculum*, London, HMSO.

DES (1990). *HMI Statement on Business and Economics Education 5–16*, London, DES.

DFE (1992). *HMI Report on 'Economic and Industrial Understanding 5–16'*, London, DFE.

EBEA (1994a). *Economics 16-19 Project Newsletter 3*, Oxford, Heinemann Educational.

EBEA (1994b). Thomas, L. (ed.), *Teaching and Learning the New Economics*, Oxford, Heinemann Educational.

EBEA (1995). *Core Economics*, Oxford, Heinemann Educational.

EBEA Business Education KS4 Working Group (1995). 'Statement on business studies at Key Stage 4', *Economics and Business Education*, vol. 3, part 1, no. 9. pp. 32–3.

Economics Association (1977). *The Contribution of Economics to General Education* (Report of an ad hoc committee).

Economics Association (1985). *Understanding Economics*, Harlow, Longman.

Economics Association (1991). 'Economic awareness in primary education', *Economics*, vol. 27, part 4, no. 116, pp. 171–4.

Edwards, G.J., Phillips, R.F.R. and Ryba, R.H. (1954). *The Teaching of Economics*, Economics Association.

Linton, T.M. (1985). 'Economics in the early years of school', in: Atkinson, G. B. J. (ed.), *Teaching Economics*, Economics Association/Heinemann.

Macfarlane, E.J. (1993). *Education 16–19 in Transition*, London, Routledge.

Vidler, C. (1995). *Economics 16–19 Project Briefing Paper*, London, EBEA.

PART 2

TEACHING AND LEARNING

5 Teaching and learning: discussion

Steve Hodkinson and Martin Jephcote

The 1990s provide a rich environment for issues and questions concerned with teaching and learning, and this book comes appropriately (as is reported in Part 1) at the culmination of a process of review in education that has as one of its focal points the raising of the quality of teaching and learning in schools and colleges. The National Curriculum, the introduction of GNVQ and the Dearing Review of post-16 education are instances of the continuous process of adaptation to new curricula and assessment arrangements (beginning with the introduction of GCSE) which teachers everywhere have grappled with over a period of some ten years. New terms and phrases have become part of our everyday teaching language – differentiation, tiered assessment, performance criteria, range statements, grading themes, competence, core skills, and many others. New targets for education and training have been developed in an attempt to underpin (or stimulate even) this increased emphasis on learning and achievement. The National Targets for Education and Training, for example, include foundation learning targets to be achieved by the year 2000:

- by age nineteen, 85 per cent of young people to achieve five GCSEs at grade C or above, an Intermediate GNVQ or an NVQ at Level 2;

- 75 per cent of young people to achieve Level 2 competence in communication, numeracy and IT by age nineteen, and 35 per cent to achieve Level 3 competence in these core skills by age twenty-one;

- by age twenty-one, 60 per cent of young people to achieve two GCE A levels, an Advanced GNVQ or an NVQ at Level 3.

New inspection arrangements in schools and colleges and in initial teacher education (see Chapters 23 and 27 by Keith Brumfitt, and Ian Chambers and Susan Squires, respectively) are intended to monitor the quality of responses by the educational professionals themselves to this broad agenda. The concept of a 'failing school' is one that a number of local communities are living with at this time.

Some of the recent focus on teaching and learning in economics and business classrooms has inevitably been bound up with developing coping strategies for this changed environment for schools and colleges. Some of the chapters in this part of the book are rightly concerned, therefore, with those coping strategies. Alison Atkinson (Chapter 14), for example, examines the issues involved in assessing the diverse evidence generated by students following GNVQ courses in business. This is an aspect of assessment which many teachers of economics and business in schools have encountered for the first time through GNVQ. Nick Heard (Chapter 12) is concerned to address the classroom issues relating to differentiation. His contribution suggests that we are all now well acquainted with the concept of differentiation as applied to examinations at Key Stage 4, but that considerable further work is needed if GCSE learning objectives are to be accessed and achieved in some form by all students. Nick Heard's analysis and examples should be of some help to subject leaders who increasingly are being asked to meet individual learning needs. Sue Hatt (Chapter 9) draws our attention once more to the fact that economics teaching can and should be handled so as to promote equal opportunities in respect of gender. Again her examples and analysis should help those of us who are trying to realize such whole-curriculum objectives in practice.

The core of this part of the book is, however, mainly concerned with issues in the teaching and learning of economics and business which comprise part of our response to our own critique of our achievements. At the heart of this critique have been concerns over the role of economics in post-16 education, the relationship between economics and business, and the contribution of our subjects to the development of core skills, particularly information technology (IT).

Concerns over the future of A level Economics have led to two major curriculum projects devoted to addressing the issues – the EBEA's own Economics 16–19 Project and the Nuffield Business and Economics Project. The outcomes of the two are very different. From the first has emerged an analysis of teaching and learning that seeks to influence the study of economics and its teaching in general and which finds form in teacher collaboration and exemplar teacher and student materials. From the other has emerged an approach to the teaching of economics rooted in links between economics and business and which finds form in an examination syllabus and related materials.

But what of significance has emerged from this process of critical self-evaluation by teachers of economics and business? Linda Thomas (Chapter 6) sees 'economic thoughtfulness' as the EBEA Project's 'seminal idea', one which 'permeated its processes and outcomes'. She characterizes it as a 'contract between teacher and learner in which the intention is to develop individuals' critical consciousness in relation to experience and ... to refine the theoretical frameworks in the process' (p. 65). She asserts that achieving it extends beyond encouraging students to argue about technicalities and the discipline's propositions or constructing exciting lessons about such matters.

Alan Hamlin (Chapter 7) and Dave Dickson (Chapter 8) add weight to these arguments, and the Project's publications, *Teaching and Learning the New Economics* (EBEA, 1994) and *Core Economics* (EBEA, 1995) add evidence and detail. Your assessment of the significance of the Project's work is 'key', for if you accept its philosophy and evidence then through it you will help to overcome an agreed fundamental criticism of A level Economics:

'A-level content is relatively mechanical, requiring only that students learn

some models and be capable of reproducing them without great thought or understanding. These models are spelled out in a vacuum of history and judgement, so that (i) the links between theory and supporting evidence are never properly made, and (ii) students do not learn the skills of assembling critical evidence towards the assessment of an idea' (EBEA, 1994, p. 51).

Achieving this would indeed be a significant contribution to our future students' education.

The Nuffield Project team members in their contributions to this book (Chapters 10 and 11) describe how their own thinking has led them to assert that it would be through the 'integration of economics and business' that the full complexities of real world problems could be addressed and that 'genuine understanding of such problems involves an appreciation of a number of different perspectives' (p. 131). Access to the Nuffield Project's work to teachers and students is assured through its availability as a University of London Examinations and Assessment Council (ULEAC) examination syllabus (at Key Stage 4 as well as at 16–19). The significance of its long term contribution to teaching and learning in our subject areas rests on the outworking of two assumptions – that integrating a discipline (economics) and an eclectic study of a phenomenon (business) is a relatively simple matter, and that economics is best taught in such a framework rather than as part of a social science curriculum.

The notion of 'core skills' has been with us for some time. It is embedded not only in National Targets for Education and Training but also in the National Curriculum and GNVQ requirements and is a central part of the Dearing 16–19 Review (Dearing, 1995). Among these core skills, IT has for a long time been assumed to be particularly appropriate and significant in the context of teaching and learning business and economics, especially in Key Stage 4 Business. Nettleship (1990), writing on behalf of the Economics Association in response to national discussion on core skills, was upbeat in his assessment of the contribution of economics. More recently, Tribe (1994) conducted a survey which did much to challenge the 1990 analysis; and Hurd (1995), in his third survey report on the use of computers in economics and business, draws attention to the continued very slow progress being made.

Peter Davies in his contribution to this book (Chapter 13) takes the discussion much further by focusing on classrooms and learning. His analysis of the current situation at Key Stage 4 questions assumed relationships not only about learning IT and learning economics and business, but also about the apparent contribution that frequent use of IT in business classrooms makes to progression in either IT or in business. Subject learning and core skills (like IT) is a major current issue and clearly one, according to Davies, where there is considerable scope for further work.

References

Dearing, Sir R. (1995). *Review of 16–19 Qualifications: Interim Report*, London, DFEE

EBEA (1995). *Core Economics*, Oxford, Heinemann Educational.

EBEA (1994). Thomas, L. (ed.), *Teaching and Learning the New Economics*, Oxford, Heinemann Educational.

Hurd, S. J. (1995). *Third National Survey of Computer Use in Economics and Business Education*, University of Staffordshire.

Nettleship, J. (1990). 'Core skills and A/AS Economics', *Economics*, vol. 26, part 4, pp.162–4.

Tribe, J. (1994). 'Core skills and A/AS Economics: some survey findings', in *Economics and Business Education*, vol. 2, part 2, pp. 84–6.

6 Promoting economic thoughtfulness

Linda Thomas

Introduction

Economic thoughtfulness was a term coined by the Economics 16–19 Project in recognition of the emphasis placed on the learner within the new A level economics espoused by the Project. Disturbed by the results of its research phase, which included an enquiry into learners' perceptions both of economics and of the outcomes of studying it, the Project mounted a three-pronged attack to effect change. A new specification of the content and structure of examination syllabuses at 16–19 was developed, an appropriate teaching and learning framework was devised, and the parameters of the task of changing economics teachers' perception and conceptualization of teaching and learning within economics classrooms was established.

Economic thoughtfulness, the Project's seminal idea, permeated its processes and outcomes. It informed and was illustrated by the Project's publications, the first of which discussed the Project's approach to the content and learning of economics within the 16–19 curriculum (Thomas, 1994). This presented the theoretical basis for its curriculum development work which was illustrated in the resulting publications for students (EBEA, 1995) and teachers (Thomas, 1995).

The purpose of this chapter is to focus on the idea of economic thoughtfulness and to provide insights into its nature and role within economics education. In the first two sections of the chapter, some of the characteristics of economic thoughtfulness are revealed as a result of its comparison with *academic competence* – the practice of teaching economics as a set of theoretical propositions – and with *operational competence* – a phrase associated with the introduction of experiential learning and General National Vocational Qualifications (GNVQs). In the third section, the concept is further developed by means of a consideration of its innovative potential within teaching and learning contexts. Finally, its nature is illuminated through an attempt to predict its effect on teaching and learning in economics classrooms into the future and on likely sources of further development. It is possible, for example, that by emphasizing thoughtfulness, economics teachers will generate a need for more open kinds of pedagogy and curricula which will make new demands on both students and teachers.

Thoughtfulness versus academic competence

Economic thoughtfulness involves developing a commitment on the part of students to the canons of behaviour established by the discipline. In the introduction to *Core Economics* (EBEA, 1995a), this is expressed as follows:

'Core Economics *assumes that the reader will behave like an economist from page 1. Each of the nineteen units uses real economic material – data or reports – and the tasks which the reader is asked to undertake are the ones that economists would use in the same circumstances'* (p. 1).

To this extent it does not differ from every other context of academic endeavour which, according to Barnett (1994), calls for:

'*... a willingness to give oneself to the demands of the discipline (in other words, self-discipline), a personal toughness in developing and propounding one's own thinking, a commitment to and ownership of one's offerings, and an ability to put an individual stamp on things'* (p. 169).

Where economic thoughtfulness may differ is in the way it defines *learning*. Economic thoughtfulness within 16–19 economics also involves developing a commitment to certain canons of learning. In an ideal world, these canons would be found within the practices of academic and professional economists and would be embedded within the traditions of the economic community. The Introduction to *Core Economics* describes this ideal world:

'Core Economics *also assumes that the reader will learn like an economist from page 1. Each situation dealt with by economists is always slightly different from anything previously encountered. Economists are therefore faced with an on-going learning process which requires them to analyse each situation afresh, to adapt their existing knowledge in the new context and to evaluate its usefulness. An economics student opening this book for the first time is different from an expert economist only to the extent that he or she has less formal knowledge. By the end of the first six pages, however, they will already have done some analysis and learnt to review their conclusions. In this way, just like professional economists, they will gradually refine their knowledge of economic models and theories as they use them to understand and predict real events'* (pp. 1–2).

However, on the basis of experience of the academic community's preoccupations, I am convinced that this is a description of what ought to be, rather than what is, in reality. So, in instituting the term 'economic thoughtfulness' the Project is in broad agreement with Barnett's (1994) description of academic perceptions of teaching and learning:

'*In the academic version of competence ... learning is essentially propositional in character. Many will say that individual facts, propositions and items of information are neither here nor there. What counts is the imparting of what it is to think as a historian or physicist and so on. That is said, certainly. But it is doubtful if many students could recognise the claim in their curriculum experience. ... After all, the academic's own learning is of a propositional kind. ... What fires academics is precisely the latest findings or heated controversy over new concepts. It is not concerns over the fundamental character of their discipline'* (p. 161).

The implication is that the academic community takes responsibility for students' learning only in the sense of accessing the discipline's propositions. It remains detached from the need to engage students with the relationship between the discipline's constructs and the challenges of human life – the latter is there either as an illustration of, or to be explained by, the former. Learning, in this context, is more likely to represent a surface, processing approach (resulting in academic competence) than a conscious engagement in the search for a critical personal stance in relation to theory and its relationship with individual experience of the economic system (resulting in economic thoughtfulness).

Learning, in the context of economic thoughtfulness, assumes that individual learners mediate between the meanings they give to their own experiences of the economic system and the propositions of economic theory. This process of mediation will give learners control over their own learning and an awareness of the value both of economic theory and of experience. Its outcome will be the development, through use and evaluation, of a *critical* framework of theory – that is, control over their own learning.

Thoughtfulness versus operational competence

The term *operational competence* was created by Barnett (1994) with the intention of signalling another area of concern for all teachers and especially those whose areas of operation, like economics, overlap with the vocational world. He argued that operational competence:

'... may lead to a narrowing of human consciousness. Understanding is replaced by competence; insight is replaced by effectiveness; and rigour of interactive argument is replaced by communication skills' (p. 37).

Mindful of this danger, members of the 16–19 Project were nevertheless impressed by some of the characteristics of the GNVQ framework as it was emerging in 1991. Three features seemed particularly promising: the emphasis on learners' self-directed learning; the awarding of responsibility for assessment to teachers, supported by a system for moderation; and the recognition that there is a need for the curriculum to confront the challenges of today's world. The Project cooperated with the National Council for Vocational Qualifications to exploit these conditions and produce, within the Business GNVQ, unit specifications in which the concept of economic thoughtfulness was embedded in the two contexts of production and employment. The aim was to allow students to develop within a framework of critical understanding and thus to escape the imposition of a closed world of instrumental action and work.

67

Within one year of its introduction, this had been abandoned. The swift replacement of the Project's framework with a conventional descriptive programme, which even succeeded in presenting *theory* as description, signified the strength of an approach which saw economics operationally (in terms of its usefulness to business). As was stated in an NCVQ paper (1995, p. 18) forecasting the change: 'It is intended that economic insights are used to understand the business environment'.

The experience demonstrated both the power and the insidious nature of the operational competence movement and gave support to Barnett's claim that it is a real danger within education, capable of permeating ideas, institutions and language. Almost without our noticing, it can affect the way we think – the medium becomes the message. Barnett suggests that ideas such as vocationalism and training, transferable skill development and capability, although seemingly distanced from education, can become embedded in its fabric. Even words and phrases that are relatively neutral, such as 'the learning society', 'underlying knowledge', 'learning how to learn', and 'critical thinking skills', may reflect the operation of a very different set of interests:

'Competence, skill, knowing-how, getting things done, technique, effectiveness, operation: all these are coming to form a constellation of concepts marking out ... a set of interests' (p. 170).

These must be constantly examined and challenged, especially when at their most persuasive, because they represent a denial of the independence of mind which should characterize a human being:

'What is sought is a response to a given situation: an input–output notion lies not far under the surface of operational competence. What is prized is not a genuine personal interpretation of a situation (for that could lead to an unduly challenging world-view) but a reprocessing of presented sense data. Real independence of mind cannot be tolerated. Real minds would be liable to challenge the given definitions of competence and outcomes. 'Mind', therefore, falls outside the constellation of concepts containing competence and outcomes' (p. 173).

Economic thoughtfulness is capable of undermining the notion of operational competence and of opening up the closed world of instrumental action. This is because it places the nurturing of the individual's critical consciousness at the heart of the economics education process. As such it had no place in GNVQ Business and was removed at the first opportunity.

Economic thoughtfulness and innovations in teaching and learning

In the previous sections I have argued that economic thoughtfulness carries with it a new vision of learning as an holistic process of enfranchisement. Through the processes of economic thoughtfulness:

- *Learners are released from the constraints of academic competence – theory without criticism.* Teachers and learners have to keep faith with their discipline and submit to its methodological rules – what McCloskey (1985) refers to as method with a small 'm', the tools of the discipline, which he describes as 'economic theory in its verbal and mathematical forms, statistical theory and practice, familiarity with certain accounting conventions and statistical sources, and a background of stylised historical fact and worldly experience' (p. 24). At the same time, they learn to view it with critical detachment and use experience to evaluate its validity for them as individual thinkers and doers.

- *Learners are released from the constraints of operational competence – action/experience without critical meaning and understanding.* Students need to be given responsibility for organizing their own reading and discussions. They need to be actively involved in learning experiences. At the same time, they need to learn to be critical of their own judgements and perspectives by constantly searching for meaning within experience.

- *Individuals learn to trust the discipline to tell the truth about their experiences*, because they see and understand that the discipline and experience are not separate, but one.

This fusion of theory and experience, which the Project advocated for economics teaching and learning, was also applied to its own developmental processes – the resulting classroom materials were intended to be practical representations of the philosophy of economic thoughtfulness. They were designed:

- to satisfy the internal demands of the discipline of economics while encouraging collaborative self-criticism in both teacher and students;

- to encourage students to engage in new thought and new action in a way which would do justice to both;

- to provide a specification for disciplined emancipation from both traditional academic and newer experience-focused operational models of teaching and learning.

Where the materials have been successful in achieving this design, they illuminate the concept of thoughtfulness. In the following examples, reference is made to a range of contexts drawn from *Core Economics* which are summarized in the quick reference sections of *Core Economics Teacher's Guide*.

All Project Units are organized into four sections. Contexts and issues are introduced using authentic stimulus materials, including newspaper cuttings, official statistics, company reports and cuttings from specialist magazines and journals. Analysis boxes draw on appropriate theory to assist the process of analysis (providing an ever-expanding background of theory). Review sections encourage students consistently to reflect on the issues encountered and on the appropriateness of theory and their own responses in that context. The tasks they are asked to undertake involve them in an iterative process in which

69

they mediate between their own experiences and the theoretical framework of economics.

Monopolistic markets

Unit 4 is about monopolistic markets:

- the impact of monopolies and monopolistic behaviour on market outcomes such as prices;
- the impact of monopolies and monopolistic behaviour on efficiency;
- the identification of monopoly power;
- government intervention to correct for the effects of the application of monopoly power.

In this Unit, stimulus materials provide information on the following contexts and issues:

- a case study of British Gas and its pricing policy;
- British Rail and the debate about competition or Government investment;
- the merger of Allied–Lyons plc and Carlsberg A/S and the intervention of the Monopolies and Mergers Commission;
- a case study of patents, monopoly power and investment in the drug industry.

Students are invited to analyse:

- the case for and against monopolies in comparison with competitive markets;
- the regulation of prices and quality and the promotion of competition by Regulators;
- cost–benefit analysis;
- types of merger.

Opportunities for review focus on:

- monopoly pricing, regulation and the promotion of competition;
- privatization and the implications for competition, efficiency and investment;
- regulating merger activity;
- patents and the public interest.

The tasks that students are asked to undertake, in collaboration with fellow students and teachers, are:

- to compare the various systems of ownership which, historically, have applied to the supply of gas (competition, state ownership, private monopoly with regulation) – and identify the information required to complete the task;

- to explore the major issues involved in the privatization of British Rail;

- to identify different views about mergers amongst the various interest groups in the brewing industry and consider the implications of such differences for the work of the Monopolies and Mergers Commission;

- on the basis of a thorough examination of information about the pharmaceutical industry, to write a report to the European Parliament about the advisability of extending the time period for which a patent on a new drug should operate.

Growth and development

Unit 14 is about growth and development:

- the meaning and measurement of growth and development;

- growth as an increase in economic capacity;

- the causes of growth;

- the consequences of growth.

Stimulus materials include newspaper cuttings, official statistics, company reports and cuttings from specialist magazines and journals, to introduce contemporary events and issues. These include:

- quotations from diarists, poets, politicians, economists and newspaper reports providing different perspectives on growth;

- statistical data on GDP and qualitative data generated through investigation;

- case study material providing information on the economies of the UK, the USA and Eastern Europe;

- commentaries and reports on the environmental and social costs of growth;

- data and information on development indicators and debt-service ratios for various regions and countries in the world; detailed information about Jamaica, Lebanon, Namibia and Tunisia.

Analysis boxes draw on appropriate theory to assist the process of analysis (providing an ever-expanding background of theory). They focus on:

- the production possibility frontier as a simple model of growth;

- the problems of using GDP as a measure of performance;

- alternative definitions of economic development;

- sources of investment in developing countries – domestic markets or international debt;

- indicators of the contrast between developed and less developed countries.

Review sections encourage students consistently to reflect on the issues encountered and on the appropriateness of theory and their own responses in that context. Students are asked to consider:

- the difference between recovery (to full capacity) and growth;

- strategies for growth and their appropriateness in different circumstances;

- the problem of identifying those benefiting and paying for growth;

- the international debt crisis, its extent and incidence;

- the universality of growth as an economic policy target.

The tasks students are asked to undertake involve them in an iterative process in which they mediate between their own experiences and the theoretical framework of economics. They are asked:

- with reference to historical and contemporary commentaries and data, to consider economic growth from a critical perspective;

- to use data and information (some generated through interviews) to explore various measures and indicators of and contexts for economic growth;

- to work through three case studies, providing data on the UK, the USA and Eastern Europe, to evaluate the success of policies designed to stimulate growth;

- to prepare for and engage in debate on the costs and benefits of growth;

- to identify differing views about development and consider their implications;

- to carry out a statistical exercise based on data about development indicators in Africa;

- to analyse the effects of debt in developing countries;

- by means of a simulation and actual data on development indicators for four countries, to evaluate different strategies for development.

Labour markets

Unit 15 is about labour markets:

- the relationship between individual aspirations and motivation and the supply of labour as a factor of production;

- deriving the demand for labour from the demand for a product;

- the characteristics of occupational labour markets and the shape of demand and supply curves in those markets;

- explanations of wage differentials in a competitive economy – discrimination, rent, and the activities of trade unions and employer organizations;

- the developing notion of the quality of the workforce and its implications for the individual supplier of labour.

Stimulus materials draw attention to contexts and issues from the economic world, such as:

- differing perceptions of the costs and benefits of part-time work;

- data and commentary on changes in full- and part-time employment;

- a simulated interview with an employer of labour from the service sector;

- job advertisements across a range of occupations;

- data on wage rates and conditions of work within one occupation in the retail trade;

- data and commentary on wage and employment differentials across ethnic and sex groups;

- perceptions of the nature and purpose of trade union activity.

Analysis boxes highlight the following theoretical propositions:

- the supply curve model of the individual's supply of labour; the effects of taxes within the model;

- marginal revenue product and the demand curve for the labour of individual units of labour;

- the effects of discrimination on wage levels;

- the use of economic rent and trade union activity to explain wage differentials within the market for an individual's labour;

- the case for and against government intervention in the market for an individual's labour.

Review sections encourage reflection on the issues encountered and on the appropriateness of theory and students' own responses to:

- the competitive market model for an individual's labour;

- the market model account of the existence of wage differentials;

- market failure and the existence of wage differentials;

- market failure and the implications for the quality and employability of individual labour.

The tasks students are asked to undertake once more involve them in an iterative process in which they mediate between their own experiences and the theoretical framework of economics. They are asked to:

- conduct surveys of attitudes to various institutions within the labour market, such as part-time work and trade unions, and analyse the data obtained;

- work through various text-based exercises to increase familiarity with graphical representations of the supply of an individual's labour

- analyse and consider explanations for trends in employment data, such as part- and full-time work;

- consider the demand for a unit of labour in terms of its value to the employer;

- work through text-based exercises using data generated from various sources, such as personal experience, national statistics and case studies, to provide explanations for the existence of differential wage rates;

- conduct their own data-gathering exercises, both in relation to hypotheses drawn from their own experience of the labour market and to assess the effects of the government's attempt to focus attention on quality and employability.

Predicting the future

The vision of teaching and learning encapsulated in economic thoughtfulness, as illustrated in the previous section, is of a particularly open kind of communicative exercise firmly grounded within practical criticism. Engagement with such an enterprise is likely to create new challenges for all concerned. For example, parents, schools and examination authorities may attempt to intervene on behalf of 'mastery' of the technicalities of the discipline.

Students who have become accustomed to conventional teaching and learning contexts may also resist the introduction of collaborative methods, as is illustrated by Jones (1995). Having engaged in a video-recorded lesson on international trade in which, in groups, students were asked to respond from different perspectives to the collapse of sterling in 1992, they were invited to evaluate the lesson. The teacher noted:

'Students felt strongly that they needed a "solid set of notes to revise from", and equally insistently, that notes should come first. A typical comment recorded on film: "It would be good if you knew the theory first ... you would know what you were talking about" ' (p. 9).

One student even resisted the introduction of group work: 'I feel class interaction is a complete waste of time with little if any educational gain. Group work is a contradiction in terms. The fact is that a group of four or five seventeen year olds given the chance will not sit in a circle discussing economics' (p. 9).

Teachers, too, may encounter problems in interpretation and implementation of their own roles, especially when they themselves tend to be as excited as academic economists about the discipline's propositions. It is easy to forget that very few young people are going to be intrinsically interested in the study of concepts and theories for their own sake and that the importation of active learning techniques in order artificially to increase the interest factor is unlikely to succeed. If the intention is to help students to amass the knowledge and skills of the discipline in the most efficient way this is what teachers should do, even if it means theory first, illustration later and the copious use of note-taking techniques.

On the other hand, if the intention is to promote economic thoughtfulness, students must be let into the teaching and learning secret and become partners in, rather than the recipients of, teaching and learning strategies. Teachers will need to remind themselves that it is not enough to encourage students to argue about technical matters, the discipline's propositions, or to construct lessons that are intended to achieve greater interest and excitement in the internal workings of mathematical propositions. Learning becomes a contract between teacher and learner in which the intention is to develop individuals' critical consciousness in relation to experience and – the other side of the coin – to refine the theoretical frameworks involved in the process.

The kinds of teaching and learning required for economic thoughtfulness thus have implications for the ways in which members of the education community think and act within their world. On a practical level it will be necessary to develop more open kinds of pedagogy, curricula and assessment regimes. On a philosophical level, it is likely to lead to a review of the meaning of human learning and development which is at the heart of the educational enterprise.

In a contribution to the National Commission on Education's commission of inquiry into education and training Hayes *et al.* (1995) argue that society is undergoing a transformation as significant as the movement from an agricultural to an industrial society. The harbingers of the transformation include the following:

- The nation state in the developed West is declining as a locus of power.

- There is an on-going shift from mass production work to work in organizations based on responsiveness and customization.

- The economy is increasingly organized around the processing of information.

- The increasing accessibility of information is helping to break monopolies of power.

- Effective action is no longer possible on the traditional military, industrial, political and public service model, with thinkers and planners instructing and controlling implementers and doers.

- Active participation is demanded from ever-wider sections of society, with

75

each individual developing the capability to bring about change at individual, organizational and collective levels – in other words, individuals can make a difference.

- Problem-solving capabilities based on the use of concepts rather than on experience are becoming essential when facing new and unfamiliar situations. Knowledge and skills are necessary, but insufficient, prerequisites for effective action.

The authors also argue that society must adapt to these new imperatives in ways that prevent total dislocation. In their view one of the most powerful tools at society's disposal is learning but only if it is in a form capable of empowering individuals, organizations and government to build bridges from the present into the post-transformation society. Economic thoughtfulness, if it encourages the development of new forms of critical communication in classrooms, may meet that criterion and thus contribute to the process of easing society into a new learning age.

References

Barnett, R. (1994). *The Limits of Competence*, Milton Keynes, Open University Press.

EBEA (1995a). *Core Economics*, Oxford, Heinemann Educational.

Hayes, C., Fonda, N. and Hillman, J. (1995). *Learning in the New Millennium*, National Commission on Education Briefing, New Series 5.

Jones, C. (1995). 'Teaching and learning the new economics'. Unpublished PGCE coursework, Manchester University.

McCloskey, D. (1985). *The Rhetoric of Economics*, London, Wheatsheaf Press.

NCVQ (1995). Mandatory Units for Advanced Business GNVQ.

Thomas, L. (ed.) (1994). *Teaching and Learning the New Economics*, Oxford, Heinemann Educational.

Thomas, L. (1995). *Core Economics: Teacher's Guide*, Oxford, Heinemann Educational.

7 Assessment by design for A level Economics

Alan Hamlin

Introduction

According to one dictionary definition, assessment is concerned with the estimation of value, magnitude or quality. But such a definition is of little practical help in approaching the topic of assessment within A level Economics unless we can be more precise about the interpretation of the underlying ideas of value, magnitude and quality in this particular context. We can only talk sensibly about alternative forms of assessment and the important details of assessment design if we have a clear idea of what we are attempting to assess, and what purposes our assessments are to serve; and we must derive these ideas from consideration of the underlying purposes of A level Economics. It is in this sense that questions of assessment are integral to the overall conception of this A level.

Of course, there are many possible conceptions of A level Economics. Some might argue that the study of economics at this level should be seen as an introduction to economic theory for an audience who might at least consider studying economics at university; others might argue that economics at A level should be concerned with providing students with particular vocational skills; still others might argue that the role of economics at A level is to provide students with a basis for understanding and participating in the popular and political debate on economic policy. Many other views are possible, but the simple point I want to emphasize is that each of these conceptions of the purpose of A level Economics will carry with it implications for the design of all aspects of the A level – syllabus content, style of delivery, source materials, and assessment.

The purpose of this chapter is to explore some of the implications of a particular view of the role and purpose of economics at A level for assessment. The particular view of economics at this level is that associated with the Economics and Business Education Association's Economics 16–19 Project.[1] My first task is, therefore, to identify some of the salient features of that approach which allow us to address the question of what we are attempting to assess, and so identify the relevant concepts of value, quantity and quality. My second task will then be to address the question of the purposes of assessment. I will then attempt to discuss the implications of these two sets of ideas for the specific question of the design of assessment methods for A level Economics. This discussion will try both to provide a relatively general statement of the appropriate style of assessment, and more specific examples of what I will argue to be good practice.

A view of A level Economics

A full account of the view of A level Economics associated with the EBEA's Economics 16–19 Project is not possible here.[2] However it is important to note that this view has both formal and substantive dimensions. That is, it says something about the appropriate mode of study for economics at A level and something about the appropriate economics to study at A level. Economics, in this view, is not primarily a body of information – facts and theories – to be absorbed, but an approach to issues to be exemplified in a wide range of particular contexts. Of course, this is not intended to imply that economics lacks informational or theoretical content, but rather that this content is most appropriately studied at A level by the process of exploring economic problems and issues. The emphasis, then, is on 'doing economics' rather than 'knowing economics', and on the encouragement of an active and thoughtful approach to economic issues and ideas.

This commitment to an active, problem-led mode of study is set alongside a commitment to the study of the operation of the market economy, so that the substantive theme that unites the various contexts and problems to be explored is that of the market system. Notice that this substantive theme is not specified in terms of particular theoretical constructs. Theoretical constructs are seen as inputs to the process of economic understanding at A level rather than as desired outputs in their own right. Thus, for example, knowledge of the theoretical analysis of, say, the concept of natural monopoly is valued to the extent that it contributes to students' understanding of specific economic issues rather than simply as evidence of abstract knowledge *per se*. Notice also that the focus on the market system is intended to unify the variety of contexts and problems faced by students and so provide a framework within which economic skills are transferable. The concentration on the market system should therefore be interpreted widely and should certainly include a range of criticisms of the market system in particular contexts.

These commitments to an active and problem-led approach to issues arising in market economies carry important implications for the approach to teaching and learning at A level. These implications may be summarized as a task-based approach. But the 'task-based approach' must be more than simply another fine phrase, it must identify a particular approach to the design of appropriate tasks. Although it is beyond the scope of this chapter to give a detailed discussion of the full range of questions arising in the area of task design, three points should be emphasized since they carry direct implications in the area of assessment:

- Tasks should be realistic but of manageable scale.

- Tasks should draw on a variety of sources of information and skills.

- Tasks should result in outputs which are recognizably of value in their own right.

These three points apply to all tasks – whether they are conceived primarily as teaching tasks or assessment tasks – but they are guidelines for good practice rather than iron rules.

This brief discussion of an approach to economics at A level has drawn attention to two aspects of assessment. Assessment should operate via tasks which themselves conform to the criteria suggested by the approach; and assessment should set out to estimate the particular values, magnitudes and qualities identified by the approach. If the approach to economics at A level is to stress a problem-led approach to issues arising in market economies, it must utilize assessment techniques designed to assess the relevant skills and abilities in appropriate contexts.

Roles of assessment

Whilst the last section identifies the central idea underlying the design of assessment tasks, it should be remembered that assessment techniques must be sensitive not only to the nature of the object of assessment, but also to the intended purposes of assessment. Two distinctions are relevant here: first the distinction between *formative/diagnostic* assessment on the one hand and *summative* assessment on the other; and second, the distinction between *internal* and *external* assessment. I suggest that the former distinction is of more fundamental importance when considering the design of assessment tasks. This suggestion follows from recognizing that almost all formative/diagnostic assessment is internal by its nature; while the distinction between internal and external assessment in the context of summative assessment arises mostly in terms of the constraints that are considered relevant.

Summative assessment

Summative assessment is concerned primarily with an overall evaluation of a student's achievements. It is clear that assessment tasks used for this purpose must conform to the central idea outlined above, so that they should allow the student to display the relevant range of skills and abilities and their application in a variety of relevant contexts. This does not mean that *each* task has to be balanced in the sense that all skills and abilities are required equally, but that all pathways through the assessment *as a whole* should be capable of assessing the range of skills and abilities as well as providing a variety of contexts in which those skills and abilities can be deployed.

The range of tasks that might be employed in such summative assessment is very wide. But other considerations might be relevant when considering specifically external assessment. For example, there may be issues of verifiability, concerns over the time-scale of some tasks, or difficulties in handling certain types of output, which restrict the range of practicable external assessment tasks. But these constraints do not really bear on the central issue of the criteria against which summative assessment tasks should be judged.

Formative/diagnostic assessment

The major function of formative/diagnostic assessment is the provision of information on progress and problems to both student and teacher. Progress and problems can be defined only in terms of the ultimate objectives of the programme of study, so it is clear that assessment tasks intended for diagnostic use must relate to the intended summative techniques in both form and content. However, this relationship need not be direct. While it will be important to use assessment tasks which require the appropriate combination of skills and abilities, it will also be appropriate to use more specific tasks which focus on particular skills or abilities. In this way, the set of assessment tasks appropriate for diagnostic purposes will be larger than the set appropriate for summative purposes.

An obvious example concerns the use of specific economic techniques or models. The approach to economics adopted here would argue that it would be inappropriate to design a summative assessment task around the knowledge of a specific technique or model – such techniques should be seen in use rather than in isolation. Nevertheless, in the course of diagnostic assessment it may be important to locate precisely the limits of a student's ability to deploy economic arguments and, in this setting, assessment tasks that focus on particular aspects of the process may be important.

Assessment tasks

The basic points to be derived from the discussion so far are that assessment tasks must be fit for the purposes they are intended to serve and that, on the interpretation of economics at A level offered by the Economics 16–19 Project, these purposes must include the encouragement of an active and thoughtful approach to economic issues arising in market economies.

Assessment tasks should, wherever possible, place the student in a situation in which the skills of economics can be employed; where the student is encouraged to react to a context, rather than recall information; and where a range of skills and abilities can be deployed. The emphasis is on integrated assessment tasks. So, what are the characteristics of such an integrated assessment task? The answer must be that they derive directly from the overall objectives of the programme of study and so might include the requirement to:

- apply and develop economic ideas in unfamiliar contexts;
- adopt a critical perspective, recognizing different approaches and viewpoints;
- select ideas and information relevant to a specific problem;
- deploy numerical skills in support of analysis;

- develop an extended discussion, synthesizing a range of arguments;

- recognize the limitations and possible biases of arguments.

Any particular assessment task (with the exception of some diagnostic tasks) should be designed to blend together several of these characteristics. While further balancing across assessment objectives can be achieved at the level of the whole assessment package, it is important to blend characteristics together within tasks rather than separate out each objective to be met by a distinct form of assessment. This importance derives from two considerations. First, the skills and abilities associated with an active and thoughtful approach to economics are essentially interrelated, and therefore should be assessed together as an essential part of the idea of assessing economics in context. And second, tasks that focus on just one assessment objective are likely to be unrealistic and artificial so that the student is not engaged in a meaningful task but simply confronted by a question.

All of this implies a shift away from the focus on alternative forms of assessment (as in the distinction between essay questions, data response questions and multiple-choice questions, for example) and towards an emphasis on the design of integrated assessment tasks.

Given this emphasis, it might be thought that integrated assessment that succeeds in blending relevant characteristics in an appropriate manner while also offering a variety of realistic and manageable contexts would be hopelessly complicated and far removed from current assessment practice. On the contrary, much that is regarded as successful in current assessment practice could (and should) be retained with only minor modification, if any. While the approach outlined here reflects a radical rethinking of all aspects of the process of learning and teaching economics at A level, it does not require the wholesale abandonment of all that has gone before. It is the approach that underlies the design of assessment tasks, and the emphasis on relatively open-ended and integrated assessment tasks that are important and novel, there is no requirement that the types of tasks themselves should be radical departures from existing good practice.

Exemplars

This final section reproduces several examples of assessment tasks that embody and illustrate some of the principles outlined above. There has been no attempt to bring together a group of assessment tasks which illustrate the full range of possibilities, or cover the range of syllabus content or assessment objectives. The idea is simply to display some of the principles of design and to provide a brief commentary on each task to draw out its strengths and weaknesses.

Most of the tasks included here are suitable for inclusion in a time-constrained, unseen examination (although they are not all of the same 'size' so that different time allocations might be appropriate). This is not the only valid form of assessment, but it is a central form of assessment and might be thought to raise the greatest difficulty for the task-based approach advocated here.

Exemplar A

This task is intended to assess understanding of some of the basic properties of markets, the interrelationships between markets, the reactions of markets to external events, and the links from market analysis to policy considerations. But the strategy behind the task is to assess these understandings through the student's ability to use these economic ideas in an unfamiliar but recognizable context and to display other skills – such as distinguishing between analysis and evaluation, recognizing the relevance of different perspectives, and showing an awareness of the limitations of arguments. This task, therefore, clearly exemplifies the basic spirit of the approach to assessment outlined above.

It is important to note that the context offered to the student is not heavily documented or finely detailed. This offers a response to one line of criticism that might be offered – that it is cumbersome and relies on the provision of detailed case-study style documentation, so that a student's ability to handle the volume of information may be more important than an ability to work with economic ideas. This exemplar shows that a meaningful and realistic context can be established briefly and without threatening *informational overload*. The task offers a relatively wide variety of opportunities for the student to display economic thinking within a clear framework.

Study the data about 'Markets in Ethiopia' and answer the following questions:

1. For each of the four markets decide which groups of people would have been buyers and which groups would have been sellers.

2. At about this time Welo suffered a prolonged drought lasting over a year. There was a complete failure of the rains so essential to sustain the agriculture of the area. How would this have affected the members of the five groups in the population?

3. (a) Food prices did not go up by much or for long in Welo as a result of the drought. Offer an explanation for this price stability.

   (b) The drought resulted in the death of nearly 100,000 people in the Welo region. Would a sharper rise in food prices have resulted in more or fewer deaths?

   (c) Many countries face the problems of famine today. Their plight has inspired many charitable relief efforts. Is pouring food aid into an area the best solution to such problems? Could it have any undesirable effects?

Markets in Ethiopia

Ethiopia is one of the poorest countries in the world. Welo is a rural region in the north

---

83

east of the country. Some twenty years ago there were basically five occupational groups in Welo:

1. **NOMADIC PEOPLE**

   These tended herds of animals, selling some to buy grain. Meat was a luxury product in Welo, being far more expensive than grain.

2. **LARGER LAND OWNERS**

   These grew crops for sale and profit. They employed farm labourers and domestic servants, and rented some land to small tenant farmers.

3. **SMALL FARMERS**

   These grew crops for themselves (subsistence farming). Some family members found labouring jobs with the larger farmers to supplement the family income. These and the labourers were the largest groups of people in the region.

4. **LANDLESS LABOURERS**

   These were dependent on casual labouring jobs with land owners. They were generally hired by the day or week.

5. **CRAFT WORKERS**

   These produced cloth, kitchen utensils, furniture and jewellery for sale.
   In the region four markets appeared to operate.

- The market for animals
- The market for grain for food
- The market for craft products
- The market for labour

Exemplar B

This task is much more tightly focused than Exemplar A, both in terms of the context offered and in terms of the range of economic ideas in play. The source material provided is relatively detailed and requires careful reading, combining numerical and text-based information. In terms of assessment characteristics, this task emphasizes evaluation and judgement skills at a number of levels within the setting of a report-writing exercise. The student is expected to marshall relevant economic arguments in a sustained discussion, and to be able to support judgements by appeal both to the evidence provided and to the economic arguments deployed. The student is also expected to recognize the provisional nature of the judgements reached, and indicate how these judgements might be improved.

The more detailed style of this task contrasts with the style of Exemplar A, but the styles complement each other in a variety of ways, thereby illustrating the flexibility of the task-based approach.

In the UK, the Monopolies Commissions asks the following questions when passing a judgement on a proposed merger.

Does the merger:

- maintain and promote competition in the UK?
- promote the interests of consumers?
- promote the development of new products and the reduction of costs?
- maintain and promote the balanced regional distribution of industry and employment?
- maintain and promote competitive activity by UK companies in overseas markets?

Study the data on the proposed merger between Allied-Lyons plc and Carlsberg A/S. How important is each of the questions in the case of this proposed merger? On the basis of the evidence provided evaluate the proposed merger. What further information might improve your evaluation?

'No decent excuse' for beer increases

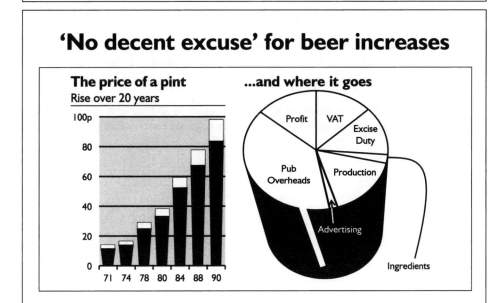

The price of a pint
Rise over 20 years

...and where it goes

James Erlichman, Consumer Affairs Correspondent

An increase in beer prices of 7p a pint, imposed this week by Allied Breweries, makers of Tetley, Burton and Ind Coope ales, takes the price of a pint to above £1.50 in most parts of London.

The rise follows one imposed two weeks ago by Bass, makers of Bass, Worthington, and Tennents, which put up prices in the West Midlands by 7p, and is likely to be followed by a 10p increase from Courage.

Pub attendances are down slightly on last year, but price increases have ensured that takings are rising faster than inflation.

85

Andrew Sangster, spokesman for the Campaign for Real Ale, said: "There is no decent excuse for these rises. Most companies respond in a recession by lowering prices to attract customers. The brewers put prices up while pub attendances are still going down."

Camra claims that most brewers used the Chancellor's budget increases on excise duty and VAT as a fig leaf to boost their prices higher than was required.

City analysts offered a "no comment" on whether the big six brewers might be engaged in an informal cartel.

Colin Davies, a brewing analyst with Barclays de Zoete Wedd, said "Most pubgoers are not interested in the price they pay for a pint. You must remember that pub amenities are far better now than 20 years ago, when spit and sawdust were the rule. People are paying for that in higher beer prices, which are, in effect, the entry fee to a nicer place to be."

Mike Ripley for the Brewers Society, said: "Then rise in beer prices does reflect the investment that has gone into pubs at the retail end."

The real price of beer (compared with wages) had fallen. "Treasury figures show it took the average man 16 minutes to earn a pint in 1970 and only 12 minutes in 1990."

In 1971, the average price of a pint of bitter in a pub was 12p.

Since 1978 the retail price index for all goods has risen by 252 per cent. By the same measure food has risen by only 207 per cent, but beer has risen by 320 per cent.

Source: *The Guardian*, 13 June 1991

THE PROPOSED MERGER OF ALLIED-LYONS PLC AND CARLSBERG A/S

In October 1991, Allied Lyons PLC and Carlsberg A/S agreed to merge their brewing and wholesaling activities by forming a new company – Carlsberg Tetley Brewing Ltd (CTL). Under the agreement Allied would continue to own its 4,400 pubs and would have a seven year supply agreement to buy all of its beer requirements from CTL (15% could be 3rd party brands stocked by CTL).

The following are extracts from the Monopolies and Mergers Commission Report on the proposed merger:

1.THE UK BEER MARKET

	Consumption m bbls	By type ale %	lager %
1960	27.6	99.0	1.0
1970	35.0	93.0	7.0
1980	40.7	69.3	30.7
1990	38.6	48.6	51.4
1991	37.2	49.0	51.0

2.There are some differences in the profile of ale and lager drinkers. Lager is a more popular type of beer for women drinkers than is ale...A survey by the British Market Research Bureau in 1990 showed that women accounted for 36% of draught ale drinkers. Lager drinking is also more popular (relative to ale drinking) with the young than older consumers; the same survey showed that nearly 50% of draught lager drinkers were aged 34 or less compared with nearly 33% of draught ale drinkers.

3.Total production of beer by UK brewers amounted to just over 35 million barrels in 1991. Imports of beer have been increasing but from a very low base. In 1991 imports were 3.3 million barrels, accounting for just under 9% of beer supplied in the UK. Of these imports, around 1.4 million barrels came from the Republic of Ireland: these included Irish-brewed ales destined for Northern Ireland and Irish brewed Guinness.

4.ESTIMATED MAJOR BREWERS' SHARES OF BEER PRODUCTION 1991

	Total	Ale	Lager
Allied	12	12	13
Carlsberg	4	0	8
Bass	22	20	24
Courage/Grand Met	21	20	22
Whitbread	12	12	12
S&N	11	13	9

5.ALLIED'S AND CARLSBERG'S MAIN BEER BRANDS 1991

ALLIED: Lagers* – Skol, Castlemaine, Lowenbrau, Wrexham lager, Swan Light (low alcohol).
Ales – Tetley Bitter, Ansells, Tetley Mild, John Bull, Draught Burton Ale.

CARLSBERG: Lagers – Carlsberg Pilsener; Carlsberg Export, Carlsberg Special Brew, Tuborg Green, Dansk LA, Tuborg Gold, Carlsberg Elephant.
*some of Allied's lager brands (eg Skol) are owned by Allied but others (eg Castlemaine) are brewed under licence.

6.PRODUCTION CAPACITY. The Brewers' Society estimates that there were some 280 breweries (production plants and not brewing companies) in the UK in 1990. These range from large breweries with a capacity of up to 2 million barrels a year to the very small micro-brewers. Despite the closure of a number of breweries in recent years there is still excess capacity in the brewing industry.

7.BRAND MARKETING AND ADVERTISING. Different marketing approaches have generally been adopted for ale and lager. The marketing of ale tends to focus on stressing its regional characteristics or its association with a particular brewery. Lager, however, is promoted on a national basis, often by means of major advertising campaigns... In 1991 Allied and Carlsberg spent around £24 million (or roughly £5 a barrel) and £20 million (roughly £13 a barrel), respectively on advertising and promotion.

8.ALLIED'S AND CARLSBERG'S ANNUAL EXPENDITURE ON ADVERTISING AND MARKETING IN 1991 (£million)

	Specific brands		Non-specific
Allied	7.2	12.3	4.4
Carlsberg	N/A	11.3	9.1

9.EFFECTS ON INDEPENDENT WHOLESALERS

In 1991 18% of Carlsberg's sales were to independent wholesalers, representing around 23% of their lager requirements... this latter percentage how now fallen to around 13% as a result of Courage's appointment as exclusive distributor of Carlsberg to the off-trade.

We received strong representations from independent wholesalers that the continued existence of Carlsberg as an independent brewer was important to them because:

- Carlsberg was the last independent source of a strong lager brand
- the Carlsberg brand was the top selling brand of lager in the free on-trade
- Carlsberg gave much better support to wholesalers than other brewers...

Exemplar C

The final sentence of this task description might easily have been taken from a traditional A level essay question. This emphasizes the continuity between much current examining practice and the approach to assessment advocated here. But placing this question in a context shifts the emphasis away from the recall of standard economic arguments and towards the use of those arguments to make sense of the information provided. This shift in emphasis is fundamental to the task-based approach.

The contrast in styles between the two pieces of source material challenges the student to make connections in a thoughtful manner, and requires the ability to move from argument to data in a flexible manner. The text-based source opens up a number of possible lines of enquiry, so that the student is faced with a relatively open-ended task, within a structured context. This task illustrates the ability of the task-based approach to assess students' abilities in the core areas of economic argument in a manner that is both fresh and realistic.

Study the tables and the article 'In love with the job'. What relevance does the information in these tables have for the arguments expressed in the article? Is there other evidence that should be sought? Assess the view that excessive pay increases will mean job losses.

IN LOVE WITH THE JOB

How can employers motivate and satisfy their workers? The usual and easy answer is to pay them more. How can trade unions enthuse or at least retain their members? The usual and easy answer is to fight for higher pay. Yet this conventional wisdom on both sides of industry is probably wrong.

According to a MORI poll conducted for GMB, the municipal and engineering trade union, pay ranks well down the list of criteria by which employees judge their well-being. When more than a thousand workers from all walks of life were asked to pick six out of 21 qualities which were important for them in their jobs, only a third mentioned pay. The factors which came out overwhelmingly ahead, and the only two that were listed by more than half the respondents, were job security and "finding the job interesting and enjoyable".

Such findings, which have emerged from similar recent surveys in many other industrialised countries, are consistent with economic theory as well as psychological observation and common sense. As society becomes richer, an additional pound of pay is worth steadily less to all but its poorest members. As people leave the bread line far behind, non-material sources of satisfaction and security begin to gain the upper hand over money.

The diminishing importance of money as the sole reason for working has obvious implications for industrial relations, business management and even economic policy – or would, were it not that people do not act as they tell the survey-merchants they feel. Never has that paradox been more evident than in the current recession.

The government keeps warning that excessive pay increases will mean job losses. But many workers do not believe there is a direct connection between their own job security and their pay; and they are not entirely irrational in this respect. Not only do the jobs destroyed by excessive pay rises usually belong to other people, there have also been cases the world over where workers in declining and uncompetitive industries have accepted deep pay cuts but have still ended up losing their jobs.

89

Lower wages alone will not make a declining industry or a badly-managed company competitive. A combination of wage restraint, product innovation and efficiency improvement is usually required. In order to achieve this combination, a company obviously needs a cooperative and flexible workforce. But it also needs a management which knows how to enthuse its workers and is seen to protect the longer term security of their jobs by using their talents to best advantage. That is why personnel management is a central executive skill, wrongly subordinated to that of accountancy in the hierarchy of so many British companies.

Source: *The Times*, 9 May 1991

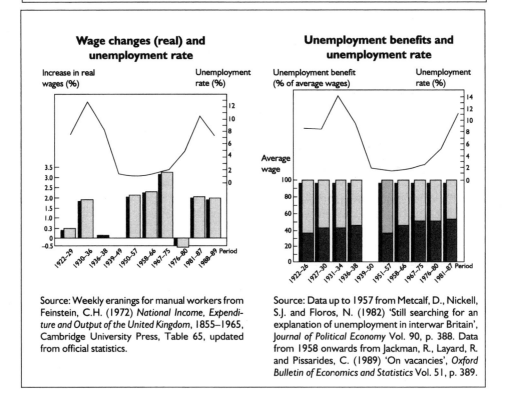

Wage changes (real) and unemployment rate

Source: Weekly eranings for manual workers from Feinstein, C.H. (1972) *National Income, Expenditure and Output of the United Kingdom*, 1855–1965, Cambridge University Press, Table 65, updated from official statistics.

Unemployment benefits and unemployment rate

Source: Data up to 1957 from Metcalf, D., Nickell, S.J. and Floros, N. (1982) 'Still searching for an explanation of unemployment in interwar Britain', *Journal of Political Economy* Vol. 90, p. 388. Data from 1958 onwards from Jackman, R., Layard, R. and Pissarides, C. (1989) 'On vacancies', *Oxford Bulletin of Economics and Statistics* Vol. 51, p. 389.

Exemplar D

This task is one in which the provision of a relatively rich and detailed context is essential. Of course, one might set the traditional essay question 'Compare and evaluate the following options for UK pensions policy ...', but such a question would presume that the topic of pensions policy had been taught explicitly; and the outputs that one might expect from such an essay question would be very different from the outputs that one might expect from the task as specified, where there is no presumption that students have had previous experience of the analysis of pensions policy.

Use the information provided to help you review the following options for future pensions policy. Taking into account the likely impact on current and future pensioners, on tax payers and on government finances in general, prepare a report which explains the reasons for your chosen option.

Possible Options

1.*Continue existing flat-rate pension for all*
£1 billion spent this way would provide an extra £0.85 per week (pw) for the poorest 40% (they would lose some income support entitlement) and £3.50 pw for the richest 40%.

Costs will rise as the number of pensioners grows and because pension increases are tied to prices. But earnings rise more quickly than prices, so workers' tax rates needed to pay for pensions will fall, typically by 5% by 2050. By that time, the pension would be worth 6% of average earnings compared with 15% in 1993.

2.*Flat-rate pension linked to earnings*
To ensure that the pension holds its current value of 15% of earnings, link pension increases to average earnings. Tax rates (needed to pay for it) up 4% by 2020 and 7% by 2030.

3.*Means-tested pensions*
£1 billion spent this way (for example as on existing income support) would add an average of £4.30 pw for the poorest 40% of pensioners and nothing for the richest 40%.

A sliding scale of payments would ensure the poorest receive pensions which hold their value compared with average earnings, while the richest receive little or nothing.

The system could be introduced as in New Zealand, where everyone receives the same pension but an extra tax is paid by the rich.

4.*Encourage private pensions*
Any change could be confined to those who will not retire for some years and so can make private provision. The private sector may need to be regulated to ensure its reliability.

BACKGROUND INFORMATION

The Current System

The *basic state pension* is a flat-rate benefit payable to all over 65 (60 for women until 2010) who have paid National Insurance Contributions for 9/10ths of their working life.

Since 1980, any increase has been linked to prices rather than earnings. The result is that a single basic pension is worth 15% of average male earnings in 1993 as against 20% in 1977.

91

The cost in 1991/2 was £24.7 billion.

In addition, 15% of pensioners receive *income support* and 30% some form of *income-related benefit*. (Total cost 91/92; £5.8 billion). This is partly because some have reduced pensions but mainly because income support rates are actually higher than the basic pension:

single person 65–75   pension per week £54.15   income support £59.15
married couple   pension per week £86.70   income support £91.95

Finally, 3 million pensioners now receive an average of £9 per week from the *State-Earnings Related Pension Scheme (SERPS)*. This scheme, introduced in 1978, links pensions to people's earnings throughout their working lives. It requires a higher rate of contribution but already the pension payments have been reduced so that the original level of 25% of average earnings is down to 20% and likely to be about 13% in 2030.

The Government's main response has been to encourage private pension provision. Occupation pensions cover around half of the work-force at any time and personal pensions are held by around 25% of the workforce.

Pensioners' income distribution

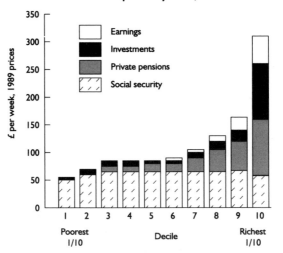

The figure illustrates the effect of the current system on income distribution amongst pensioners. The average income for the top tenth (decile) is more than four times that of the lowest tenth (decile). Moreover, because social security levels have risen little relative to investment levels and occupational pensions, the gap between the groups is growing.

Source: *Fiscal Studies*, Nov. 1992
Published by Institute of Fiscal Studies, p.10

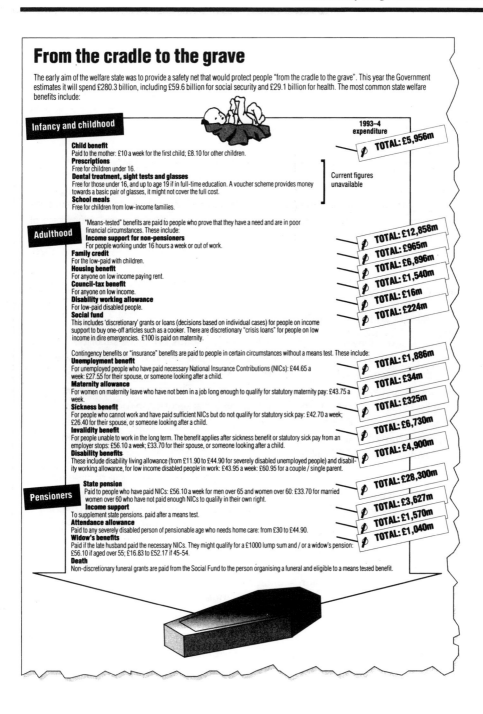

From the cradle to the grave

The early aim of the welfare state was to provide a safety net that would protect people "from the cradle to the grave". This year the Government estimates it will spend £280.3 billion, including £59.6 billion for social security and £29.1 billion for health. The most common state welfare benefits include:

Infancy and childhood

1993–4 expenditure

£ TOTAL: £5,956m

Child benefit
Paid to the mother: £10 a week for the first child; £8.10 for other children.
Prescriptions
Free for children under 16.
Dental treatment, sight tests and glasses
Free for those under 16, and up to age 19 if in full-time education. A voucher scheme provides money towards a basic pair of glasses, it might not cover the full cost.
School meals
Free for children from low-income families.

Current figures unavailable

Adulthood

"Means-tested" benefits are paid to people who prove that they have a need and are in poor financial circumstances. These include:
Income support for non-pensioners
For people working under 16 hours a week or out of work.
£ TOTAL: £12,858m
Family credit
For the low-paid with children.
£ TOTAL: £965m
Housing benefit
For anyone on low income paying rent.
£ TOTAL: £6,896m
Council-tax benefit
For anyone on low income.
£ TOTAL: £1,540m
Disability working allowance
For low-paid disabled people.
£ TOTAL: £16m
Social fund
This includes 'discretionary' grants or loans (decisions based on individual cases) for people on income support to buy one-off articles such as a cooker. There are discretionary "crisis loans" for people on low income in dire emergencies. £100 is paid on maternity.
£ TOTAL: £224m

Contingency benefits or "insurance" benefits are paid to people in certain circumstances without a means test. These include:
Unemployment benefit
For unemployed people who have paid necessary National Insurance Contributions (NICs): £44.65 a week: £27.55 for their spouse, or someone looking after a child.
£ TOTAL: £1,886m
Maternity allowance
For women on maternity leave who have not been in a job long enough to qualify for statutory maternity pay: £43.75 a week.
£ TOTAL: £34m
Sickness benefit
For people who cannot work and have paid sufficient NICs but do not qualify for statutory sick pay: £42.70 a week; £26.40 for their spouse, or someone looking after a child.
£ TOTAL: £325m
Invalidity benefit
For people unable to work in the long term. The benefit applies after sickness benefit or statutory sick pay from an employer stops: £56.10 a week; £33.70 for their spouse, or someone looking after a child.
£ TOTAL: £6,730m
Disability benefits
These include disability living allowance (from £11.90 to £44.90 for severely disabled unemployed people) and disability working allowance, for low income disabled people in work: £43.95 a week: £60.95 for a couple / single parent.
£ TOTAL: £4,900m

Pensioners

State pension
Paid to people who have paid NICs: £56.10 a week for men over 65 and women over 60: £33.70 for married women over 60 who have not paid enough NICs to qualify in their own right.
£ TOTAL: £28,300m
Income support
To supplement state pensions. paid after a means test.
£ TOTAL: £3,627m
Attendance allowance
Paid to any severely disabled person of pensionable age who needs home care: from £30 to £44.90.
£ TOTAL: £1,570m
Widow's benefits
Paid if the late husband paid the necessary NICs. They might qualify for a £1000 lump sum and / or a widow's pension: £56.10 if aged over 55; £16.83 to £52.17 if 45-54.
£ TOTAL: £1,040m
Death
Non-discretionary funeral grants are paid from the Social Fund to the person organising a funeral and eligible to a means tested benefit.

Source: *Education Guardian*, 1 June 1993

Population projections for Great Britain (in millions, and percentage of total)

Age group	1990	2010	2030	2050
Children (0–15)	11.2 (20.1)	11.8 (20.2)	11.9 (19.9)	11.2 (19.3)
Number of working age (men 16–64, women 16–59)	34.3 (61.5)	35.3 (60.6)	33.7 (56.6)	33.7 (58.0)
Number of pensionable age (men 65+, women 60+)	10.3 (18.4)	11.2 (19.2)	14.0 (23.5)	13.2 (22.7)
Totals	58.8 (100)	58.3 (100)	59.6 (100)	58.1 (100)
Number of working age people per person over pension age	3.3	3.2	2.4	2.6

Source: *Government Actuary*, 1990

SOCIAL SECURITY

Old problems and new solutions

Last year, Central Government spent £74 billion pounds on social security. That's about thirteen hundred pounds for each person in the country. Put another way, it would cover the entire defence budget three times over with cash to spare. The chart below shows just what the £74 billion was spent on. The government's projections say that by 1999, we'll be spending £88 billion on social security, in today's prices. The chart also shows what DSS experts think the pattern of spending will look like then. They have assumed that Britain grows at a rate of 2.5 per cent each year, and that unemployment falls to 2.25 million.

By far the largest area of expenditure both now and at the end of the decade is the state retirement pension. This will continue to grow until 2030, without some reform. Over the next decade however, the largest growth is likely to come not from spending on the elderly but on disabled people, those with high rents and on lone parents.

It has been difficult to escape the impression in recent months that Britain's social security system has become unsustainable and is in need of radical pruning. But it might be argued that £88 billion – in an economy that will have grown – is quite sustainable. On the Government's central assumption, the share of benefit spending in national income will, at 12.4 per cent, be virtually the same at the end of the decade as it is now.

There are clearly grounds for concern. The current Government wishes to balance the budget. This implies either making people worse off through tax increases, or benefit cuts, or cuts in other spending.

If unemployment stays at its present level and economic growth is poor, then social security will take up a larger share of national income by the end of the decade.

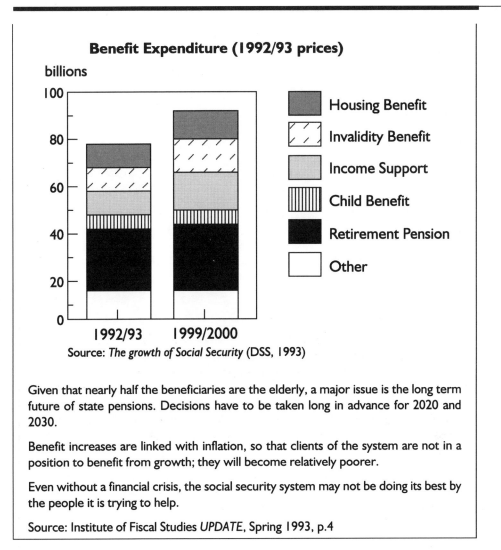

Benefit Expenditure (1992/93 prices)

billions

Legend:
- Housing Benefit
- Invalidity Benefit
- Income Support
- Child Benefit
- Retirement Pension
- Other

1992/93   1999/2000

Source: *The growth of Social Security* (DSS, 1993)

Given that nearly half the beneficiaries are the elderly, a major issue is the long term future of state pensions. Decisions have to be taken long in advance for 2020 and 2030.

Benefit increases are linked with inflation, so that clients of the system are not in a position to benefit from growth; they will become relatively poorer.

Even without a financial crisis, the social security system may not be doing its best by the people it is trying to help.

Source: Institute of Fiscal Studies *UPDATE*, Spring 1993, p.4

This task assesses a student's ability to extract relevant information from a range of sources and then deploy that information in a relatively complex evaluative setting. The ability to use economic skills and ideas to make sense of information and policy options lies at the heart of the task-based approach to the nature, purpose and content of economics at A level, and to its teaching, learning and assessment.

End notes

1. This chapter draws on a working paper prepared under the auspices of that Project by Alan Hamlin, Steve Hodkinson and Frank Livesey. While I am happy to acknowledge my debts to these people and others working within the Project, I retain responsibility for all errors and obscurities. I

should also emphasize that I am writing here as an individual rather than as a representative of the Project.

2. More detailed statements can be found in Chapters 6 and 8, and in *Teaching and Learning the New Economics* (EBEA, 1994).

8 16-19 economics: reflecting on change

Dave Dickson

Introduction

In 1992, I was approached to lead the Bristol and West of England Regional Team as part of a project seeking to review the nature of economics education for the 16–19 age group. The team were colleagues I had successfully worked with before in a number of projects related to the production of stimulus material. Our first year focused on debating the economic content to be delivered and the teaching and learning strategies to be commended to colleagues in schools and colleges. The debates were rigorous, informed and challenging with agreement often difficult to find. From this the national team developed the notion of 'economic thoughtfulness' (see Chapter 6) which underpinned our regional work on styles of teaching and learning and the production of stimulus material for the text *Core Economics* (EBEA, 1995).

The team met frequently and agreed a style to reflect the national meetings and to retain a unique regional flavour. For us this was the provision of materials that would stimulate further analysis as students developed the skills of economic thoughtfulness as explicit elements of their everyday life. This approach follows closely the style and operation of the now defunct Wessex project which did much to enhance the teaching of economics within a context. In terms of originality, editing and the need to produce a coherent text, the final output has lost some of our original thinking, but we feel the end-product offers a clear access point to teachers who are seeking to operate the new subject core for economics and above all to make the study of economics more accessible and relevant to young people.

What follows is a personal reflection of how the project developed, and discussion of a series of issues that require consideration from both supporters and detractors of the change. One would expect nothing else from a social science desirous of seeking truth through the constant and consistent examination of challenging evidence. My approach in this brief review is to frame the text around a series of questions that were asked frequently during regional meetings with colleagues as we detailed the progress of the project and sought opinions to inform our contributions to the project groups on content and teaching and learning.

From these issues related to change and how the process was enacted, the chapter moves to a more pragmatic dimension using the *Core Economics* text as an illustration of good practice in designing stimulus materials for classroom use. The theme of economic thoughtfulness as defined within the Economics 16–19 Project is integral to the piece and is revisited throughout the text.

Process and outcome

The Economics 16–19 Project sought to reshape not only the content of economics offered post-16, but also to develop a new pedagogy for teachers and to emphasize a mode of learning that was student-centred and experiential. In *Teaching and Learning the New Economics* (EBEA, 1994), Barry McCormick and Chris Vidler write:

'This book documents the work of the NDGs for Content *and for* Teaching and Learning, *in collaboration with other members of the project. Their work on the nature of economics and its teaching and learning has allowed the project to determine* what *students might learn in economics and* how *they might do so. They argue that:*

- The new economics *assists students to appreciate the power of economics as an important tool to analyse, explain and evaluate the strengths and weaknesses of the market economy in which they live and work, to establish the need for intervention and to assess the appropriateness and impact of different forms of intervention. It requires us to generate learning activities which distinguish between economics and the economic system which is the focus of study.*

- The new economics *expects students to develop their theoretical knowledge, skills and understanding through investigation and analysis of the economic institutions, issues and phenomena with which economists routinely deal. It requires us to abandon the 'theory followed by application' rule which is common in economics texts but which does not reflect the way that economists develop or apply their tools of analysis in practice.*

- The new economics *encourages students to approach the task of learning economics as a whole, to bring the full range of knowledge and expertise which they possess to bear on the exploration of each new context and to recognize the need to develop and expand existing concepts and skills. It requires us to emphasize the inter-relatedness of the disciplines's constructs rather than their fragmentation.*

- The new economics *challenges students to become actively and thoughtfully involved in the learning process, to locate new insights in relation to their existing knowledge of the economic system and to respond creatively to the challenges involved in generating new meaning. It requires us to provide opportunities for students to review and reflect on their understanding at every stage in the learning process.'*

So what is new? In order to respond to this question it is necessary to explore briefly what is generally meant by *pedagogy*. Certain groups regard it as the science of teaching, incorporating a wide range of professional techniques to stimulate the learning process and to support students in their pursuit of knowledge. As Vygotsky (1963) said: 'pedagogy ... must be oriented not to-wards the yesterday of development, but towards its tomorrow'. Those of us who are teachers of economics have in the main striven to develop within our students an awareness of 'real' economic understanding, but have often been frustrated by the way in which students' learning or our own pedagogy com-partmentalizes the knowledge base. Invisible Chinese walls appear to frus-trate the integration of knowledge that will produce the understanding and analytical skills that are the hallmark of the successful economics student. The Project attempted to remove these walls and, through the learning materials, provide within a critical framework a focus for an holistic pedagogical process focusing on the market economy and its strengths and weaknesses, and the role of government.

Is this different? 'Yes and no' would seem a good answer from an economist, and in many ways it is the correct perspective. Knowledge has a part to play, but the emphasis is on understanding, application and analysis in the 'real' world. In terms of teaching we are now equally concerned about both what our students know and how well they can use this knowledge thoughtfully to discuss economic issues and gain insights based on evidence and understanding.

Economic thoughtfulness is defined by the Teaching and Learning team as the ability '... to clarify the relationship between active, effective and rigorous learning and to provide insights into the process of interaction between teach-ers, learning tasks and students' (EBEA, 1994, p. 30). To achieve this the teacher is faced with developing both a style of teaching that is informed by an understanding of the learning process, and also the ability to develop structured tasks that will support individuals and groups in attaining this.

For many teachers this is not a new phenomenon, but one that began with the developments in the Economics Association's Economics Education 14–16 Project and which are continued through today. If, as a colleague argues, we are defining only *process*, where is the economic *perspective* in economic thoughtfulness? In defining the content for the core and option elements in economics and advising the SCAA group, an enormous amount of debate took place. The groups achieved consensus on the need for young people to be provided with a syllabus that centred on an ethos of real economics in a current context. The organizing principle highlighted was that the 16–19 cur-riculum in economics 'should be organized around the central ideas that both explain the behaviour of the market economy and account for its weaknesses.' Crucial to this is the move to use the 'primitive concepts' identified by McCor-mick and Vidler as tools of analysis to achieve insights into economic activity. The application of microeconomic analysis to macroeconomic issues is a fun-damental principle of *Core Economics* and underpins the desire to enable students to select data more effectively and to develop economic argument in

Economics students at 16–19 need to work in applied settings so as to be able to do the following:

- Explain how individuals gain from trade with other individuals in goods and services.
- Explain what is meant by economic efficiency for an economy as a whole.
- Use provided data to construct and interpret a production possibility frontier for a simple economy.
- Relate this to the behaviour of a competitive economy which satisfies certain assumptions.
- Show what is meant by an efficient allocation of resources within the specific organizational context of a firm and non-market institution, such as a school, prison or hospital.
- Explain how a single shock to a market economy – for example, the collapse of demand for coal – leads to a series of repercussions, and to predict (i) in which markets repercussions would be large or small, and (ii) where the greatest mobility of inputs would be required.
- Show how the resources used by an industry are changed if (i) the cost structure of producing the industry's output changes, (ii) the demand for the product changes, (iii) the product is supplied by a monopolist, and (iv) an input becomes more scarce.
- Show how an entrepreneur making a business investment, or a decision to enter a market, is influenced by both the micreconomic circumstances faced by the individual firm and the various monetary and fiscal instruments which determine the macroeconomic environment.
- Show how government policy may raise economic efficiency in certain specific contexts: namely, where there exist monopolies, externalities or public goods.
- Identify the presence of monopolies, externalities and public goods in different market contexts (for example, housing, education, health) and thus operationalize understanding of the circumstance in which economists regard that governments should and should not intervene in a market economy.
- Analyse the implications – in the short and long run – of prices being fixed at levels different from market clearing prices.
- Analyse the implications, for unemployment levels and inflation, of wages set above market clearing levels.
- Analyse the broad factors which may have influenced the success of firms in certain economies relative to those elsewhere.
- Explain how the nature of the firm has changed in the twentieth century, and why firms in certain economies have prospered while those elsewhere have been less successful.
- Explain the distribution of earnings and total income between different types of household, and be able to relate this to educational achievement and worker experience (and be able to analyse whether economic discrimination is arising in a workplace).

- Explain the objectives of negotiators representing firms and trade unions and show the likely consequences of their behaviour for the decisions of the firm.
- Explain the overall budgetary problem faced by a Chancellor of the Exchequer seeking to meet the demands for various expenditures and also the objections to taxation and higher levels of government borrowing.
- Analyse (i) recent monetary and fiscal policy, (ii) the recent two decades of a central microeconomics feature of the economy (e.g. the changing market for higher education or that for housing).
- Carry out simple interpretative exercises using data.
- Distinguish arguments to support a proposition and be able to recognize that correlation and causality differ.
- Use statements involving probability.
- Qualify their conclusions as necessary by language such as 'on the basis of this data' and be able to set out their results and interpretations in a full and meaningful way to include a clear statement of the assumptions upon which their analysis is based.

Figure 8.1 Applied skills (EBEA, 1994, pp. 13–14)

order to answer questions related to policy change. An extract from *Teaching and Learning the New Economics* (see Figure 8.1) details the range of questions we would expect students to answer effectively after taking a course in economics.

Managing the change: issues for economic educators

Is there a loss?

Certain areas of the current syllabuses have been reduced in an attempt to produce a level of content more accessible to the average A level student. Rigour has not been abandoned, if by rigour we mean the definition given above of 'economic thoughtfulness'. However, the selected content areas do reflect the particular values held by the content group. Not everyone agrees with the defined content and compromises were reached along the way. Maybe the question should be: Have we gone far enough? For the teacher of economics the shift in emphasis may not be unexpected, broadly reflecting on-going changes in some texts and some syllabuses in the micro and macro core.

Do the outcomes of the Project match the intentions?

Core Economics reflects the outcomes of the Project's process. One misapprehension is that it is a source book that can be used to produce learning materials utilizing the stimulus material alone. However, this is to miss the main reason for the text which is the combination of resources designed to support the development of new knowledge and to engender economic thoughtfulness in the reader. The material will date, as does all topical material, but it is the selection of exemplar material that should enable students to develop their own research skills and alongside this economic thoughtfulness, using the text as a supportive element in their learning and final understanding.

The newspaper article reproduced here as Figure 8.2 reflects a situation that

Where do all the tickets go?

lawing black marketeering have little chance of succeeding.

For the ticket touts it's business as usual. A spokesman for Welshman Rugby Services, which is offering champagne packages which include meeting rugby stars at £199 a ticket, said he had no difficulty in obtaining tickets but declined to reveal his sources.

"I'm sworn to secrecy about where I get my tickets But I have no trouble getting them and even less selling them for a game like this. It hasn't affected us at all," he said.

Most of the 60 clubs taking part in the official hospitality scheme are outside the Heineken League and for many giving up a maximum of 10 stand tickets per game means cashing in on about half their allocation for £500 each time.

Mr Price said without this income some small clubs "would go down the pan."

Former England and British Lion rugby star Mike Burton added: "Over the years I have always bought international tickets from the clubs and sold them to clients in corporate hospitality packages. I don't call it a black market, I prefer to call it a secondary market."

Despite the official blessing of the WRU, corporate hospitality is a source of controversy to ordinary rugby supporters.

Former Western Mail sports editor John Billot said: "Corporate hospitality has always been a bone of contention to ordinary supporters.

"You do get a lot of grumbling from the man in the street who doesn't think sufficient tickets are going in his direction."

He said the "vice presidents" deal where fans pay inflated prices to become vice presidents of clubs to guarantee tickets for internationals was now accepted by the majority of people.

WRU fails to stamp out the black market

WELSH rugby's attempt to stamp out black marketeering in international rugby tickets by running an official corporate hospitality scheme is already being thwarted.

With tickets for Saturday's Wales v England match like gold dust, ticket touts say they are having no problems obtaining tickets on the black market or selling them off to high-paying companies and individuals.

The WRU has followed in the wake of other countries by launching an official corporate hospitality package managed by a man once known as King of the Touts, Mike Burton, who has been running the unofficial variety for years.

WRU commercial executive Jonathan Price believes corporate hospitality is a fact of life but without an official scheme the profits would not be ploughed back into rugby union.

Under the WRU's controversial ticket touting operating, clubs sell stand tickets at £50 each, guaranteeing them £3,000 over the next three years.

The WRU, in partnership with Mike Burton, hopes to make a £1m profit over the next six home internationals with 600 ticket-official-hospitality packages based at Cardiff Castle at £285 a ticket.

But any hopes the WRU has of out-

KING TOUT: Mike Burton now offers hospitality packages in league with the WRU

Figure 8.2 From *Wales on Sunday*, 31 January 1993

is constantly occurring and shows economics at work in the real world. It can be applied to a wide range of situations where secondary markets are likely to develop. Students require knowledge of supply and demand theory and must apply it to understand the complex issues involved in this particular market situation. As we know, the initial clear-cut interpretation gives rise to a number of 'real' problems that students have to explore carefully to develop

How are health care products and services paid for?
How could they be paid for?

The NHS is paid for out of taxation in Britain, which has a reputation for valuing and resourcing a substantial public health care system. This section considers the evidence for this claim and the problems associated with public funding of health care. It also explores the costs and benefits of alternative payment systems.

How Britain compares

TASK

Study the information, headed 'How we compare' which provides comparative data on health care spending in various countries.

To what extent does this information support the claim that Britain values highly its public health care system? What kinds of questions are raised by such data?

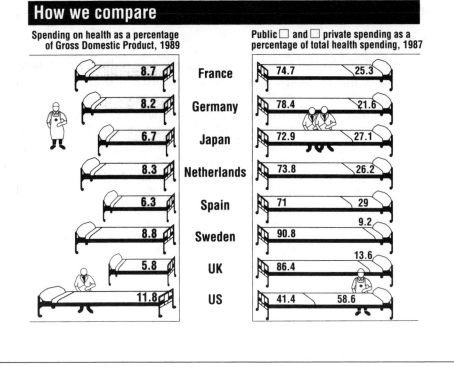

How we compare

Spending on health as a percentage of Gross Domestic Product, 1989

Public ☐ and ☐ private spending as a percentage of total health spending, 1987

Country	Health as % of GDP (1989)	Public (%)	Private (%)
France	8.7	74.7	25.3
Germany	8.2	78.4	21.6
Japan	6.7	72.9	27.1
Netherlands	8.3	73.8	26.2
Spain	6.3	71	29
Sweden	8.8	90.8	9.2
UK	5.8	86.4	13.6
US	11.8	41.4	58.6

Figure 8.3 From *Core Economics* and *The Guardian*, 25 June 1991

an analytical perspective on this particular situation. In this instance the real problems are the fact that the market is determined by the realities of fixed supply and an allocative system that does not wholly recognize price as the main means of distribution. From this, secondary markets develop that function around the price system, but are obviously lucrative to the original suppliers if they can exert some control and move into price discrimination. Students begin to engage with the economics of economic thoughtfulness very early and the complexities become inherent in their research skills. It is in this exploration of their own research data that students begin to engage with the real issues of economics, and it is at this time that they need the support of their teachers in overcoming the obstacles to understanding that will present themselves. Crucially, the interaction of teachers and students will enhance the learning process, as it usually does.

In the example given in Figure 8.3, elements previously studied are brought together in order to investigate the National Health Service. But does this really encourage economic thoughtfulness? It does not if the student has not been prepared for this type of analysis, and the task becomes irrelevant if the student has not been given a critical frame of reference within his or her exploration of economic thoughtfulness. The ability of students to engage with this type of approach will be determined by both intellectual competence and the pedagogic processes that have underpinned their learning. Students move from a view, often expressed, of 'Why are we studying this?' to 'Why is this the case in this market?'.

What about learning?

The material in the Project appears to be modelled on Kolb's (1984) theory of learning – allowing the learner to access the material over a range of instances, which will suit those learners who prefer concrete experiences and are action-oriented while allowing those who are more reflective to deliberate and observe. For some students an ability to formulate abstractions and develop theories is important, and for others the testing of a concept or idea will be more appropriate. Students in the classroom will follow these diverse routes to understanding, with preferences often changing according to competence and confidence in the learning situation. Without being prescriptive, the learning material developed in the Project text supports all styles of learning when it is contained within a carefully constructed learning programme.

For example, if we analyse the material on minimum wage rates in Figure 8.4 using Kolb's learning cycle, the learner is able to access each aspect as appropriate with concrete experiences provided in the analysis box, and there is a range of materials designed to stimulate reflection on existing knowledge of supply and demand theory as well as the need to theorize about the market model and test the hypothesis using 'real' experiences.

Figure 8.4 From *Core Economics* and *The Times*, 7 April 1992

Analysis

Minimum wage

Putting faith in labour markets clearing to reduce unemployment leads to views such as the following:

- high unemployment benefit paid to those out of work will prevent the labour markets from clearing
- workers are motivated by changes in their wages.

If labour markets *did* clear, the predictable effect of the introduction by the government of a minimum wage set above the equilibrium would be an increase in unemployment.

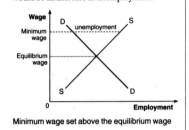

Minimum wage set above the equilibrium wage

Britain bargains too hard for the minimal effect of minimum wage

Wolfgang Münchau

Landmark changes in social policy have never been introduced without furious protests. Be it the abolition of slavery, the introduction of health and safety legislation, or equal pay for women: each time fears were raised that such policies would be inflationary and damaging to the country's competitiveness. Some people might want to draw parallels with the arguments raging in Britain today over a statutory minimum wage.

Rules or agreements imposing minimum wages are commonplace in the European Community and also exist in America. Even in Britain, wages have been fixed by statutory bodies in some traditional low-wage industries for three generations. The debate is about whether Britain should follow suit in imposing a general minimum wage. The Labour party thinks it should, and plans to introduce a minimum wage at £3.40 an hour, equivalent to about half the average of male earnings, by next year.

The most unedifying aspect of this debate is the way everybody seems to exaggerate the measure's likely impact. Supporters claim that it would improve the living conditions of the poor dramatically. Opponents say it would render the British economy uncompetitive and would lead to a massive rise in unemployment.

The experience of a minimum wage in Europe would suggest that neither claim holds true. The social justice claim is an exaggeration, while assertions that a minimum wage would wreck the country's economy do not bear scrutiny. Those who make such claims rely on the assumption that the economic effects of a minimum wage are predictable. This is not so.

Since the majority of economists have proved incompetent even at forecasting the rate of economic growth over a 12-month period, one should treat with suspicion claims that they can predict accurately the effects of a policy whose outcome would become visible only in the medium term and which depends entirely on how employers will react to it. The problem of forecasting the impact of minimum wages is well established, and any serious analysis of this subject carries a methodological health warning.

This minor inconvenience has not deterred some producing wild claims about the direct reduction in employment resulting from a £3.40 minimum wage. These estimates range from 8,800 (Liverpool university), to 49,100 (City university) or 102,400 (the Treasury). The Confederation of British Industry even claimed that unemployment would soar by 150,000 and Michael Howard, employment secretary, suggested an ultimate figure of about 2 million, including indirect effects.

A better way of finding out about the minimum wage is to look at the situation elsewhere in Europe and draw qualitative rather than quantitative conclusions. From a British point of view, the most comparable country is probably France, where a minimum wage is statutory, as proposed by Labour, and not based on industry-wide agreements as is common in Germany. The French minimum wage works out at about equivalent to Labour's proposal of £3.40 an hour. In Germany, the effective minimum wage is about £1 higher, the precise amount depending on region and industry.

France has a problem of youth employment, although the official youth unemployment rate has improved considerably since 1985. According to an analysis by Stephen Bazen and John Martin, published in OECD Economic Studies a year ago, a minimum wage increased youth unemployment to some extent. There are still doubts about cause and effect. "We have not been able to establish satisfactorily, however, that increases in real youth labour costs have had a negative impact on youth employment even though we believe this to be the case," they wrote. Notably, the impact of a minimum wage on adult employment "appears to be zero".

A minimum wage does not appear to threaten adult employment but has a small effect on youth unemployment (15 to 24-year-olds). It has, however, a large effect on youth earnings. The authors recommend that the rise in minimum wages should lag behind average earnings, or that "special sub-minimum wages for young workers" should be introduced.

This has happened to some extent in France, where the government introduced special training and community work schemes at pay rates below the minimum wage. This amounts to differential pay scales and may be one of the factors that has led to a fall in French youth unemployment from 34 per cent in 1985 to 18.4 per cent in 1989.

The problem with a statutory minimum wage is that it tends not to take account of regional and industrial differences. In Germany, minimum wages form part of industry-wide bargaining agreements and these differ for each region and industry. There are also loopholes. Only 90 per cent of the workforce is covered by these agreements.

Opponents argue that a minimum wage would set in motion a wage-price spiral, because higher groups would want to maintain wage differentials. The effect of differentials is thought to be marginal in industry, although there might be a problem in the public sector especially the national health service, where pay is strictly graded. Comparisons with France, however, would not support the differential theory. France has a lower average wage, for production workers, than Britain, despite the minimum wage.

There is, however, a big difference between continuing a minimum wage regime and introducing one. If employers pass on the extra costs in higher prices, a minimum wage could prove inflationary, but no more than a rise in VAT, and the rise in inflation should be temporary. Unemployment might go up to some extent, or profits might come down, or both.

Only a few, not necessarily well-performing, industries, would be hit. The impact on the economy as a whole is likely to be limited. Positive impulses would come from greater purchasing power and higher tax revenues. The combined effect of all these measures would be difficult to predict.

Most of the reputable economic analysis on the subject concludes with ample health warnings about methodology, that the overall economic impact of a minimum wage is small. Equally, there is little evidence that a minimum wage has any measurable effect in eradicating poverty, as its proponents claim.

According to a study by Paul Gregg for the National Institute Economic Review, the national minimum wage is well-targeted only for the poorest families, where at least one member is at work. "However, a national minimum wage is weakly targeted on all poor families for the reason that most are poor as a result of not having a job." Confirming the experience in France, Mr Gregg comes to the conclusion that "targeting on families who are likely to spend long periods in poverty would be much improved by a reduced rate for youths that is related to their age. This would also reduce the cost to the economy by around a quarter."

Read the article 'Britain bargains too hard for the minimal effect of minimum wage'. The author argues that the effects of a minimum wage are *not* predictable despite what economic theory suggests (see the Analysis box on minimum wage, p. 89).

Does this mean that the theory is not helpful in researching and writing articles like this?

Review◀

Wages and unemployment

Evidence has been presented in this section to show that labour markets do not clear – but those who are beguiled by the simple solution to unemployment that cutting wages provides, have to find ways of restoring their faith in a clearing labour market. One way that this can be done is to call those who will not respond to an offer of a job at a lower wage *voluntarily* unemployed, and then to find the means to make them change their minds. The possibilities suggested for this include reducing unemployment benefit to 'starve' them back to the labour market to sell their labour at the market clearing wage, or to train them so that the market becomes an attractive place to trade their new skills (although there is no guarantee that any employer will want to buy them).

It is important to be aware that there are other suggested solutions for unemployment which do not depend on the assumption that labour markets clear. A discussion of these appears in Unit 10 of this book – which expands upon this crucial area of economics.

A minimum wage and unemployment

Economic theory helps to answer the question of what would be the effect of the government introducing a minimum wage, because the assumptions of the theory can be questioned to find out why its prediction is unreliable. Questioning the assumptions could provide the basis for an investigation. Questions such as the following could be asked:

- Can workers be assumed to be the same or does the existence of differences between workers lead to problems in applying the theory in its simple form? For example, in the article 'Britain bargains too hard for the minimal effect of minimum wage' the author distinguishes between adult and youth employment and explores the differential effect on these.

- Is it, in fact, as easy for employers to hire and fire workers as the theory assumes?

In the same article the author points out that the effect of introducing a minimum wage is unclear. 'Unemployment might go up to some extent, or profits might come down, or both.'

On completion of such an investigation, it should be possible to identify the causes of differences in the wage rates paid to workers of different age, sex, race and skill in different industries and occupations. It should be possible also to say something about the potential effects on an economy of the introduction of a national minimum wage. ◀

Figure 8.4 From *Core Economics* and *The Times*, 7 April 1992 (*continued*)

Developing resources

Economics education has a surfeit of resources available to students and staff. A problem is always time and the ability to be selective in the face of such a diverse range of material included in current texts and documents. Gaining access to stimulating and relevant material that can be quickly used in the classroom is an ongoing issue for all economics educators. Understanding how you approach the task of resource development in a critically reflective mode can aid in making you a more effective and efficient practitioner.

Are you a peruser and filer who just sees material and thinks generally how it may be used, or are you goal-oriented with clear ideas of the area, and objectives you want to achieve? In fact it is likely you are both of these as you try to develop resource banks for your students and specific learning materials.

What follows below is a very brief outline of how the team approached the development of our sections for the *Core Economics* text. It is not prescriptive, but indicative of the thought processes used by a group of practising economics educators in selecting material for their students.

Stage 1: Setting the aims for a unit of work

We had a very clear view of how we wanted the material to be developed. It had to provide factual knowledge, encourage independent research from a supportive base, and maintain the rigour of the subject area. The resources also had to recognize the needs of different learners, but maintain the pedagogic imperatives of the teachers involved – not least of which was the students passing their particular examination.

In our case the areas were given and we worked accordingly. We found this was a very good discipline because it prevented too much wandering off the point and any temptation to create the 'ultimate integrated resource'.

Looking for example at the area of 'markets that fail to clear', it becomes essential to carry out the following principles of practice:

- How can we use the knowledge and experience of our students?
- What concepts are we working with, and within what framework will students undertake tasks?
- How can we design a structure in our teaching that clearly identifies student- and teacher-focused work clearly?
- How can we provide regular points for evaluation and reflection on our original learning outcomes, and assess the development of economic thoughtfulness?

If we have defined the content clearly and specified with rigour the outcomes we wish to achieve in the classroom, it should now be possible to develop a more effective experience for our students.

Stage 2: Developing the content

We had to be very specific about the outcomes we wished to see from each section, and about how we would maintain some flexibility for the teacher and learner. This was, of course, a daunting task. In our original copy we preferred a clearly annotated section detailing the main aspects of theoretical understanding to be developed in this particular topic area. It was to provide a bank of knowledge that indicated clearly to the students both new and old aspects of learning. We were, however, becoming too prescriptive and had to return frequently to the original teaching and learning aims of the Project and the concept of economic thoughtfulness to aid us.

This is a dilemma that many teachers go through in designing resource material. How much do we give students in leading them towards an answer, and how much do we allow them freedom to develop their own under-standing? To repeat the textbook seems pointless, but to include a Key Points section on your stimulus sheet seems to be a good idea, as long as the details are relevant to the skills and understanding you are seeking to develop. The resource is not a programmed learning sheet – it will elicit a range of opinions and answers that will have some variety, reflecting the abilities, interests and experiences of your students.

As teachers we often forget the powerful role we can play in developing ma-terials that are specific to our own students' needs. Other sources will always be second-best to your own carefully planned materials, but they can be adapted and used to support a variety of in-class activities.

Stage 3: Searching for materials

Sources for this were many and varied, but we often found the regional news-papers more accessible to students initially than the *Financial Times* or *The Economist*. In fact we had to edit many of the articles to focus the content into the areas we wished to highlight. This is crucial in developing such materials to introduce students to economic discussion and encourage their own inde-pendent reading as they progress.

Each article or photograph was chosen to highlight a specific aspect of the topic we were covering. In many cases material that was too general or painted too broad a brush for learners was 'dropped'.

Selecting the issues to be raised by the material was therefore relatively sim-ple, but too much questioning arguably could limit the level of engagement by students and therefore their ability to develop economic thoughtfulness. We think the text balances this reasonably well with quite specific closed ques-tions amply supported by open-ended questions linked to the stimulus material. A real benefit is the inclusion of student responses to the questions, because these indicate the need for further evidence and thinking.

Stage 4: Layout and design

When we have the content and the stimulus material, they need to be put together in an attractive layout that will stimulate interest and encourage the reader to stay with the text. Often our attitude to design is poor. Many excellent resources are poorly presented, so eroding the benefit that may be gained. In these days of desktop publishing templates and easy-to-use scanners, we no longer have any excuse for boring layouts and poorly presented text.

The material must be structured to include activities that balance with the extent of students' learning as they progress through the text. Initially one may want to have more Key Points and shorter stimulus pieces, gradually building towards more complex pieces both in length and intellectual analysis.

The layout should adopt the principle of less rather than more and aid the

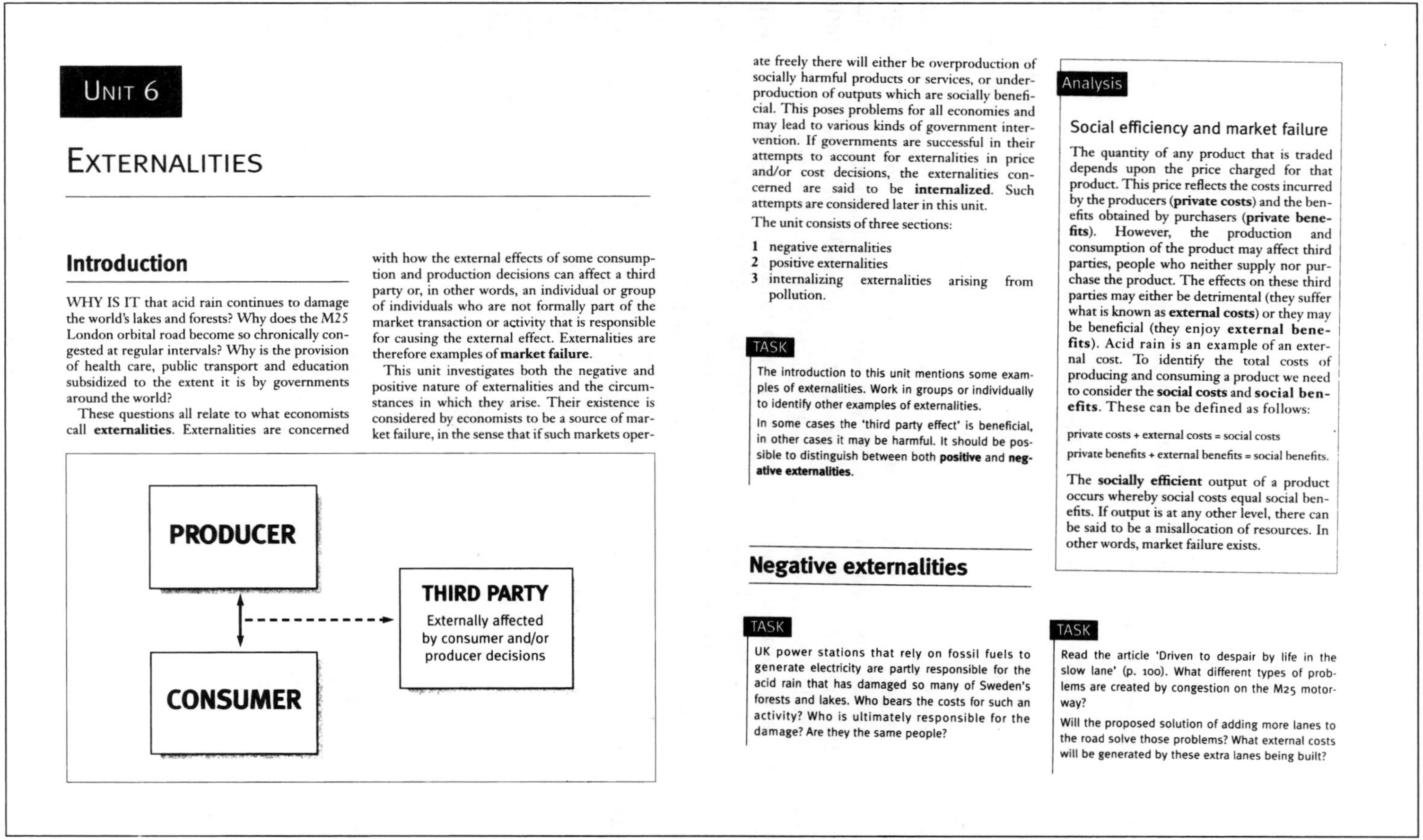

UNIT 6

EXTERNALITIES

Introduction

WHY IS IT that acid rain continues to damage the world's lakes and forests? Why does the M25 London orbital road become so chronically congested at regular intervals? Why is the provision of health care, public transport and education subsidized to the extent it is by governments around the world?

These questions all relate to what economists call **externalities**. Externalities are concerned with how the external effects of some consumption and production decisions can affect a third party or, in other words, an individual or group of individuals who are not formally part of the market transaction or activity that is responsible for causing the external effect. Externalities are therefore examples of **market failure**.

This unit investigates both the negative and positive nature of externalities and the circumstances in which they arise. Their existence is considered by economists to be a source of market failure, in the sense that if such markets operate freely there will either be overproduction of socially harmful products or services, or underproduction of outputs which are socially beneficial. This poses problems for all economies and may lead to various kinds of government intervention. If governments are successful in their attempts to account for externalities in price and/or cost decisions, the externalities concerned are said to be **internalized**. Such attempts are considered later in this unit.

The unit consists of three sections:

1 negative externalities
2 positive externalities
3 internalizing externalities arising from pollution.

TASK

The introduction to this unit mentions some examples of externalities. Work in groups or individually to identify other examples of externalities.

In some cases the 'third party effect' is beneficial, in other cases it may be harmful. It should be possible to distinguish between both **positive and negative externalities.**

Negative externalities

TASK

UK power stations that rely on fossil fuels to generate electricity are partly responsible for the acid rain that has damaged so many of Sweden's forests and lakes. Who bears the costs for such an activity? Who is ultimately responsible for the damage? Are they the same people?

Analysis

Social efficiency and market failure

The quantity of any product that is traded depends upon the price charged for that product. This price reflects the costs incurred by the producers (**private costs**) and the benefits obtained by purchasers (**private benefits**). However, the production and consumption of the product may affect third parties, people who neither supply nor purchase the product. The effects on these third parties may either be detrimental (they suffer what is known as **external costs**) or they may be beneficial (they enjoy **external benefits**). Acid rain is an example of an external cost. To identify the total costs of producing and consuming a product we need to consider the **social costs** and **social benefits**. These can be defined as follows:

private costs + external costs = social costs

private benefits + external benefits = social benefits.

The **socially efficient** output of a product occurs whereby social costs equal social benefits. If output is at any other level, there can be said to be a misallocation of resources. In other words, market failure exists.

TASK

Read the article 'Driven to despair by life in the slow lane' (p. 100). What different types of problems are created by congestion on the M25 motorway?

Will the proposed solution of adding more lanes to the road solve those problems? What external costs will be generated by these extra lanes being built?

PRODUCER

CONSUMER

THIRD PARTY
Externally affected by consumer and/or producer decisions

Figure 8.5 Style layout in *Core Economics*

109

reader without disjointed boxes and irrelevant graphics creeping in to disrupt the pattern of learning.

Unit 6 on 'externalities' (see Figure 8.5) gives a good example of the style of layout that can be achieved with comparatively straightforward DTP software. The Key Points are defined clearly and the main issue defined with a straightforward activity to stimulate discussion. The analysis section provides further support for students' understanding while they begin to tackle the two tasks detailed. In principle the piece has a number of learner access points, supporting the illustration from Kolb mentioned above.

Stage 5: Designing appropriate assessment

As students progress through the work it is vital that an assessment takes place that tests the abilities of the whole student cohort effectively, and also reflects the styles of teaching and learning that have taken place.

Core Economics has been designed with assessment as an integral element in the learning process. This is reflected in the tasks set within the Units and the inclusion of specific assessment tasks from various examining boards. Crucial to the text and to the development of relevant materials is the need to provide our students with assessment tasks that prepare them for the external examinations they are about to undertake. The whole construct of *Core Economics* and the underpinning ethos of 'economic thoughtfulness' is about preparing students to demonstrate their understanding and ability to synthesize and evaluate economic phenomena in a variety of contexts.

One of the advantages of a teacher preparing his or her own materials lies in the close links that can be developed to the specific syllabus the students are undertaking. Thomas (1986) rehearsed the nature of economics attainment in a paper presented to the International Seminar on Research and Development issues as 'a synthesis of procedures and content'. In her concluding paper she states that to achieve economics understanding in any context is 'to understand the nature and function of the relationships which anchor specific skills, concepts and information to a general framework'.

Conclusion

The Economics 16–19 Project allowed teachers and other professionals to have an active say in the development of existing approaches in post-16 education, while at the same time recognizing the overload in many syllabuses for teachers and students. The Project was concerned with accessibility and to an extent the demystification of economic theory so that theory can become a useful tool in the analysis of everyday problems. Above all it was prepared to engage with areas that do not conform to glib mathematical models and to recognize the need for students to develop critical thinking in their approach to the subject.

When undertaking this brief review I was struck by the extent to which we really haven't changed anything. Much of our work cemented the foundations of good practice rather than changed our whole view of economics education. However, it is clear that the process of delivering the message of economic thoughtfulness will be fraught with problems if we do not adopt a pedagogical stance that includes the learner as a central focus for our teaching. Extending and developing the EBEA network may be the way of encouraging hard-pressed staff to engage with this task on a joint basis.

Resources that are locally and topically focused are always more effective in classrooms, but it may be that we can encourage students to develop these inputs of real economics through a teaching style that encourages presentations, and peer group assessment. This is where the structure of the *Core Economics* text is most helpful in providing a base for extended research and development linked to students' needs.

References

EBEA (1994). Thomas, L. (ed.), *Teaching and Learning the New Economics*, Oxford, Heinemann Educational.

EBEA (1995). *Core Economics*, Oxford, Heinemann Educational.

Kolb, D. A. (1984). *Experiential Learning: Experience as the Source of Learning Development*, Englewood Cliffs, NJ, Prentice-Hall.

Thomas, L. (1986). 'Assessment of achievement in economics', in: Hodkinson, S. and Whitehead, D. W. (eds), *Economics Education Research and Development Issues*, Harlow, Longman.

Vygotsky, L. S. (1963). 'Learning and mental development at school age' in: Simon, B. and Simon J. (eds), *Educational Psychology in the USSR*, London, Routledge & Kegan Paul.

9 Gender issues in economics

Sue Hatt

An inclusive curriculum in economics

'Rational economic man' is a phrase which many economists nowadays try to avoid; it is not consistent with equal opportunities, it is not politically correct. We speak instead of rational actors or rational agents. Yet changing the language we use is not sufficient to ensure an inclusive curriculum. Social science should help us to understand social behaviour – that is the behaviour of both men and women. The particular focus of economics is on the production and distribution of goods and services within society. These activities can take place within markets or in the non-marketed sector of the economy. Firms produce motor vehicles, electrical circuits and agricultural commodities and supply these in markets to consumers, who are willing and able to demand them. Household production includes growing vegetables, washing clothes, preparing meals and caring for young children. These are also productive activities although the goods and services never reach the market; they are consumed within the household.

Market production and consumption has become the focus of economics; household production is often overlooked. Market-based production is visible and its extent is relatively easy to estimate. Gross domestic product includes the market value of goods and services; it omits household production from the accounts. Household production, though, is far from insignificant – it amounts to goods and services whose value has been estimated to account for between one-third and a half of marketed GDP. Waring (1988) provides a thorough examination of the valuable, yet invisible, contribution women make to national output. The size of this contribution will vary considerably from country to country depending upon the level of development, the fertility rate, the social structure and so on.

Household production in a developed country will include activities performed by both men and women. Studies show that men often take responsibility for car maintenance, interior decoration and gardening whilst women prepare meals, feed babies, fetch children from school and wash clothes (Warde and Hetherington, 1993). Omitting household production from economic analysis might appear to be gender-neutral; we exclude certain aspects of both men's and women's work. But these household tasks are not shared equally between men and women. Women usually spend about twice as long as men on household work even in households where both partners are in paid employment

(Coré, 1994). Since household work, even in industrialized countries, falls disproportionately upon women, its omission as an economic activity renders women's role in production less visible than that of men.

Men and women play different roles in the productive process in the market-based sector too. Whilst women have been moving into paid employment in increasing numbers in recent decades, their work histories and employment patterns differ from those of men in several significant respects. Men predominate in manufacturing industry whilst women outnumber men in the service sector of the economy. Men who lose their jobs will appear in the statistics for the unemployed whilst women who lose their jobs often become non-participants in the labour force. Part-time employment has been an important growth area in the British economy in recent years, yet 86 per cent of these jobs are occupied by women. In paid work, as well as within the household, women are found doing different jobs from those which men undertake.

In Britain, government statistics document differences between men and women in the labour force and between people from different ethnic backgrounds, but it is important to remember that women are not all the same. (Many government statistical sources classify some groups of men and women by their country of origin – e.g. Bangladeshi – whilst others are identified by colour.) Class and race will also affect labour force participation. West Indian and Guyanese women are more likely to be economically active than white women, whilst Pakistani and Bangladeshi women have the lowest rates of economic activity. Only 24 per cent of Pakistani or Bangladeshi women are economically active, as opposed to 71 per cent of West Indian or Guyanese women (OPCS, 1992). The strength of small businesses amongst the Asian population is reflected in the high proportion of these women who are self-employed; 10 per cent of Indian women and 12 per cent of Pakistani and Bangladeshi women are self-employed whilst for white women the proportion is only 7 per cent. These distinctions between women are interesting, but this chapter will focus upon the differences in the economic positions of women and men.

Many introductory textbooks are already trying to use inclusive language and to provide examples of both men and women in their case studies. Chapters on labour markets will often include a section on women and ethnic minorities. This is certainly helpful but it is not sufficient. The particular role of women in the productive process needs to be identified and to be made explicit throughout an introductory economics syllabus.

There is a small, but growing, body of literature that is especially helpful to teachers wishing to introduce gender issues into their courses. Blau and Ferber (1992) is a useful North American textbook which uses neoclassical economic theory to explain the roles that men and women play in economic activity. Jacobsen (1994) is a welcome addition to the literature and provides a very thorough analysis of gender issues from a neoclassical perspective.

Adopting both an economic and a sociological perspective, Dex (1985) provides a helpful examination of research on gender issues in labour markets in Britain particularly. The wider philosophical issues are examined in a collection of contributions from American economists (Ferber and Nelson, 1992).

Journals too are beginning to address these issues. The most significant journal articles in this area have been published in a collected edition (Humphries, 1995) which provides an essential reference source. The *Economic Review* has carried several articles which investigate the different positions of men and women in paid employment and examine the impact of the changing economic structure upon these two groups (Turner, 1993; Rice, 1994; Dex, 1990). The economic basis for the domestic division of labour is discussed by Hatt (1994) in *Economics and Business Education*, and a worksheet is provided for classroom discussion.

There are many ways in which teachers of economics can make gender issues visible throughout an introductory economics course. Economic issues concerning gender and work in Britain and Europe provide the focus for an accessible new book in this area (Hatt, 1996). This text should provide a useful introduction for A level students of economics and business studies and for first-year undergraduates. The inclusion of gender issues in introductory courses will help to enlighten the new generation of students and make them more aware of the different impacts that economic policy can have upon men and women. This chapter identifies three areas of an introductory economics syllabus – the production possibility curve, the minimum-wage debate, and unemployment – where gender issues can be discussed.

Production possibility curves and opportunity cost

One of the fundamental concerns of economics is the efficient use of scarce resources. The more efficiently resources are deployed to produce goods and services that people want to consume, the higher the standard of living will be. Productive and allocative efficiency are both important. The labour resources of an economy include men and women. Men, throughout their working lives, participate in the working population, engaging in paid work and spending their income in product markets; the roles they play in economic activity are visible and easy to analyse. Their output is included in the neoclassical analysis of the production possibility curve which is based upon accepted norms and conventions and is drawn to include the marketed and the government sector of the economy.

For women the position is different. They move into and out of the labour force during the period of family formation and will often work on a part-time basis whilst their children are of pre-school age. The care of pre-school children in Britain takes place mainly within the household and involves women's unpaid labour; these women are providing valuable services bringing up the future citizens of our country, the workers of the twenty-first century. This household production affects the standard of living and represents a considerable

115

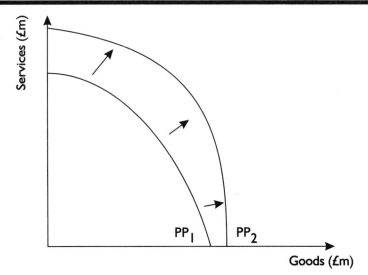

Figure 9.1 Production possibility curve including household production

addition to total output. A more inclusive approach would include household production in the production possibility curve.

Many of the unpaid activities in the invisible domestic sector of the economy involve the production of services rather than goods. Meals are prepared, clothes are washed, rooms are cleaned and children are cared for. If the production possibility curve of an economy is drawn to include these non-market transactions, then the production possibility frontier will shift outwards. This new curve will not be parallel to the old one since the largest proportion of these unpaid activities are services. The curve will both move and rotate as well, to reflect the fact that the production of services in the unpaid sector is greater than the production of goods.

In Figure 9.1 the original curve, PP_1, shows the economy's potential output of goods and services in the visible sector of the economy; it includes production in the private sector and the provision of goods and services by the government. The standard of living is influenced by household production too. The second curve, PP_2, indicates the level of output that this economy is capable of producing if all the productive activities performed within the household were included as well. The second curve provides a more comprehensive measure of the economy's potential output. Since women's contribution to the unpaid domestic economy is greater than that of men, the area between the two curves contains more activities provided by women than by men.

Women's productive activities within the household constrain their participation in paid employment. The typical pattern of labour market participation for women in Britain is bimodal or M-shaped. Many women withdraw from the working population, work on a part-time basis or will be prepared to accept less-skilled jobs while their children are small. Their household production is at the expense of their full participation in the marketed visible sector of the economy. In an economist's terms, household production involves an opportunity cost, the output that could be produced by these women if they were employed in their next-best alternative use. In April 1993 a woman accountant in Britain could earn an average of £422.80 a week, whilst a woman employed as a restaurant manager would typically be earning £258.90 (DoE, 1993). These figures provide some estimate of the opportunity cost of well qualified women withdrawing from the labour force.

Economists need to consider whether this traditional division of labour, whereby women are responsible for the care of their own children, represents an efficient use of scarce resources. Preparing meals, caring for the sick and

OPPORTUNITY COST AND THE PRODUCTION FRONTIER

1. If women's average weekly earnings are two thirds of those received by men in the same occupations, discuss the ways in which this will affect the market economy in its allocation of scarce resource between alternative uses.

2. Discuss the role which men and women play in the non-marketed sector of the economy.

3. The data in Table A represents the average gross weekly earnings for some professional occupations in April 1993:

Table A: Weekly earnings of men and women

Occupation	Men (£ per week)	Women (£ per week)
University lecturers	552.50	441.70
Pharmacists	453.30	415.20
Cleaners/domestics	195.20	153.70
Child care/care assistants	195.00	180.90

Source: *New Earnings Survey*, 1993

Using the data given in the table, calculate the opportunity cost of the following activities if the person concerned must take unpaid leave from their occupation in order to perform them (assume one week's work usually means 5 days):

(a) One week spent cleaning the house by a female pharmacist.

(b) One week spent caring for an elderly relative by a male cleaner.

(c) Two days per week spent in household work by a female university lecturer.

(d) Two weeks spent in child care by a male university lecturer.

Figure 9.2 Opportunity costs

elderly, washing clothes and raising children are all important productive activities; but they should not necessarily be the mother's sole responsibility. There might be significant benefits for the whole of society if young children were cared for by a wider group of adults. Fathers would have the opportunity to develop a stronger bond with their children, the children themselves would have a variety of role models, and women would have greater opportunities to develop their productive potential. The use of a woman's unpaid labour within the household has clear implications for her lifetime earnings and economic autonomy, but it might have wider implications as well. It might involve productive inefficiency as the economy is failing to make full use of its productive resources.

Some examples of activities that might help to stimulate students to evaluate the roles women play in the economy are included in Figure 9.2. Questions 1 and 3 highlight the fact that, even 20 years after the implementation of the Equal Pay Act, women still earned less than men. Since women's weekly earnings are lower than those of a man they have less spending power, less ability to make their demands effective in the market, and less power to affect the allocation of scarce resources. These issues can be discussed in the context of question 1.

Furthermore the opportunity cost of non-market work varies between men and women as a consequence of the earnings gap. Question 3 asks students to calculate some examples of the opportunity cost of various non-market activities in order to raise discussion about the standard of living of the household as a whole. The appropriate division of labour between household members can be discussed either in the context of a sharing of domestic tasks between men and women or through the employment of domestic labour. Teachers might wish to discuss both the long- and short-term costs and benefits of complete specialization on paid work and household work.

Changes in the working population

The position of the production possibility curve depends partly on the labour resources at society's disposal. Over the last 30 years, the United Kingdom has experienced an increase in its total labour resources and a change in their composition. There were 3.5 million more workers in 1990 than in 1960, a fall of 0.3 million men and an increase of 3.8 million women. The British economy has thus acquired more labour resources, causing an outward shift in its production possibility curve. Provided the economy makes full and efficient use of its resources, it is now possible to produce more goods and services than in 1960. Table 9.1 shows the changes that have occurred in the working population in the UK since 1960.

Over this same period there has been a decline in employment in the manufacturing sector in Britain. In 1966 it provided for over 8 million jobs, employing one worker in every three; by 1990 there were only 5 million workers employed in British manufacturing industry and employment in the service sector had increased. Some economists have suggested that the growth of public sector services has *crowded out* manufacturing employment, causing the economy to move around its production frontier.

Table 9.1 The working population (UK, millions)

Year	Total	Men	Women
1960	25.0	16.6	8.4
1970	25.6	16.4	9.2
1980	26.4	16.1	10.3
1990	28.5	16.3	12.2

Source: *Annual Abstract of Statistics*, various issues

This argument assumes that there has been no change in the labour resources in the economy; it states simply that more workers employed in services must lead to a reduction in the number employed in manufacturing. Such an explanation of deindustrialization ignores the fact that the production frontier has been extended over this period by the movement of women into the working population. The extra women seeking employment were largely employed in the public sector of the economy producing the extra services; but this change did not in itself necessitate the reduction in manufacturing jobs. Approximately 70 per cent of the employees in British manufacturing industry are men whilst the service sector of the economy employs a predominantly female workforce.

Had full employment been maintained, then the increasing number of women entering the workforce would have enabled the British economy to increase employment in its service sector whilst also maintaining jobs in manufacturing. We could have moved out onto a new production possibility curve had we made full and efficient use of the available labour resources. In fact, though, deindustrialization was accompanied by rising unemployment, especially amongst men. Since the mid-1970s Britain has been operating within its production possibility frontier and has failed to make full and productive use of its labour resources.

The efficient use of scarce resources

Full employment of resources does not necessarily ensure the efficient allocation of resources. To use resources efficiently, an economy must not only be producing out on its production frontier; it must also be at that particular point on its frontier which gives the most highly valued combination of goods and services. Allocative efficiency, as well as productive efficiency, must be considered.

119

Within the marketed sector, the pattern of goods and services produced and consumed will depend upon the distribution of income and spending power within that society. In a world where women earn less than men, men will have a greater command over the nation's resources and the pattern of production will be weighted towards their preferences. In 1991, women earned on average 71 per cent of male hourly earnings in Britain, in France the percentage was 81 per cent, whilst in Japan it falls to 51 per cent (ILO, 1993).

In the neoclassical model, allocative efficiency depends upon the particular distribution of income. If some groups find it hard to express their preferences through the market mechanism, then this will affect the allocation of scarce resources. Women work unpaid within the household and women's demands upon the allocation of scarce resources are often not visible within the market economy. It is difficult in practice to ensure that the deployment of resources is allocatively efficient if we have imperfect information about the consumer preferences of one section of the community. In our society men have more opportunity than women to make their preferences felt.

The minimum-wage debate

The social and economic dimensions of the European Union are closely intertwined. Hence the launching of the Single European Act brought the Social Charter in its wake. In 1994, ten out of the twelve member states of the European Union had a minimum wage; only in Britain and Ireland was the determination of workers' wages left to market forces. Whilst our partners have committed themselves to the protection of workers' rights, the UK government has doggedly proceeded with labour market deregulation. A majority of the other member states have a national minimum wage, but Britain has abolished wages councils and left the determination of pay and conditions of work to market forces.

A minimum wage would establish the lowest wage rate that could be paid to a worker. Its introduction would thus raise the wage rate of any worker earning less than the minimum, but it would not directly affect those already earning wages above this level. It is therefore important to identify the level at which the minimum wage might be introduced in order to establish which groups of workers might be affected by its introduction.

The Trades Union Congress has expressed concern over the three million British workers who earn less than £3 an hour. The Labour Party has suggested a figure of £4 an hour or half of male average earnings. The Low Pay Unit is committed to a decency threshold of two-thirds of male median earnings, giving £197 a week or £4.56 an hour on 1992 figures (EOC, 1993). There were approximately 9.5 million workers earning less than this rate in 1992, concentrated in industries like retailing, catering and hairdressing. It is these workers who would be most affected by the introduction of a minimum wage.

One of the most striking features of contemporary employment patterns is the extent of occupational segregation. Retailing, catering and hairdressing are traditionally women's areas of employment. In 1994 in Great Britain, women constituted 66 per cent of employees in food retailing, 63 per cent in hotel and catering and 91 per cent of hairdressers (calculated from *Employment Gazette*, September 1994). These are sectors in which workers earning below the proposed minimum wage are likely to be employed. The introduction of a minimum wage is therefore likely to have a greater impact upon women's wages than upon men's.

In many occupations, even when both male and female workers are employed, there is a considerable difference between the earnings of these two groups of workers, as Table 9.2 shows. The reasons for this gender pay gap are well documented in any introductory economics textbook. The extent of their domestic commitments, the lack of labour market mobility, lower levels of experience and qualifications are all cited as explanations of women's lower earnings. In food retailing and in mixed retailing, men earn an average wage above the decency threshold whilst women's average wages fall below this level. The majority of those earning below the decency threshold are women, so the introduction of a minimum wage would, in many cases, affect women's wages whilst leaving men's unchanged.

Table 9.2 Average hourly earnings

Occupation	Men (£)	Women (£)
Counter clerks and cashiers	7.08	6.17
Sales assistant and checkout operators	4.53	3.86
Bar staff	3.98	3.33
Footwear workers	5.17	3.69
All occupations	8.10	6.38

Source: *New Earnings Survey*, 1993

Women earning low wage rates would therefore experience an increase in their wages were a minimum wage to be introduced. But is this an unambiguous gain? Many politicians and economists argue that there is a catch – minimum wages, they say, cost jobs. Economics provides a clear analysis of the consequences of introducing a minimum wage above the market equilibrium level. At the market equilibrium wage rate, employers seek to employ all those workers who are prepared to work at the going wage rate. The market clears as the supply of labour equals the demand. But if a minimum wage is introduced above the market equilibrium level, then this will cause a reduction in the demand for labour. A profit-maximizing employer will seek to equate the wage rate with the worker's marginal revenue product and, since there are diminishing returns to the employment of labour, an imposed rise in wages will cause firms to cut job opportunities.

Clearly there is a trade-off here between those workers who retain their jobs at the higher wage rate and those who lose their jobs as the firm can no longer afford to employ them. The extent of the job loss will depend upon the level of the established minimum and the elasticity of demand for labour. The Conservative Party argued in the 1992 general election that the introduction of a minimum wage by the Labour Party would cost about two million jobs; many of these would be women's jobs. Some women would gain because they would be earning higher wages but others would lose their jobs.

Whilst this argument is unassailable in competitive labour markets, very few markets in practice conform to this ideal. In many labour markets there is some degree of market power either through trade union collective bargaining or through a single employer of labour. If a monopsonist employer is facing a competitive labour supply then the position is very different. In this case the cost of employing one extra worker, the marginal cost of labour, will be greater than the average cost of labour which represents the supply curve of labour. A profit-maximizing employer will seek to equate the marginal cost of labour with the marginal revenue product but will be able to pay a wage below the marginal revenue product. The wage rate need only reflect the average

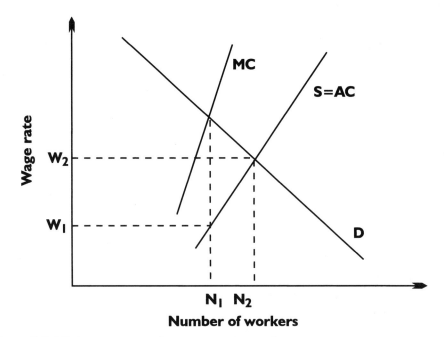

Figure 9.3 Minimum wage and a monopsonist employer

cost of labour. In Figure 9.3 the profit-maximizing firm will want to employ N_1 workers at a wage of W_1. In this case a monopsonistic employer is in equilibrium when both the wage rate and the number of workers employed fall below the competitive market level.

In such a situation the introduction of a minimum wage can improve the workers' position in both respects. If a minimum wage is introduced at the competitive market equilibrium, W_2, then this wage rate will represent both the marginal and average cost of labour. The employer will move along the supply curve for labour from N_1 to N_2 offering more jobs as wage rates rise. When the market equilibrium is reached at W_2N_2 the minimum wage is equal to the worker's marginal revenue product. Women are less likely to be unionized than men and often have less bargaining power with respect to employers; they could well find themselves working under these market conditions. In such circumstances they would stand to gain through the introduction of a minimum wage.

Evidence seems to suggest that minimum wages rarely cost jobs. The Centre for Economic Performance at the London School of Economics has examined the impact of the defunct wages councils on employment and has found that, if anything, there is a positive correlation between minimum wage levels and employment (Machin and Manning, 1992). Studies in both Britain and the United States have reached the conclusion that in many cases wage increases can be accompanied by increases in employment levels too. The most striking evidence comes from New Jersey which increased its minimum wage yet employment in fast-food restaurants rose (Card and Krueger, 1992). If this is the case then women can benefit from the introduction of a minimum wage; their rate of pay will be increased without any loss of jobs.

The questions in Figure 9.4 provide an opportunity for students to explore the different effects that the introduction of a minimum wage would have upon male and female workers in paid employment. The introduction of a minimum wage only directly affects those whose pay is initially below the proposed

---

MINIMUM WAGES FOR MEN AND WOMEN

1. In April 1993, a male teacher in a primary school earned on average £443.80 per week whilst a women in the same profession earned £369 per week. What factors are likely to account for this difference in earnings between men and women?

2. Using the data in Table 9.2, identify those workers whose pay will be affected by the introduction of a minimum wage were one to be introduced at half of the average (mean) male hourly earnings in all occupations.

3. Discuss the factors that will determine the extent to which the introduction of a minimum wage will affect the level of employment.

Figure 9.4 Questions on a minimum wage

minimum; since women earn less than men the initial impact will be felt by more women than men as question 2 makes clear. Over a longer period, though, workers might try to restore their differentials and thus even those above the proposed minimum could find their wage levels and their job opportunities affected by the introduction of a minimum wage. These wider issues could be discussed in response to question 3.

The unemployment of men and women

Unemployment can prove an interesting macroeconomic topic through which to discuss the distinctive roles that men and women play in economic activity. Britain is unusual amongst the developed countries of the world in that the rate of unemployment of men is higher than that of women. In 1993 there were 2.2 million men, or 14 per cent of the male working population, included in the claimant unemployed as opposed to 0.6 million women or 5.6 per cent of the female labour force. This difference has persisted through all phases of the trade cycle and despite the significant growth in women's participation in the working population that has occurred over the last few decades. Women account for 44 per cent of the working population, 49 per cent of employees in employment and 52 per cent of the adult population, but only 25 per cent of unemployed workers: women are under-represented amongst the unemployed. Since unemployment is usually associated with a fall in the worker's living standards and their sense of well-being, women might, at first sight, appear to have an advantage in this area.

Table 9.3 Men's and women's rate of unemployment (UK)

Year	Men	Women	Total
1971	4.5	1.2	3.3
1973	3.5	1.0	2.6
1976	7.0	3.1	5.5
1979	6.5	3.7	5.4
1982	15.5	8.3	12.5
1986	13.7	9.1	11.8
1990	7.6	3.6	5.8
1993	14.0	5.6	10.4

Source: *Employment Gazette*, various issues

One of the main types of unemployment is demand-deficient or cyclical unemployment and in Britain this is experienced by both men and women. As Table 9.3 shows, in the 'Barber boom' of 1973, 3.5 per cent of the male labour force and 1 per cent of the female labour force were registered as unemployed, and at the height of the recession in 1982 men's unemployment stood at 15.5 per cent whilst unemployment for women had risen to 8.3 per cent. Both men and women are likely to experience cyclical unemployment. But here the similarity ends. At every point on the trade cycle there are more men than women registered as unemployed.

It has sometimes been suggested that women constitute a 'reserve army of labour' upon which the economy can draw in times of high demand and which can be easily discarded when the downturn arrives. If this were the case, cyclical unemployment would be a greater problem for women than for men. Women would then constitute a higher percentage of the unemployed in times of recession than in the boom years as they will be more likely than men to lose their jobs. The evidence from the statistics for the claimant unemployed does not seem to support this argument. In 1982 women accounted for nearly 27 per cent of the claimant unemployed whilst at the peak of the boom in 1990 they still represented 26 per cent of the total.

The claimant count, based as it is upon eligibility to benefits, inevitably distorts the true extent of unemployment. Returners to the labour force are not eligible for benefits since they have not been paying National Insurance contributions, and workers seeking part-time jobs are not included in the unemployment statistics. Women are more likely than men to be in these categories. The typical work history for a woman will include a career break to care for pre-school children and will involve some period in which only part-time work is undertaken. A comparison between the *Labour Force Survey* (OPCS, 1992) and the claimant count suggests that in 1989 only 39 per cent of women who were regarded as unemployed in the survey were registered as claimants whilst 90 per cent of men unemployed were so registered (Pissarides and Wadsworth, 1992). The claimant count not only understates the full extent of unemployment, it also distorts women's unemployment to a greater extent than men's and thus helps to account for the under-representation of women in the unemployment statistics.

Structural unemployment occurs when changes take place in the pattern of demand in the economy so that workers made unemployed from one sector of industry find difficulty in obtaining new employment in another sector. The British economy has undergone significant changes in the pattern of demand such that manufacturing industry which accounted for one job in every three in the mid-1960s now provides less than one job in five. The loss of jobs in British manufacturing industry affected more men than women; about one million men became unemployed in the early 1980s as opposed to half a million women. Furthermore the changes that occurred in the pattern of demand in Britain in the 1980s favoured the employment of women rather than men. The boom of the late 1980s led to a tremendous growth in the demand for services and the service sector has traditionally been a major employer of women's labour. As the economy recovered from the recession, the new jobs created were increasingly occupied by women and their unemployment fell accordingly. Male unemployment proved harder to reduce and so structural unemployment in Britain has been predominantly a man's problem!

As the British economy recovered from the recession of the early 1980s, government policy emphasized the importance of market forces. With regard to labour markets, this implied that all restrictions and controls were to be removed as far as possible and the markets should be left free to respond to the pressures of supply and demand for labour. Accordingly, wages councils were abolished, the power of trades unions was curtailed and the economic climate encouraged the introduction of flexible working practices.

These policy changes impacted upon men and women in the labour market in different ways. Over the decades more women have entered paid employment, but the terms upon which women are prepared to accept jobs are very different from those that men seek. Eighty-six per cent of part-time jobs are filled by women and many of the new employment opportunities in Britain, which have arisen since the mid 1980s, have been for part-timers. If women are more willing than men to consider these vacancies, then this helps to explain the lower rate of unemployment amongst women. The introduction of flexibility into labour markets has encouraged the growth of part-time rather than full-time jobs. Such positions are more likely to be filled by women than men and thus women's unemployment has been lower than men's.

Women are indeed under-represented in the unemployment statistics, but it is debatable whether this is to their economic advantage. The emphasis upon the claimant count hides the true extent of women's unemployment and has contributed to the neglect of the topic by both economists and policy-makers. The changes in the British economy have impacted differently upon men and women. Women might be less likely to be unemployed than men but they are more likely to be working part-time. Part-time jobs bring in part-time wages; until very recently part-time workers did not receive the same entitlement as full-time workers to pensions and other fringe benefits; part-time workers will often experience a cut in their working hours if business moves into recession. All these factors make women as workers especially vulnerable in this brave new world of flexible labour markets.

In Figure 9.5, the questions on the employment and unemployment of men and women in Britain provide students with data to explore the distinctive ways in which men and women participate in the working population. Whilst women are nearly as numerous as men in employment they are far less likely to be claiming unemployment benefit. The questions stimulate students to examine the reasons why men and women come to be registered as unemployed.

EMPLOYMENT AND UNEMPLOYMENT IN BRITAIN

Table A Employment and unemployment (December 1992, thousands)

	Men	Women
Employees in employment	10,695	10,314
Claimant unemployed	2202	664
Employees in Manufacturing	2988	1286
Employees in Services	6505	8749
Part-time employment	1105	4717

Source: *Employment Gazette*, 1994

Using the data provided in the table, answer the following questions:

1. Calculate the rate of unemployment for (a) men and (b) women in 1992. To what extent does the unemployment experience of men and women workers differ?

2. In 1979, 37 per cent of men and 23 per cent of women were employed in the manufacturing sector of the economy. Calculate the relevant percentages in 1992 and discuss the factors that have affected these trends.

3. The service sector of the economy employed 6 068 000 men and 6 937 400 women in 1979. Identify the changes that had occurred by 1992 and consider whether these have affected the rate of unemployment for men and women.

4. Calculate the percentage of men and women employees who were employed part-time in 1992. What factors might help to explain these figures?

5. Distinguish between cyclical unemployment and structural unemployment. To what extent do you consider that these types of unemployment affected both men and women in Britain in 1992?

Figure 9.5 Employment and unemployment

Conclusion

If economics is to contribute to the understanding of society as a whole, then an introductory syllabus should consider the production and consumption activities of both men and women. Omitting household production from the analysis excludes productive activities on which many women spend a significant part of their working lives.

Over the past three decades the British economy has undergone considerable changes in its industrial structure, in the extent of government intervention and in the composition of its labour force. These changes do not affect men and women in the same ways; men and women often work in different sectors of the economy and exhibit different patterns of labour market participation over their life cycle. If economics is to justify its place amongst the social sciences, the discipline needs to become more inclusive and to consider the different ways in which men and women contribute to the economy. This chapter and the specimen questions are intended to provide some indication of how gender issues can be introduced into an introductory syllabus without reinforcing traditional stereotypes.

References

Blau, F. and Ferber, M. (1992). *The Economics of Women, Men and Work,* Englewood Cliffs, NJ, Prentice-Hall.

Card, D. and Krueger, A. (1992). 'Minimum wages and employment: a case study of fast food in New Jersey and Pennsylvania', National Bureau of Economic Research Working Paper 4509.

Coré, F. (1994). *Women and the Restructuring of Employment,* OECD Observer no. 186, Feb/March, pp.4–12.

Dex, S. (1985). *The Sexual Division of Work,* Brighton, Harvester Wheatsheaf.

Dex, S. (1990). 'Women and unemployment', *Economic Review,* vol. 8, no. 1, pp. 37–41.

DoE (1993). *New Earnings Survey,* London, HMSO.

Employment Gazette, various issues, London, HMSO.

EOC (1993). *Men and Women in Britain,* Manchester, Equal Opportunities Commission.

Ferber, M. and Nelson, J. (1993). *Beyond Economic Man,* Chicago, University of Chicago Press.

Hatt, S. (1994). 'Microeconomics: a woman friendly approach', *Economics and Business Education,* vol. 2, part 4, no. 8, pp. 160–2.

Hatt, S. (1996). *Gender, Work and Labour Markets,* London, Macmillan.

Humphries, J. (1995). *Gender and Economics,* Aldershot, Edward Elgar.

Hunt, A. (ed.) (1988). *Women and Paid Work: Issues of Equality,* London, Macmillan.

International Labour Office (1993). *Yearbook of Labour Statistics.*

Jacobsen, J. (1994). *The Economics of Gender,* Oxford, Blackwell.

Machin, S. and Manning, A. (1992). 'Minimum wages, wage dispersion and employment: evidence from UK wages councils', Centre for Economic Performance Discussion Paper 80.

Office of Population Censuses and Surveys (1992). *Labour Force Survey,* London, HMSO.

Pissardes, C. and Wadsworth, J. (1992). 'Unemployment risks', in: McLaughlin, E. (ed.), *Understanding Unemployment,* London, Routledge.

Rice, P. (1994). 'The changing face of the labour force in Britain', *Economic Review,* vol. 12, no. 1, pp. 22–4.

Turner, P. (1993). 'Changes in the structure of employment', *Economic Review*, vol. 11, no. 1, pp. 26–8.

Warde, A. and Hetherington, K. (1993). 'A changing domestic division of labour?', *Work, Employment and Society*, vol. 7, no. 1, pp. 23–45.

Waring, M. (1988). *If Women Counted: A New Feminist Economics*, London, Macmillan.

10 Economics and business at A level: an integrated approach

Nancy Wall, Stephen Barnes, Jenny Wales and David Lines

Introduction

It is quite possible to study economics or business up to degree level and to think little about the nature of either subject in relation to the other. People may think casually of economics as being concerned primarily with theory. It may seem obvious that business studies is about what businesses do in the real world. It may even seem unremarkable that the two subjects differ so greatly in approach. But can it be right that two subjects with an obvious and strong common element are so often taught and developed almost in isolation from one another?

The writers of this chapter have all been involved in the Nuffield Economics and Business Project. We started curriculum development work with little more than a conviction that students might derive great educational benefit from a joint subject approach. We began the process of creating a new A level course in 1991. The first 3500 students started the course in September 1994. We saw the integration of economics and business studies as a means by which the full complexities of real-world problems could be addressed. Genuine understanding of such problems involves an appreciation of a number of different perspectives. Our view was that an integrated, joint-subject approach would give students the greatest possible command over the thought processes which can lead to a full understanding of the real world.

When the Nuffield Project started work, there was no received wisdom on the joint subject approach. The team thought through the means by which the subjects might be integrated. The syllabus was devised with the help of a team of seconded teachers. The resources we wrote were carefully trialled by nearly 40 teachers in four different LEAs. The ideas that emerged had undergone a process of continuous adaptation in the light of experience. Our views are therefore the outcome of the practical process of setting up and resourcing a new course. The examples given here grew out of our experience in writing about problems that can be analysed using the concepts of both subjects.

This chapter seeks first to examine the real differences between the two subjects. Having explored the contrasts in approach, it goes on to consider more fully why we might want to integrate the two subjects and how this may best be achieved. Finally the chapter moves on to look briefly at the work of major thinkers who have straddled the boundaries between the subjects, and at the way a joint course may fit into the wider academic framework.

What's the difference?

Both economics and business are concerned with the allocation and management of scarce resources. But the perspectives are different. Economics is essentially a detached analysis of the forces that act to bring about a given resource allocation. Business concerns itself with the human management of enterprises within the environment of forces which economics identifies.

In defining the differences in more detail, it is important to explore the two subjects' respective places in the framework of human knowledge. Economics is a discipline. This means that it has a structure based upon a set of logically connected relationships. These are the theories that model the behaviour of the real economy. They can be applied to economic problems and will give us predictions as to what may happen in the future. Business studies, on the other hand, is multidisciplinary. It incorporates knowledge drawn from a wide range of disciplines and uses them in appropriate ways to shed light on practical issues. It makes use of sociology and psychology in the study of human resource management; of economics in the study of business decisions; of politics, and of accountancy and many other disciplines in lesser degrees.

This does not imply that there is some sort of hierarchy of knowledge. Interdisciplinary studies have a long history of respectable intellectual development. Medicine, for example, draws upon biology, chemistry and physics in order to study the best ways of treating health problems. However, if we wish to teach a discipline and a multidisciplinary subject together, there are implications which we should consider carefully.

Helburn (1986) in her analysis of the nature of economics as a discipline, and the implications of this for teaching, discusses how a single paradigm view of economics is preserved and protected by the economics profession in the USA, despite the existence of alternative approaches. Political events since the partial demise of communism after 1989 have tended to reinforce the primacy of this paradigm. Values are, therefore, an important part of the discipline, in that they may determine the *way* in which its fundamental principles are understood and applied.

The study of business proceeds in a rather different way. Its primary focus is upon decision-making, in the context of any organization, be it in the private or the public sector, or charitable in its objectives. It seeks to create informed approaches to decisions, by identifying different kinds of information that may be needed, and procedures that may aid the analysis of the available information. It does not have a formalized paradigm which binds its logical structures together. There is no parallel to the competitive market model which underpins most economic theory. Instead it draws on a wide range of ideas that may be deemed helpful in the decision-making process. These in turn draw upon a number of different disciplines.

It should go without saying that economics and business studies are entirely valid as separate subjects at degree level and at A level. There are many students who will want to pursue specific interests for whom the choice of a single-subject approach is appropriate. But we believe it is also the case that an integrated approach can provide an internally consistent and rigorous course of study.

The possibility of gaining insights from both subjects

Economics has a theoretical structure that is internally consistent. It uses models which effectively allow us to abstract from some of the complexities of the real world in order to simplify the picture to the point where we are able to analyse it effectively. The value of these models depends not upon the degree of realism they are able to incorporate, but on the accuracy of their predictions.

These are the strengths of economics. The capacity for abstraction makes it possible for students to delve beneath the surface of economic problems to investigate the underlying forces that the theory suggests to them. However, with this capacity for abstraction goes a tendency to become detached from the realities of economic life.

Business brings different strengths to the integrated approach. It can complement economics by rooting the student experience in practical issues to which a wide range of ideas may be applied. It can take up where economics leaves off. A combination of logical approach with real-world relevance should give considerable student appeal, creating motivation to explore in depth.

In fact, because there is a difference between the two subjects, we have found that students gain greater insights by using the concepts of both. For example, there are a number of areas in which both subjects have little to say. Take efficiency, a concept that economics defines very clearly, as referring to the minimization of costs in real resource terms. Although in economics efficiency is an important goal, the subject has little to say about how a firm may actually increase efficiency. Business, however, explores a multitude of ways in which firms may seek to improve efficiency by adopting well-known strategies in the field of human resource management, the organization of production and so on.

On the other hand economics can help us to broaden our view of efficiency by including allocative as well as technical efficiency. In economics, we find that welfare is increased as much as possible when resources are used in an allocatively efficient way. In other words, we are looking for ways of achieving the greatest possible degree of personal satisfaction with the smallest expenditure in real resource terms. The composition of overall output should match the value people place on its individual components.

Business emphasizes customer orientation. This of course is an important aspect of the way in which firms satisfy consumer demand. But the notion of

133

allocative efficiency is a long way from the study of marketing, and in this area economics can do much to enrich the study of business. By drawing on both subjects, therefore, the concept of efficiency can be explored in much greater depth than either subject alone can support.

The outcome of an integrated approach to economics and business should be the creation of a single toolkit which would equip students to handle all of the problems which currently confront us in the economy and in business. From this integrated kit the student would select the tools which seem most relevant to the question in hand. This does not mean that two bodies of theory have to be in some way amalgamated into a single coherent discipline. That would anyway be impossible. But it does mean that the student is encouraged to identify and use the tools of analysis which provide the most far-reaching insights in any particular situation.

Some practical benefits

At A level, business studies does draw upon economics to a degree. However, teachers are supposed to fit this economics in along with the usual business content of the course, and in the time available it is difficult for them to do it justice. Our experience is that some students emerge from their A level course with a sense that economics was on the syllabus, but it was not very relevant to the rest of the course.

Drawing on economics in this way may simply reinforce the view of economics as theoretical and irrelevant. It may do nothing to highlight the explanatory power of economic concepts and their usefulness in analysis. In the integrated approach that we propose, the role of economic concepts in relation to business concepts is, however, made explicit and clear. They are used both to broaden and deepen understanding.

Many of the people who plan to teach business studies at A level were trained as economists. They may have little formal training in the business field, and even less business experience. An integrated approach should provide a highly effective way for them to retrain as business teachers, because it should relate business concepts to what they already know.

There is a general consensus that A level study must incorporate a degree of rigour. No one questions the presence of rigour in economics, but business studies is sometimes seen as being in want of it. An integrated body of economic theory can provide the rigorous framework that gives coherence to the subject. Yet, business decisions are not based on theory alone; they are subject to cultural, political, social, psychological, emotional and intuitive forces that make complex interplay with quantitative evidence and pathways of rationality. Decision-makers do not behave with mechanistic single-mindedness. The integrated approach can accommodate this and address the range of considerations within its analytical framework. In this way the two subjects should complement one another.

134

Ways of integrating economics and business

An integrated approach to the two subjects does not imply that they are invariably equally represented in every area of the course. There are times when it is necessary to concentrate on one or the other. It does imply that the study of decision-taking and of resource allocation are seen as two aspects of the same process, and that the insights of both subjects are freely available for use in analysis as appropriate.The question then is, how should ideas and factual material be grouped in order to facilitate this?

An issue-based strategy

This allows ideas to be grouped according to their applicability to a particular problem. For example, if the focus was upon the impact of exchange rate changes, economics can contribute important predictions about the effect on prices and profits, while business can contribute an understanding of the range of options that firms might use to exploit opportunities through marketing strategies and market orientation. However, if a course is to be issue-based, judicious selection of the issues is needed and care must be taken to avoid those which will date.

Common elements

Another approach is to look for the common elements in the content of the two subjects and exploit the areas of overlap. For example, an understanding of the nature of the business cycle is of great and obvious value within both subjects. An understanding of the impact of cyclical change upon firms can develop hand in hand with understanding of the dilemmas of government policy-making. The whole creates a degree of grasp which is far broader and more balanced than the student can realistically expect to obtain from a single-subject approach.

A thematic approach

Another, related, approach is to explore themes. This can be combined with a gradual build up of ideas in the form of a spiral curriculum. It allows the student to preserve an overview of the subject area while working on a particular area of it. A wide range of concepts is introduced early in the course, but each is defined as simply as possible and an element of naivety is accepted at the beginning. As the course proceeds, students' understanding can be built upon as they repeatedly use the concepts in different contexts.

A stakeholders approach

A model for integration is provided by the grouping of ideas around the study of different stakeholders. The student explores the subjects and the issues from the viewpoint of the consumer, the employee, the manager, the shareholder and society as a whole. This creates considerable breadth of vision and balance, because the student must appreciate the multiplicity of interests.

The Nuffield economics and business approach

The thinking that underlies the Nuffield Project's approach to integrating economics and business is detailed elsewhere (Wall *et al.*, 1992, 1994; Wales *et al.*, 1995).

Courses are based upon themes, with a spiral approach. They are divided into six sections, of which the first four are integrated and follow the themes of Objectives, Efficiency, Expansion and Uncertainty. They proceed deliberately from local, small-scale scenarios in Objectives; through explanations of business and consumer behaviour in Efficiency; towards an understanding of large businesses, the national economy and the international framework in Expansion. The fourth stage broadens still further to consider expected and unexpected change and how people and organizations adapt to it.

Within each of these stages, the content is grouped around three questions, which are set out in the course structure diagram in Figure 10.1. The unit 'How is a profit made?' provides an opportunity to examine added value, supply and demand, breakeven analysis, profit and loss accounts and marketing. Initially, each of these is treated at a low level, but the concepts become available for application in subsequent units, and repeated use in fresh contexts should deepen student understanding.

We saw the selection of the questions around which the course is built as being important. They had to reflect significant issues, and not date; highlight crucial concepts in both subjects and provide a framework for the integration of ideas. They had also to embody an element of progression, so that students could digest ideas in a coherent sequence. For example, the question 'How do firms expand?' (Unit 3/1) involves the student looking at changes in the technology and technical efficiency, changes in the nature of the market, organic versus inorganic growth, market share, and so on. Some of these ideas would have been encountered earlier in the course and some are introduced in the context of this question.

It should be pointed out that the Nuffield courses are set up with a clearly specified expectation about teaching approaches. Investigation is central to the process of learning the fundamentals, and all concepts are expected to be taught in the context of real-world examples, case study material and situations. The objective is to proceed from the concrete to the abstract, making the course material as accessible as possible and, at the same time, making the complexities of the real world as clear as possible.

The difficulties in an integrated approach

So far we have dwelt on positive aspects of an integrated approach, but there

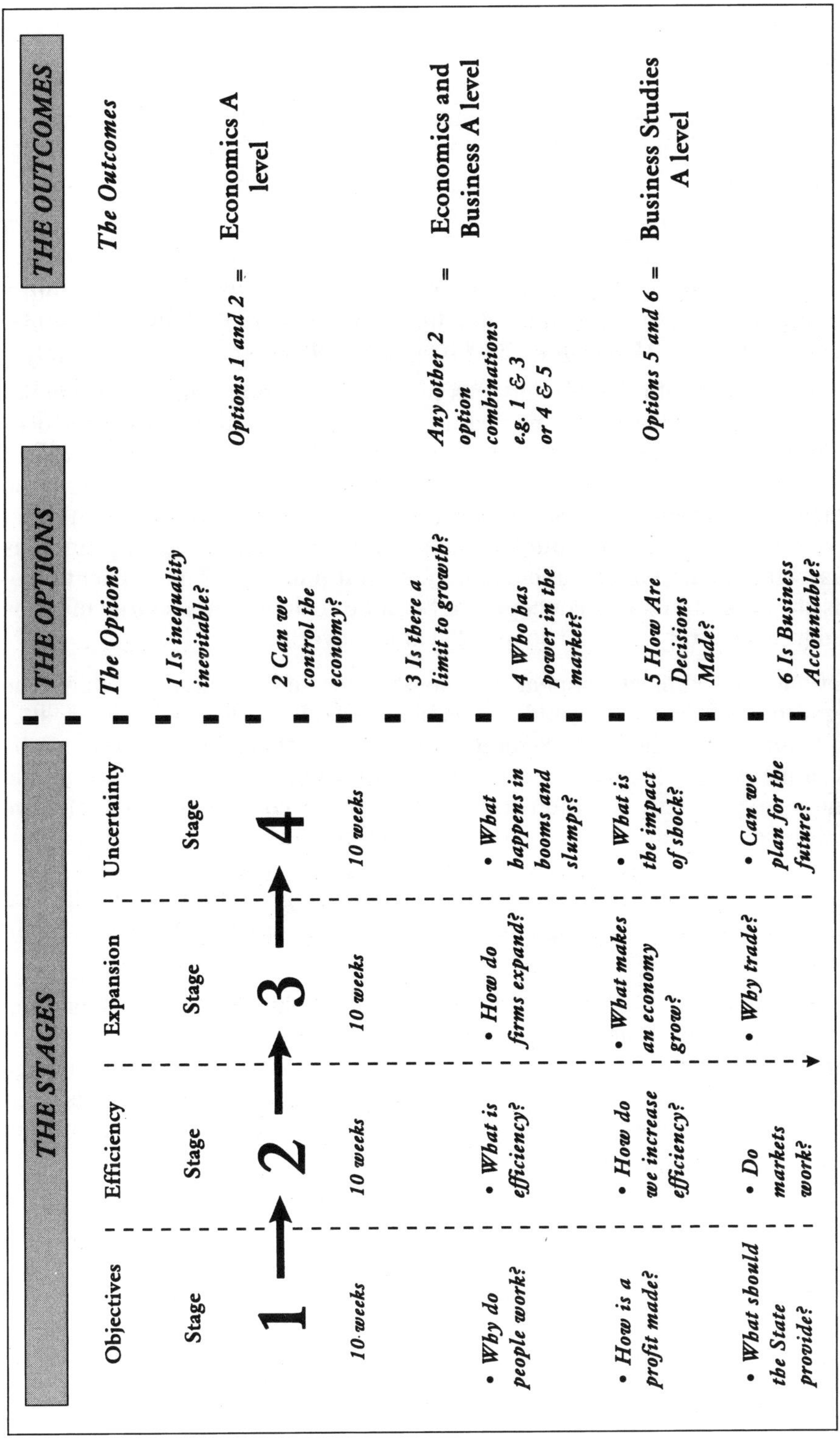

Figure 10.1 The course structure of the Nuffield Economics and Business Project

are difficulties. A discipline provides a set of rules, or procedures, which can be used to analyse problems. In a multidisciplinary context there is no unique set of rules, but a series of approaches, all of which may offer some degree of insight into the nature of the problem. In other words, it is still possible to be analytical in approach, but there will be a wider range of conceptual strategies.

Given this basic problem, what practical issues are encountered in creating an integrated economics and business course? First, there is the fact of having to accommodate two sets of jargon. The two subjects have acquired two cultures and two languages. In some cases the same words may be used but have subtly different meanings. The student may feel bewildered.

Thinking about profit exemplifies this problem. Economics distinguishes between economic, accounting, normal and supernormal profit. Business uses accounting conventions that take a completely different line. Where the economic categories are conceptual, the business categories have to do with the practical measurement of gross, operating, pre-tax profit and so on. In practice, students must become familiar with all these and know which definitions are associated with which subject, and for what purposes. The implication of this is that the number of concepts that can be included in a course must be considered carefully in order to avoid syllabus overload.

Sometimes the subjects appear to speak different languages. It might be thought that productivity would be a concept which would unite the two subjects. Economists refer to it frequently. It has a practical function and can be used to measure efficiency. It could be useful in business. Yet conventional business texts hardly mention it. They are more concerned with effective human resource management, an idea which might be thought to have considerable bearing on productivity. Similarly, many economists hardly know what human resource management is. In the integrated approach the two ideas are used appropriately, both separately and together. However, again there is the possibility of syllabus overload.

Different attitudes are also visible in the two subjects. Business has been described as focusing on the entrepreneur, the view from the manager's chair, looking out from the inside of the production process. Economics in contrast takes a detached view, looking at firms from the outside. Again students must be alive to both viewpoints in the joint approach. But they should benefit from the diversity of vision that can be acquired.

One area that can create problems is that of costs. Do we expect students to have a thorough grasp of fixed and variable costs, and of direct and indirect costs, the relationships between them and their respective uses? At A level the answer must be yes, but these cost concepts have been on traditional business studies syllabuses for many years and a great many teachers and students appear to be surmounting the problem already.

Will an integrated approach be successful?

It is too soon to say how successful this approach will be at A level in terms of attracting teachers and students. However, there are thinkers who are teaching and writing now who began as economists and gradually shifted to an approach that is very much akin to that of the business specialist. Their work can show how authoritative figures explain current problems, without necessarily giving their views a very specific subject base.

Perhaps the foremost of these in Britain is John Kay, Professor of Economics at the London Business School. His article 'Economics and business' (Kay, 1991) is essential reading for anyone interested in the links between economics and business studies. He accuses economists of an 'inability, or unwillingness, to probe within the boundaries of the firm itself'. He accuses business specialists of having failed to produce a well-ordered body of thought. He shows that this situation is now changing as economists become increasingly interested in aspects of game theory which seem likely to yield interesting results. Also potentially powerful is the work being done on the internal organization of firms. He concludes:

'Economics is the natural integrative discipline for much of management science. But its past relative neglect of the firm as a unit of organisation has severely limited the role which it has to play. That is now changing, and that can mean that economics in the next hundred years will have a quite different, and much wider, range of policy applications than those it has exercised in the century that has passed.'

Another important thinker in this field is Michael Porter. Though he avoids much of current economic theory, his ideas are rooted in the traditions of economics. Yet they speak clearly to the world of business. *The Competitive Advantage of Nations* (Porter, 1990) explores the nature of business success in many countries.

Writers such as Kay and Porter are not alone in this field, although they are perhaps exceptional in their impact. The more common pattern, as yet, is for people to perceive economics and business as opposing views of the way the world works. Many have an intense loyalty to one subject or the other. They may tend to look down on protagonists of the other subject. Business specialists may speak of the abstract, theoretical nature of economics, its tendency to be irrelevant to real-world problems. Economists may see business studies as fuzzy, perhaps relatively unacademic, in nature, and lacking in rigour.

Both views, though deeply simplistic, have links to more soundly based criticisms. As we have seen, by its nature business studies lacks a systematic framework, precisely because it is multidisciplinary in approach.

At the same time, economics has come under fire from some economists. *The Death of Economics* (Ormerod, 1994) examines the theoretical foundations of the competitive market model. In recent years it has become the underlying principle for the formation of much government policy. Deregulation, internal markets, competition policy and trade policy have all been based on an attempt to bring real-world markets closer to the competitive model. Ormerod points out how recent research has shown the weaknesses of this very pervasive model. Economists at the forefront of the profession have themselves shown how the existence of widespread market failure calls into question many of the policies that have been used to try to enhance the workings of various markets. He argues that the frequency with which markets fail makes it inevitable that policies based on the logic of the competitive model have disappointing if not disastrous results. If economics is to serve society well, it needs new methods of analysis which will provide a better basis for policy prescription.

One way of accommodating both these criticisms is by adopting an integrated course. The multidisciplinary approach allows the student to incorporate aspects of a range of disciplines, each of which can contribute to understanding of real-world problems. Economics can provide the logical structures that give coherence to the study of business. In particular the market model can illuminate some of the fundamental relationships between firms and people that characterize the process of wealth creation.

Conclusion

The Nuffield Project team has found that an integrated approach can offer great benefits. For students whose formal education will cease at 18, it offers a firmer, broader, more practically applicable body of knowledge than can either subject on its own. For the potential specialist it provides an excellent foundation for specialising in either economics or business. In our experience the intellectual synergy and the reciprocal strengthening of the academic framework of each subject provide stimulus and a capacity for analysis. Students appear to develop a sense of being able to address important issues with a range of techniques that are potentially both powerful and sensitive. The ideas themselves may be quite simple but the range of capability developed by students appears to be considerable.

References

Helburn, S. (1986). 'The selective use of discipline structures in economics curricula', in: Hodkinson, S. and Whitehead, D.J. (eds), *Economics Education: Research and Development Issues*, Harlow, Longman.

Kay, J. (1991). 'Economics and business', *Economic Journal*, vol. 101, pp. 57–63.

Ormerod, P. (1994). *The Death of Economics*, London, Faber and Faber.

Porter, M. (1990). *The Competitive Advantage of Nations*, London, Macmillan.

Wales, J., Barnes, S., Wall, N. and Lines, D. (1995). 'The Nuffield way', *Economics and Business Education*, vol. 3, part 1, spring, pp. 25–8.

Wall, N., Lines, D., Wales, J. and Barnes, S. (1992). 'Business and economics: the case for a joint course', *Economics*, vol. 28, part 4, winter, pp. 171–4.

Wall, N., Barnes, S., Lines, D.and Wales, J. (1994). 'The Nuffield economics and business project', *Economics and Business Education*, vol. 2, part 1, spring, pp. 23–5.

11 Case study design for learning and assessment

Stephen Barnes, Jenny Wales, Nancy Wall and David Lines

Introduction

Documented experience has always been recognized as a powerful learning resource in any area of study. Consider the significance of the General Strike in the history of labour relations; or the impact of tourism on agriculture in the Loire valley; or the discovery of radium by Madame Curie; or Van Gogh's struggle with mental illness. Extrapolation away from the particular towards the general is shot through with caveats, uncertainties and paradox but it remains an essential and irresistible way of knowing about phenomena when knowledge is incomplete.

There is quite a long tradition of using case studies in teaching and learning about business. Curriculum developers and teachers alike have recognized the illustrative power of stories and scenarios whether factual or fictional. The early development of the Cambridge A level course from the late 1960s embraced the use of case studies, and they have had a significant place in every course designed since.

The value of case studies

'At 8:30 a.m. on 13 April 1988, the Swiss chocolate group Suchard launched a "dawn raid" on the shares of Rowntree. In a thirty-five minute buying spree they bought £160 millions of Rowntree's shares on the London stock market – 14.9 per cent of the British firm's share capital. This was achieved by offering shareholders 630p for shares worth 475p the previous day.'
Marcuse (1994)

This was, of course, the trigger for a spectacular battle between Rowntree, Suchard and Nestlé. A good case study allows concepts to be explored in context. Students are encouraged to recognize the theoretical content of a scenario and to apply the appropriate tools of analysis in attempting to make decisions and to solve problems. Each case contains a unique mix of human and operational factors placing a premium on the transferability of skills to unfamiliar situations.

By its nature, a case study is a more complex vehicle for learning than conventional test-style questions. This does not necessarily mean that more is required of the student, but any questions or tasks in a case study are embedded in the multidimensional context that is typical of the real world. In this sense, the case allows the integration of business or economic ideas rather than testing students on isolated applications of single concepts. This is particularly important in business studies where the subject's intrinsic validity has depended on the integration of ideas drawn from several disciplines.

Through case studies students can learn to select useful and relevant information. They must prioritize and assign weights to the evidence available while being prepared to discard irrelevancies. This process of selection also encourages them to synthesize new evidence from the raw material of the case. Moreover, a case study can serve as an encouragement to students to make their own assumptions and advocate their own ideas.

Case studies are ideally suited to group or team work. Different aspects of the problem can be identified by different students in a realistic setting which lends itself to discussion and argument.

Finally there is the issue of empathy. Problems that are purely specimens of abstraction do not prompt the emotional engagement of most students. This potential for personal and emotional identification with the scenario is a key strength of the case study method.

Most young people respond well to a story with human characters and even better to well-written drama. Business and economics are human dramas that can be analysed and understood through the use of academic ideas. These ideas can take on urgency and personal meaning when activated in the context of a good case study.

Cases in the classroom

The case study method is highly adaptable and can be used in a number of different formats, each with its own distinctive value. The most widely used is the traditional narrative scenario with a structured question to follow. This can capture major benefits of the case study approach but tends to be presented to the class as a somewhat static and assessment-orientated device, and may have a contrived, synthetic quality.

Certainly the design of the questions or tasks that are based on the case predicate the kind of learning that takes place. The most functional and convergent styles can make a case little more than a comprehension exercise, perhaps with some contextual calculation. At the other end of the spectrum a case may be creative and divergent, asking students to make their own decisions or to devise their own outcome.

Should the case be fictional or authentic? There are undoubtedly areas of subject-matter where fiction is the simple and effective answer.

In the example in Figure 11.1 overleaf, the need was to reach inside the consumer experience to extract a concept: the fiction is, in a sense, authentic. Fiction is usually applied in costing cases simply because reality is almost always too complex. However, it can be equally productive to strip down a real

To assist small children in spending their pocket money, a sweet shop offers a tray of assorted items all priced at 10p. An 8-year-old enters the shop, asks to see the Ten Pence Tray and is soon engrossed in making complex and painful choices. What is the best buy? Aniseed balls or a 'mega-chew'? A sherbet fountain or a candy stick? Chewing gum or a jelly bear? The aniseed balls, the candy stick and the chewing gum are all rejected on the grounds of not being worth 10p. The 'mega-chew', the sherbet fountain and the jelly bear are all 'worth it' – but which to choose? Not having the jelly bear is thinkable, but the 'mega-chew' and the sherbet fountain are both magic. Perhaps the 'mega-chew'? But the price of choosing the 'mega-chew' is not having the sherbet fountain ... too awful! It must therefore be the sherbet fountain. The child hands over the 10p. The shopkeeper hands over the sherbet fountain. Both are satisfied.

Figure 11.1 'The Ten Pence Tray' (Nuffield, 1994)

Coca Cola was introduced to America in 1885 and first bottled for mass distribution in 1913. By the early 1980s it was still the country's leading soft drink brand but was losing market share to the sweeter-tasting Pepsi. In response Coca Cola set about devising a new formula for the drink. A $4 million market research programme took two years to perfect 'New Coke', with a smoother, sweeter taste. After conducting over 200 000 taste tests the company was reassured to find that 60 per cent of consumers preferred the new product.

In 1985 a high-profile marketing campaign launched 'New Coke' and sales briefly took off. But soon the reaction began. As the sales curve faltered and fell, complaints poured in to company HQ – including 1500 telephone calls each day – and consumer pressure groups formed, demanding the return of the old formula. After three months the company reintroduced the traditional product as 'Coke Classic', and sold it alongside 'New Coke'. Sales of 'Coke Classic' rapidly overtook those of 'New Coke', and despite every effort by the company to retrieve the situation, the decline of 'New Coke' seemed unstoppable. At the end of the 1980s the original formula was outselling 'New Coke' in a ratio 10:1.

In retrospect the market research was perfectly correct within its limited terms of reference: 60 per cent of consumers *did* prefer the taste of 'New Coke'. But Coca Cola is about more than taste. As a brand and a drink it is a powerful symbol of American life and culture. It carries a huge hidden agenda relating to image, style, youth, memories, history and nostalgia. In the words of one of the Coca Cola company's own slogans: 'You can't beat the feeling'.

Figure 11.2 'The New Coke Disaster' (Nuffield, 1994)

scenario, simplify the circumstances, reduce the number of variables and respecify the data.

Generally, an authentic case has the advantage of a certain vitality and credibility that is usually (but not necessarily) lacking in fictional cases. For example, the story surrounding the 1958 launch of the standard Bic Crystal 'shilling throwaway' ball pen is a good case on pricing and also an insight into the origins of a classic product. In any case a certain *frisson* is to be had in probing behind the scenes in famous companies and understanding the genesis and true nature of familiar products. There is also real value in students recognizing the fallibility of the mysterious 'they', who appear to make decisions with such gravity and objectivity. Better to recognize that Coca Cola could conduct 'scientific market research' and still launch the classic disaster of New Coke in 1985 (see Figure 11.2 opposite below).

Much also depends on the scope and scale of the case. A quick, short case may only be intended to illustrate a single concept or technique. Longer cases can be used to link several related ideas or integrate freely across the whole subject area.

Whatever the objectives of the case, there is likely to be some mix of quantitative and qualitative evidence. This reflects the realities of economic and business decision-making and can contribute to overcoming the tendency of textbooks to 'cover' a numerate topic without adequate regard for its human and circumstantial context. However, there is a risk that students will become rather fixated on the numbers in the case, believing that they carry a special significance in being difficult to 'crack' and yet rich in marks. Indeed, badly designed cases do contain pockets of numeracy where students can equally be ambushed or rewarded by the mark scheme. Too often this leads to some students becoming almost superstitiously fearful of numbers and perceiving the numerate evidence in a case as booby-traps waiting to explode. Clearly, quantitative and qualitative data need integrating to form a fluent narrative where numbers are a useful shorthand and not a separate language.

Perhaps, in economics especially, there has been a tendency to underplay qualitative evidence. Traditional textbooks were prone to supplying 'exercises' in which theory was 'applied' yet without a convincing context. Another problem has been the use of extracts from journals and the broadsheet press where a graph and a table of numerate data are surrounded by a barrage of heavyweight prose. For students less confident with or less motivated by statistical data, such material can seem extremely unfriendly. And in the process of assessment, too, the term 'data response' has meant for some exam boards a question rooted primarily in numerate relationships.

The situation, however, is changing. *Economics Explained* (Maunder *et al.*, 1995) was early in offering full-length and authentic case studies, while Alain Anderton's *Economics* (1995) extended the principle to include a stream of short case examples as well as longer studies. The Nuffield Economics and Business Project's *Student Book* (1994a) uses contextual case material to

145

introduce almost every element of theory. Likewise the Economics and Business Education Association's *Core Economics* (EBEA, 1994) ensures that theory is convincingly tested in case contexts supplied by its teacher-writers.

In any event, the case study method can be an effective route to more active and student-centred learning. One useful approach is to supply students with the case material in tranches, so heightening the sense of drama and allowing them to develop and modify their decisions as more information becomes available. This mimics what is often the reality of decision-making and enables variable time lapses to be incorporated into the case.

For example, the class might divide into small groups and be supplied with details of a firm's existing product and its major competitors. There could also be a sheet of market research data, some macroeconomic indicators and perhaps some estimates of price and income elasticities. 'Is there a gap in the

---

Part I THE PROBLEM

It was 1975. Rowntrees was an independent British chocolate and confectionery manufacturer and its marketing department faced an intriguing problem.

The chocolate market in Britain was (and is) very large – worth nearly £800m in terms of sales. It was dominated by three companies – Cadburys, Mars and Rowntrees – who controlled 80 per cent of the total market through long-standing, popular brands, nationally distributed and advertised. Rowntrees owned some of the most successful among these brands, such as KitKat (launched 1953), Quality Street (1937) and Black Magic (1935). Yet in the block chocolate market they held only a weak 5 per cent market share.

Sector	Volume (tonnes)	Rowntree's market share (%)
Milk solid blocks	40000	8
Milk ingredient blocks	25000	0
Plain solid blocks	7000	4
TOTALS	72000	5

The clear market leader was Cadburys with Dairy Milk – originally launched in 1905. However, sales of the smaller, lower-priced blocks had been in recent decline. These had been significantly reduced in thickness by Cadburys as a response to sharp rises in sugar and cocoa prices. Research showed that thin bars were not liked by consumers: large, thicker family blocks were selling better.

Against this background, Rowntrees pondered the problem of how to obtain a major national presence in the block chocolate market. Analysis of market research findings revealed a range of consumer needs, and each of these was matched with a new product concept, including edible samples, packaging and advertising material.

Figure 11.3 'Yorkie' (Nuffield, 1994)

market?', the students may be asked, and 'What would be the characteristics of a possible new product?' After making group presentations to the class, the students might then receive information on the firm's actual decision and the product launch that followed. This could lead on to the evaluation of subsequent sales data, a post-launch SWOT analysis and a 'with hindsight' look at the problem again. 'Yorkie' in the Nuffield materials adopts this type of approach (see Figure 11.3 opposite).

Multi-part cases have the great advantage of making the scenario dynamic and experientially uncertain. It may even be possible to feed into student groups only the information that they have requested and to run some kind of charging system to simulate the opportunity cost of research and delayed action. Students will then reach different conclusions depending on both the nature of their response and the evidence that they actually collected.

A further exciting development is to arrange an active or 'live' case study where the decision-cycle is recreated by a representative of the organization concerned. The teacher sets up the event with an external decision-maker such as a local banker, entrepreneur or council officer who becomes the key presenter. He or she identifies a situation or decision where the outcome was particularly successful or disastrous (or just surprising). Either in the classroom or – better still – at an office or boardroom, the students are presented with the initial scenario and the evidence available at that time. Working in groups, the students then make their own decisions, which they justify to the presenter and the class. The actual decision taken is then disclosed and evaluated by the students. This leads to the revelation of the real outcome and a final retrospective analysis.

In general, the more the students are personally involved in case study work, the better. An interesting experiment is to ask students in pairs or small groups to write case studies for one another (or for a different level, such as GCSE). Ironically it is quite possibly more educational to write a case than to use one for study. The process of conceiving the scenario, eliminating bugs in the numbers and designing foolproof answers is extremely testing and does not allow less than mastery of the topic. Students can set their cases as challenges for others in the class and later explain and justify the answers.

In many areas of case study design and application, the use of IT can be valuable. Spreadsheet programs are especially effective in persuading students to pursue 'what if ...?' investigations and to manipulate numerate data creatively. It is a pity that so relatively few exercises of this type are readily available, but only a little expertise is necessary for teachers to write their own material. Databases can also be an important research facility in writing and tackling case studies. The SECOS series (Statistics for Education, 1995) now includes a Nuffield Investigations and Data disk that features case studies based on the music, fashion textiles and motor industries. These can be used to encourage students to explore the database and to use the data-handling facilities.

Subject to copyright restrictions, the technology of wordprocessing has also helped the case study approach to move forward. Although there are now some excellent books of case studies with extensive student and teacher guidance, there is a sense in which a book is inherently unsuitable as the medium for presenting case studies. Students need to feel that each case is a unique experience with its own ambience and character. A book imposes visual uniformity, allows no new sequencing of case material and – on its own – can conceal no secrets or surprises. Wordprocessing of inhouse or other material, and printing from disk, makes the presentation of multi-part cases easy and opens possibilities for customization and original graphic design. Devices of this kind go a long way towards avoiding the risk of 'case study *ennui*' and keeping alive a sense of delight among the students.

Simulations and role-play exercises

From the position above it is only a step to simulations and role-play exercises. Understandably some teachers feel doubtful about the practicalities and skills involved. In practice, although the problems do need serious thought, the potential for learning is huge. Role-play can allow students to empathize with the case scenario while making demands that are affective as well as cognitive. The teacher can move literally off-stage and becomes 'producer', facilitator and observer. The students can become far more intensely engaged with the problem than would be likely in a conventional exercise.

The Nuffield materials (1994b) include a good example that dramatizes the problems faced by a government in setting the framework for the Budget. Students take on the roles of cabinet ministers who must establish relative spending priorities and settle taxation-expenditure tradeoffs. The fallacy of the 'free lunch' is brightly illuminated and the concept of opportunity cost moves into sharp focus.

Role-play can be a particularly effective method when confronting a topic that students find 'difficult' or excessively theoretical. The treatment of ratio analysis in David Myddelton's *Financial and Accounting Decisions* (1993) is ideally suited to learning through role-play. Written as part of the main text, the case concerns Hamilton Pumps, a small engineering firm in difficulties. Performance is deteriorating: the shareholders are dissatisfied, the bank manager is losing patience, the creditors are pressing for payment and the workforce are demanding a pay rise. The students can be given the basic background and a set of this year's and last year's accounts. Role-play scenes can then be built around the company AGM, meetings with the bank and the creditors, and negotiations with employee representatives. Trying this out with students showed no lack of commitment among them in analysing the accounts and in framing searching questions to direct at other participants. Even shy or reticent students were able to find useful roles as 'extras' – shareholders at the AGM or 'workers' at a union meeting.

It is probably worth the time and effort to add touches of reality to the staging of role-plays. Arrangement of furniture, name placards, OHP transparencies and even lighting effects all increase the sense of occasion and once any initial reluctance is overcome, help the students to identify with their roles. If time and equipment permit, a video recording can be valuable. It puts students on their mettle and allows a critical retrospect on the whole event.

The role of case studies in assessment

There has been a long tradition of using case study materials in business studies assessment both in the formal examination and as course work. In the formal setting, they have varied from shorter pieces offered by the Associated Examining Board to longer, pre-issued scenarios supplied by the University of Cambridge Local Examinations Syndicate. In some course settings students in effect develop their own case studies to meet the requirements of the project.

Ideally, assessment should reflect the best pedagogical strategies of a course. This would mean that formal examinations would match as closely as possible the classroom activity in which the students have been engaged. Reality, of course, all too often endorses the reverse logic. The 'timed essay' and 'bet it's C, ah no, it's E' are familiar words to teachers and students. But would the multiple-choice test and essay against the clock be preferred methods of learning? This is the great strength of the case study approach. It is an assessment strategy but it is also an effective and enjoyable vehicle for learning.

Examiners are always seeking effective methods to discriminate between candidates. The case study can provide such opportunities because the related questions can be ranked in order of difficulty and allow able candidates to develop answers and therefore show their ability in terms of higher-order skills. Equally the combination of accessible text and structured questions can enable weaker candidates to show their capabilities.

Answers to problems in economics or business studies are rarely single-faceted. In both subjects, students are asked to draw upon ideas learnt throughout the course in order to demonstrate their understanding of the integrated nature of the subjects. Case studies can be a powerful medium for learning and assessing these skills of integration. In selecting or writing a case, it is possible to decide on the range of ideas that students should be handling simultaneously while allowing the most able to use their conceptual menu more creatively. This ability to integrate and synthesize is a powerful measure of achievement and an effective tool in discriminating between students.

Although economics has used data response or stimulus type questions for many years, few syllabuses have ventured far into the case study mode. The Wessex Project and Nuffield have both used real, or lightly disguised scenarios as a means of encouraging students to demonstrate economic skills and understanding. There are many opportunities to bring the subject to life by presenting students with material to which economics theory can be applied in solving problems. An element of human interest does not detract from the quality of analysis or evaluation and may well prove attractive to students who are beginning to find economics less appealing.

An issue often raised in discussions about case studies in assessment is the value of pre-issuing. Some boards make the material available several weeks before the date of the examination and therefore give teachers and students time to prepare more fully. At its best, this strategy provides a culmination of the course in which teachers help students to draw together all the threads of their learning in order to deal with potential questions. By doing so, the integrated nature of the subjects is reinforced in a concrete way which assists everyone, whatever their level of achievement. At its worst, it leads to teachers providing lengthy sets of photocopied notes they hope will meet every eventuality. The former is very beneficial, the latter is hard to avoid.

Despite such drawbacks, the case study provides a method of assessment that meets many of the requirements of high-quality testing. In the longer run, it is likely to be a format that is developed more fully in economics. This shift is starting to take place in the recently approved syllabuses where some boards (e.g. ULEAC Nuffield Business and Economics at A level) have introduced focused studies (Vidler, 1995) and have moved towards a case study style in their data response questions.

Conclusion

Case studies aim to contextualize knowledge and connect academic ideas with the vitality and complexity of the real world. They can be highly motivating for students and can open the way to some innovative assessment techniques. Like any specific approach to learning, the case study method is liable to inappropriate or excessive use. Cases are no substitute in themselves for a proper understanding of theory. The need is for students to take personal ownership of that theory and to become confident in its application. This goal suggests a realistic specification of the theory to be learned and a major role for case studies in the process of learning.

References

Anderton, A. (1995). *Economics*, 2nd edn, Ormskirk, Causeway Press.

EBEA (1995). *Core Economics*, Oxford, Heinemann Educational.

Marcusé, I. (1994). *Case Studies*, 2nd edn, Harlow, Longman.

Maunder, P., Myers, D. and Wall, N. (1995). *Economics Explained*, 3rd edn, London, Collins Educational.

Myddelton, D. (1993). *Financial and Accounting Decisions*, Harlow, Longman.

Nuffield (1994a). *Nuffield Economics and Business Project: Student Book*, Harlow, Longman.

Nuffield (1994b). *Nuffield Economics and Business Project: Teachers' Resources*, Harlow, Longman.

SECOS (1995). *Nuffield Economics and Business*, Statistics for Education, 5 Bridge Street, Bishop's Stortford, Herts CM23 2JU.

Vidler, C. (1995). 'The new market place', *Economics and Business Education*, vol. 3, part 1, no. 9.

12 Differentiation at Key Stage 4

Nick Heard

Introduction

For a number of years differentiation has been something of a buzz-word in educational circles. The call for a broad, balanced, relevant and differentiated curriculum in *Better Schools* (DES, 1985) led to differentiation being recognized as a key element of the statutory curricula introduced in England, Wales and Northern Ireland as part of education reform, and was followed by a number of initiatives and much writing on the topic. In Scotland a national differentiation project funded by the Scottish Office Education Department and coordinated by the Scottish Consultative Council on the Curriculum (SCCC) was launched in 1993 to help schools develop their approaches to differentiation within the 5–14 programme.

Numerous articles have been written and a great deal of guidance, support and INSET material has been developed which has attempted to suggest how the goal of a differentiated curriculum could be translated into practice – see, for example, Barthorpe and Visser (1991), Stradling and Saunders with Weston (1991), Peter (1992), Visser (1993), Dickenson and Wright (1993) and SCCC (1994). However, much of this work has occurred within the context of the statutory curriculum and has been directed toward teachers of pupils in Key Stages 1–3, with the emphasis on making programmes of study accessible to pupils at their own level. That which has been written about differentiation at Key Stage 4 and its role in optional subjects has tended to concentrate on GCSE assessment – see, for example, Davies (1991). This chapter attempts to broaden the discussion of differentiation to include wider teaching and learning considerations in economics and business education at 14–16.

The chapter does not attempt to explore in any detail the political and social values that underpin the contrasting views of differentiation described below. However, I would subscribe to the view that education should provide all students with an equal opportunity to demonstrate their true capability. The subsequent discussion of the rationale and practice of differentiation attempts to show how differentiated teaching and learning can help to achieve this goal.

What is meant by differentiation?

Definitions of differentiation abound and reflect differing, and sometimes conflicting, educational beliefs and practices. As Stradling and Saunders (1991) have shown, contrasting perceptions of differentiation can broadly be grouped into two categories – those that focus on differentiation between groups and those that emphasize differentiation between individuals. The former view is one that identifies with grouping strategies such as streaming, setting and banding as the most practical ways of implementing a differentiated approach. The latter perspective, on the other hand, stresses the applicability of the same broad and balanced curriculum for all and concentrates on the need to tailor teaching approaches and processes to the different learning needs of individuals.

Teachers of economics and business at Key Stage 4 are unlikely to have sufficient numbers of students following their courses to allow for separate classes grouped according to ability, even when they teach in schools in which this is the policy for some subjects. Moreover, Stradling and Saunders (1993) argue that differentiation between groups does not do justice 'to the different and changing needs of individual pupils across their whole curriculum'. There are those such as Dowling (1990) and Hart (1992) who go further and argue that differentiation reinforces and perpetuates existing inequalities. Hart makes the case for a fundamental shift in focus away from the abilities and characteristics of learners to the composition of the curriculum. She suggests that the responses of learners may tell us as much about the appropriateness of the curriculum as about individual abilities and characteristics, and she therefore emphasizes the importance of continual evaluation of existing curriculum content, organization and pedagogy.

However, notwithstanding the aforementioned critique of differentiation, there does appear to be an increasing acceptance of the need, even within classes in which students have been grouped together according to their broad similarity in terms of ability, to take account of individual differences. One definition of differentiation which encapsulates this approach has been provided by Stradling and Saunders (1993) who refer to it as:

'... the process of matching learning targets, tasks, activities, resources and learning support to individual learners' needs, styles and rates of learning'.

Why differentiate?

As Weston (1992) has pointed out, learners differ from one another in a number of ways – not only in ability but also, for example, in respect of their interests, experiences, motivation and learning style. Given this diversity, she suggests, learners and teachers will require a wide range of strategies and flexibility of timing and approach if they are to achieve their common curriculum aims. So, though a course in economics or business studies at Key Stage 4 may have a set of broad aims which apply to all students embarking on the particular course (for example, the development of the abilities to make effective use of appropriate terminology, concepts and methods, to apply knowledge and understanding to a range of problems and issues, and to evaluate data in order to make informed judgements), the ways in which individual students may be best helped to achieve these aims throughout the course may be many and varied.

How can we differentiate?

The concept of differentiation has important implications for the curriculum, assessment and examinations. Teachers of economics and business are perhaps most familiar with differentiation in the context of GCSE assessment. The Schools Curriculum and Assessment Authority regulations for GCSE syllabuses (SCAA, 1995) refer to differentiation as 'the provision of opportunities for candidates across the attainment range to show what they know, understand and can do'. The regulations require each syllabus to include a scheme of assessment which specifies the means by which differentiation is to be achieved. In this respect differentiation is mainly achieved by a combination of task and outcome or response.

Differentiation in examinations

In GCSE assessment, terminal examinations with tiers of entry are provided to cater for different levels of ability. Therefore at least some questions on a foundation tier-of-entry paper targeted at grades G–C would be worded or structured differently from those on a higher-tier paper targeted at grades D–A*. This differentiation by task may be achieved in a number of ways:

- The balance of questions on the papers may differ. For example, more short-answer questions and fewer essay questions might be asked on the foundation tier paper.

- Students may be asked to respond to case study or data response material which differs in terms of its level of complexity or readability.

- Questions for the higher-tier paper may put more emphasis on higher-order analytical or evaluative skills or be more open-ended and less guided than those on the foundation tier paper.

Within any tier of entry candidates are differentiated by outcome through their response to the questions asked. It is important, therefore, that a substantial proportion of questions are sufficiently open-ended to allow for responses at different levels.

Differentiation in coursework

Similarly within GCSE coursework there may be differentiation by task and/or outcome. Students may be set different tasks appropriate to their levels of ability or common tasks may be set which allow for different levels of response.

Four other forms of differentiation in coursework can be identified:

- The *content* on which coursework is based may differ from one student to another, with students working on parts of the syllabus in which they have a particular interest.

- Where coursework forms an integral part of the day-to-day teaching process, differentiation by *support* is also relevant here. The teacher acting as the 'research tutor' may offer varying degrees of support to students in the different stages of the coursework such as planning, collecting, organizing and presenting data, analysis, evaluation and drawing conclusions. Assessment schemes for coursework normally take account of this, so that candidates are rewarded for their ability to carry out the task largely independently whereas those requiring extensive guidance during each stage of the task are penalized.

- Coursework may also provide an opportunity for differentiation by *resource* as students working on the same task may be guided by their teacher towards those resources most appropriate to their abilities, interests or learning styles.

- Teachers may also differentiate by *pace* of work in coursework, requiring students who are known to work more slowly to begin a task further in advance of a deadline for submission than others who are able to work more quickly without impairing quality.

Differentiation in the classroom

Whilst teachers of economics and business at Key Stage 4 are increasingly conversant with the above strategies for differentiation in terms of examinations and coursework assessment, they would appear to make less use of them in their day-to-day classroom teaching and assessment. Despite teachers' recognition of the diversity that is to be found within any class of students, for a large part of their courses students are often fed an undifferentiated diet. Lack of adequate differentiation in the planning and organization of learning experiences is an area that has been highlighted by school inspection reports over a number of years. This has been supported by research studies across the curriculum. For example, Daugherty *et al.* (1991) in their study of the GCSE in Wales found in relation to differentiation in the classroom 'little evidence of fully developed strategies to cater for the differing capabilities of pupils'.

A not untypical practice would be that the teacher provides students with the same textbooks and handouts, presents them with the same exposition of a topic, asks them the same type of questions and sets them the same classroom tasks and homework. Whilst this approach may be justified initially in terms of equality of treatment and the need to get to know a class of students, and whilst a teacher could claim that the students are still differentiated by their responses to the work they are set, this way of teaching is inevitably restrictive. These practices run counter to the broad educational goal to which most teachers subscribe, namely to enable all students to develop their diverse talents and fulfil their potential. By treating a class of students as an homogeneous group rather than as individuals with differing needs, the teacher may often fail to get the most out of students, just as a producer in imperfect competition may restrict profits by charging the same price for a product in separable markets!

The result may be that some students find lessons go 'over their head' and switch off or drop out. Some may find that they are insufficiently stretched or the content bears little relationship to their experiences or interests. Others may find that, though the content is pitched at the right level, they do not have opportunities to learn in the ways which suit them best, and yet others may find the pace of learning too rapid or too slow to maintain their interest and motivation.

Recognition of individual differences is not intended to imply that 'individualized learning programmes' are the solution. As Weston (1992) has pointed out, 'It goes against the grain, and requires an unusual effort of professional imagination and discipline, to take [students'] differences as the starting point for curriculum planning.' However, within the common framework in which any class of economics or business studies students is working there is room to take account of individual needs. This may be achieved by students working as members of small groups, in pairs and as individuals depending on the task. Where pair or group work is appropriate, students may be grouped according to ability, interest or friendship, or they may be allocated to mixed groups that ensure a balance of interests and abilities needed to complete a particular task. Moore (1992) draws attention to the benefits that can accrue from changing the composition of the group to suit the task. Flexibility of teaching and learning approaches and skilled intervention from the teacher emerge as important elements of successful differentiation.

As indicated earlier, teachers of economics and business are familiar with strategies for differentiation in examinations and coursework. What is needed is for these and other strategies to become more a part of day-to-day teaching and learning. Many teachers do make use of some or all of these strategies, either deliberately – for example as part of a whole-school or departmental initiative on differentiation – or less consciously as an aspect of what they consider to be normal good practice.

Figure 12.1 summarizes some of the main forms of differentiation. It is not intended to be exhaustive, and in practice the form or forms of differentiation a teacher employs will depend on a number of factors including the subject matter of what is being taught, the teacher's and students' preferences for particular teaching and learning styles, the physical classroom environment, the availability of teaching and learning resources, and the educational values and ethos of the school.

Of course, the hard-pressed economics or business teacher may retort that differentiation is all very fine in theory but that practice is a different matter. When faced with the heavy demands of a full syllabus, coursework

By content

While the broad content of economics and business courses is defined by the syllabus or course specification, teachers may devise schemes of work that allow students to work on different aspects of a particular topic appropriate to their needs, abilities, experiences and/or interests.

By task

Differentiation by task involves setting different learning objectives for groups of students within a class to take account of their varied needs, abilities, experiences and/or interests. Basic tasks may be extended or modified for particular students or groups of students or different tasks may be set. In some instances a range of tasks may be provided to allow for student choice, or alternative learning routes may be built into a piece of work.

By outcome or response

This occurs when a common task is set for all students which allows for responses at different levels. Such tasks tend to be relatively open-ended and can provide useful formative assessment information to which the teacher can respond by offering the student further guidance and planning appropriate future work which sets learning targets to build on strengths and remedy weaknesses.

By support

Some students often require more help than others to make progress in their work or to complete a task. Such assistance may be provided in a variety of ways, including individual support to the student by the class teacher, support from other adults such as support teachers or business personnel working alongside the classroom teacher, peer support from other students, support from appropriate educational technology, or the tutoring of small groups of students.

By resource

Differentiation can be achieved by allowing students to work with different resources that are appropriate to their individual needs. This may involve the provision of resources which vary according to reading difficulty, the replacement or supplement of class texts with resources that make use of a variety of media, the use of study guides that can be personalized to the needs of individual students, the provision of accessible storage facilities and retrieval systems for learning resources, and the development of students' study skills to maximize their effective use of the available resources.

By pace

This occurs when students undertake similar activities but work at varying speeds. The teacher allows some students more or less time than others to accomplish a particular task.

Figure 12.1 Forms of differentiation – for a fuller explanation and illustration of some of these strategies readers should consult Dickenson and Wright (1993)

assessment, records of achievement, staff, departmental and parents' meetings, together with the day-to-day requirements of preparing lessons, teaching and marking work for large classes, it is difficult to find the time to devise and implement strategies for differentiation. This is an understandable response, but giving students more responsibility for their own learning and helping them to become more independent as learners can free teachers to respond to individual needs.

Flexible learning approaches have much to commend them in this context. These approaches emphasize the role of regular planned tutorial meetings between teachers and small groups of students, the availability and accessibility of a wide range of resources, the use of study guides to help students organize their tasks, resources and general planning, and efficient classroom organization and management. There is not space within this short chapter to describe flexible learning in any depth, but two publications that do are Waterhouse (1990) and Hughes (1993).

To the extent that the development of differentiated approaches in the classroom requires teachers to acquire new skills, then there is an obvious need for appropriate training and professional development. Teachers require opportunities to familiarize themselves with appropriate teaching and learning strategies and time to develop confidence in making use of these with their students. Experience suggests that small-scale incremental change has a better chance of achieving long-term success than attempts at immediate wholesale transformation of existing practice. Initially experimenting with one form of differentiation with one class and regularly reviewing progress before attempting further development is a realistic way forward for most teachers.

Classroom illustrations

The remainder of this chapter is devoted to illustrations of ways in which differentiation may be achieved within the classroom. The examples illustrate two approaches to differentiation in the classroom. In the first, differentiated tasks are provided for students. In the second example, the main focus is on differentiation by support and resource. Commentaries on the examples draw attention to some of the potential benefits and drawbacks of each approach.

Example 1: Market research
(differentiation by task – see Appendix 1)

In the Northern Ireland Curriculum Council's *Guidance Materials on Business Studies* (NICC, 1992) teachers are provided with an example of how differentiation by task might be achieved. The example centres around a unit of work designed to introduce GCSE Business Studies students to the idea of market research.

After an introduction from the teacher and whole-class discussion of the meaning and types of market, the students are given one of two sets of tasks to complete according to their level of ability. The first two tasks are completed individually and the third in small groups of similar ability.

In the first task, the lower-ability group (Group A) are given four products or services and asked to identify, giving reasons, whether the market for each one is local, regional, national or international. The higher-ability group (Group B) are given a similar task but they are asked to suggest their own products or services.

After a class discussion of the outcomes of the first task, the students are each provided with a case study of the launch of the Yorkie chocolate bar taken from *Business Studies* by David Butler (1989). They are then given their second task in the form of a worksheet with questions relating to the case study. There are two worksheets again differentiated according to the ability of the student. The worksheet for Group A students begins with more straightforward opening questions. These students are also given additional guidance as, for certain questions, they are provided with a range of possible answers from which they can select whereas the relevant questions for Group B students are open-ended. One of the questions for Group A is also more directly related to the students' own experiences. To complete this task, Group B students are given an additional extension question which is not included on Group A's worksheet.

For the final task all students are provided with the same scenario of an owner of a hairdressing salon in a busy shopping centre who wishes to research the market to find out how best to promote the business and attract customers. They are required to discuss in their small groups how to research the market, to prepare a report on their conclusions and to appoint a spokesperson to present the report to the rest of the class. Students from Group A are guided towards a number of points to consider in preparing their report, whereas for Group B students no further guidance is given.

Commentary. By providing differentiated tasks the teacher is better able to ensure that the range of abilities within the class is catered for and that all students are motivated to work. When tasks are differentiated in this way there is less chance of students becoming disaffected, as may occur when tasks are either too diifficult or insufficiently demanding. However, it could be argued that simply having two sets of differentiated tasks for a class of 20 or 30 students is a rather blunt instrument to fashion a solution to the multifaceted problem of catering for individual students' needs, abilities and interests. Teachers also need to be aware of the possible adverse effects that grouping by ability may have on the self-esteem, expectations and attitudes of lower attaining students. Over-reliance on this form of differentiation may in the long run prove counter-productive.

Example 2: Managing the economy
(differentiation by support and resource – see Appendix 2)

Flexible-learning study guides have been produced commercially by Network

Educational Press for Business Studies GCSE/Economic Awareness, for A level Economics and for other subjects across the curriculum. In addition many teachers have produced their own study guides for particular units of work using a similar format. This example describes one such unit designed to assist GCSE Economics students develop their understanding of how governments attempt to manage the economy and some of the problems they face in doing so.

At the beginning of the unit all students in the class are provided with the same study guide. The guide begins with an 'advanced organizer' with a visual portrayal of the main areas to be studied (unemployment, inflation, economic growth and the balance of payments) and a list of aims so that all students are aware at the outset of how the various activities in the unit fit together.

Near to the front of the study guide a box is provided for the students to note important information such as deadlines for the completion of the work, personal targets, the length of written work required and how the work is to be assessed. This is followed by space where useful resources such as books, newspaper articles, video resources and information technology can be listed. The rest of the guide is devoted to a number of group and individual activities in which the students explore their initial understanding of the topic, check their existing ideas and views against evidence, and examine economic policy tools and problems. Throughout the guide space is available for margin notes.

The use of a study guide allows the teacher to use available resources flexibly and effectively whilst helping to create time for support to individuals and groups of students. The teacher or student can 'personalize' the guide by making use of the white space provided in the margins and boxes to make notes, record decisions and list learning targets. The teacher can draw students' attention to resources that are particularly suited to individual abilities, needs and interests, can advise students on the most suitable approaches to particular activities, and may suggest that some activities are not attempted by some students whilst providing extension activities for others. The students are also provided with suggestions for alternative ways in which they can present their report in the final activity, thus allowing for individual strengths and preferences.

Commentary. The achievement of effective differentiation in which individual needs are addressed is one of the main advantages of flexible learning. Hughes (1993) has indicated that, as individual students are able to work at their own pace for most of the time, far greater progress is made than would normally be expected. He draws attention, in particular, to the way in which flexible learning succeeds in stretching the most able students more than in whole-class teaching situations. The approach does make considerable initial demands on the teacher in setting up a systematic way of working in the classroom and familiarizing students with it, and in the preparation of study guides. However, evidence suggests that the initial investment of time and energy pays dividends in the long run through a reduction in time-consuming administrative tasks for teachers and increased opportunities for them to help their students to learn. These in turn are accompanied by gains in student motivation, behaviour, responsibility and attainment.

Conclusion

Forms of differentiation are not mutually exclusive and may all be used at various times as particular needs and circumstances dictate. They all offer opportunities to take greater account of individual needs but are not perfect solutions or without drawbacks. Differentiation should be viewed as an integral part of effective teaching and learning which encourages progression and higher attainment for all students.

As Moore (1992) has pointed out: 'The most important and essential feature of successful differentiation is good planning.' In devising units of work, providing suitable support for individuals and groups of students, and selecting the most appropriate methods of assessment, teachers of economics and business need to think carefully about how common curriculum objectives can be translated into learning experiences which take account of the needs of individual students. In order to differentiate effectively teachers need to develop a thorough knowledge of their students as individuals. There is therefore a clear link between formative, diagnostic assessment and improving differentiation in the classroom. It is only when teachers are fully aware of what students already know, understand and can do that appropriate targets can be set for further learning.

Teachers of economics and business studies are often at a disadvantage here compared with teachers of other subjects as they do not usually encounter their students in a teaching situation until those students embark on their Key Stage 4 courses. Teachers therefore may have little prior knowledge of their students to guide them in the early stages of the course, though records of students' performance in other related subjects can provide useful pointers.

Differentiated approaches are likely to flourish best in schools that have long-term, whole-school strategies with the full support of senior management. There are therefore implications for staff development and for school organization and resource allocation. Evidence suggests (e.g. Stradling and Saunders, 1993) that learning support coordinators and staff may have a great deal of relevant expertise that other teachers can draw on in developing their own approaches to differentiation. However, even without a coordinated whole-school approach, economics and business studies departments and teachers can still make progress in adapting their classroom practice to take greater account of individual differences among their students. By reviewing existing approaches, preferably in conjunction with colleagues and students, and by experimenting gradually with new strategies, expertise can be developed and refined. In the long term, differentiation should become an accepted feature of day-to-day teaching and not just of end-of-course assessment.

References

Barthorpe, T. and Visser, J. (1991). *Differentiation: Your Responsibility.* Stafford, National Association of Special Educational Needs.

Butler, D. (1989). *Business Studies,* Oxford, Oxford University Press.

Daugherty, R. *et al.* (1991). *GCSE in Wales,* Cardiff, Welsh Office.

Davies, P. (1991). *Differentiation in the Classroom and in the Examination Room: Achieving the Impossible?,* Cardiff, Welsh Joint Education Committee.

DES (1985). *Better Schools,* Cmnd. 9469, London, HMSO.

Dickenson, C. and Wright, W. (1993). *Differentiation: A Practical Handbook of Classroom Strategies,* Coventry, National Council for Educational Technology.

Dowling, P. (1990). 'The Shogun's and other curriculum voices', in: Dowling, P and Noss, R. (eds), *Mathematics versus the National Curriculum,* Basingstoke, Falmer.

Hart, S. (1992). 'Differentiation: way forward or retreat?', *British Journal of Special Education,* vol. 19, no. 1.

Hughes, M. (1993). *Flexible Learning: Evidence Examined,* Stafford, Network Educational Press.

Moore, J. (1992). 'Good planning is the key', *British Journal of Special Education,* vol. 19, no. 1.

NICC (1992). *Guidance Materials for Business Studies,* Belfast, Northern Ireland Curriculum Council.

Peter, M. (ed.) (1992). *Differentiation: Ways Forward,* Stafford, National Association of Special Education Needs (reprinted from *British Journal of Special Education,* vol. 19, no. 1).

SCAA (1995). *Regulations for the General Certificate of Secondary Education (GCSE) and Regulations for Other Syllabuses Designed for Pupils of Compulsory School Age,* London, School Curriculum and Assessment Authority.

Scottish CCC (1994). *Learning and Teaching: Making Sense of Differentiation,* Dundee, Scottish Consultative Council on the Curriculum.

Stradling, R. and Saunders, L., with Weston, P. (1991). *Differentiation in Action: A Whole School Approach for Raising Attainment,* London, HMSO.

Stradling, R. and Saunders, L. (1993). 'Differentiation in practice: responding to the needs of all pupils', *Educational Research*, vol. 35, no. 2.

Visser, J. (1993). *Differentiation: Making It Work*, Stafford, National Association of Special Educational Needs.

Waterhouse , P. (1990). *Flexible Learning: An Outline*, Stafford, Network Educational Press.

Weston, P. (1992). 'A decade for differentiation', *British Journal of Special Education*, vol. 19, no. 1.

Appendix 1

Market research: The launch of the Yorkie Bar

The aim of this unit is to introduce Key Stage 4 students to the idea of market research. The outline below illustrates how the unit has been devised to allow for differentiation by task between students of different levels of ability. Task 2 is based on the case study of *The Launch of Yorkie Bar*. Worksheets for Tasks 2 and 3 follow the case study.

Students who are working at lower levels of attainment	Plan of action	Students who are working at higher levels of attainment
Task 1 Students are given four products or services eg soda bread, mushrooms, Tyrone Crystal, hairdressing. They are asked to identify the market for each one ie local, regional, national or international and indicate the reason for their choice.	1 Introduction – what is a market Class discussion. Begin with a discussion about the local market and then consider larger markets. 2 Students should carry out Task 1. 3 Class discussion of outcomes from Task 1. 4 Students are given the case study entitled. The Launch of Yorkie Bar. After some discussion students should carry out Task 2.	**Task 1** Students are asked to choose four products or services and identify the market for each one ie local, regional, national or international. They should indicate the reasons for their choice.
Task 2 Students should complete Worksheet A.		**Task 2** Students should complete Worksheet B.
Task 3 Students should complete Group Activity A.	5 Students should carry out Task 3 which relates to market research for a service as opposed to a product. This activity should be carried out in groups of students of similar abilities. 6 Each group should be asked to give a short report of its findings.	**Task 3** Students should complete Group Activity B.

The Launch of Yorkie Bar

Background

The market for chocolate in the UK is a very competitive one and is dominated by Cadbury-Schweppes and Rowntree-Mackintosh. During the 1970s, sales of bars of chocolate were declining. This was partly due to a rapid rise in the price of cocoa, which made the bars more expensive, and partly due to change in tastes. The manufacturer's responses to rising cocoa prices was to make the bars thinner and this was also proving to be unpopular with consumers. It was against this background that Rowntree-Mackintosh decided to develop a new product line.

How Rowntree-Mackintosh researched the market

Rowntree-Mackintosh spent several years researching the market for bars of chocolate. They did this in a number of ways:

- They looked at existing data available on sales of chocolate products, market shares and consumer trends.
- They used survey information already collected by various market research agencies. These agencies maintain information on people's spending patterns, who buys what and when, what television programmes they are likely to watch, which newspapers they are likely to read, etc. This type of information enabled Rowntree-Mackintosh to *target* the groups of consumers who were most likely to buy a new line in chocolate.
- Further research was carried out on existing brands to find out why people bought them, what made them switch brands and their attitude towards advertising claims.
- Rowntree-Mackintosh, together with their advertising agency, J Walter Thompson, came up with five new product concepts. These were tested on four different groups of consumers. Consumers tasted each new product and looked at *mock ups* of the type of advertising that would go with the product image. Four out of the five ideas were very rapidly rejected but there was considerable interest in the remaining product, This product was call Rations and was a thick, sustaining bar which was associated with open-air activities. The advertising image showed pictures of mountaineers and used slogans such as 'When you've got to keep going'.
- Although market research showed the consumer liked Rations, it also showed they did not like the name. Several alternative names were thought up, together with different wrapper designs. These were again tested by market research and eventually the name of Yorkie was chosen.
- Finally, a range of advertisements was tested on consumers in order to select the right image for the product. The idea of the long-distance truck driver proved to be the most popular and this formed the basis of the advertising campaign.

The outcome

- The Yorkie Bar was launched in 1976 and proved very popular, taking 20 per cent of the market for bars of chocolate.

Worksheet A

Answer the following questions.

1. Who is Rowntree-Mackintosh's main competitor?

2. Why did the sales of chocolate bars decline during the 1970s?

3. Rowntree-Mackintosh spent a long time researching the market for chocolate bars. For which of the following reasons do you think they carried out this market research:

   - to find out about sales of other chocolate bars;
   - to find out the most popular chocolate drink;
   - to find out what people spend money on;
   - to find out who is most likely to try a new chocolate bar;
   - to find out what percentage of truck drivers eat chocolate bars;
   - to find out why people buy existing chocolate bars;
   - to find out if people are influenced by advertising;
   - to find out the best ways to advertise a new chocolate bar?

4. From the list below, select the different ways by which Rowntree-Mackintosh obtain the information they required.

   - Asking people to answer questionnaires.
   - Posting leaflets through letterboxes.
   - Allowing people to taste different chocolate.
   - Interviewing people.
   - Interviewing all the lorry drivers they could find.
   - Looking at statistics from other market research findings.

5. Rowntree-Mackintosh carried out further market research on existing brands of chocolate to find out why people bought them. Respond to questions (a) and (b) below.

   (a) What is your favourite chocolate bar?
      Think about:

      - its wrapper;
      - its taste;
      - how it is advertised;
      - its price;
      - similar chocolate bars.

   (b) Why is it your favourite chocolate bar?

6. Do you think the market research carried out by Rowntree-Mackintosh was successful? Give reasons for your answer.

Worksheet B

Answer the following questions.

1. Explain the meaning of the following terms as they are used in the case study entitled 'The Launch of the Yorkie bar':

   (a) product image;
   (b) competitive market.

2. Why did Rowntree-Mackintosh decide to develop a new product line?

3. Rowntree-Mackintosh spent a long time researching the market for chocolate bars. What were the purposes of this research?

4. In what different ways did Rowntree-Mackintosh obtain information?

5. Some of the early market research was used to identify the target group of customers. For what purpose did Rowntree-Mackintosh subsequently use this information?

6. Do you think the market research carried out by Rowntree-Mackintosh was successful? Give reasons for the answer.

7. A manufacturer wishes to research the market for washing machines. In what way could this market research be carried out using methods:

- similar to that of Rowntree-Mackintosh?
- different from that of Rowntree-Mackintosh?

Researching the market for a service

Group Activity A

Within the group, consider the case of an owner of a hairdressing salon in a busy shopping centre. The salon owner wishes to research the market to find out how best to promote the business and attract customers. Discuss how to research the market for the hairdressing service.

YOU MAY FIND IT HELPFUL TO CONSIDER THE FOLLOWING POINTS:

– The amount of money to spend on this market research is limited.
– What information is available currently?
– What information might be supplied by existing customers?
– What information might be supplied by people who do not already use the salon?
– How might the required information be collected?
– What other sources of information might be available?

Prepare a short report on the group's conclusions and appoint a spokesperson to present the report to the whole class.

Group Activity B

Within the group, consider the case of an owner of a hairdressing salon in a busy shopping centre. The salon owner wishes to research the market to find out how best to promote the business and to attract customers. Discuss how to research the market for the hairdressing service.

Prepare a short report on the group's conclusions and appoint a spokesperson to present the report to the whole class.

This example is adapted from the Northern Ireland Curriculum Council (NICC) Guidance Materials on Business Studies *(1992). Task two of the materials centres around a case study reproduced with permission from pages 186–187 of* Business Studies *by David Butler (1989).*

Appendix 2

Study Guide : Managing the economy

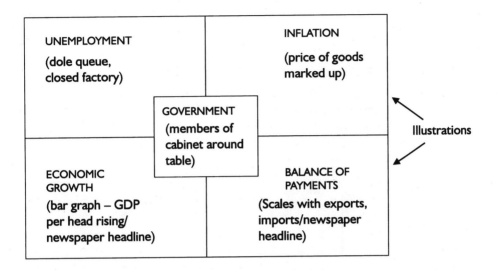

In this unit of work you will learn about how and why the government is important to the economy and some of the problems it faces in trying to manage the economy.

Aims

Margin notes

This guide will help you to:
- find out more about economic terms such as unemployment, inflation, economic growth, the balance of payments, monetary and fiscal policy;
- examine how the UK economy is performing and make judgements about how successful it is;
- understand how the government attempts to manage the economy and some of the problems it experiences in doing so;
- present your findings and ideas clearly and in a suitable form.

Use this box for important information – deadlines, personal targets, length of work, assessment, etc.

Resources

Margin notes

Books
-
-
-

Newspaper articles
-
-

Video resources
-
-

Information technology
-
-

Use this box to note any other suitable resources or sources of information you can think of.

Activities

You may not need to do all of the activities in this guide. Read through the activities first and discuss with your teacher which ones you should attempt.

Activity 1: What do you already know?

In this activity you are going to check what you already know (or think you know!) about this topic. In your group, and without looking at textbooks or other resources, discuss and if possible agree answers to the following questions:

(a)What is meant by:
 –unemployment
 –inflation
 –economic growth
 –the balance of payments?
(b)Do you think that the UK economy is performing well at the moment? Give reasons for your answer.
(c)Do you think your area is doing better or less well than the rest of the UK? Give reasons for your answer.

Activity 2: Checking your 'facts'

In this activity you are going to check your existing ideas and views against the evidence.

(a)Using your textbooks check the meaning of unemployment, inflation, economic growth and balance of payments. Write down economic definitions of each term.
(b)Use your textbooks to help you explain how each of these variables is measured in the UK and what problems are experienced in making these measurements.
(c)Study the newspaper articles listed in your resources. Do they confirm or contradict your group's answers to Activity 1b and 1c? Explain your answer.

Activity 3 : What can the government do?

In this activity you are going to examine what the government can do to manage the economy and to examine some of the problems it has in doing so.

(a) Working in a group of four, take one each of the four economic variables you have looked at so far and explain how you think the government could help to improve the current situation Discuss your answers with the rest of the group.

(b) Government policy for managing the economy is often divided up into monetary policy and fiscal policy. Find out the meaning of these terms and explain how they can be used to deal with economic problems. You may wish to present your answer in the form of a table such as the one opposite.

(c) Governments often find it difficult to achieve success in dealing with all their economic problems at once. They find that the nearer they get to achieving one aim the further away they get from another. Explain with the aid of examples why you think this might be.

(d) Some people think that the government should have other aims for economic policy beside those already mentioned, for example, improving the environment or making the distribution of income more equal. Take one of these aims or suggest another alternative and produce a brief report setting out:

- why you think the aim is important;
- your assessment of the extent of the problem at present;
- what you think the government could do to improve the situation;
- any possible conflicts with other aims of economic policy.

You could make your report in a number of ways, for example:

- an illustrated talk or lecture;
- an illustrated written report;
- the script for an investigative TV or radio programme;
- a campaign poster or leaflet.

Economic problems and possible solutions

	High unemployment	High rate of inflation	Low economic growth	Persistent balance of payments deficit
Monetary policy				
Fiscal policy				

Effective use of information technology

Peter Davies

Introduction

The focus for this chapter is the relationship between IT skills and learning economics and business studies. I shall argue that a good understanding of this relationship provides the basis for the effective use of IT in the classroom, and refer to examples that show what this might mean in practice. In particular, I will argue that the descriptions of IT capability in the National Curriculum provide a good basis for planning the complementary development of IT skills and understanding of economics and business. In contrast to some other descriptions of IT capability, the National Curriculum emphasizes the skills of processing data *in the light of what the data mean*. The meaning of the data comes from the ideas that are used to make sense of data and the context from which the data are drawn. Economics and business are rich in contexts which provide suitable data for the development of these skills. In addition, pupils' skills of data processing can be harnessed to help them to recognize patterns, to challenge their preconceptions, and to build models of relationships in economics and business.

It is important to recognize at the outset that a large proportion of schools' experience with IT in the classroom is not consistent with the argument I have just summarized. Approximately two-thirds of all computer use in economics and business is accounted for by word-processing, desktop publishing and related 'integrated packages' (Hurd, 1995). Practice in other subjects is similar (DES, 1993). This software is used primarily to improve the presentation of work rather than to help pupils to process and learn from data. Available research evidence (Cochran-Smith, 1991) suggests that pupils do not revise the meaning of their writing when using a word-processor. The first two answers to the question 'Why are you (the pupils) using a word-processor in this lesson' given by business studies teachers and pupils interviewed by Davies (1991) were 'Because it makes the work neater' and 'That's what you do in business studies'.

Researchers (e.g. Beynon, 1993) who have studied the use of a wider range of software have also concluded that the ratio of the development of new IT skills compared with pupils' time spent using IT is low. Neither is there any encouragement to be drawn from research evidence on the impact of the use of computers in helping pupils to learn economics and business studies. A number of studies (Siegfried and Fels, 1979; Wood, 1982; Khandkher and

Wehrs, 1990) have compared the effect of teaching with computers with 'normal methods' using tests before and after the teaching. None of these studies showed any net advantage for using computers.

What reason is there to feel optimistic about IT in the face of this evidence? The argument advanced in this chapter is that the usefulness of the practice reviewed in the literature quoted above was undermined by insufficient attention to how pupils learn. This applies equally to the progression in pupils' IT

The National Curriculum for England and Wales (DFE, 1995)

Level 3 – Pupils use IT to generate, amend, organize and present ideas ... use IT to save data and to access stored information, following straightforward lines of enquiry ... use IT-based models or simulations to help them make decisions, and are aware of the consequences of their choices ... describe their use of IT, and its use in the outside world.

Level 5 – Pupils use IT to organize, refine and present information in different forms and styles for specific purposes and audiences ... select the information needed for different purposes, check its accuracy and organize and prepare it in a form suitable for processing using IT ... explore the effects of changing variables in a computer model ... communicate their knowledge and experience of using IT and assess its use in their working practices.

GCSE Business and Information Studies (NDTEF, 1994)

2.1 Create a spreadsheet
2.2 Enter numeric data; text; formulae; +, -, *,/average and sum
2.3 Delete data; text; formulae
2.4 Replicate text
2.5 Replicate numeric data
2.6 Replicate formulae; relatively
2.7 Replicate formulae; absolutely
2.8 Replicate a cell
2.9 Add a row
2.10 Add a column

GNVQ Core Skills (Information Technology) (NCVQ, 1993)

Element 2.2: Edit, organize and integrate information from different sources

Performance criteria:

4. Editing/search/calculation routines minimise the number of steps/stages needed
5. Editing/moving/copying routines minimize risks of deleting/disrupting information
6. Information is saved/arranged in a form which makes it most amenable to transfer
7. Any discrepancies between the source material and new files/records are corrected if necessary.

Figure 13.1 Extracts from descriptions of IT skills

skills and the role which the processing of information can play in learning economics and business studies. Some attempts to use IT in the teaching of mathematics and science (Hoyles and Sutherland, 1989; Brna, 1991; White and Horwitz, 1990) provide encouraging evidence of how careful thought about pupils' learning can lead to a more effective use of IT. Ideas from these sources are used later in some of the examples.

The first part of this chapter concentrates on the development of IT skills, and the second part examines the usefulness of ideas about how pupils learn when planning the use of IT in teaching economics and business studies.

How do information technology skills develop?

Two aspects of this question are examined here:

- How should descriptions of IT skills refer to the meaning of data?

- What is the difference between low and high levels of skill?

Answers to these questions imply particular views of how higher levels of skill develop and how teaching might be organized to achieve them.

Learning outcomes in IT are described in levels of skill. The examples shown in Figure 13.1 on the previous page are referred to throughout the first part of the chapter.

How should descriptions of IT skills refer to the meaning of data?

The three descriptions of learning outcomes in Figure 13.1 differ in purpose and progression. The purpose of the National Curriculum is to be found in phrases such as 'following straightforward lines of enquiry', 'help them to make decisions', and 'for specific purposes and audiences'. The GCSE and GNVQ lists, on the other hand, do not refer to the meaning of the data, merely to procedures used in their manipulation. This implies a difference in underlying purpose and carries implications for the organization of teaching. These implications are summarized in Figure 13.2 opposite.

Figure 13.2 suggests that if the purpose of teaching is to help pupils to use IT in the course of a task they initiate or manage, then descriptions of IT skills should include reference to the meaning of data. In these circumstances pupils need to judge when and why to use IT. The sharper vocational purpose in preparation for 'clerical' (GCSE Business Studies) or 'technical' (GNVQ) employment implies that descriptions of IT skills should make no reference to the meaning of the data. In these circumstances the skill is to accurately carry out the required technique.

The implied aim in descriptions of IT skills carries a prescription for the organization of teaching. The purpose of the National Curriculum implies that teaching should be organized such that 'subject content' and 'IT' are inte-

Description of IT skills	Focus	Implied aim
National Curriculum	Use of IT 'fit for purpose'	To help people to know when and how to use IT in the course of any data-related task in employment or at home
GCSE Business Studies	Acquisition of specific techniques	To develop specific skills for 'office work'
GNVQ	Developing efficient working routines	To equip pupils for data preparation and data management roles of 'computer operator' type jobs

Figure 13.2 Differences in purpose implied by definitions of IT skills

grated. This is necessary in order to provide opportunities for pupils to develop a higher ability in judging when, why and how to use IT. Whilst this kind of integration might also be adopted within GCSE or GNVQ, it is ultimately the decision for the individual teacher, rather than a direct implication of the purpose of the curriculum.

In these circumstances it is common to find 'basic IT skills' taught in isolation before pupils are asked to use these skills in the manipulation of data about business or the economy. The case for this approach to teaching IT skills rests on the large amount of highly specific knowledge (e.g. 'how to highlight text', 'how to select a field', 'how to copy a formula') which pupils need before they can begin to exercise some independence at the keyboard. An illustration of the depth of detailed knowledge required is shown in the written instructions provided by a teacher for a Year 7 class (Figure 13.3).

The need for instructions that are this detailed arises when pupils are asked to learn how to use new software or new procedures through creating their own data. Even instructions that are this detailed may leave some pupils unsure. For instance, the reference in Figure 13.3 to 'data type' (in 'Setting up your class file') leaves the jargon unexplained. The major problem with this type of instruction is that pupils are not asked to think about what to do next or why each step is the right one. It is quite possible that a number of pupils will understand the significance of defining fields and choosing data type from the teacher's verbal introduction, and that others will infer this significance from the tasks as they carry them out. However, it is likely that a number of pupils in each class will follow the sequence of instructions without a clear sense of how they all fit together.

To get into the database programme
Click and hold mouse on the apple picture (top left)
'Drag' down the mouse to highlight 'CLARISWORKS'
Let go of the mouse

You have now entered ClarisWorks
Click on 'DATABASE' (black dot will appear in circle)
Click on OK

Setting up your Class File
Steps : (1) Define Fields
 (a) Type in 'SURNAME' (capitals!)
 —Click mouse on data type required
 —e.g. surname = 'TEXT'
 —Click on 'CREATE'
 (b) Type in 'NAME'
 —Click mouse on data type required
 —Click on CREATE'
 etc. until you have entered all the fields

Figure 13.3 Extract from a set of written instructions to a class from a lesson which introduced databases

An alternative approach is to introduce new software and new techniques through examples of data that are 'pre-prepared'. Such an approach asks pupils to consider the meaning of data without having an extensive knowledge of the software. Figure 13.4 shows an extract from a database on Excel that can be used to investigate the question 'What makes one can of fizzy drink more expensive than another?' The 'records' 1 to 25 are sellers of fizzy drinks. The 'fields' are prices of drinks and factors that might affect those prices. Pupils can be introduced to 'records' and 'fields' through examples. They can develop their repertoire of database skills in a sequence that is led by their need to understand and manipulate the data rather than by a sequence that is led by how the database works.

For instance, the database in Figure 13.4 includes two data types: alpha-numeric (letters or numbers) in fields two to five, and numeric in the others. The significance of data type is apparent through the character of each field and in the kinds of investigation that can be carried out. Alphanumeric fields classify fields so that investigations can check the number of records in each class and, crucially, the relationship between classes. (The latter is an example of a 'complex line of investigation' referred to in the National Curriculum as typical of Level 7.) Classes are created in numeric fields through the imposition of rules such as '>40', '>30' AND '<40'. Further fields (such as the fifth and sixth fields in Figure 13.4) can be created through calculations on numeric fields. Field 6 shows the average price of cans of fizzy drink in each place.

Record Number	Retailer	Type of Place	Independent or Chain	Type of Seller	Number of Brands	Average price of Cans	Britvic 55	Cherry Cola	Citrus Spring	Coke	Diet Coke	Caffeine Free Coke
1	Chemist	S	I	SS	6	33						
2	Chester Rd. Off Licence	S	I	OL	12	40.7	46	39		39	39	
3	Esso Garage	TC	C	G	21	44	49	43	43	43		43
4	Fish & Chip	TC	I	TA	12	40				40	40	
5	Papas Takeaway	S	I	TA	4	50						
6	Shell Garage	S	C	G	13	40.9		40		40	40	
7	Spar	S	C	S	11	35.5				36	36	
8	Thresher	S	C	OL	11	43.4	46		42			
9	Sandwich Bar	IC	I	SS	6	37.8				35	35	
10	Tescos	TC	C	S	18	33.1			33	33	33	
11	Inter-City Buffet Bar	TR	C	TA	4	73				73	73	
12	Railway Station Stall	TR	I	SS	13	38.7			43	35	35	
13	Fish & Chip	IC	I	TA	9	45		45		45	45	
14	Newsagent	IC	I	SS	10	40.8				40	40	
15	Baker's	IC	I	SS	10	40.3				40	33	
16	General Store	IC	I	SS	8	35.4				35	38	
17	Fish & Chip	TC	I	TA	5	50						
18	Victoria Wine	TC	C	OL	14	43.1	55	43	43	43	33	
19	Baker's Shop	TC	I	SS	3	40					40	
20	Baker's Shop	TC	I	SS	4	42						
21	Don Miller's	TC	C	SS	9	40				40	40	
22	Newsagent	TC	I	SS	14	42			42	42	42	
23	General Store	IT	I	SS	5	38				38	38	
24	Fish & Chip	IT	I	TA	3	40				40		
25	Spar	IC	C	S	16	35.4				36	36	

Figure 13.4 Extract from a 'fizzy drinks database'

What is the difference between low and high levels of skill?

It is important to be clear about what constitutes lower and higher levels of IT skill so that opportunities can be planned for pupils to move from one to the other. The three descriptions of IT skills in Figure 13.1 present different views of this progression. The descriptions provided in GCSE and GNVQ present lists of skills to be 'ticked off'. It is hard to see how any one skill is more advanced than another. In contrast, the National Curriculum does present a genuine view of progression precisely because it is concerned with information handling in a wider sense than that found in the GCSE Business Studies course or GNVQ. One way of discerning lines of progression within the National Curriculum's definition of IT skills is presented in Figure 13.5.

Level	Sense of purpose and audience	Exploring models	Translating information	The usefulness of IT
4	Aware that GIGO; interprets findings; need for care in framing questions	Uses models to explore simple predictions	Combines different forms of information; adds, amends interrogates	
5	Organizes, refines & presents info. for different purposes and audiences; selects info. for purpose; checks accuracy	Explores effects of changing variables		Assess use of IT in their working practices
6	Clear sense of audience and purpose; follows complex lines of enquiry in testing hypotheses	Use and vary rules in complex models; assess validity of models		Discuss wider impact of IT on society
7	Presents to unfamiliar and critical audience; pros and cons of different IT applications	Designs computer models to meet needs	Translate enquiries in everyday language into forms required by a system	Considers limitations of IT tools and the info. they produce
8	Select appropriate IT for particular tasks. taking account of ease of use and suitability for purpose; design and implement systems for others		Design means of capturing and preparing data	Discuss in an informed way the social and economic issues raised by IT

Figure 13.5 Strands in the 'Level Descriptors' for the revised National Curriculum for Information Technology

The value of trying to identify strands of progression in this way is that it helps in planning schemes of work and in setting targets for pupils with different levels of attainment in the same class. For instance, the 'exploring models' strand suggests a very clear line of progression which is easily translatable into a series of tasks:

- use a model to predict;

- change variables and record effects;

- vary rules in a model and assess its validity; and

- design a model.

If this sequence accurately describes progression in attainment for a majority of pupils, it has strong implications for teaching. For example, it suggests that asking every pupil in a mixed-ability Year 10 class to design their own break-even model is inappropriate. That is, if pupils don't know how to vary the rules in a complex model and are not able to make 'reasoned judgements' about whether a model represents reality in an appropriate way, then they are not *ready* to design a model.

The level descriptions in the National Curriculum do, of course, beg a number of substantial questions. Research evidence on the progression of IT attainment is very thin. For instance, we do not know how far ability to vary the rules in one complex model transfers to ability to vary the rules in another. The transferability of ability to assess the validity of models is even more problematic.

Nevertheless, using strands in the National Curriculum to help sort out what pupils 'are ready for' is part of effective teaching with information technology. This is certainly true when considering how to use IT to help pupils in their understanding of business and the economy. IT provides pupils with opportunities to process information in ways which should help them to perceive patterns and relationships in business and economic behaviour. Pupils' level of IT attainment places a ceiling on the kind of processing they can carry out and, therefore, on the kinds of task it is appropriate to give them. For instance, they are likely to learn more from complex than simple lines of enquiry when working with a database (Underwood and Underwood, 1990) and they are more likely to learn more from exploring the rules of a model than from changing variables. However, if pupils' IT skills have not reached these levels then such tasks may be worse than useless in developing understanding of business and the economy.

Putting this into practice in IT-based lessons rests on setting and monitoring clear learning targets for individuals or groups of pupils. This is no easy matter for three reasons:

- It is easy for the teacher's attention to be swallowed up by the need to keep pupils on task: avoiding congregations around the printer whilst 'printouts' are awaited; responding to procedural problems that pupils encounter, and checking that pupils have not switched to another task or even another piece of software.

- The fact that pupils are engrossed in their work does not mean they are not ready to move on to learning higher skills. They may be learning little that is new even if they are very 'active'. For example, it is easy for large amounts of pupils' time to be absorbed in refining the appearance of their work and in rehearsing skills they have already acquired.

- The descriptions of IT skill in the National Curriculum, GCSE Business Studies and GNVQ do not create a picture of smooth progression between key stages. There are clear differences in purpose that are reflected in the attention (or lack of it) paid to the purpose of the data to be processed. Skills such as 'widening columns' and 'copying formulae' which have been used to describe attainment in GCSE courses would merit no more than a Level

5 on the National Curriculum scale. In an era of 'concern about standards' this is a hotchpotch of major proportions.

How can IT skills be harnessed to help develop understanding of economics and business?

Four themes in using pupils' IT skills to help them learn economics and business studies are outlined:

- the link between progression in IT skills and learning economics and business studies;

- the role of IT-based tasks in a sequence of activity;

- the degree of autonomy that should be given to pupils; and

- collaboration between pupils.

There is a gradual shift in emphasis in this sequence of themes: from the kind of information processing that IT helps; to the role of this processing in learning; to the degree of guidance needed from the teacher to ensure that pupils' activity is productive; to the way in which pupils can help each other to learn from these activities.

The link between progression in IT skills and learning economics and business studies

The first three strands in Figure 13.5 can be used to help plan IT-based lessons to teach pupils economics or business studies. The abilities described in these strands are to:

- organize information with a sense of purpose and audience;

- translate information from one form into another;

- explore and create models.

Tasks can be devised in which pupils use these skills to learn from economic or business data and to develop new ideas about economic and business relationships. Figure 13.6 suggests some styles of task which could be set for pupils and some learning issues that are raised by each style.

The following discussion examines the first two elements in Figure 13.6 in more detail. The role of 'organizing information with a sense of purpose and audience' can be illustrated with reference to the fizzy drinks database in Figure 13.4. Two of the characteristics of Level 6 attainment in the National Curriculum are 'using complex enquiries' and 'having a clear sense of audience'. It can, however, be difficult to decide whether an enquiry is simple or complex because there are several sources of complexity. The three enquiries in Figure 13.7 can be used to illustrate these.

Type of IT skill	Example task	Learning issues
Organizing information with a sense of purpose and audience	Selecting appropriate data from a database; inferring a pattern in a relationship between two classes in a database	The ability to infer patterns depends on knowledge of the meaning of the data as well as a general ability to draw inferences
Translating information from one form into another	Working out a formula for a relationship; describing a statistical trend in words	The task will only engage pupils' thinking if they are doing the translating or carefully selecting the type of translation they want the computer to carry out
Exploring models and creating models	Changing variables in a spreadsheet; devising a spreadsheet model of demand	Making sense of relationships in a model depends substantially on pupils' ability to handle relationships e.g. only changing one variable whilst keeping others constant

Figure 13.6 IT skills and tasks for pupils

1. The owner of a small general store just outside a town centre (record 23) explains how he decides what price to charge: 'quote'. Is this shop owner typical in the prices he charges?

2. Which type of seller – supermarkets, small shops, garages, takeaways, or off-licences – tend to be the cheapest and which tend to be the most expensive?

3. Why do some retailers charge more for fizzy drinks than others?

Figure 13.7 Examples of 'Enquiries' on the fizzy drinks database

- *The number of variables to be handled.* The first enquiry only requires investigation of one field, the second enquiry requires investigation of two fields (average price and type of seller) whilst the third requires attention to each of the five general fields.

- *The mathematical complexity of criteria for selecting records.* Pupils might approach the first enquiry by getting data on each type of seller and calculating the average price of each. They might also use an inequality

183

(e.g. all the records with average price less than 40) to isolate the cheapest retailers. Either of these enquiries is more difficult mathematically than the second enquiry.

- *The methodology involved in choosing a type of enquiry.* The first enquiry also includes a greater methodological problem because the second style of enquiry (using the criterion 'all records with an average price of under 40') clearly has a weakness which ought to be spotted by pupils who have attained Level 5/6 in mathematics – i.e. 14-year-olds of average mathematical ability. As there are more small shops in the sample than any other type of retailer there is a disproportionate chance of finding examples of this type of retailer in the records with an average price under 40 pence.

- *The complexity of the context.* The final enquiry invites pupils to infer explanations from their understanding of the economic context of the data. An answer that merely refers to which kind of retailers tended to be more expensive – even if this answer refers to several fields – only goes part way to answering the question. Behind these differences lie issues of local monopoly, the size of business, and the degree of impulse buying in different circumstances.

Two points arise from this discussion of 'using complex enquiries'. First, individual pupils may be relatively stronger in one of these areas than the others so there are good reasons for setting different enquiries to different pupils. Second, as pupils develop an ability to handle more fields in enquiries, use more mathematically sophisticated criteria and choose methods more wisely, they will be able to process data in more subtle ways. This greater subtlety will increase the likelihood that they will draw inferences from the data which promote their understanding of economics and business studies.

An example of a 'transformation of information' task (element 2 in Figure 13.6) is the organization of information provided in text and numbers into a spreadsheet. Denby (1993) describes a lesson in which GCSE pupils produced a spreadsheet to summarize the costs and revenues which could be predicted for a planned concert tour by a rock group. In transforming the information into a spreadsheet pupils became aware of the problem of calculating revenue simply on the basis of the capacity of the venues at which the group might play. They became aware of this problem when their first version of the spreadsheet showed that the group would earn far more from playing at the largest venues. They decided that their spreadsheet really ought to take account of the price that would be charged at different venues and the popularity of the group. In this activity pupils were learning to 'translate enquiries into the language required by a system' (National Curriculum Level 7; see Figure 13.5), and this activity encouraged them to think about the relationships between 'production' and 'revenue' in a different way.

The role of IT-based tasks in a sequence of activity

It makes sense for IT work to be included within a sequence of activity, rather than for some units of work to involve no IT whilst others are 'all IT'. This approach is more likely to help pupils to relate their processing of information to their understanding of the world. There is a tendency for pupils to perceive models in a spreadsheet or simulation as self-contained and unreal if they conflict with their own preconceptions. Connections between the model, pupils' conceptions and other evidence can be established through work away from the computer (Davies, 1994).

A   Identifying and articulating 'rules' governing relationships

1.   Pupils are given the opportunity inductively to explore a simple model (e.g. using a spreadsheet) which will clearly confront simple ideas and lead pupils to a more complex understanding.

2.   Pupils are asked to articulate their understanding of the rule(s) governing the model, firstly through deciding whether each of a set of 'rules' is true or false, and then through writing their version of the rule.

3.   Pupils are given a simple situation which is accessible to them on the basis of their experience and are asked to explain it to see whether they employ the more sophisticated 'rule' which they have developed.
(from: White and Horwitz, 1990; Brna, 1991)

B   Using a model to evaluate decisions

1.   Pupils are introduced to a situation (e.g. the provision of bus services in a town) through data and associated tasks not involving the computer.

2.   Pupils are able to alter variables in a model (simulation or spreadsheet) to explore the effect of different decisions.

3.   Pupils evaluate the impact of decisions in writing in the light of the evidence from their paper-based and computer-based work.
(from: Davies, 1991)

C   Using a database to evaluate decisions

1.   Pupils are presented with (paper-based) data on an economic or business problem (taken from a fixed point in a time series database) and asked to suggest an appropriate economic or business response.

2.   Pupils use a database which has time series data to identify the response which was actually made and to draw inferences about the effects of that response.

3.   Pupils evaluate the actual response in the light of their evidence of the events which followed from it and then reconsider their original suggestion for a response to see if they can improve upon it.

Figure 13.8 Examples of sequences of pupil activity in an IT-based lesson

Conversely, if pupils are to make probing enquiries with a database or construct their own models on a spreadsheet, they need substantial preparation beforehand. This preparation could be managed through data and activities using a computer, but if pupils are thrust too quickly into using the computer to carry out investigations into data or building models they are likely to be led into superficial responses (e.g. 'I wonder what's on that table of data', 'Let's make a graph') by opportunities that the software presents. Three examples of the effective use of IT that could be incorporated in a sequence of activity are shown in Figure 13.8 on the previous page.

The use of IT for processing information is found in the first stage of example A in Figure 13.8 and in the middle stage of examples B and C. Other stages in the sequence might be handled through IT. (An example of using IT for each of the stages in example A can be found in Davies (1995)). However, the key point at which IT skills are used in the learning sequence is in the processing of information.

The degree of autonomy that should be given to pupils

As in all teaching, the decision over how much autonomy to allow the pupil is a difficult one. The danger of allowing considerable autonomy is that pupils' work may get bogged down in irrelevancies or reduced to guessing. Typical instances of this are: waiting for a network printer to produce a printout, endless changing of the format of a display, and changing levels of variables in a simulation or spreadsheet without any serious thought to how these changes are expected to affect the model. As a result, some writers (e.g. Laurillard, 1987) regard the provision of a tight structure as essential. Others (e.g. diSessa, 1986) regard a large measure of 'pupil freedom' as the essential ingredient. The degree of pupils' autonomy is influenced by the tightness with which the task is specified and the nature of the support given by the teacher whilst pupils are working. It has been argued in this chapter that tasks should be designed which lead pupils into the level of complexity they are just ready for and that this may well mean setting different tasks for different pupils in a class.

The decision as to how much help to give pupils whilst they are working on a task should take account of the kind of problem they are confronting, the demand the task is placing on their current abilities, and the help that is available in the software they are using. If the problem facing pupils is how to carry out a particular technique they need someone to demonstrate or tell them what to do. If they are struggling to interpret some data then they are likely to gain more from a less directive approach. In principle, a lot of support could be available on the software itself. For instance, much software include extensive pages of 'Help'. The problem with much of this 'help' is that it starts from what the package can do rather than from the particular problem the user wants to resolve. An alternative, with Excel, is to write your own help (using text boxes, dialog boxes and/or macros) which is pertinent to tasks.

It may also be helpful to ask a colleague to help review the kind of help you give to pupils whilst they are working on a task. For example, Hoyles and Sutherland (1989) developed an inventory (Figure 13.9) which can be used to analyse 'interventions by the teacher' whilst pupils are working with IT.

This inventory could be used in the form of a grid to record how many of each type of help is given in a lesson. It could be useful to further distinguish between help that is directed towards overcoming a technical or a terminology problem and help that is directed towards understanding the meaning of data, building a model, or how to set about a task.

Motivational	
Reinforcement	e.g. 'That's good'
Encouragement	e.g. 'Try it'
Reflection	
Looking forward	
(a) Process	Encouraging pupils to reflect on and predict the process
(b) Goal	Encouraging pupils to reflect on their ultimate goal
Looking back	
(a) Process	Encouraging pupils to reflect back on problem-solving
(b) Goal	Encouraging pupils to reflect on their goal
Directional influencing and/or changing the focus of the pupil's attention	
Nudge	e.g. 'Do you want to clear the screen?' 'How about doing your square?'
Method	Encouraging pupils to use suitable methods of problem-solving (which are already familiar to them)
Building	Encouraging pupils to apply a particular piece of new information which is necessary to enable the pupils to continue
Factual	
(a) New	Supplying a particular piece of new information which is necessary to enable the pupil to continue
(b) Recall	Reminding pupils of a piece of information (referring them to the handbook)
Powerful idea	Introducing a 'new powerful idea' or 'procedure' such as the REPEAT statement or the idea of a variable
Mathematical idea	Introducing a new mathematical idea

Figure 13.9 Categories of intervention (Hoyles and Sutherland, 1989, p. 142)

Collaboration between pupils

Decisions have to be made over whether to ask pupils to work individually, in pairs or in larger groups. Points specific to the use of IT have been the subject of research (summarized by Light, 1993). Work with IT provides a good stimulus for conversation between pupils and this conversation is important to their learning. The research of Johnson and Johnson (1986) and others suggests that pupils are likely to learn more from their IT work if they are encouraged to work together. Johnson and Johnson found that the most gains in learning were achieved when pupils worked collaboratively, rather than competitively, in small groups of two or three. This was found to be especially true for the girls in the study. Competition between pupils over who was most successful was found to have an especially debilitating effect on girls. These findings are of particular importance in the use of computer simulations such as 'business games'. Although competition may be a way of encouraging involvement (particularly of boys) in the task, it may have a negative impact on learning.

Conclusion

Some of the opportunities created by IT – competition within groups on a business game, typing and revising the form of text, using the computer as an electronic textbook – may not be at all helpful in getting pupils to learn economics and business studies. The opportunities created by IT will continue to expand, the Internet being an obvious example. However, if the use of IT in schools is driven by what the technology makes possible rather than by a careful review of how pupils learn, then teachers' and pupils' time may be wasted in ever more copious amounts.

A reasonable description of progression in IT skills can be found in the National Curriculum and these skills can be harnessed in helping pupils to learn economics and business studies through inferences from data and building models. In this way, the role that the subject area has established in the delivery of IT skills can be enhanced and the quality of learning in economics and business studies can be promoted. The design of tasks and sequences of classroom activity which put these principles into practice need to take account of the growing literature on how the organization of opportunities to process information using IT affects the quality of pupils' learning.

Economics and business studies have had a high profile in the use of IT in classrooms in the UK. Indeed, this was a very important element in the growth of business studies during the 1980s. The maintenance of this position rests on improving the quality with which IT and learning economics and business studies are integrated. Learning from experience in other subject areas should be one part of this process.

References

Beynon, J. (1993). 'Technological literacy: where do we go from here?', *Journal of Information Technology for Teacher Education*, vol. 2, no. 1, pp. 7–37.

Brna, P., (1991). 'Promoting creative confrontations', *Journal of Computer Assisted Learning*, vol. 7, pp. 114–22.

Cochran-Smith, E., (1991). 'Wordprocessing and writing in elementary classrooms : a critical review of related literature', *Review of Educational Research*, vol. 61, part 1. pp. 107–55.

Davies, P. (1991). 'Information technology in economics and business studies classrooms: practice and purpose', in: Davies, P. (ed.), *Information Technology in Economics and Business Studies Classrooms*, London, Economics Association, pp. 4–19.

Davies, P. (1994). 'Learning through computer simulations', *Economics and Business Education*, vol. 2, part 2, no. 5, pp. 30–5.

Davies, P. (1995). 'Integrating information technology and teaching economics and business studies', *Economics and Business Education*, vol. 3, part 3, no. 10, pp. 123–9.

Denby, N. (1993). 'Fostering learning through a spreadsheet investigation', *Economics and Business Education*, vol. 1, part 1, no. 1, pp. 23–8.

DES (1993). *Statistical Bulletin 6/93*, London, HMSO.

DFE (1995). *Information Technology in the National Curriculum*, London, HMSO.

diSessa, A. (1986). 'Artificial worlds and real experiences', *Instructional Science*, vol. 14, pp. 207–27.

Hoyles, C. and Sutherland, R. (1989). *LOGO Mathematics in the Classroom*, London, Routledge.

Hurd, S. (1995). *Third National Survey in Computer Use in Economics and Business Education*, Centre for Economics and Business Education, Staffordshire University, Leek Road, Stoke-on-Trent ST4 2DF.

Johnson, R. T., Johnson, D. W., and Stanne, M. B. (1986). Companion of Computer Assisted Co-operative, Competitive and Individualistic Learning, *American Educational Research Journal*, 23, 3, pp. 382–92.

Khandkher, A. W. and Wehrs, W.E. (1990). 'Integrated microcomputer graphics and simulations in open economy macroeconomics', *Journal of Economic Education*, vol. 21, no. 2, pp. 167–80.

Laurillard, D.M. (1987). 'Computers and the emancipation of students: giving control to the learner', *Instructional Science,* vol. 16, pp. 3–18.

Light, P. (1993). 'Collaborative learning with computers', in: Scrimshaw, P. (ed.), *Language, Classrooms and Computers*, London, Routledge, pp. 40–56.

NCVQ (1993). Core Skills Units for GNVQ2 and GNVQ3, London, National Council for Vocational Qualifications.

NDTEF (1990). Business and Information Systems Single Option Syllabus, National Design and Technology Educational Foundation.

Siegfried, J. J. and Fels, R. (1979). 'Research on teaching college economics: a survey', *Journal of Economic Literature*, vol. 17, pp. 923–69.

Underwood, G. and Underwood, J. M., with Turner (1993). 'Children's thinking during collaborative computer based problem solving', *Educational Psychology*, vol. 13, nos. 3 and 4, pp. 345–55.

White, B. and and Horwitz, P. (1990). 'Computer microworlds in science', in: Boyd-Barrett, O. and Scarratt, R. (eds), *Computers and Learning*, Wokingham, Addison–Wesley, pp. 51–63.

Wood, K. (1983). 'Computer assisted learning in a sixth form course', Research Paper in Economics Education, University of London Institute of Education, Bedford Way, London, WC1H 0AL.

4 Assessing diverse evidence in GNVQ

Alison Atkinson

Introduction of the general national vocational qualification (GNVQ) has required tutors to become familiar with an assessment strategy that is different from that used for GCSE and A level awards. Tutors need skills and expertise in assessing a variety of types of evidence, against the nationally set performance criteria, and taking into account grading themes that focus on students' abilities to plan, carry out and evaluate their work as evidenced in a portfolio. This chapter considers the requirements for the assessment of diverse evidence, whilst placing such evidence within the wider context of increasing the range of teaching and learning situations appropriate to all involved in vocational education in business.

Types of diverse evidence

Taking the evidence types as identified in the D33 specifications in order (natural performance, simulations, projects and assignments, questioning, candidate and peer reports, candidates' prior achievement and learning), we can see that assessment strategies need not be more complex or time-consuming for one type of learning activity than another.

The following ideas are designed to stimulate you to produce your own assessment procedures for a variety of types of evidence generated by students.

Natural performance

Evidence for assessment will be generated during routine work in the classroom. This will be especially so for the core skills that are integral to learning activities. As such, checklists of performance criteria (as in Figure 14.1) can be usefully applied to the assessment process.

Simulations and presentations

An essential element when assessing these is that the tutor and the student agree in advance what is to be assessed. Unless video evidence is being used, assessment is carried out at the same time as the activity, which gives relatively little time for reflection. It is generally a good idea to have, associated with the performance criteria, an assessment scale, which enables tutors to identify where strengths or weaknesses are perceived. For instance, assessment for a presentation might include a scale such as that in Figure 14.2.

191

Application of Number: Level 3

Performance criteria	Activity	Date	Tutor
Makes decision about what data should be collected			
Chooses and uses techniques that suit the task			
Performs the techniques in a correct order			
Chooses and works to an appropriate level of accuracy			
Records data in appropriate units and in an appropriate format			
Makes sure that records are accurate and complete			
Identifies sources or error and their effects			

Figure 14.1 A checklist of performance criteria

Assessment sheet for presentations

5 = very good; 4 = good; 3 = adequate; 2 = inadequate; 1 = clearly inadequate

Images selected that clearly illustrate points being made	1	2	3	4	5
Images suitable to audience, situation and purpose	1	2	3	4	5
Images used at appropriate times and places	1	2	3	4	5

(Performance criteria are for Communication Element 3.3)

Figure 14.2 Assessment sheet for presentations

Projects and assignments

Performance criteria play a major role in assessing projects and assignments. It is important that the tutor keeps in mind the range statements which give insight into the depth and breadth of the work expected, and the evidence indicators which can be useful in deciding whether or not a piece of work provides adequate evidence of achievement within an element or unit. Recent specifications include amplification and guidance on what is acceptable, which can aid in both planning and assessing.

Questioning

The use of questioning, both written and oral, is an important part of GNVQ assessment, as it can be used to provide evidence of underpinning knowledge which was, perhaps, missing from an assessment task. Written fixed response questions, with clear right or wrong answers, constitute the end-of-unit tests that accompany most of the GNVQ units. There are three formats for these questions, the multiple-choice, the true/false and the classification set. Although sometimes unpopular as an assessment device, these do have advantages of ease of administration and of marking, and are an acceptable part of an overall assessment strategy.

The use of oral questioning for the production of supplementary evidence is difficult, although the value of a one-to-one question and answer session between student and teacher is undisputed. Such sessions may be taped, and the tape submitted as part of the portfolio. Witness statements may be used, in which another tutor or verifier signs a statement confirming that a student met specified performance criteria within an oral assessment. These should be reasonably detailed, and should specify the date, place and context of the questioning.

Candidate and peer reports

These can be useful in identifying to students not only how well they are doing, but also how they could improve their performance. As such, they are an important tool in the development of skills which will enable students to achieve higher grades under the GNVQ grading criteria. Although self and peer reports will vary in detail, they should always identify the performance criteria being attempted. Students might be asked to justify whether or not they felt that the criteria have been met, identify particular problems encountered, and make an overall comment on the assessment task. Peer reports may be in the form of a critical appraisal of a piece of work, or of an individual's contribution to a group project. To aid both self and peer assessment, the criteria should be laid out in a format that is both easy to read and linked to the assessed work. The Oxford Centre for Staff Development (1992) project offers some criteria for assignment self-assessment, over and above the GNVQ performance criteria. These include questions such as:

Is the assignment easy to understand? Does it make sense? Is it presented logically? Is all the material relevant? Are examples of what you are referring to given at all possible times? Are opinions and assertions backed up in some way?

Candidate's prior achievement and learning

This is dealt with later in the chapter, when looking at the issue of reliability.

Strategies for assessment

GNVQ assessment strategy divides the assessment process into three component parts: negotiation with the student which allows opportunities for evidence collection to be identified; the collection and assessment of evidence; and feedback to the student following the assessment process.

Negotiation

Assessment tasks are undertaken throughout the award, and any given task may be either formative or summative, depending upon where the student is in terms of achievement against the performance criteria. This flexibility should enable students to develop a personalized learning programme that reflects their own needs and which allows for differentiation to take place as an integral part of the learning process. For one student, a task may be used as evidence that certain performance criteria have been achieved, whilst for others it may identify gaps in understanding or proficiency which still need to be addressed. Time constraints often make it difficult for teachers and tutors to make use of this facility effectively. As a result there is a tendency to utilize all GNVQ assessment as summative, with a new task being set when evidence is inadequate, without the diagnostic aspect of the portfolio being fully implemented.

One difficulty for teachers in this is that, whilst a certain type of activity, such as groupwork, may be appropriate as an assessment strategy for a cohort, it may become inappropriate for an individual working alone. Thus diversity of evidence may not only refer to the evidence within an individual student's portfolio, but may also apply to different evidence for assessing the same performance criteria.

Because of the potential for personalized learning, initial action planning is essential for students' success. It also ensures that both student and tutor have a common understanding of what evidence will be presented, and how it will be assessed. Whilst this is to a great extent defined by the performance criteria and the evidence indicators, there should be the opportunity for students or tutors to suggest alternatives to a set task.

For instance, within the Advanced GNVQ in Business (Element 3.1, PC 1) a student is asked to discuss marketing principles and marketing functions. The range statements explain what must be covered within this discussion, and the evidence indicators require 'a record of a discussion about marketing principles and marketing functions with supporting notes ...' The evidence for this discussion could come from a structured debate within the cohort, from a meeting with adults other than teachers coming into the school or college, from attendance at a marketing meeting of either the school or college, or at a work placement, or from a session with the tutor/assessor.

Students running a mini enterprise or organizing a school event may find that such a discussion takes place almost as a matter of course, within the context of group meetings. For example, students following a business course at an agricultural college arranged a horse show and gymkhana as part of their coursework. This was a large affair attracting competitors from all over the south of England, and involved the students in a wide variety of business activities. The group had to decide what activities and events would attract competitors and spectators, and what practical needs would have to be met in the way of shelters, availability of food and drink for horses and people, toilet and parking facilities etc. They also had long discussions on whether or not it was primarily a profit-making event, or one that had the marketing of the college as a primary function. They had to arrange for AA signs on the local roads, ensure that their show was not competing with any similar events locally on the same day, as well as producing posters, flyers and programmes.

Students in the foregoing example may wish to present a video of their discussions, a structured debate might be watched specifically for assessment purposes, whilst students offering evidence from attendance at a meeting may wish to submit the minutes of that meeting in support of their claim for accreditation against the performance criteria. The result for the tutor is a diversity of evidence to assess in relation to the same performance criteria.

Collection and assessment of evidence

With any assessment technique, there are generic issues that need to be considered, and appropriate application skills which need to be developed.

Stephen Steadman, writing about the assessment of outcomes, writes: 'The desirable properties of an assessment system are that it should have the confidence of the population, be demonstrably efficient (inexpensive), fair to all candidates, relevant, reliable and valid' (Burke, 1995).

Gilbert Jessup (1991), one of the original designers of NVQs, added 'sufficient' to this list and wrote, in relation to NVQs: '... assessment is related directly to the elements ... and sufficiency of evidence is the key concept'. He added: '... we should just forget reliability altogether and concentrate on validity, which is ultimately all that matters'. Jessup was, clearly, being provocative and not referring directly to GNVQ assessment, but his pointers have much relevance for GNVQ.

Sufficiency of evidence requires that the evidence is enough to demonstrate that the assessment criteria have been met. Within a GNVQ framework, this is generally taken to mean that students demonstrate that they have met a given performance criteria more than once. The argument runs that if any one criteria is met only once within a full-time course, this could suggest that a student produced the evidence almost by chance, by a fluke perhaps. If tutors encourage students to place within their portfolio two or more items of evidence to match the same performance criteria, they can be certain that the student has demonstrated the ability to meet those criteria.

Validity refers to the extent to which the evidence actually does match the performance criteria. The current evidence indicators should remove the need for tutors to concern themselves with issues of validity, if they are followed closely. However, these are indicators, not requirements, and if a student did ask to put forward alternative evidence, its validity would then become a key feature of the decision on whether or not to accept it.

In order to ensure validity, tutors need to be sure that they know exactly what is being assessed. Although performance criteria should make this explicit, they do have to be read carefully to be sure that the evidence presented really does match the desired outcome. For instance, the Foundation level performance criterion which asks students to explain how employees can benefit from business profit is supported by a range statement that defines such benefits as share ownership, bonuses, incentives, profit-sharing. A student who produced evidence to match this performance criterion which consisted of a statement to the effect 'Employees could benefit from the profits of a business by buying shares, receiving bonuses or incentives, or by taking part in a profit-sharing scheme' could not be said to have met the performance criteria. There is no element of *explanation* within that answer, and although it appears to demonstrate some degree of knowledge there is nothing to demonstrate understanding.

This *is* of course a situation where the use of diverse evidence could be implemented to allow students to demonstrate that they have achieved the desired outcome. A tutor using the written statement as a starting point could employ a question and answer technique, in order to assess whether or not the student did have greater understanding of the issues and to encourage the student to explain the concepts.

Reliability is perhaps the most difficult requirement to meet when assessing diversity of evidence. Reliability requires that the assessment process be consistent. Alison Wolf (1993) found that when the first full-scale assessment of National Curriculum SATs for 7-year-olds was carried out, reliability was compromised in two areas. One was in the variation of the actual administration of the SATs, and the other was in the differences in the way that assessors interpreted pupils' achievements. Wolf writes that the differences were so wide that 'the reliability of the results was highly questionable'.

Her findings have implications for the assessment of diverse evidence. If reliability requires identical assessment tasks, taken in identical situations, then clearly this will not be achieved. However, there are ways in which reliability can be assured. The requirement that all GNVQ assessors have either the D33 award or the new GPA awards is one attempt to ensure consistency. The use of internal and external verifiers, who moderate/verify assessment within and across institutions, is a second technique. Other techniques include the use of second markers, of assessing as a team for oral work, and the use of team meetings to discuss assessments.

One situation within GNVQ assessment in which a degree of reliability is relatively easy to achieve is in the assessment of prior achievement/learning (APA/L). Here there is often a need to have a standardized measure of equivalence against which evidence produced in support of APA or APL can be placed. Although a diversity of evidence may still be accepted, it is probable that diversity will be clearly defined. For example, an institution that had a large number of mature students joining its part-time GNVQ Business courses found that tutors were spending an inordinate amount of time discussing with students whether or not work previously carried out on other courses or in the workplace could be used to gain APA/L, with consequent exemption from some units of work. It was decided that instead of deciding each case separately, there would be a description of the types of acceptable evidence. Students would then have the responsibility of putting together a portfolio of evidence that would demonstrate they had already met the requirements for particular units of work. The institution decided that it would accept certificates of courses or awards, transcripts of courses or awards, authenticated portfolios of coursework, and institutional statements identifying core elements of courses. Although witness statements and either a contemporaneous or retrospective logbook supporting the documentary evidence were welcomed, they were not to be acceptable on their own.

The need to avoid bias is central to any assessment technique, and failure to do so should automatically invalidate the assessment. Avoiding bias may be easier when students are submitting different types of evidence for assessment. The diversity of evidence should preclude any student or group of students being disadvantaged over time by being asked to submit types of evidence that cause them particular difficulties.

Because GNVQ assessment is based upon outcomes assessed against published performance criteria, it has an inbuilt protection against tutor bias. However, there is the potential for inequality within the evidence accepted by the assessor, and care needs to be taken that students are not being assessed in ways which undermine reliability.

Feedback to students

From the student's point of view, the single most important element of assessment is the provision of feedback following the assessment decision. The assessment of any one part or type of evidence is intended to lead the student on to the production of further evidence or, if necessary, to return to the original work and to add to it. Assessors need to ensure that not only do they give clear and constructive feedback, but that it is also appropriate to the student's level of confidence. It also needs to be accessible to the candidate.

In 1992, the Oxford Centre for Staff Development in its findings from a PCFC project entitled 'Teaching More Students', concentrated in part on effective,

197

Structure Clear, logical structure	I	2	3	4	5	Confused list
Sources Properly referenced	I	2	3	4	5	References lacking or incorrect
Grammar, spelling Correct	I	2	3	4	5	Many errors

Tutor's comments

Figure 14.3 An essay feedback list

Rating for assessment of contribution to the team

5 = well above average; 4 = above average; 3 = average; 2 = below average;
I = well below average

Attendance at and preparation for the group sessions	I	2	3	4	5
Quality of contribution to the group	I	2	3	4	5
Receptiveness to the ideas of others	I	2	3	4	5
Facilitation of group cohesion	I	2	3	4	5

Tutor's comments:

Suggested mark:

Figure 14.4 Assessment of a piece of group work (Oxford Centre for Staff Development, 1992)

198

student-centred assessment strategies. They concluded that feedback techniques will vary with the evidence being assessed. However, they should always allow a student to understand how work could be improved. With formal essay and report type assignments, a feedback sheet which looks at component parts of the assignment and places them on a scale of 1–5 may be useful. For instance, an essay feedback sheet might look like that in Figure 14.3, and that for the assessment of a piece of group work like that in Figure 14.4.

Students need to be reassured that evidence will be assessed if it matches performance criteria, and that evidence does not need to be produced by following a common assessment task for the whole group. They should be encouraged to look at their learning in a holistic manner, and to identify elements within their learning that might be submitted as evidence of achievement. This should include activities that might not traditionally be formally assessed, such as work experience and role-playing sessions.

Recognition of the need to encourage diversity rather than conformity is an essential element in our future prosperity. GNVQ has much to contribute to this.

References

Burke, J. (ed.) (1995). *Outcomes, Learning and the Curriculum*, Brighton, Falmer Press.

Jessup, G. (1991). 'The evidence required to demonstrate competence', in: *Outcomes: NVQs and the Emerging Model of Education and Training*, Brighton, Falmer Press.

Oxford Centre for Staff Development (1992). *Teaching More Students*, Oxford, PCFC.

Wolf, A. (1993). *Assessment Issues and Problems in a Criterion-Based System*, London, Further Education Unit.

PART 3

THE WHOLE CURRICULUM

15 The whole curriculum: discussion

Martin Jephcote and Steve Hodkinson

In pre-16 education the concept of a 'whole curriculum' was developed as a response to the perceived limitations of the National Curriculum, introduced in 1988. It was felt by some that the Basic Curriculum comprising the National Curriculum (core and foundation subjects, and for schools in Wales, Welsh) plus religious education did not describe adequately what was already taught in many schools and nor did it encompass what many believed to be the totality of a broad, balanced and relevant curriculum.

In response, the Curriculum Councils for England, Wales and Northern Ireland argued that the National Curriculum should be supplemented with cross-curricular themes. In England, these were careers education and guidance, environmental education, health education, economic and industrial understanding (EIU) and education for citizenship. In Wales, education for citizenship was replaced with community understanding, and in Northern Ireland there were six themes: education for mutual understanding, cultural heritage, health education, careers education, economic awareness, and information technology. In addition, emphasis was also given to cross-curricular competences/skills, including communication, numeracy, problem-solving and study skills together with cross-curricular dimensions such as equal opportunities.

In post-16 education there was also concern about the narrowness of the curriculum, especially where students were given a choice in what subjects or courses to study and where lip service only was paid to arrangements for complementary programmes in areas such as study skills or personal and social education. The Technical Vocational Education Initiative (TVEI) had done much to broaden the curriculum and was especially successful in introducing a work-related curriculum focused on work experience and other industry links. At a time of increased calls from government and industry to link post-16 education and training, and especially further education, to the needs of employers, attention was given to the notion of an 'entitlement' curriculum.

The National Curriculum Council (NCC, *Core Skills 16–19,* March 1990) did attempt at first to establish the idea of a post-16 'whole curriculum framework'. They suggested that the five cross-curricular themes identified for England were also essential in the post-16 curriculum where more emphasis would need to be given to scientific, technological and creative understanding. However, the focus soon became those aspects of an entitlement curriculum, described as *core skills*, which were seen as of more direct relevance to the world of work. EIU and other cross-curricular themes appeared to be regarded as too much a part of a general and liberal education.

Debate about the purpose and content of the curriculum, and the case for the inclusion of an economic dimension, can be traced back over many years. It is widely accepted that the 1976 speech by the then Prime Minister, James Callaghan, both summarized the prevailing mood and led to what is referred to as the 'Great Debate'. Callaghan's call for education to be more responsive to the needs of industry spawned many initiatives aimed at creating a better partnership between schools/colleges and the wider business community. Subsequently, providing answers to questions concerned with the purposes and content of the curriculum in schools and colleges has largely been taken out of the control of teachers and lecturers. It remains critical, however, for our professional futures for us to assert our principles and to engage in debate about the importance of an economic dimension to the education of all young people.

Teachers of economics and business assert that 'economics' and/or 'business' should be an aspect of everyone's education. Many groups and individuals endorse this assertion as recent attempts to find an appropriate framework serve witness. In pre-16 education, the combination of the imposition of a National Curriculum with emphasis on core and foundation subjects, lack of government support for cross-curricular themes and what is described as 'curriculum overload' do, however, provide a difficult backcloth for future development. In post-16 education effort seems to be geared towards the promotion of vocational education and importance is attached to a narrow range of core skills. Moreover, in both pre- and post-16 education it must be tempting, given the change of fortunes as shown in increasing numbers taking GNVQ Business, to think that there is no real cause for concern. Promoting economic understanding may, however, still prove to be a difficult task. Economic understanding may not necessarily come about through greater work relatedness or from following courses in business. Indeed, Linda Thomas suggests in Chapter 6 that the revised specifications for GNVQ Business (Advanced) illustrate an abandonment of a framework for critical understanding in preference for a descriptive programme. And, of course, we have yet to resolve how economic understanding will be extended into the curriculum for everyone.

There seem to be no ready-made solution. Experience has shown that the promotion of economic understanding is problematic. In the early development of economic understanding solutions were sought from those concerned, teachers and managers, in schools and colleges. This development can be characterized as a partnership between teachers, providers and the business community. However, the overall national picture is of a rather fragmented and piecemeal development. Attempts at linking economic understanding to National Curriculum attainment targets and programmes of study met with limited success, in part explained by the overload situation in schools at the time to which this very attempt no doubt added. Collectively, however, we have a substantial body of experience, knowledge and expertise on which to draw – though it is not immediately obvious how this may be used at the present time. As a starting point, there is a need to take stock of what has been achieved, to record the process and to identify ways forward. Many chapters in this book assist in developing this record and those in this section are particularly relevant.

Next, we suggest, there is need for an agreement on the part of teachers – especially economics and business teachers – to support the promotion of economic understanding for all, together with acceptance of some responsibility in their own classrooms and, for some, the added responsibility for promotion at a school or college level. We owe it to our students to help in their preparation for the rights and responsibilities of adult life in a market-oriented world.

Individual teachers can explore their own classrooms and the opportunities they provide for developing students' economic understanding. Our experience suggests, however, that those teachers who accept this responsibility need help to identify opportunities, to prepare tasks and materials for their own classroom, and to review their experiences with colleagues. Economics and business teachers may have a role to play in providing this help and perhaps, too, may take on the wider development and coordination at a school or college level.

No matter what one's role or intention, subscription is, we believe, preferable to conscription; teachers are likely to engage in the development of their students' economic understanding because they recognize the benefits to their students. External initiatives and projects have been shown to be important change agents but their long-term success is dependent on developing long-term commitment which outlives the life of a particular project. An obvious limitation of the project approach is that they have a finite life. So, what happens, for example, when another initiative comes along? Can we argue that economic understanding is more important than drugs awareness or the need to promote parenting skills? Whereas we would not suggest that economic understanding can be a vehicle for every other relevant issue it does lend itself to the analysis of a number of important questions which underpin other issues. Invariably, facing issues involves decision-making and is about weighing up the alternatives, assessing the costs and benefits, allocating resources and about making difficult choices. These are, inherently, economic as well as social and political issues.

Neil Denby and Heather Stretch (Chapter 18) illustrate a number of features of whole-school whole curriculum development. The need, from the outset, for teacher ownership of an initiative is seen as important. Neil Denby, an economics and business specialist, recognized the need for a broad whole curriculum approach and took on the responsibility of planning the introduction of economic awareness and liaising with other colleagues. As the school's coordinator he drew on the support of senior managers at the school and set about the introduction of a 'permeation' model. Initial auditing, raising staff awareness and collaborating with colleagues at a classroom level all featured in his strategy. He also helps us to think about how we might begin to judge progress with respect to this aspect of curriculum development by reference to three sets of indicators:

- enabling indicators that provide evidence that support structures are in place;

- process indicators that provide evidence of classroom activity; and

- success indicators that include evidence of student learning and links with outside agencies.

Heather Stretch teaches English and has taken on the role of the school's EIU coordinator. Her case study illustrates the importance of getting in place appropriate procedures and structures. These include a school policy statement and an organizational structure which draws together persons with responsibility both inside and outside the school, focusing on a range of activities for pupils and staff. EIU has featured significantly in the school's curriculum for more than six years and indications are that it continues to have an established place. In part this has been achieved by recognizing and acting upon the constraints to the development of EIU which are to do with the institution and people within and outside the institution. There can be little doubt that the continued high profile of EIU owes much to the hard work and enthusiasm of the coordinator and her colleagues and to the support given by senior managers.

Alma Harris (Chapter 17) draws on a literature which underlines the importance of subjects in the curriculum and a set of evidence which suggests that the whole curriculum and cross-curricular themes in particular have suffered mixed fortunes. She suggests that cross-curricular approaches are not the best means of providing breadth in the curriculum, not least because they remain an optional element within the curriculum. She argues for a reconceptualization of the work-related curriculum which defines learning outcomes constructed on students' age-related experiences; in effect, she argues for a work-related curriculum that would be recognized by all as a subject in the curriculum. Through the 'Pathways to Adult and Working Life' project, Alma Harris provides a clear illustration of how 'effective teaching and learning' is to be achieved. The approach draws on experiential learning theory with learning derived from an individual's experiences. Again a partnership approach is emphasized, although it is not immediately clear who the partners are or what role, if any, specialist teachers of economics and business are to play.

Contributions from Nigel West and Ken Webster (Chapters 19 and 20) argue the need for economic understanding to embrace the whole curriculum issues of global and environmental perspectives. Nigel West asserts that if as teachers our aim is to equip students with the skills to understand the world better, then they need to appreciate and draw on a knowledge of different theoretical perspectives and lived experiences of the world. He reminds us that our own view of the world and the way in which we make sense of our experiences is limited, and calls for a global dimension to what we teach. Ken Webster bases his case on the premise that anyone who teaches economics and business will find an environmental perspective 'inescapable'. This gives rise to a dilemma: teachers accept it as it is or they give thought to what it is they are teaching and why. He argues that economics and business education teachers will not escape what he describes as a fundamental process of change, and he hopes that this emerging future will be 'embraced willingly'.

An alternative whole curriculum concept is that of the 'entitlement curriculum', where the focus for planning the curriculum moves from the needs of society (industry) as defined by central planners to the needs of individuals. The concern, as Chris Leonard describes in Chapter 16, is with the empowerment of the individual enabling him or her to lead a fulfilled life. 'Entitlement' is, however, a term that needs to be qualified. Is it, for example, an aspect of the curriculum that is provided but made optional, or is it something in which students are compelled to partake? Perhaps, as he suggests, there is a case to negotiate the entitlement curriculum with students. He adds that economics and business education are important aspects of an entitlement curriculum provided that they promote a critical awareness and understanding of experiences that will affect students' lives.

16

The post-16 entitlement curriculum

Chris Leonard

Introduction

In a well-known Marx Brothers film, three hero-aviators are interviewed about their repeated attempts to fly across the Atlantic Ocean. One of the aviators says 'The first time we tried we almost get there, but then we run out of gas and we got to go back.'

Perhaps this might describe the situation for many colleagues, who as hero-innovators have been working so hard to weave economic and business education into the 5–16 curriculum. Much has been achieved, but with all the changes to the National Curriculum, together with the problem of time constraints, cross-curricular themes in general have been forced to 'turn back' or, at least, no longer command what limited attention they enjoyed in the past. Jamieson and Harris (1994, p. 19) refer to informal feedback from OfSTED reports which indicate that cross-curricular themes are not seen as a priority by schools. However, in common with HMI (1990, p. 9) they have suggested that the notion of an economic and business education entitlement for all is more likely to secure a permanent place in the curriculum if it is focused in the 16–19 age group. The reasons for this are given later in this chapter, but it leads us to the question of what constitutes an entitlement curriculum in post-16 education.

The post-16 entitlement curriculum

There are now in excess of 14 000 qualifications available to young people in the 16–19 age range. In addition to these, there are an enormous variety of experiences and activities that contribute to the post-16 curriculum. In a review of 16-19 qualifications, Dearing (1995) has stated that the scale and complexity of the existing framework is such that it will be a difficult task to achieve a coherent picture for all of the stakeholders.

Central to this issue of complexity is of course the continued existence of a two-track system, represented on the one hand by the A level 'gold standard' of the liberal education tradition, and on the other hand by the plethora of qualifications forming the emerging vocational tradition. The continued separation of these two traditions or cultures has been deemed as falsely dichotomous by, amongst many others, Crombie-White *et al.* (1995). They point to the evolution of the Technical and Vocational Education Initiative (TVEI) which, since its inception in 1983, has repeatedly shown that the utilitarian objectives associated with vocational activities can do much to enhance and enrich the tradition of liberal education, and vice versa.

The main thrust of the TVEI was to promote the relevance of what was studied in schools and colleges by reference to the world of work. As a condition of membership of the initiative, schools and colleges were asked to identify an entitlement curriculum for all students in the 16–19 age range (DoE, 1991). This entitlement, or irreducible minimum, was described by the Further Education Unit (FEU) in 1989 as follows:

'This minimum entitlement should comprise negotiated content, negotiated and pre-specified outcomes, individual progression opportunities and learning experiences which are the same for everyone.'

The purpose of an entitlement curriculum is to ensure breadth, balance, relevance and coherence in every student's programme of study, so that a smooth transition can be made through the various phases of education and training to a creative and fulfilling working life.

Phil Hodkinson (1994) notes that an entitlement curriculum should help young people take control of their lives in a rapidly changing and fragmenting world. He calls for a curriculum that empowers young people, so enabling them to be proactive and independent rather than passive and reliant. It would seem important, therefore, that young people be given the opportunity to negotiate a significant part of their curriculum, and in this respect he underlines the definition given by the FEU. To some extent this happens when a student negotiates to do a particular GNVQ course or to select two or three A levels. However, once this choice has been made, it is arguable how much negotiation occurs thereafter. This is particularly the case when the whole of a student's programme is considered, and especially the way in which it is taught and assessed. Curriculum planners have omitted the important aspect of negotiation to their cost. Many have worked hard, with the very best of intentions, to produce an entitlement package through additional or supplementary studies to the main course, only to find to their disappointment that the students do not want this entitlement!

Statements of curriculum entitlement such as those given in Figures 16.1 and 16.2 exist in most Local Education Authorities, schools and colleges. Teachers of economics and business education will be gratified to note that this is included in most, if not all, statements in one form or another. However, the following questions need to be addressed:

- What consultation process was undertaken when drafting the statement (were students involved)?

- How was the statement integrated with institutional, curriculum and staff development plans?

- How is the statement monitored and evaluated?

- When was the statement last reviewed and revised?

... and, for teachers concerned with economics and business education:

- How are the features of entitlement articulated in economic and business courses?

- What is the 'irreducible minimum' of content, concepts and skills that might be included in an economic and business education entitlement for all students?

Jamieson and Harris (1994, p. 20) note that this last question is very controversial. They suggest that without an agreed working definition any further sensible debate about economic and business education is difficult. In practice it might be a very empowering and effective process if students and teachers from across an institution took part in attempting to define their economic and business entitlement. Alternatively, perhaps this is a new challenge for the Economics and Business Education Association (EBEA), building upon their recent work in the national Economics 16–19 Project?

Core Skills	Health, Leisure and Recreation
Careers and Work-Related Education	Expressive Arts
Economic, Environmental and Political Education	Modern Foreign Language
	Scientific and Technical

Figure 16.1 Dorset TVEI's post-16 submission to the TVEI Unit

Personal, Social and Health Education	Environmental Awareness
Creative Arts	Citizenship
Technology	Equal Opportunities
Information Technology	Careers Education and Guidance
Communication	Residential Activities
Numeracy	Work-Related and Community Activity
Economic and Political Awareness	

Figure 16.2 Dimensions of a unified common core 14–19 (Crombie-White *et al.*, 1995)

Phil Hodkinson (1990) has provided two broad classifications of the strategies used in the implementation of an entitlement framework:

- *Enhancements:* improvements in quality within a particular subject or course. This would include such things as changes in teaching methods, assessment and the contexts in which learning takes place – for example a visit to a hotel as part of a Leisure and Tourism course.

- *Enrichments:* improvements to a student's programme as a whole by means of additional elements, such as a timetable suspension for a 'Challenge of Industry' day.

The terms 'enhancement' and 'enrichment' can be very useful when attempting to make sense of what is already in place in the post-16 curriculum. Enrichment activities are easy to see because they tend to be institution-wide. However, with course or subject enhancement the picture is not so easy to assess without resort to an audit. The situation is made more difficult by the fact that entitlement criteria need to be drafted, shared and applied so that their meanings can be constructed by everyone in the school or college. It is understandable, therefore, that in most schools, and some colleges, aspects of curriculum entitlement are addressed through the provision of a discrete course of general, additional or supplementary studies.

HMI (1989) found that many A level and vocational course students viewed compulsory non-accredited supplementary or 'liberal studies' courses as irrelevant, distracting and, in some cases, even patronising. However, four years later the Audit Commission noted that HMI were finding students better disposed towards supplementary studies with the quality of work being 'unusually good' in 60 per cent of the lessons observed. (Whether the impact of the TVEI in the post-16 curriculum had anything to do with this would be a matter for further research.)

In Further Education Colleges the situation is slightly different where supplementary studies courses have almost entirely disappeared from programmes offered to vocational students probably due to cost factors and student resistance. Nevertheless, the Audit Commission (1993) state:

'There is a general move, especially in larger institutions of all kinds, to establish general support and a range of supplementary studies and activities, to develop the knowledge and skills important to adult life.'

The place of economic and business education in the post-16 entitlement curriculum

In the United Kingdom, participation rates have been rising steadily so that nationally in 1992/93 the percentages were 67 per cent at 16 dropping to 50 per cent at 17 and 35 per cent at age 18. International statistics reveal that, by comparison with other nations, the UK is at the bottom of the league table. The government, prompted by the Confederation of British Industry and others, has argued that, if the UK is to remain internationally competitive and retain a world-class workforce, then higher levels of participation, completion and attainment will be required in schools and colleges. In the White Paper *Competitiveness: Forging Ahead* (1995) the government produced revised National Training and Education Targets. If these are to be achieved, as Dearing (1995) observes, there will have to be an increase in advanced level vocational courses since A level may well have reached the limits of the market for which it was designed. (One has to wonder how many products or services would have survived in the market place if they had remained largely un-changed since their inception in 1951 without having to resort to government protection.)

Whatever the outcome of Dearing's review of post-16 qualifications, it seems likely that work-related and vocational elements will be apparent in all courses of study available to this age group; so an economic and business understanding would seem vital if students are to make sense of these ele-ments. The framework of enhancement and enrichment outlined above can be used to identify areas where economic and business education is most likely to take place.

Enhancement activities

General and National Vocational Qualifications

The introduction of GNVQ places considerable demands on students and teachers to develop their economic and business understanding. Unlike GCSEs, these courses are vocational with criteria designed to promote compe-tence,experience and understanding of the world of work. Learning in these courses could be said to be incomplete if it does not reflect an awareness and understanding of the economic and business phenomena that affect the very existence of the industry for which the student is being vocationally prepared.

Some teachers may feel particularly vulnerable when addressing certain ele-ments of these new courses. For example, it cannot be taken for granted that an Art teacher will feel comfortable when addressing all the performance criteria in the unit entitled 'Business and Professional Practice' (Advanced GNVQ Art and Design, Unit 5). Similarly, it is not unreasonable for a colleague with a background in Geography to feel uncertain about units like 'Marketing', 'Finance', and 'Business Systems' (Advanced GNVQ Leisure and Tourism, Units 3, 4 and 5). In larger institutions a degree of cross-faculty servicing will be in place, but in smaller establishments this may not be possible.

Flexible learning and supported self-study materials such as those produced by teachers involved in the Wessex Project can help; but, whatever the internal arrangements, it is important that economics and business education teachers be involved in direct support of colleagues teaching on these courses. They can either be given time to join course teams or provide in-service sessions. An-other way is to ensure that economics or business education teachers are involved in the assessment and validation procedures of these courses. In this way the outcomes of learning can be used to provide in-service and staff development opportunities.

Gillmon (1992) asserts that the roles of economics and business education teachers will have to change, as will that of the coordinator. She argues that there will be no place for the isolated specialism of previous times and calls for a generalist capable of coordinating all those elements of the curriculum that enable a student to understand the business and economic processes that will affect their lives. (She also notes that this shift in roles will have obvious implications for initial teacher education and training.)

School and college managers will have to redefine the role, function and timetabling arrangements of their economics and business education teachers or risk the possibility that learning in some aspects of vocational courses becomes purely descriptive and superficial. Again, reference to any school or college statement on student entitlement to economics and business education will confirm the need to do this.

A and AS level courses

At the end of the 1980s pressure continued to mount to reform post-16 quali-fications and there was a suggestion that all A levels should be 'broadened' to contain reference to economic and industrial understanding. Disappointingly, when the most recent *Code of Practice* for GCE A and AS level was published by SCAA (1994) there was only reference to syllabuses providing, where appropriate, the dimensions of health, environment and Europe.

Whilst it is true that all A level syllabuses have the potential to develop eco-nomic and business education entitlement, there is considerable evidence from lessons learned in the 14–16 curriculum that this is problematic. Jephcote and Williams (1994) conducted a number of interviews into teacher receptivity to economic and business understanding. They found that the clas-sical, subject-centred perspective predominated, with the more utilitarian vocational perspective receiving less support. There was a concern that cross-curricular working detrimentally affected student attainment and that the time constraints facing the teacher when dealing with an extensive list of content made such activity difficult.

Perhaps it is not so much a case that the non-economic and business education specialist lacks the necessary knowledge to feel confident when confronted with economic or business phenomena, but that they do not have the back-ground, culture and values to work in this way. Could it be that teachers themselves exercised a vocational choice when they became teachers and, in a sense, rejected the culture of commercialism and business? In my work, first as a classroom teacher and then as an Education Business Partnership Coor-dinator, I have encountered all sorts of fears, uncertainties, prejudices and outright rejection, by some, of any notion that education ought to be linked to the world of work.

Jamieson and Harris (1994) refer to teachers who felt that cross-curricular themes 'interfered' with normal subject discourse and, anyway, this was all that was needed to explain various phenomena. This subject-centred myopia meant that teachers, understandably perhaps, were more confident when getting on with 'real' science or mathematics rather than becoming embroiled in the type of metacognitive exercise required by interdisciplinary study of the world. Nevertheless, they argue that, in the post-16 phase, students have begun to specialize in those areas where they are most comfortable with the structure of subjects and where the subject discourse has become more firmly embedded. In this phase both students and teachers feel more confident to branch out and consider cross-curricular themes in parallel with the main subject being studied.

Overall though, the evidence suggests that it will not be easy to use the enhancement approach to permeate A and AS level courses with economics and business education. Coles *et al.* (1992) refer to a whole sixth-form college strategy developed under the auspices of TVEI. The success of this development seemed to be based upon the following key features:

- There was full support from the college vice-principal.
- Additional resources were allocated to the task using, in this case, a TVEI budget.
- A Business Studies and Economics Project Officer was created by enhancing an existing post. This person was also responsible for the Work-Related Curriculum, meaning that he was well placed to locate contexts where economics and business issues could be developed.
- Teacher in-service education and training time was given for the whole staff to address issues.
- There was support and critical friendship from an outside agency, in this case Manchester University.
- A lot of thought went into designing an auditing device that suited the user group and promoted rather than hindered development.
- Colleagues 'auditing' their subject for opportunities to promote economic and business education received support from specialists.

Even with all these critical features in place, the pace of development was described as slow and the college decided to use modules in complementary studies to ensure some minimum student entitlement to various core themes and skills.

Enrichment activities

General, additional, complementary or supplementary studies

Most, if not all, of these courses, and certainly all of the accredited courses on offer, refer to economics and business education in one form or another. Such courses often use real-world contexts to provide relevance. Adults other than teachers are frequently used, and this again provides opportunities to develop cross-curricular themes like economics, business and careers education.

For example, in one General Studies course, the coordinator used the local Teacher Placement Service in order to spend time in a bank. This led to the redesigning of key parts of the course and the involvement of bank personnel during implementation. It is important that economics and business education teachers be included in teams who are responsible for designing such courses.

Work experience and experience of work

In some schools and colleges, experience of work is seen as an entitlement for all students. In courses such as the Certificate of Pre-Vocational Education, the Diploma of Vocational Education, and BTEC's First and National Diplomas, these experiences were a prerequisite of accreditation. Many schools and colleges have now moved away from these courses and have replaced them with GNVQs where work-related experiences are strongly recommended but are not compulsory.

The numbers of students involved in work-related experiences post-16 continues to grow along with the rapid increase in participation rates referred to earlier. Far too often the objectives of these activities are neither clearly defined nor do they reflect the opportunities offered to develop economics and business education entitlement. In short, they are seen as an entitlement in themselves. There is of course a danger that students can embark on work experience or experience of work activities overloaded with objectives, but it is important that economics and business education teachers be involved in, at least, the planning, preparation and follow-up of these activities.

Industry days and other work-related activities

At the end of a recent 'Challenge of Industry' conference a student was overheard to say to her adviser from a local firm, 'Thank you very much, I really enjoyed myself and I learned a lot.' At a subsequent debriefing of the conference by the advisers this remark was discussed, and all the participants wondered what the students had actually learned. The Industrial Society, which initiated the 'Challenge of Industry' concept, gives clear guidelines to advisers that the conferences are designed to promote, amongst other things, an insight into the range of opportunities available in industry, commerce and the public sector and to raise awareness of the skills required. Students are encouraged to consider the things that industry creates for the community and there is a particular emphasis on the development of leadership skills.

All of the advisers agreed that each problem-solving activity or simulation was 'typical' of those encountered in business, but each admitted that they were not sure exactly what the learning focus had been. Certainly each exercise generated many issues, but as the day progressed excited 'busy-ness' tended to displace 'thoughtfulness' and reflection. It is possible to become oversensitive about this lack of certainty over what has been learned. However, it is probably true to say that, once again, a lively activity had caused all of the participants to become oriented to the input process rather than to the output. It is all a question of balance, and much depends on the ability of the advisers to keep at least two ideas in their heads simultaneously. As HMI (1990) have stated, student involvement in business and economic activity does not necessarily generate economics and business understanding.

There is a whole raft of other work-related activity similar to the very worthwhile 'Challenge of Industry' conference, and each has the potential to promote and contribute to economics and business education entitlement. Activities include:

Work shadowing

Teacher placement in industry and the community

Problem-solving activity for business and community organizations

Curriculum projects

Visits to industry

Mock interviews

Visitors from industry

Careers interviews and lessons

Young Enterprise

Industrial mentoring

Vocational tasters

Projects in association with training providers

The key questions here, as with all aspects of the entitlement curriculum, are:

- Who has an overview of these activities?

- Is there a management information system in place to assist with this overview, or does this reside in an individual student's Record of Achievement?

- Is there a list of objectives, rather than broad aims, that facilitates coherence and progression? (It may well be worth focusing on one or two minimum objectives for each activity.)

- What are the expected outcomes?

- Is there a statement of entitlement to the work-related curriculum?

- Is there an economic and business education template, or set of objectives, that can be used as part of this entitlement?

Teaching and learning styles in economics and business entitlement

The most significant, if perhaps rather obvious, contribution made by the Teaching and Learning Group to the EBEA's Economics 16–19 Project was that participative teaching and learning approaches engender what has been described by Vidler (1993) and others as 'classroom thoughtfulness'.

Participative approaches create an opportunity for a plurality of perspectives to emerge when viewing a specific issue. Without this active learning approach it is likely that partial views and interpretations will occur. The meanings attached to various phenomena are, in short, socially constructed. Jephcote (1992) suggests that participative critically aware classrooms are more likely to secure economics and business understanding because students' prior knowledge and ideas are respected, challenged and used to tackle issues. The outcomes are then to do with shared meanings and may involve students shifting from 'taken for granted' or received views of the world to a more informed, empowered and enlightened personal view.

As mentioned earlier, Phil Hodkinson (1994) argues for empowerment as an entitlement and gives three characteristics of this that will be easily recognized by teachers of economic and business education:

- *personal effectiveness* – involving collaborative achievement as well as individual effort. Hodkinson mentions the term 'synergy' which is frequently used by industrialists to describe collaboration between otherwise highly individualized inputs to a process;

- *community* – the recognition that, in a pluralistic society, there is a need to consider the needs, aspirations and position of other individuals and groups;

- *critical autonomy* – primarily to do with ensuring that the educational process enables all young people to think for themselves.

In the 'Challenge of Industry' conference mentioned earlier, one activity required a group of students to be allocated the roles of managers and shop stewards. Stimulus materials revealed that redundancies would be necessary for the firm to move to a new phase of development and survival. In the first meeting of the two groups, management put the case and shop stewards had very little to say except that there were some concerns about washing facilities at the plant. During a 'time out' the adviser asked the students to give more thought to the position of their colleagues whose redundancy was imminent. In the next phase of the simulation, discussions covered the reasons for redundancy as well as the economic and business context within which the firm operated. 'What did you do to those "shop stewards" during the time-out?' asked one of the 'managers', referring to the more balanced debate that had occurred towards the end of the exercise. This accords with what Hodkinson (1994) refers to as critical autonomy, community and personal effectiveness when he argues that students involved in simulated business activity should be encouraged to explore critically the power and pay structures that many people take for granted. Critically aware and thoughtful classrooms are an important aspect of any consideration of economics and business education in the post-16 entitlement curriculum.

The status of 'core skills'

For some time now there has been considerable discussion as to whether core skills should be included in the post-16 curriculum. HMI (1989), in a 'non-definitive' paper, suggested that there was a case for all students to acquire core skills. The National Curriculum Council (1990) called for core skill performance to be assessed and reported in different contexts including A and AS certification as part of a record of achievement. Subsequently, core skills have been redefined several times and have been included in GNVQs at all levels as follows:

- Application of Number (compulsory)
- Communication (compulsory)
- Information Technology (compulsory).

In addition there is a suggestion that other generic skills may become compulsory in GNVQ as follows:

- working with others
- improving own learning and performance
- problem-solving.

Dearing (1995), in his review of 16–19 qualifications, has been asked to consider the case for the adoption of core skills in a wider range of post-16 provision. (In Scotland core skills are mandatory in some awards and are 'encouraged' in all post-16 programmes of study.) The implication is that core skills may well be included in programmes of study for A and AS level students. How this will be achieved is open to debate, but there are considerable logistical difficulties associated with integrating, assessing and accrediting core skills at A and AS levels. The main problem will be finding valid ways to assess things like 'working with others' or 'problem-solving' in a three-hour examination paper!

It is possible that additional activities will be recommended such as those used in the University of Liverpool's Curriculum Enrichment Programme or the University of Bath's Post-16 Curriculum Enrichment Programme. Both these developments used industrial contexts to develop core skills and then 'accredit' them in a record of achievement. Core skills require a context for their implementation and a business or community setting is used for this purpose. This means that once again there is a need to consider the implications for economics and business entitlement when work-related contexts are used to address core skills.

Smithers (1995), in a fairly damning article, considers core skills to be a 'digression' (where has this been heard before?), arguing that subjects are no longer subjects when they become vehicles for delivering core skills.

Is it perhaps too fanciful to hope that what emerges from the current post-16 debate will be a new paradigm? This paradigm would use modules that enabled students to associate skills and subject knowledge in real-world contexts. In other words, instead of using core skills and work-related contexts to augment the post-16 curriculum, the modules would in fact give it a new orientation. (Grubb Institute, 1989). Any new orientation of this kind would undoubtedly require an economics and business education entitlement.

Conclusion

In the post-16 phase of education and training, young people move through a phase of economic dependency towards independence. Important to this transition will be the provision of an entitlement curriculum that is broad, balanced, coherent and progressive. The government has not indicated, except through things like the TVEI, what this entitlement curriculum should be like. This provides an opportunity for schools and colleges to work with students on the design of this curriculum. Economics and business education is an important entitlement for students because it promotes a critical awareness and understanding of phenomena that will affect their working lives.

Whatever the outcomes of Dearing's review of post-16 qualifications, there is already undoubtedly a shift in the orientation of the post-16 curriculum to incorporate work-related skills, content and contexts. The role of the economics and business education teacher will need to widen to accommodate this new orientation. Perhaps it is time, once again, for the hero-innovators of economics and business education to refuel, don their flying helmets and venture forth!

References

Audit Commission and HMI (1993). *Unfinished Business: Full-Time Education Courses for 16–19 Year Olds*, London, HMSO.

Coles, A., Cheshire, B. and Hodkinson, S. (1992). 'EIU and curriculum enhancement in a sixth form college', *Economic Awareness*, vol. 4, no. 3, pp. 22–7.

Crombie-White, R., Pring, K., and Brockington, D. (1995). *14–19 Education and Training: Implementing a Unified System of Learning*, London, RSA.

Dearing, Sir Ron (1995). *Review of 16–19 Qualifications: Summary of the Interim Report*, London, Central Office of Information.

DoE (1991). *Guidance for Authorities Preparing Proposals for the 16–18 Phase*, London, TVEI Unit.

Gillmon, E. (1992). *Business Education in the Secondary School: A CTC Response*, City Technology College Trust Ltd, 15 Young Street, London W8 5EH, CTC Trust Publications.

Grubb Institute (1989). *Technical and Vocational Education Extension: Towards a Paradigm for Total Learning*, Grubb Institute, London N1 6HO, (Cloudesley Street).

HMI (1989). *Post-16 Education and Training: Core Skills*, London, Department of Education and Science.

HMI (1990). *Statement on Business and Economics Education 5–16*, London, HMSO.

Hodkinson, P. (1990). 'A framework for providing TVEI post-16', in: Hodkinson, P. (ed.), *TVEI and the Post-16 Curriculum*, Exeter, Wheaton Education.

Hodkinson, P. (1994). 'Empowerment as an entitlement in the post-16 curriculum', *Journal of Curriculum Studies*, vol. 26, no. 5, pp. 491–508.

Jamieson, I. and Harris, A. (1994). 'Can schools prepare young people for adult economic life?', Economic Awareness, vol. 6, no. 3.

Jephcote, M. (1992). *Understanding Economics or Economic Understanding*, EATE Research Report 4, October 1992, Department of Employment.

Jephcote, M. and Williams, M. (1994). 'Teacher receptivity to the introduction of economic and industrial understanding', *Quarterly Journal of the Economics and Business Education Association*, vol. 2, part 4, no. 8, pp. 163–7.

National Curriculum Council (1990). *Core Skills 16–19*, York, NCC.

Saunders, L. (1992). 'The work related curriculum: the new entitlement?', *British Journal of Education and Work*, vol. 6, no. 1, pp. 75–89.

School Curriculum and Assessment Authority (1994). *GCSE 'A' and 'AS' Code of Practice*, London, Central Office of Information.

Smithers, A. (1995). 'How many core skills can be balanced on a pinhead?', *Times Educational Supplement*, 6 Oct.

Vidler, C. (1993). 'Start making sense', *Economics and Business Education*, vol. 1, part 1, no. 4, pp. 178–81.

17

Reconceptualizing the work-related curriculum

Alma Harris

This chapter argues that the work-related curriculum has an important part to play in developing economic and industrial understanding in young people. It acknowledges that, to date, there has generally been a lack of progression, continuity and coherence in this important area of the curriculum. The chapter outlines a new approach to implementing and delivering the work-related curriculum. It concludes by suggesting that this approach has much to offer economics and business studies teaching.[1]

Background

Over the last decade or so, the phrase 'work-related curriculum' has established something of a currency in the UK. Despite the difficulty of describing this curriculum area in any specific detail, there are general characteristics of the work-related curriculum that are easily defined (Jamieson, 1993). It is most readily identified as being a curriculum area concerned with vocational preparation coupled with work-related activities such as work experience, industry weeks and mini-enterprise. These work-related activities are often integrated within the mainstream curriculum and contribute to particular programmes of study (Jamieson *et al.*, 1988).

To date, the work-related curriculum has been primarily geared towards secondary school pupils. Mainly viewed as a prevocational option involving general preparation for the world of work, young people have come into contact with this curriculum through pre-vocational courses, through PSE and through relevant aspects of the GCSE. In contrast, the work-related curriculum has been relatively underdeveloped in primary schools (Craft, 1995). Where work-related activities have taken place in the primary sector, mostly they have contributed to general topic, or themed work and have most often comprised mini-enterprise or industry-specific projects (Ross, 1995).

The existence of the work-related curriculum has always been heavily dependent on it having a secure place in educational provision. The arrival of the National Curriculum has done little to strengthen the position of the work-related curriculum. Based on traditional subject divisions and a single transmission model of knowledge, the National Curriculum has been viewed as quite incompatible with many work-related activities (Jamieson, 1993). Indeed, it could be argued that the National Curriculum has substantially weakened the position of this curricular area.

It also remains highly debatable whether the National Curriculum has been able to meet fully the requirements of Section 1 of the Education Reform Act 1988. This stipulates the necessity to provide a broad and balanced curriculum that:

- promotes the spiritual, moral, cultural, mental and physical development of pupils at the school and of society;

- prepares pupils for the opportunities, responsibilities and experiences of adult life.

Initial concerns about this issue led to widespread support for the notion of the 'whole curriculum' and the education of the 'whole child'. There was much anxiety that an over-emphasis on a fragmented curriculum could shift the process of teaching and learning away from the 'whole child' to a much more instrumental and narrow focus. As a result of this particular lobby, the Curriculum Guidance paper *The Whole Curriculum* was published (NCC, 1990), followed closely by the five cross-curricular themes.

Much of the subsequent research evidence concerning the 'whole curriculum' and the cross-curricular themes has not been very encouraging. In particular, there is a wide range of literature documenting the mixed fortunes of the cross-curricular themes (e.g. Ross, 1995; Harris and Jamieson, 1992; Whitty *et al.*, 1992). One recent study has shown that economic and industrial understanding has fared the least well of the five themes in teaching and learning terms (Saunders *et al.*, 1995). Similarly, another study showed that pupils had rarely heard of economic and industrial understanding and very few thought they had been taught any (Rowe *et al.*, 1993; Whitty *et al.*, 1992).

The research findings repeatedly underline the difficulty of learning without a clear subject context and subject discourse (Vass, 1995; Harris and Jamieson, 1992; Saunders *et al.*, 1995). It has been suggested that teaching in a cross-curricular way 'interferes' with the subject discourse. From the perspective of the learners, cross-curricular activities appear to be a confusing distraction to the emerging 'rules' of the subject, unless they arise 'naturally' as part of subject discourse (Jamieson and Harris, 1994). This would suggest that cross-curricular approaches are not the optimum means of providing breadth in the curriculum. Moreover, it emphasizes the fact that economic and business-related learning cannot be left to the chance fortunes of a singular cross-curricular theme, or to a largely optional work-related curriculum.

Reconceptualizing the work-related curriculum

Two fundamental weaknesses exist in the work-related curriculum as it currently stands. The first relates to progression and coherence between the key stages of learning. Unlike many traditional school subjects areas, many pupils derive a significant amount of knowledge about work from outside the school – for example from part-time work or relatives. Work experience takes place off school premises and is largely out of sight and control of the teacher.

Consequently there are no generally accepted schemes for what experiences should take place, when and in what order certain concepts should be encountered within the work-related curriculum (Trainor, 1992, p. 17)

The second weakness relates to the fact that the work-related curriculum has systematically failed to provide clearly defined learning outcomes related to the National Curriculum's key stages. This has resulted in work-related learning being accepted as being implicit in activities, rather than explicitly defined. With a National Curriculum so tightly bound up in specifying learning outcomes, it seems reasonable that by comparison the work-related curriculum appears a rather ill-defined and unstructured curricular option.

It would appear, therefore, that some reconceptualization of the work-related curriculum is needed in order to successfully deliver economic and industrial related learning. It is suggested that careful consideration of children's age-related acquisition of economic concepts and principles should be planned for and included (Schug, 1990; Linton, 1990). There is sufficient research evidence to support the view that children understand those socio-economic ideas that they experience directly (Holroyd, 1990).

Furthermore, it is suggested that well constructed age-related experiences are needed to encourage young people to rethink and reconstruct their views of economic phenomena. Consequently, any reconceptualization of the work-related curriculum should necessarily include clearly defined learning outcomes, prescribed in much the same way as for other national curriculum subject areas. Without a clearly defined 'subject' discourse, the work-related curriculum will, it is argued, continue to be undermined and steadily marginalized within the National Curriculum.

On this particular issue, one is led inevitably to the position of arguing for a discrete work-related curriculum component within the National Curriculum. Such suggestions are not new, neither are models of successful courses (see Stenhouse, 1980). Also, the fact that the review of the National Curriculum, under the chairmanship of Sir Ron Dearing (Dearing, 1993; SCAA, 1994) has left the principle of the 'whole' curriculum untouched is both important and timely. The draft proposals for the post-1995 National Curriculum remain most compatible with the requirements of the 1988 Educational Reform Act for a broad and balanced curriculum. This means that there is still the opportunity for the work-related curriculum to make an important contribution to the whole curriculum. In this respect, it is posited that a reconceptualized work-related curriculum which provides a holistic framework for work-related teaching and learning is long overdue.

The 'Pathways Toward Adult and Working Life' project (1995)[2]

'Pathways Toward Adult and Working Life' is a project that has been developed to provide a work-related curriculum framework such as that discussed above. Piloted in three quite diverse LEA contexts – Cheshire, Doncaster and Lewisham – the 'Pathways' project provides a curriculum 'Framework' from ages 5 to 16 for all work-related activities. One of the chief aims of the project is to develop economic and industrial understanding in young people of all ages. Its purpose is to provide a coherent work-related 5–16 curriculum and to ensure that work-related learning outcomes are planned for, and built upon, at each successive key stage.

The Framework deliberately does not prescribe *how* the student outcomes should be met, as it recognizes that this is clearly the domain of schools and their partner organizations. It is recognized that individual schools will be in slightly different positions regarding this area of the curriculum and will need to work from their own starting points in terms of the learning processes needed to meet the pre-specified student outcomes.

Planned learning outcomes

To assist in this process, the 'Pathways' Framework documentation provided for schools is also a planning tool. In addition to the prescribed learning outcomes at each key stage, the document includes *six* headings, arranged over blank columns, aimed at assisting schools to plan and develop this area of the curriculum. The aim of these blank columns is to ensure that quality work-related experiences are carefully planned for all pupils, and that all *partners*, including both large and small employers, play an active role in delivery. The column headings are:

- Existing school practices dedicated to assisting learners achieve the outcomes
- School plans to assist learners, including management and monitoring issues
- Details of partners' existing work with the school
- Partners' plans for working with school to assist learners, including management issues
- Anticipated benefits to partners: a commentary
- Evidence that student outcomes have been achieved.

The Framework has four main sections. These are as follows:

1. Knowledge and understanding of the developing self and personal skills
2. Knowledge and understanding of opportunities, choices, responsibilities and rights
3. Knowledge and understanding of work and of business
4. Knowledge and understanding of the influences of the economy and the environment on life.

225

Sections 1 and 2 therefore concentrate on personal and social development with an emphasis on careers and citizenship, while sections 3 and 4 concentrate primarily on developing economic and industrial understanding in young people.

Sections 3 and 4 both outline concepts related to economics and business in the form of *generic learner outcomes.* So, learners must show that they:

- know how businesses create wealth (3.1)

- know how services are provided in different sectors of society (3.2)

- know about the scope and range of work and business (3.3)

- know the legal responsibilities of employers and employees (3.4)

- know about political systems and processes (3.5)

- understand that they live in a pluralistic society (3.6)

- can record and review what they have learned about the world of work (3.7)

and

- know about and can investigate the interrelationship between the economy and the environment. (4.1)

- can analyse and interpret information about the economy and environment. (4.2).

Each generic learning outcome is then translated at each of the key stages to ensure progression and to reinforce learning throughout the Framework. Taking *learning outcome 3.1* as an example, the specific age-related learning outcomes at each of the key stages are as follows:

- *Key Stage 1* – Students can use money in simple buying and selling transactions and can barter with other goods.

- *Key Stage 2* – Students can give examples that show they know and understand about real costs and benefits to themselves and others of personal transactions.

- *Key Stage 3* – Students know and understand about various costs, benefits and added value in a given business context and, with help, can analyse these economic elements.

- *Key Stage 4* – Students can understand how businesses create wealth on a national and international scale, and make profits, and know why profits are essential for improving and developing products, creating employment, providing taxation and funding community development.

For all of the generic learning outcomes identified in each of the four sections, specific outcomes related to the key stages have been provided. This pattern gives the overall structure of the Framework.

Content

Moving from the structure of the Framework to its economics- and business-related *content*, there are several points to make. Firstly, the Framework has taken as its starting point the fact that economics is a discipline with a number of interrelated concepts that are reiterated and amplified as one's knowledge of the subject develops. Research has shown that there are a number of basic economic concepts within the comprehension of primary school children between the ages of 5 and 11 (Linton, 1990; Schug, 1990; Ryba, 1990). Consequently, these concepts have been taken as the starting point for the economic content within the Framework and necessarily relate to a range of business knowledge and skills.

The concepts are as follows: demand and supply; value and price; costs and benefits; wealth creation and distribution; resource allocation; profit; ownership (private, public, voluntary sectors); competition; trade and exchange; labour; and externalities.

These key economics- and business-related concepts are reinforced at each successive key stage and they are implicit in the learner outcomes outlined in sections 3 and 4 of the Framework. The purpose of defining learner outcomes at each key stage in this way is to ensure continuity, coherence and progression in pupils' learning.

A second issue relating to the economic content of the Framework concerns its ideological origin. Unlike 'Economic and Industrial Understanding', the representation of economic and business concepts in broad learner outcomes avoids overly narrow interpretations. Unlike EIU, the Framework 'does not have a clear line of descent from Sir Keith Joseph's obsession with what he saw as a lack of capitalistic virtue' (Ross, 1995, p. 83). Neither is it a 'front for inculcating monetarist economics in the young' (Blyth, 1994). Instead, the Framework is premised upon effective teaching and learning about the world of work. It is not dominated, or driven, by any one ideological stance but is concerned primarily with the process of learning through *individual experiences*.

Discussion

Vass (1995) has argued that there is little point in constructing economic meaning through an 'integrated curriculum'. His viewpoint is that the economic descriptors in EIU 'fail to encapsulate our local, fragmented and contingent feel for contemporary experiences' (p. 5). In other words, learning rarely takes place in a neat integrated way but is the result of personal experience and the construction of individual meaning.

In this respect, the theoretical basis of the 'Pathways' project lies in a subscription to experiential learning theory. Experiential learning theory is premised on the assumption that children learn through their activity and build their minds through the kinds of behaviour in which they participate. In Dewey's words (1916, pp. 89–90), the task of education accordingly 'is that reconstruction or reorganisation of experience which adds to the meaning of experience and which increases ability to direct the course of subsequent experience'. The 'Pathways' project is concerned to develop the individual's capability to learn from experience by providing a learning context, or frame for the experience. Such 'pedagogic procedures' are among those that have repeatedly been found to promote economic and business understanding (Thomas, 1991, 1994; Hodkinson and Thomas, 1988, 1989, 1991).

Preliminary evaluation data have revealed that the Framework is providing opportunities for discussion and experimentation within the context of work-related learning (Harris, 1995). Pupil data have revealed that at all key stages learners are engaged in economic learning appropriate to their stage of development. Unlike previous curriculum development in this area, the Framework is giving *all* pupils at *all* key stages the opportunity to be involved, to some degree, in economics and business thinking. In addition, the evaluation evidence has revealed that the Framework is providing an important platform for cross-phase liaison centred upon the stipulated learning outcomes.

There will inevitably be those who view 'Pathways' as presenting a disempowering, conventional view of economics and business knowledge. There are two related points to be made here. First, there is no such thing as a 'conventional economic view' of economic and industrial understanding but more usually a series of competing views. Cole (1986, 1993) has argued this point most forcibly by suggesting that even where there is a 'role-centred' approach to learning economics – based upon the young person as consumer, producer and citizen – these roles implicitly accept an orthodox conception of the nature of economic theory and economic literacy.

Second, the objective of the 'Pathways' project is not to reinforce a particular theoretical perspective, or economic orthodoxy, but rather to equip young people to be more economically aware, or *thoughtful*. It is this latter view that is consistently found in recent economics education literature and numerous published papers (Hodkinson and Thomas, 1988, 1989, 1991, Vidler, 1993). As Craft (1995, p. 167) notes, economics and business learning can only be empowering 'if it involves a wide range of economic and industrial affairs, if it involves a range of models and views and, most critically, children are strongly encouraged to think independently about these, to reflect and be critical rather than accept the way things are'. The 'Pathways' project adheres to all of these important fundamental principles.

Conclusion

The 'Pathways to Working Life' project is premised upon a clear and shared sense of purpose. This purpose is the preparation of young people for adult and working life. The net result of this common purpose should be to introduce a 'new' concept of partnership extending beyond superficial education-business liaison. The central aim of this 'new' partnership is to work towards common learner objectives and learner outcomes. These objectives and outcomes will be based upon what young people should be able to achieve and demonstrate at the age of 16 which collectively represent a preparation for adult and working life.

As Ahier and Ross (1995) point out, the National Curriculum can never be developed in asocial terms. Similarly, the work-related curriculum cannot be viewed out of its historical or social contexts. For twenty years or so, traditional conservative thinkers have been at odds with conservative modernizers about the purpose of a work-related curriculum (Ball, 1990). The latter have tended to argue for a set of educational changes more suitable to what they see as a rapidly changing economy.

There is now widespread acknowledgement that the post-industrial economy will necessitate new skills and aptitudes from young people. As a result of increased corporatism, European union and economic globalization, the power of ownership has in many cases become further removed from the site of production (Murray, 1989). The consequence for employment, regional economies and labour/management relations will inevitably result in less stability over time (Gilbert, 1995). These economic changes will impact upon young people. The post-industrial economy will increasingly draw on a more diverse range of skills which will necessitate much closer linkage between education and the economy.

Consequently, if schools are serious about preparing pupils for adult and working life, then the curriculum provision cannot be piecemeal. Experience has shown what happens with a curriculum model of subject 'leftovers' where important social and economic learning becomes a matter of chance, rather than entitlement. This only serves to denigrate the importance of children's social and economic learning.

Progression, continuity and coherence need to be paramount in future curriculum planning for economics- and business-related learning. The 'Pathways' project represents a step in this direction as a curriculum 'framework' *for all pupils, at all stages of their development.* If this project is successful, it should serve to secure and strengthen the position of economics and business studies teaching from 5 to 16. If unsuccessful, the work-related curriculum might well collapse through the forces of the market, and economics and business studies will be denied the curriculum status both deserve.

References

Ahier, J. and Ross, A. (eds) (1995). *The Social Subjects Within the Curriculum*, Brighton, Falmer Press.

Ball, S. (1990). *Politics and Policy Making in Education*, London, Routledge.

Blyth, W. A. L. (1994). 'Beyond economic and industrial understanding: an economic perspective in the primary curriculum', British Journal of Education and Work, vol. 7, no. 1, pp. 11–17.

Cole, K. (1986). *Economic Literacy and Development*, Education Discussion Paper 193, School of Development Studies, University of East Anglia.

Cole, K. (1993). 'New directions in teaching economics', *Journal of Economics and Business Education*, vol. 1, part 1, no. 2, pp. 79–84.

Craft, A. (1995). 'Indoctrination or empowerment? The case of economic and industrial understanding', in: Ahier, J. and Ross, A. (eds), *The Social Subjects Within the Curriculum*, Brighton, Falmer Press.

Dearing, Sir Ron (1993). *The National Curriculum and its Assessment : An Interim Report*, York and London, National Curriculum Council/ Schools Examinations and Assessment Council.

Dewey, J. (1916). *Democracy and Education*, New York, Macmillan.

Gilbert, R. (1995). 'Education for citizenship and the problem of identity in post modern political culture', in: Ahier, J. and Ross, A. (eds), *The Social Subjects Within the Curriculum*, Brighton, Falmer Press.

Harris, A. (1995). 'Preliminary evaluation findings from the Pathways pilot project', unpublished report, London, LENTA.

Harris, A. and Jamieson, I. M. (1992). 'Evaluating economic awareness. 2: Teaching and learning issues,' *Economic Awareness*, vol. 5, no. 1, pp. 23–8.

Hodkinson, S. and Thomas, L. (1988). 'What is economic awareness?', *Economic Awareness*, vol. 1, no. 1, pp. 1–4.

Hodkinson, S. and Thomas, L. (1989). 'Balancing act', *Times Educational Supplement*, 2 Oct.

Hodkinson, S. and Thomas, L. (1991). 'Economics education for all', in: Whitehead, D. and Dyer, D. (eds), *New Developments in Economics and Business Education*, London, Kogan Page.

Holroyd, S. (1990). 'Children's development in socio-economic ideas: some psychological perspectives', in: Ross, A. (ed.), *Economic and Industrial Understanding in the Primary School*, London, Polytechnic of North London Press.

Jamieson, I. M. (1993). 'The rise and fall of the work-related curriculum' in: Wellington, J. (ed.), *The Work-Related Curriculum*, London, Kogan Page.

Jamieson, I. M., Miller, A. and Watts, A. G. (1988). *Mirrors of Work: Work Simulations in Schools*, Brighton, Falmer Press.

Jamieson, I. M. and Harris, A. (1994). 'Can schools prepare young people for adult economic life', *Economic Awareness*, vol. 6, no. 3, pp. 19–24.

Linton, T. (1990). 'A child's eye view of economics', in: Ross, A. (ed.), *Economic and Industrial Awareness in the Primary School*, London, Polytechnic of North London Press.

Murray, R. (1989). 'Benetton Britain', in: Hall, S. and Jaques, M. (eds), *New Times: The Changing Face of Politics in the 1990s*, London, Lawrence & Wishart.

National Curriculum Council (1990). *Curriculum Guidance 4: Economic and Industrial Understanding*, York, NCC.

Ross, A. (1995). 'The whole curriculum, the National Curriculum and social studies', in: Ahier, J. and Ross, A. (eds), *The Social Subjects Within the Curriculum*, Brighton, Falmer Press.

Rowe, G., Aggleton, P. J. and Whitty, G. J. (1993). 'Subjects and themes in the school curriculum', in (mimeograph): *Working Papers of the ESRC Project: Assessing Quality in Cross Curricular Contexts*, London, Institute of Education.

Ryba, R. (1990). 'Exploring the Economic Concepts of Young Children', in: Ross, A. (ed.), *Economic and Industrial Awareness in the Primary School*, London, Polytechnic of North London Press.

Saunders, L., MacDonald, A., Hewitt, D. and Schagen, S. (1995). *Education For Life: The Cross Curricular Themes in Primary and Secondary Schools*, Slough, NFER.

Schug, M. (1990). 'Research on children's understanding of economics: implications for teaching', in: Ross, A. (ed.), *Economic and Industrial Awareness in the Primary School*, Polytechnic of North London Press.

Stenhouse, L. (ed.) (1980). *Curriculum Research and Development in Action*, London, William Heinemann.

Thomas, L. (1991). A new perspective on learning: what does it mean for economics?', *Economics*, vol. 27, part 2, no. 114, pp. 79–83.

Thomas, L. (1994). 'Preparation for adult life: the case for subject-based classroom relevance', *Economic Awareness*, vol. 6, no. 2, pp. 7–12.

Trainor, D. (1992). 'Coherence, progression and continuity in work related teaching and learning', in: Richardson, W. (ed.), *Work Related Teaching and Learning in Schools*, Centre for Education and Industry, University of Warwick.

Whitty, G. J., Aggleton, P. J. and Rowe, G. (1992). *Cross-Curricular Work in Secondary Schools: A Summary of Results of a Survey Carried Out in 1992* (mimeograph), London, Institute of Education.

Vass, J. (1995). 'Narrations of "self" and "world" through the "economic and industrial understanding"', in Ahier, J. and Ross, A. (eds), *The Social Subjects Within the Curriculum*, Brighton, Falmer Press.

Vidler, C. (1993). 'Economics 16–19 Project teaching and learning strategies' (unpublished paper), London, Institute of Education.

End notes

1. I would like to thank Malcolm Brigg OBE for his helpful comments on initial drafts of this chapter.

2. Further details of the 'Pathways to Working Life' project can be obtained from Mike Goodfellow, LEntA, 4 Snow Hill, London EC1A 2BS.

18 Economic and industrial understanding in the 11–16 curriculum: two case studies

Neil Denby and Heather Stretch

Editors' note: This chapter consists of two independent case studies to illustrate the development of 'economic and industrial understanding' (EIU) as a cross-curricular theme. One is taken from England and the other from Wales.

EIU was promoted by the National Curriculum Council (NCC) in England, and by the Curriculum Council for Wales (CCW), each providing non-statutory guidance: *Curriculum Guidance 4* (NCC, 1990) and *Advisory Paper 7* (CCW, 1990). The Northern Ireland Curriculum Council (NICC, 1989) identified 'economic awareness' as a cross-curricular theme, which later became a statutory requirement to be delivered through other subjects.

Support was given to Local Education Authorities (LEAs), schools and teachers in their attempts at developing school structures, classroom strategies and materials. This support was provided by a host of agencies and projects, resulting in a partnership between LEAs, schools, teachers, government departments (including the Department for Education and Science and the Department for Employment), the business community and universities and other providers. The Economics Association (now the EBEA) can take some credit for promoting and supporting the development of EIU and acting as an important link in the partnership.

Both of the case studies here, in addition to illustrating a whole-school and a whole-curriculum approach to the development of EIU, illustrate aspects of the partnership approach. Neil Denby focuses on his own role as the EIU coordinator, drawing on the support of the Economic Awareness Teacher Training Programme (EcATT) based at the University of Manchester. Heather Stretch shows the importance of the Technical Vocational Education Initiative (TVEI) in supporting her work and in establishing consortium arrangements. Both studies illustrate the benefits of links with the business community.

* * *

Case Study One – Neil Denby
A whole-school approach to EIU

The introduction of the National Curriculum – and the fact that it left out both economics and business studies – led to a need to define these areas of study more broadly in terms of the whole curriculum. While neither 'economics' nor 'business studies' appears as a core or a foundation subject, there is a place for them in the secondary school curriculum. This place is twofold: they have a contribution to make as specialist subjects – as options within the curriculum – and as part of the 'cross-curricular loom' on which the rest of the whole curriculum may be woven.

According to the National Curriculum Council (NCC, 1989, p. 1), the Education Reform Act 1988 'places a statutory responsibility upon schools to provide a broad and balanced curriculum'. The same NCC publication states that, as part of that breadth and balance, the ten National Curriculum subjects should be augmented *inter alia* by 'an accepted range of cross-curricular elements'. These elements are to come in three varieties: dimensions, skills and themes. The themes encompass environmental education, citizenship, health, careers education and guidance, and economic and industrial understanding (EIU).

Pearce (1989, p. 10) outlined his thinking about economic and industrial understanding in the following way:

'The educational rationale for economic and industrial understanding is clear. Everyone is involved in the economy where decisions are made about the use of limited or available resources. Such decisions affect employment, living standards, economic growth, services and government policies and so relate to careers, health, environmental and citizenship education.'

According to Pearce, the *themes* were to be delivered at each key stage – in the primary sector (at Stages 1 and 2) through methods such as investigative topics, factory visits, shopping and budgeting; and in the secondary sector (at Stages 3 and 4) through 'permeating appropriate contexts of National Curriculum subjects and forming further discrete programmes of study'.

Implementation must involve an organized and managed format and a structured approach. The main alternatives open to delivery of the themes are:

- through GCSE at Key Stage 4;
- as discrete units in the curriculum;
- through a whole-school approach.

The first of these limits economic and industrial understanding to the 14–16 age range and is clearly inappropriate. The second lacks context or continuity. The third, however, provides an opportunity to give both context and continuity and to enhance the delivery of other subject areas. For this to take place it is necessary to have considerable planning and to liaise with subject specialists.

Background to the case study

I was appointed to an 11–16 High School in 1990 with a brief to raise the whole-school profile of 'economic awareness' (as it was then called) and to devise a method or methods whereby the theme could be delivered in accordance with the available curriculum guidance. I had already been involved in

234

the transition from GCE and CSE to GCSE, and in the writing and development of several economics courses. Involvement in teacher training, and links with local universities and colleges, had given insights into current trends.

My previous post involved me in the development of a student-led approach to the delivery of many courses. Group work, course work, mini-enterprise and self-directed student learning were integral parts of the curriculum. All aspects of these experiences were to prove useful in my new position. I was. however, the only teacher in the school with a specialist knowledge of economics and business, and so had no one with whom to discuss ideas. This was at least partially solved through working with the Economic Awareness Teacher Training (EcATT) programme at Manchester University and, eventually, by writing up my experiences as a dissertation for a Masters degree (Denby, 1993, 1994).

From the outset I was convinced that the best way to deliver EIU was through a process of permeation – delivering the theme through other subjects. However, I was mindful of HMI (1990) concerns over a whole-curriculum approach:

'Involvement in business and economic activity ... does not generate economic and business understanding unless the teachers specifically set these as objectives, preparing and debriefing the activity accordingly. The provision of an economic and business focus lessens the impact of the activity as a source of learning in maths, science, geography.' (§ 12)

'... an encounter with business and economic content which is not focused in both preparation and follow-up by the teacher, does not produce understanding.' (§ 15)

I was also aware that the appointment of a theme coordinator was only one approach to implementation. The work could have been given to a coordinator whose job was already cross-curricular in nature, such as a PSE or careers coordinator; it could have been delegated to the head of a curriculum area already considered to be delivering many elements of the theme, such as the head of Humanities; or it could have been given to a senior member of staff with responsibility for all the cross-curricular themes. My investigations into the methods of delivery used in schools in West Yorkshire showed that all these alternatives were used.

The responses to my questionnaire survey indicated, however, that the most successful approach was that of a theme coordinator with a whole-school responsibility for delivery and with support from the senior management team. With all these elements in place, the evidence suggested, it was possible to embark on a structured programme of delivery permeating all curriculum areas.

My own approach to implementation was in three stages: first, to conduct an audit of what was currently being delivered; second, to raise the awareness of the staff in a non-threatening manner; and third, through observation and delivery, to actually take part in the enhancement of curriculum area lesson delivery through planning and participation.

The audit

The initial move in this 'permeation' approach was to find out what was already being delivered and by whom. The Key Stage 3 audit carried out at my school was based on the headings provided in *Curriculum Guidance 4* (NCC, 1990). A grid was produced using those headings: 'economic concepts', 'business enterprise', 'industry and work', 'consumer affairs' and 'government and society'. Curriculum teams were asked to decide where delivery currently took place and complete the appropriate box in the grid – this was then returned to me for overall analysis. This gave a snapshot picture of where EIU was being delivered, either in some depth or superficially, and allowed me to consider where best to intervene.

Further detail was provided by curriculum coordinators through one-line statements indicating where and when each particular element of EIU was being delivered. (for example, 'in the second term of Year 7 during a study of ...').

Raising awareness

The need to raise staff awareness came at a time when teachers were beginning to suffer from 'innovation fatigue' as a result of the introduction of the National Curriculum. It was essential for any new development to appear in a favourable light and not appear to create extra work.

A report on the audit was published. It showed that many of the elements of the theme were already being delivered in a number of curriculum areas. Those areas which appeared to be offering least to the theme (in particular, English and Mathematics) were approached individually. Lesson plans and examples were prepared to illustrate how economic awareness could be integrated into courses and to show how it would enhance the subject. Together we produced teaching materials that added to existing lesson plans, and I provided examples of new approaches in published material (e.g. articles in the journal *Economic Awareness* and in *Forum*, the NCC publication on economic awareness, and reports of LEA projects).

Next, a series of meetings was held with representatives from different curriculum areas at which the positive benefits of delivering the theme through subject areas were discussed. For example, links between Music and Business Studies were used to look at the music industry, and between Modern Languages and Physical Education to look at how sports facilities could be promoted to foreign visitors. Obvious links with Careers Education, PSE and with the mini-enterprise activities carried out in the Key Stage 3 Technology curriculum were also explored.

The logical next port of call appeared to be to present a school-based definition of 'economic awareness' and a policy statement outlining what was intended. *HMI stresses the importance of policy statements for EIU*. It is argued that such statements help subject specialists to 'recognize sufficiently how they could contribute to economic understanding' (DES, 1987, § 23) and to provide a firm foundation for teachers to 'develop adequate strategies for assessment and evaluation' (§ 23).

The implication of the various HMI reports is that a policy statement is a necessary if not a sufficient condition for successful implementation. Davies (1991, p. 3), in his summary of the HMI reports, states:

'This implies that a whole school policy statement can only emerge from the whole of the staff as a consequence of some initial work by them on what Economic Awareness means in their work.'

In my school a policy statement was developed by a cross-curricular group –a 'management' group – which represented each curriculum area. A whole-school staff meeting was held where the draft policy was explained and discussed and where a description of economic understanding was presented as a kind of mission statement for the school (see Figure 18.1).

Economic and Industrial Understanding within the curriculum is concerned with enabling young people to know and understand certain basic economic concepts; to equip them with the critical and analytical skills to investigate economic issues, make judgements and take decisions and to develop attitudes necessary for them to participate in economic life, whether information is presented in words, images, numerically or statistically. It is broad, ranging over issues as diverse as industrial relations and the nature of enterprise; and balanced, embracing the needs of producers and consumers. It makes provision, at all levels, for the study of the institutions, individuals and processes involved in economic decision-making in local, regional, national, European and global contexts. It involves controversial issues and demands a balanced presentation of opposing views, encouraging young people to explore the values and beliefs held by themselves and others.

Figure 18.1 A description of 'economic understanding' in the form of a mission statement

The meeting was designed to raise the profile of the theme. To help to do this in a non-threatening way, a lighthearted quiz was used to pinpoint economic issues about which pupils should be aware. As a result I felt able to pursue the third part of my strategy – lesson observation and enhancement.

Collaboration

Observing lessons in other curriculum areas involves allocating time and resources. In my case it involved juggling with time made available by examination classes on study leave and by using my own non-contact time. Achieving this type of collaboration is vital if the permeation model is to work. Sharing lessons provides the basis for joint review and provides a foundation on which to build. It seemed that help and advice derived from these shared experiences was more likely to be accepted.

One example of this sort of collaboration involved a Year 9 group studying German who successfully combined language learning, economic awareness and sports studies in a series of lessons. As part of the language curriculum, students were told of the place and importance of German sports centres and provided with the specialist vocabulary. The local sports centre allowed free access to certain facilities, provided students with publications, and agreed to display their finished work. During the visit students learnt about the management of the centre (pricing policies and the reasons for different price bands at different times, elements of marketing the centre), used the facilities, and then designed a number of foreign-language brochures for the centre to use. The visit to the local sports centre was a focus for the learning that had gone before, and was an opportunity for the head of languages and the EIU coordinator to review what had taken place.

An advantage of this approach is that the students are encouraged to see learning as drawing on knowledge and skills from the whole curriculum. I currently give support to the permeation model by helping to prepare subject material, by taking pressure off subject teachers, and by monitoring progression and continuity.

There are, of course, drawbacks. If a coordinator is to work collaboratively – for example, to help with syllabuses and teaching plans, observe lessons, and assist in the delivery, monitoring and assessment of them – then considerable time is needed. Permeation is a slow process. Lack of enthusiasm may be encountered from subject teachers who are constrained by a single-subject approach. Moreover, without careful management and monitoring there might also be a lack of overall coherence.

Judging progress

In order to judge the success of this curriculum initiative, I identified three types of progress indicators: enabling indicators; process indicators; and success indicators.

- *Enabling indicators* provide evidence that structures and resources to support a theme are in place. These include group meeting times, places, agendas and membership; communications and report structures; delegation of tasks; provision of relevant information and resources; provision for review and feedback.

- *Process indicators* provide evidence that classroom materials and processes are being piloted; a high level of participation and involvement; that working definitions are established; and evidence of people working collaboratively.

- *Success indicators* provide evidence of outcomes, including student learning; the use of appropriate external resources; links with relevant agencies; publication and dissemination of practice.

In my school, enabling indicators were put into place quickly. Group meetings were well-attended, in all but one subject area, by the head of the curriculum area. A whole-staff agenda was drawn up. Tasks were delegated to curriculum areas, and feedback obtained through curriculum area meetings as well as directly by me.

As a way of reflecting on progress in my own school, I compared progress with other schools. To this end I conducted a questionnaire survey in 38 schools in West Yorkshire. In those schools where an action plan existed (the majority), where there was a policy in existence or in preparation (two-thirds), and where the awareness of all or most of the staff was said to have been raised (one-third), three common factors were present:

- There was an appointed coordinator.
- There was support from senior management.
- An audit had been carried out at Key Stages 3 and 4.

In those schools where little senior management support was said to exist (40 per cent), there appeared to be a lower percentage of completed action plans (50 per cent), fewer policy statements (30 per cent) and lower staff awareness.

I drew encouragement from these responses because it was possible to place my own school within the group that had procedures in place and appeared to be developing effectively. I drew comfort that, in these schools, as in my own, classroom-based development was at an early stage but was considered to be possible because support systems existed.

Conclusion

Is there, then, a single set of criteria for measuring the success of introducing the theme in a school? Common factors are the appointment of a coordinator; the support of the senior management team, and a planned programme of introduction which involves the whole staff in an institution. If all three of these factors are present then the theme is likely to be on the way to being successfully implemented. If any of these three factors is missing there appears to be less chance of success. If all are missing, then the status of the theme is likely to remain extremely low and progress will be slow. In schools where the theme was thought to be well-established and growing, 80 per cent enjoyed the positive support of senior management. Where the theme was less established and all these factors were missing, then only 25 per cent saw the theme as having any future.

* * *

Case Study Two – Heather Stretch
Developing and coordinating EIU

The forging of closer links between schools and industry has been a declared aim of many schools for a number of years, in response to the growing calls – mainly from politicians and industrialists – for schools and industry to work in closer cooperation. The links should make a contribution towards the preparation of young people for the world of work so that they are able to play a full and active part in the community. The links are not being created to provide young people with specific labour skills, but are concerned with providing them with insights into industry and the world of work. The design of programmes should be such as to encourage young people to develop a constructive yet critical approach to what they see and experience, so broadening their knowledge and understanding, skills and attitudes.

Gwendraeth Valley Comprehensive School is an 11–18 school situated in the village of Drefach at the heart of the Gwendraeth Valley in Dyfed, South Wales. The school draws its 600 pupils from a large catchment area in a rural setting in which the major industries are agriculture and services. With the decline of the mining industry the local unemployment rate is high.

The school is one of five secondary schools in the area which work closely together in the Dinefwr Compact (of which more later). It has its intake from primary schools in the surrounding villages, many of which are small two-teacher schools. Gwendraeth is noted for its close links with these primary schools, with parents, and with the village communities, and for maintaining and developing the 'homely and caring' ambience of the valley. A large proportion of the village communities speak Welsh and the bilingual nature of the valley is reflected within the school. The towns of Carmarthen, Llanelli and Ammanford are within easy reach and the school has developed links with organizations and establishments within these towns to supplement the support they receive from the valley. The variety of links that the school has with the surrounding area suggests that it is a school at the heart of its community.

The wider development of EIU: a rationale

Given the thrust of TVEI to increase teaching about the world of work across the school's curriculum, together with the designation of EIU as a cross-curricular theme in the National Curriculum, the school sought to face the challenge of developing EIU across the curriculum for every year group. This meant that appropriate strategies for the implementation and development of EIU had to be devised so that staff members could play their part. An essential first step was the production of a school policy statement which indicates both the school's commitment to EIU and its rationale. The introduction to the school's policy statement reads:

'EIU has been identified as one of the five cross-curricular themes in the curriculum in Wales, along with health education, careers education,

240

community studies and environmental studies. As such it should permeate the aspects of learning which make up the whole-curriculum. Elements of EIU which are contained in the programmes of study of core and foundation subjects are statutory requirements; other elements are not statutory but are an essential part of the whole curriculum if schools are to provide an education which promotes the aims of the Education Reform Act 1988, namely the spiritual, moral, cultural, mental and physical development of pupils and their preparation for the opportunities, responsibilities and experiences of adult life'.

The need for EIU has been emphasized in various HMI, Welsh Office, TVEI and LEA documents. The TVEI Task Group Report *Economic and Industrial Understanding: A Pupil Entitlement in the National Curriculum in Wales*, published in the autumn of 1989, stated that:

'As a preparation for responsible adulthood young people are entitled to understand more about economic life. For the future health of society there is a need for young people to leave school having been introduced to the economic and industrial aspects of the wider community'.

And in 1990 the CCW *Advisory Paper 7: Economic and Industrial Understanding*, stated:

'EIU is seen as an essential component of pupils' education if they are to be properly equipped to perform their roles as consumers, producers, providers and citizens in a fast changing economy. If the Welsh and UK economies are to make the most of their resources and respond to the needs of society as a whole in an increasingly complex, open and competitive international environment, then they will depend heavily on young people who are well-educated, adaptable and aware of the society around them. EIU has a central part to play in meeting this need'.

Stages in the development of EIU

The development of EIU was seen as a long-term goal extending over a number of years. The appointment of a coordinator, the production of a school policy statement and making available INSET time for staff to plan and implement EIU are seen as important parts of the overall strategy. The following took place at an early stage of the development.

- *Appointment of a coordinator.* The brief of the coordinator was to work closely with the management team, especially the deputy headteacher with responsibility for the curriculum, and to develop and maintain links with those in the local community.

- *Drawing-up a policy statement.* The statement, which includes the rationale for EIU, sets out the objectives of different subject areas together with expected learning outcomes, and strategies for implementation.

- *Development of a cross-curricular project.* This attracted CCW attention and was subsequently included as an example in CCW teacher support materials. This project gave staff and students a focus for EIU; it successfully demonstrated the relevance of EIU and the benefits of working across departments.

- *Whole-staff INSET.* This was to raise staff awareness of EIU and cross-curricular themes in general. It was led by the deputy headteacher (curriculum) and the EIU coordinator. The purpose of the day was to introduce and discuss a policy statement and to begin an initial audit of where EIU and other themes contribute to the curriculum.

- *Auditing of EIU.* An initial audit helped to identify those departments where it was felt a contribution to EIU could be made.

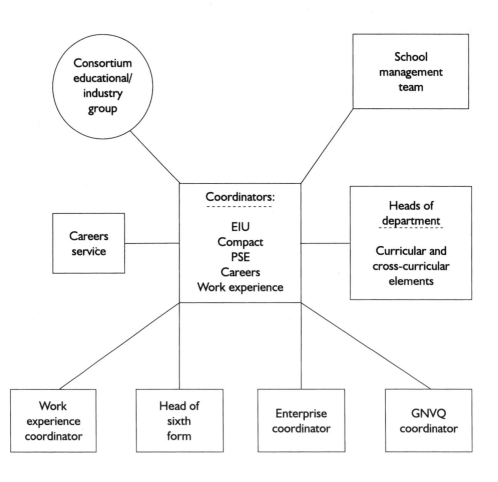

Figure 18.2 Organization structure of EIU in Gwendraeth

Strategies for implementation

Organization and structure

Figure 18.2, taken from the school's EIU policy, illustrates the organizational structure which facilitates the implementation of EIU. This illustrates the position and relationship of the EIU coordinator to other school and LEA curriculum managers.

The school receives valuable assistance from the LEA, particularly from the EBP Manager, who visits the school and is involved in the various discussion groups both at school and at Consortium level.

EIU activities

The development and extension of pupils' EIU is undertaken in a number of ways and includes subject and cross-curricular approaches. Integral to the implementation of EIU activities is the opportunity for staff development and for formal discussion between staff to plan and coordinate these activities. The following are some of the activities:

- Subject teachers discuss the impact of industry and enterprise activities and are encouraged to develop economic and industrial understanding within their own subject areas and consider the cross-curricular links between subjects.

- There is experience in mini-enterprise, both within discrete subjects (e.g. business studies) and across the curriculum (e.g. through cross-curricular projects, general studies, foundation programmes, and pre-vocational courses).

- There is work experience for all Year 10 and 12 students, and some Year 11 students, for at least one week.

- There are initiatives designed to promote EIU, such as work shadowing, conferences, careers advisory functions and industrial visits.

- Members of staff undertake visits and work placements, with a view to reflecting these experiences in their teaching.

- There is involvement in LEA-initiated projects designed to strengthen links with industry. Members of staff also initiate school-based projects in which they link with local industry.

- People from industry are invited into school to speak to various groups on industrial matters.

- Students visit industrial and commercial organizations to allow them to witness 'real life' situations and to undertake investigations.

- A module is included in the PSE/tutorial programme for all students from Year 9 onwards. For example, Year 9 pupils investigate the world of work and the contribution workers make to the local community. Year 10 pupils look at the world of work through enterprise activities where emphasis is given to developing their initiative and leadership skills as well as their understanding of business.

- Cross-curricular work includes: (i) an EIU-focused project on the tourism and leisure industry in the Gwendraeth Valley; and (ii) a cross-phase project involving the school working with a feeder primary school on an EIU-focused project sponsored by the Economic Development Unit.

- Lessons related to EIU have been developed. For example, the English curriculum requires a variety of forms, audiences and outcomes, some of which are natural EIU vehicles. The EIU Coordinator, as a teacher of English, explored, among other themes, that of looking after a pet when studying *The Battle of Bubble and Squeak* by Phillipa Pearce, and the students wrote their own books on the theme. When studying the poem *The Gas Man Cometh* by Flanders and Swann, the students dramatized the chaos caused by the visiting workmen. While studying *Summer of the Swans* by Betsy Byars, Year 8 wrote questionnaires and carried out a survey on people's attitudes to footwear as one activity, and Year 9 students, while studying *Boy* by Roald Dahl, investigated through questionnaires the sweet-buying habits of different age groups. In Science, Year 9 students study steel production using a variety of materials including a pack from British Steel, videos and a computer program. In Design & Technology, a module on Business and Industry is taught at Key Stage 3.

In all these aspects of the development of EIU the school benefits from its membership of the Dinefwr Compact and shares ideas with other schools and industrialists in this forum.

The role of the EIU coordinator: a personal reflection

I was appointed EIU Coordinator at Gwendraeth Valley Comprehensive School in 1989 when EIU was recognized as a cross-curricular theme within the National Curriculum. Prior to this appointment I had been the PSE/Careers Coordinator for three years, so the type of work involved was not entirely new to me and the experience I had gained in this role was relevant to my new position within the school.

In 1989 an EIU-focused project on the 'Tourism and Leisure Industry in the Gwendraeth Valley' was implemented in the school. This was recognized by CCW as a relevant contribution to their Teacher Support programme and gained its financial support. The project gave me, as coordinator, an opportunity to work with departments across the school, and it helped me to develop leadership and managerial skills. I also had the opportunity to work with CCW personnel and to further my professional development. This project could be considered to be the launching pad for EIU work within the school. Its success showed that EIU could be developed across the curriculum to the benefit of both staff and students.

After the completion of this project, the auditing of EIU provision was carried out. As coordinator, I was able to meet with heads of departments and discuss with them the provision made within their subject, offering them assistance in contacting outside agencies who could enhance their curriculum.

In 1992 another opportunity arose for implementing an EIU-focused project. This time it was supported by the Economic Development Unit and involved 30 pupils from Gwendraeth's Year 7 working with Year 6 of a feeder primary school (Tumble CP). As the secondary school's coordinator of the project, I again had the opportunity to work closely with departments across the curriculum and gain an insight into the primary school's curriculum.

Problems and constraints

There are a number of constraints acting on the development of EIU in the school. These can be classified as: (a) institutional, (b) people within the institution, and (c) people outside the institution.

Institutional constraints

A key constraint to any curriculum development is the availability of the resources needed to facilitate its growth. This includes classroom materials to support work at that level, and it also includes the making available of financial support to meet the cost of, for example, staff INSET. A capitation allowance is allocated to help further the development of EIU and external agencies have also given financial support for specific initiatives.

Time is an additional constraint. Time needs to be allocated for liaison with colleagues, outside agencies and students. In this day and age time is often a rare commodity. However, time can be 'bought', now that the school controls its own budget. This has occasionally been done when projects have been in the planning/evaluation stage. Also, colleagues are very supportive in providing cover when other staff are on visits. 'Extra-curricular' time, however, is often drawn upon for the day-to-day implementation and monitoring of EIU.

The coordinator can do much to support the work of individual teachers and departments, and this can be a vital contribution in securing the goodwill of colleagues. This includes, for example, arranging visits to firms and contacting appropriate speakers. The school has tried to minimize disruption to normal lessons by endeavouring to conduct EIU activities, including cross-curricular projects, within the existing timetable.

People within the institution

It is essential that management and staff be supportive of any developments, and this is made easier if there is a flow of information between all those involved. Staff are encouraged to become involved in the development and

245

claim ownership of it, and they can readily see the importance and relevance of EIU through successful outcomes.

In ensuring an adequate flow of information the EIU coordinator adopts formal and informal strategies. Formally, regular reports are given in staff meetings and, informally, the coordinator tries to keep in touch with staff through more casual discussions. Students, too, need to see the relevance of what they are doing and should be motivated by what they do. Staff and students are likely to respond more positively to activities that are purposeful and well planned.

People outside the institution

The success of links between the school and local industry – and therefore the successful development of students' EIU – depends on a good relationship with all those involved in this partnership. These are employers, parents, the LEA, careers service, and the EBP. This requires regular and effective liaison.

Parents should be kept informed of developments and their help and support for initiatives should be encouraged. The community at large should also be made aware of initiatives through, for example, newsletters, newspaper articles and other publications.

The schools in Dinefwr have joined the Dinefwr Compact, for which I am the Schools Compact Coordinator. This should give me the opportunity to consolidate the work being done in the school and to enhance it with Compact initiatives.

Conclusion

At the time of writing EIU has continued to form an integral part of the school curriculum, fully supported by the senior management. Its relevance and status have been consolidated by the introduction of the Compact initiative – which has itself been integrated with the school's National Record of Achievement procedures. EIU as a cross-curricular theme, therefore, seems to be sustainable. Staff clearly see the importance of EIU and are willing to give their time and energy to ensure a depth of provision. Many staff have commented that they appreciate the opportunity EIU provides to liaise and sometimes work with other departments.

The EIU/Compact Coordinator acts as a resource for the development of departmental activities and coordinates whole-school activities. Such activities are financed either from Compact funding or from the school budget. The 1995 Work Experience initiative has enhanced the school's programme in that area, and Dyfed EBP fully supports the school in the development of links with industry.

Acknowledgements

EIU at Gwendraeth is one of many initiatives that owe their success to a former headteacher, the late Mr R. W. Garrero. His support and encouragement enabled staff to develop and enhance the provision, to ensure that all students have the opportunity to benefit from what is provided, thus preparing them for the opportunities, responsibilities and experiences of adult life.

* * *

An earlier version of this case study first appeared in Williams, M., and Jeph-cote, M. (1993), *Economic Awareness as a Curriculum Entitlement in Wales*, Final Report, University College of Swansea, Department of Education.

References

CCW (1990). *Advisory Paper 7: Economic and Industrial Understanding*, Cardiff, Curriculum Council for Wales.

Davies, P. (1991). 'Review of HMI reports on economic awareness, 1977–90', *Economic Awareness*, vol. 1, no. 1, pp. 26–30.

Denby, N. (1993). 'EIU: sorting it out at Key Stages 3 and 4', *Economic Awareness*, vol. 5, no. 3, pp. 6–11.

Denby, N. (1994). Unpublished dissertation, University of Manchester.

DES (1987). *Economic Understanding in the Curriculum*, London, HMSO.

HMI (1990). *Statement on Business and Economics Education*, unpublished, distributed through LEAs.

NCC (1989). *Curriculum Guidance 3: The Whole Curriculum*, York, National Curriculum Council.

NCC (1990). *Curriculum Guidance 4: Education for Economic and Industrial Understanding,* York, National Curriculum Council.

NICC (1989). *Cross-Curricular Themes: Consultation Report*, Belfast, Northern Ireland Curriculum Council.

Pearce, I. (1989). 'Putting Perspectives into Perspective – A Personal Exploration of the Meaning of Economic Awareness in Economics', *Forum*, London, National Curriculum Council, spring 1989.

TVEI (1989). *Economic and Industrial Understanding: A Pupil Entitlement in the National Curriculum in Wales*, Cardiff, Technical and Vocational Education Initiative, Task Group Report.

9 Global perspectives

Nigel West

Why global perspectives are essential

This chapter begins with a question for the reader: 'Why do you teach your students economics or business studies?' There will, undoubtedly, be a number of different answers to that question, but one of them must be 'to make sense of the world in which we live'. The course you teach should equip the students with the skills to understand the world better.

As consumers, they will have to make choices between different goods and services, and they should be aware of the implications of those choices (for example, there are wide variations in the proportion of the retail price paid to the growers of different brands of coffee). As producers, they should be aware of the changes that are taking place in production processes (an example here might be the connection between the expansion of textile production in Asia and the increased unemployment in the UK textile industry). Perhaps most importantly, as citizens who should be encouraged to play an active part in the social and political life of their community, they need to be able to make sense of the different economic policies being proposed by different political parties and political commentators. Students need to realize that there are different approaches to interpreting economic experience, implying different theoretical perspectives for the explanation of economic activity.

It is also important to recognize that the perspectives of the majority of the world's people, who live in countries of 'the South' (see the note at the end of the chapter), will often be very different from the perspectives of British or American textbook writers and teachers. For example, how does Odhiambo Anacleti's perception of the global economy (see Figure 19.1) match those presented in your students' standard texts?

Sadly, this is rarely recognized in many introductory texts for teaching economics, either as a discrete subject or as part of a business studies course. All too often, students' first experience of 'economics' is as a body of theory that is presented as neutral, uncontroversial, scientific and value-free. This conflicts with their everyday experience of seeing argument over the appropriateness of economic policies on the news almost daily. I believe strongly that such teaching not only misleads and confuses students, but also puts a number of students off the subject, as not being relevant to the real world. I would like to see students being taught within a framework where they approach all study of economics and business, from day one, with an awareness of the range of

Odhiambo Anacleti is from Tanzania. After many years working for his government, he joined a large non-governmental development agency and became their Country Representative in Tanzania, before moving to the UK, where he is now a Communications Officer. He was asked to contribute the passage below, giving his perspective on 'How the global economy works'. It is a perspective to which students of economics are rarely exposed. It is shared by many others, but should not be seen as 'the African perspective'.

'The greatest mistake made in the twentieth century is the assumption that once the Cold War was over, everybody would be happy thereafter. As in any war, the Cold War ended with the celebrations of the victors and left the victims licking their wounds. The mistake was that the victors never thought ahead to what they would do with the conquered territories, especially those that had been endowed with political ideology but very little economic base.

'Up to the end of the cold war these countries had got assistance, both political and economic, provided you sang the right war song. After the cold war there was only one war song, of free trade and the power of the market. The victors of the Cold War were in competition with each other; but they have made rules which do not harm themselves.

'The poor countries have been divided among the victors. Given the colonial and neo-colonial experience, the victorious West decided that it would profit from the victory but would not take care of the drop off from the war. At the same time the West realized it could not ignore these countries, especially in Africa. The West therefore resorted to history and borrowed a chapter from the League of Nations in 1919.

'The poor countries, including the defeated Eastern Bloc, were therefore economically mandated to the Bretton Woods institutions (the IMF and World Bank) to administer and rule economically. The conqueror nations through G7 ensured the political order was maintained. The new sanction to make the countries obey was AID. Those countries that did not comply with the new rules would be denied the aid. Such a step would be recommended to the powers by the IMF and World Bank.

'However, it was not realized that the IMF and World Bank were established to manage finances and not production. Hence what has happened is that while all countries have been instructed to manage their financial systems, many have never developed their production systems. As a result fewer and fewer goods have been produced, leading to less and less money, and more and more control by the Fund and the Bank. No wonder the Fund has turned into what (former Tanzanian President) Nyerere recently called the "International Ministry of Finance".

'The global economy now works on the basis of conqueror takes all. The Western powers that won the political ideological war have also assumed political economic control, and are guarding it jealously against any newcomers. This is proved by the way the East Asian countries are praised with fear, and how Chinese and Vietnamese economic success and growth rates are kept as top secrets in the Western media and economic circles.

'One could say that the world economy is being controlled by economically declining powers who want to prove that decline is a success.'

Figure 19.1 An African perspective on the global economy

perspectives. Economic literacy implies that students are able to understand debates about the economy and thus evaluate the relative merits of different perspectives on economics; but how can this be achieved if their teaching is based upon *the* economics perspective rather than addressing *alternative* theoretical approaches? This chapter outlines a framework for an approach using different perspectives. Examples of classroom activities are given, and some sources of resources are listed towards the end of the chapter.

Even within a more conventional approach to teaching economics and business, there are opportunities to bring more of a global dimension to examples throughout the course. It would be interesting, for example, to explore the supply and demand curves for a cash crop such as coffee. If the demand for coffee is relatively inelastic, what will be the result of a large number of Southern countries increasing their supply, in line with economic policies of 'structural adjustment' implemented as part of an IMF package? Will the producer countries actually gain if they all increase their coffee exports? If not, who might gain, and why have these policies been introduced?

A framework for teaching different viewpoints

It is possible for students to approach economic theory within a framework that enables them to make sense of the different viewpoints that may be held. In a three-year curriculum development project based at Leeds Development Education Centre, the project team focused on *exchange* as the key concept. Specialization, or what economists call 'the division of labour', is a characteristic of almost all societies. As consumers and producers, we all carry out exchange. How is the 'rate of exchange' (or price) between consumers and producers determined? This rate can be interpreted as reflecting the preference of *consumers* who are seeking to maximize utility; the costs faced by *producers* in providing commodities; and the interdependence between producers and consumers reflecting people's role as *citizens*.

Since producers and consumers are part of every economic transaction, potentially there is controversy over the understanding of any economic issue. The differences arise from assumptions about who the key player is within such transactions – is it the consumer, the producer, or the citizen? People with different life experiences, and different ideologies, will make different assumptions and interpret economic reality differently. Analyses based on these different assumptions can each be logically consistent and internally coherent, can each account for actual experience and produce 'facts' to support their conclusions, and can each provide policy prescriptions for perceived problems.

If the consumer is seen as the economic dynamic, then the value of a commodity (as reflected in price) ultimately reflects the utility (pleasure) enjoyed by the individual in its consumption. Consumers have their own subjective preferences, requiring a free market environment through which these can be expressed.

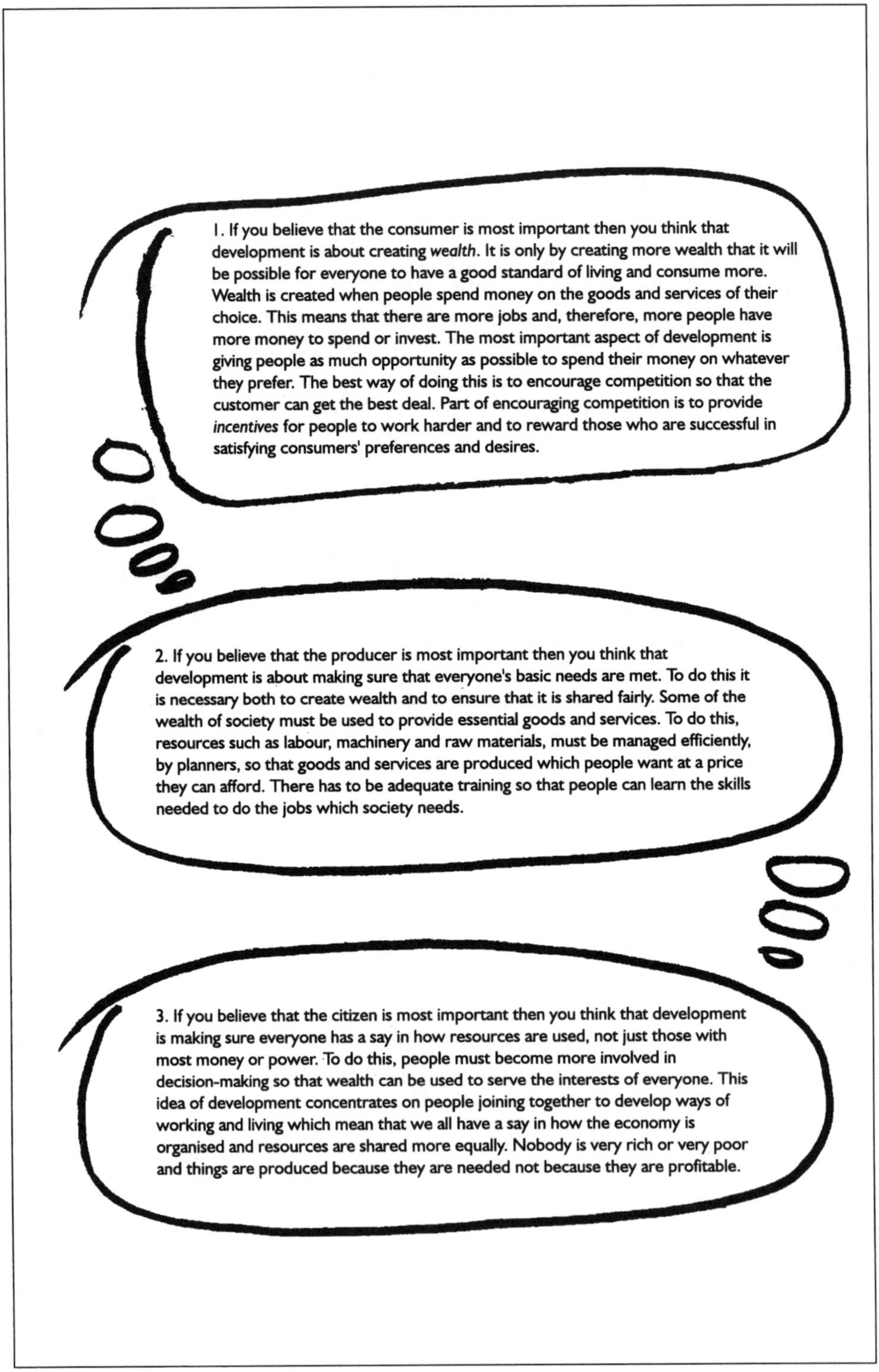

1. If you believe that the consumer is most important then you think that development is about creating *wealth*. It is only by creating more wealth that it will be possible for everyone to have a good standard of living and consume more. Wealth is created when people spend money on the goods and services of their choice. This means that there are more jobs and, therefore, more people have more money to spend or invest. The most important aspect of development is giving people as much opportunity as possible to spend their money on whatever they prefer. The best way of doing this is to encourage competition so that the customer can get the best deal. Part of encouraging competition is to provide *incentives* for people to work harder and to reward those who are successful in satisfying consumers' preferences and desires.

2. If you believe that the producer is most important then you think that development is about making sure that everyone's basic needs are met. To do this it is necessary both to create wealth and to ensure that it is shared fairly. Some of the wealth of society must be used to provide essential goods and services. To do this, resources such as labour, machinery and raw materials, must be managed efficiently, by planners, so that goods and services are produced which people want at a price they can afford. There has to be adequate training so that people can learn the skills needed to do the jobs which society needs.

3. If you believe that the citizen is most important then you think that development is making sure everyone has a say in how resources are used, not just those with most money or power. To do this, people must become more involved in decision-making so that wealth can be used to serve the interests of everyone. This idea of development concentrates on people joining together to develop ways of working and living which mean that we all have a say in how the economy is organised and resources are shared more equally. Nobody is very rich or very poor and things are produced because they are needed not because they are profitable.

Figure 19.2 Views on development

Alternatively, economic prosperity can be seen as a result of the activity of producers. Value and price now reflect the cost of production, and only the *amount supplied* reflects consumers' preferences. The costs of production are determined by the technical use of natural resources and productive inputs, and the price paid for these inputs. The relevant policy concerns are no longer the 'freedom' of markets, but the *management* of markets to create an economic environment conducive to producers (e.g. managing interest rates, exchange rates and consumers' 'effective demand'), the technology of production processes and distributional equity.

Alternatively, individuals' activity as consumers can be understood to reflect their activity as producers – people perform both roles, and it is their power as citizens that is significant in explaining economic behaviour. People are interdependent within society, and it is the social power structure that limits the ways in which people are able to behave both as producers and consumers. Economic questions become questions of social power.

This is a simplified version of an approach that can be found in detail in the book *Why Economists Disagree* (Cole *et al.*, 1991), which provides a model for using this approach to cover both economic theory and the work of individual economists. It provides a framework whereby students can gain an understanding that different perspectives can be logically coherent, although different people will gain and lose as a result of different policy prescriptions that arise. Students at some point will have to choose which analysis is most relevant to their experience and interests. Figure 19.2, taken from the *Economics for Change* series (Holmes and Marshall, 1989), demonstrates how this approach can help students to understand some of the different views on 'development' that are propounded. As teachers, it is important that we present students with a range of viewpoints on such issues, enabling them to make up their own minds. Without such a framework, the classroom activities shown later in this chapter become merely games to use in the classroom.

Methodology: active learning approaches

For the development education worker, 'development' is a process in which we are all involved. At community level, whether in Africa or the UK, this entails people being involved in changes within their community, and taking part in decision-making. A similar approach – of students being actively involved in lessons, with the teacher acting more as facilitator than as expert hander-down of knowledge – is an integral part of good development education resources. Students should be actively involved in the lesson, and use the experience to make up their own minds about the range of viewpoints that are offered.

Active learning methods offer a number of benefits. First, they broaden the range of skills that students are able to develop. In *Triumph of Hope* (Routledge and Harrison,1994), a teaching pack about development and participation in Eritrea, students have to make difficult choices about the allocation of resources to meet needs for food, security and health. The students are divided into six groups, each representing different social groups in Eritrea, such as agropastoralists, town dwellers, crop growers and returned refugees. Meanwhile representatives from the national women's organizations try to ensure that women's interests are recognized. This type of activity encourages students to listen to each other, reach consensus in their small group, develop their communication and debating skills, and gain a deeper understanding of other people's viewpoints. It means that students' learning takes place not only in the 'cognitive', knowledge-focused domain, but also in the 'affective' domain. Students develop some feeling of empathy with the people whose roles they are playing, and gain some insight into how they might view the world. The students are more likely to remember the issues raised because they felt involved in it.

In addition, the above example provides students with information that will increase their knowledge and understanding of real dilemmas in the allocation of scarce resources between competing groups who have different priorities, as well as promoting debate on the meaning of both 'development' and 'democracy' (voting doesn't feel very democratic if you are always in a minority, as tends to happen to the agropastoralists in this activity). For most students, it is also enjoyable and therefore motivating. Some students do not like role-playing, but an activity that allows them time to prepare and present their case as a small group is much less threatening. Finally, and most importantly, a role-play can enable students to explore a range of viewpoints (and may involve them presenting a case they do not personally agree with). This not only ties in with the framework outlined in the previous section, but also allows the teacher to teach about controversial issues such as inequality, without pushing a particular 'line'.

As well as role-plays and simulation games, development education resources make extensive use of group activities using photographs. These can be particularly useful for the teacher to discover what assumptions students bring to a topic, as well as developing a range of skills. For example, they can be used to raise questions about the economist's definition of 'production' – if 'work', according to the economist, has to be paid for, what are the implications for those people, most notably women, involved in unpaid domestic work?

Activities for the classroom

International trade and structural adjustment

Few economics textbooks bring a range of perspectives to their study of international trade. 'Free' trade and the reduction of tariffs is generally seen as 'a good thing'; it is rare to find discussion of the unequal power relationships between the countries involved, debate usually being limited to the utopia of 'perfect competition'. An interesting case study is that of bananas, covered in the short and readable pamphlet *A Buyer's Market* (Dalton,1994).

The 1994 GATT ruling, ending protection to 'ACP' banana producers such as the Windward Islands, is likely to have a catastrophic impact on them, because they will be unable to compete with large plantations in Central America. These plantations are owned by huge US fruit companies. The social (and ecological) costs of their operations, often with the connivance of local elites, have led to increased landlessness and poverty in Central America, but the economies of scale they 'enjoy' over small producers in the Windward Islands means that their costs are much lower. So in this case 'free' trade will benefit a small number of multinational companies, and possibly Northern consumers; but will damage the economy of several Caribbean islands – especially small farmers and their families – and possibly lead to further landlessness in Central America.

Of course, 'free' markets do not extend to the 'free' movement of labour between countries. If the theory of comparative advantage is at all valid, this would lead to increased migration from low-wage to high-wage economies, and a move towards more equal wage rates globally. This would reduce poverty in Southern countries; but since it would also reduce wages in Northern countries, barriers to migration prevent it happening. Similarly, the theory would imply that capital should flow to low-wage economies, whereas in fact the opposite is the case.

Role-play can be used to explore a range of perspectives on these issues. Many Southern countries have been compelled, by the 'debt crisis', to adopt Structural Adjustment Programmes (SAPs) at the behest of the IMF. These SAPs include measures to attract foreign investment and open up markets to 'free' competition, denying the ideals of 'social responsibility' that were formerly at the heart of development policy in, for example, Tanzania, which nationalized foreign plantations after independence in an attempt to reduce capital outflows, prioritize food security and retain control over the national economy. Since 1988, when the first IMF agreement was signed, this policy has been reversed, and multinational companies (MNCs) are now returning.

Working in groups, students explore the issues and make decisions from three perspectives –of a multinational company, of the Tanzanian government, and of the peasants who are currently farming the land. In each case, students can carry out simple cost–benefit analysis, and then report back their decisions to the whole class.

Inevitably, final discussion will focus on where real power lies. The students' analysis may look something like Figure 19.3.

While the MNC has a serious analysis to carry out (which would depend on alternative locations), the Tanzanian government has little choice but to offer encouragement (perhaps including tax incentives). The peasant farmers can be asked to decide whether to seek work on the plantation, try to farm more marginal land, or head for the city. The options open to women and men will be different, and students should discuss this also.

MULTINATIONAL COMPANY

BENEFITS

- Cheap land; government needs to sell, due to debts.
- Low wages
- Government policy (SAP) to encourage investment
- History of political stability
- New markets; South Africa

COSTS

- Poor infrastructure (roads, communications)
- Socialist traditions; mistrust of MNCs
- Little experience of 'free enterprise' culture

TANZANIAN GOVERNMENT

BENEFITS

- Foreign exchange (needed urgently; 60% of earnings go on debt repayments)
- Investment (government has no money for this)
- Jobs and training
- Will please the IMF; more chance of future loans

COSTS

- Profits will leave Tanzania
- Lack of control over the company's plans
- Land used for cash crops, will reduce food output for domestic food security
- Cash crops could undercut Tanzanian growers
- Must pay compensation to dispossessed farmers

TANZANIAN PEASANT FARMERS

BENEFITS

- May be jobs for some on the MNC plantation
- May be compensation payment

COSTS

- Loss of land
- Alternative land likely to be more marginal and/or smaller plots

Figure 19.3 Specimen student analysis following a role-play

The background information needed for this activity is available (West, 1995), as is an alternative version using tobacco production in Brazil (Holmes and Marshall, 1989).

Gender and development

Women's experiences of the economy – whether in a 'Southern' or 'Northern' country – are generally different from those of men. As Sue Hatt comments in Chapter 9, the role of women has only recently, if at all, been recognized in most economics texts. The experience of poor women from 'Southern' countries is doubly excluded. In the Tanzanian example given above, it is likely to be men who control money from cash cropping (and are more likely to obtain higher-paid work on the plantation), while women will be primarily responsible for subsistence crops and domestic work. In all societies, the economist's 'tradeoff' between paid work and 'leisure' will seem absurd to women as they carry out a disproportionate burden of domestic work.

STATEMENTS FOR DIAMOND RANKING

WOMEN HAVE CHILDREN

Women don't need to be financially independent of men because all they do is get married and have children.

YOUR OWN CHILDREN

It is up to women themselves to decide what they want to do. It isn't up to other people, like the government, to interfere. Anyway, there's nothing wrong with being a housewife or a mother.

WOMEN SHOULDN'T WORK

In a time of high unemployment women should not expect to go out to work. It's better if they stay at home and look after the children so there there are enough jobs for men.

WOMEN DO IT ALL

Women are financially worse off than men because men are lazy and con't do any of the housework or childcare, so women have to do it all and they don't get paid for it.

WOMEN HAVE SKILLS

Women have many skills and abilities which they learn whilst running a home but these are not recognised by employers when women apply for paid work.

WOMEN DO UNPAID WORK

Women are economically worse off because society does not take responsibility for child care, looking after the elderly, people with disabilities and so on, but leaves this to women to do for nothing.

WOMEN NEED NEW SKILLS

To improve their economic position, women need help to develop the skills necessary to get them paid work.

MEN WON'T CHANGE

Women are economically worse off than men because men won't change as they are worried that change will mean that they lose out. If men won't change then it's up to women to change things for

NEED LAWS FOR EQUALITY

Women are economically worse off because there hasn't been enough government support for laws to promote equality.

Figure 19.4 Why is women's work paid less than men's?

257

The activity in Figure 19.4, taken from *Economics for Change* (Holmes and Marshall, 1989), provides nine possible 'reasons' why women's work is on average paid less than men's. These can be photocopied, cut up, and discussed and ranked by students, working in small groups. They will have to give reasons for choosing which of the statements is most important. This can be followed up by relating the statements to the viewpoints outlined earlier, and to aspects of economic theory previously taught.

Teaching about an unequal world; should there be a moral dimension?

Enough has been written, in this book and elsewhere, to convince teachers of economics and business that their teaching of the subject cannot be objective. To quote from the popular *Economics Explained* (Maunder *et al.*, 1987):

'Do not get the impression that a textbook author will be able to keep his or her values out of the book. They will slip through. In fact, the choice itself of which topics to include in an introductory textbook involves normative economics.'

Teaching about global issues brings up discussion of poverty and inequality on a large scale. There will be issues that are outside the scope of economics; it is no bad thing for students to recognize that the subject has limits. But economics and business studies have a great deal to offer if poverty is to be understood and tackled. Teaching materials need an economic dimension; it won't do to see the problems as caused simply by people not being fair to others. There are economic reasons for global inequality.

The example in Figure 19.5, taken from *Hanging by a Thread* (Borowski and West,1992), requires students, in groups, to argue the case for how much each stage of the production process *ought* to receive for their contribution to a pair of jeans. (Each group receives more information to support their case.) Even though they know that little goes back to the producer country, they are shocked to discover how little (around 60p). Of course, even less goes back to the farmers themselves. In discussing why this is the case, there is need for economic analysis – supply and demand, factors determining wage rates, international trade, tariff barriers on manufactured goods, etc. But this still offers only a partial explanation; the student will also need to understand political, social, historical and geographical factors. Similarly, students are often shocked to discover that, in recent years, capital flows from 'South' to 'North' have greatly exceeded those (including aid) in the opposite direction.

The reaction of most of us to the extreme poverty that makes the TV news is that it is unacceptable; hence the millions of pounds donated by the public to the development agencies. Where economics can contribute is in suggesting some prescriptions for tackling the situation, but it cannot of course be tackled by economics alone.

A PIECE OF THE ACTION

A pair of ordinary 100% cotton jeans, made in the UK, sold by a large British retailer using their own brand name costs about £24.

The diagram below shows the production sequence of a pair of jeans from the cotton on a bush in Tanzania to the finished garment on the peg in a high street shop.

You are part of this production sequence. How much of the £24 do you think you should get?

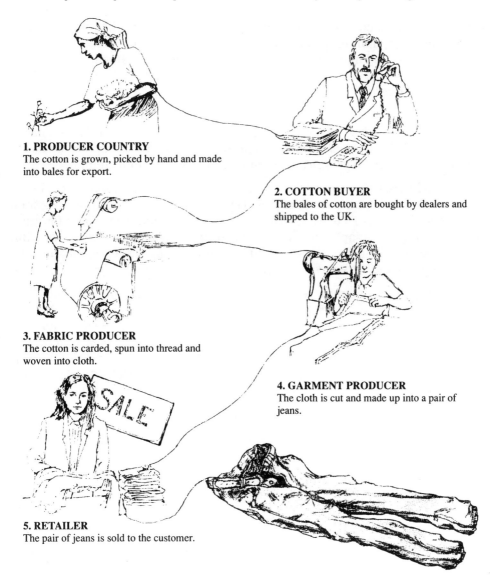

1. PRODUCER COUNTRY
The cotton is grown, picked by hand and made into bales for export.

2. COTTON BUYER
The bales of cotton are bought by dealers and shipped to the UK.

3. FABRIC PRODUCER
The cotton is carded, spun into thread and woven into cloth.

4. GARMENT PRODUCER
The cloth is cut and made up into a pair of jeans.

5. RETAILER
The pair of jeans is sold to the customer.

Figure 19.5 Teaching about an unequal world

Sources of resources

New development and global education resources appear regularly, and often have a short print run. With a little effort, teachers of economics and business studies can keep themselves up to date with a rewarding selection of materials. Most useful can be regular visits to the local Development Education Centre (there are around 50 in the UK, although some are very small). The Development Education Association can put you in contact with your nearest centre. It is also worth obtaining the annual education catalogues from Oxfam, and the Development Education Dispatch Unit, both of which handle materials from a number of different publishers. ActionAid, Christian Aid, CAFOD and Save the Children Fund produce their own educational catalogues.

Background reading

Oxfam and Christian Aid also produce regular, adult-level reports that are useful to teachers. *The Trade Trap, For Richer for Poorer* and *A Simple Guide to Structural Adjustment* (all published by Oxfam) and *Banking on the Poor: The Ethics of Third World Debt* (Christian Aid) are current examples.

Why Economists Disagree: The Political Economy of Economics by Cole, Cameron and Edwards (Longman, 1991) provides a detailed analysis of different theoretical perspectives on economics, and is invaluable reading for anyone wanting to adopt this approach in their teaching. *Understanding Economics* by Cole (Pluto Press, 1995) is an interesting resource, making use of flow charts and cartoons to illustrate the different perspectives.

On gender and economics, teachers are recommended to read *Beyond Economic Man: Feminist Theory and Economics*, edited by Ferber and Nelson (University of Chicago Press, 1993). Also useful, although written for the American market, is *Race and Gender in the American Economy: Views from Across the Spectrum*, edited by Feiner (Prentice-Hall, 1994). *Half the World, Half a Chance* is one of several resources on gender and development published by Oxfam.

Resources for classroom use

Probably the best-known resource is Christian Aid's classic *Trading Game*, where students 'compete' to produce specific shapes from paper – the rich countries have the technology, the poor have only raw materials. Enjoyable to play, the game's ultimate effectiveness depends on the debriefing (and, again, an awareness of inequalities within, as well as between, countries). A more complex adaptation, *Market Trading*, focuses on the impact of the European Single Market on Southern countries; it takes time to prepare, but students learn a great deal. Other games that look at trade include *Trading Trainers* (CAFOD) and *The Coffee Chain Game* (Oxfam).

Leeds Development Education Centre has emphasized economic perspectives in many of its active learning resources. The *Economics for Change* series consists of five units (Sexism, Racism, Class Inequality, Development, and Power and Decision-Making), with activities suitable for the 14+ age range. *Hanging by a Thread: Trade, Debt and Cotton in Tanzania* explores the problems of dependency on cash crops whose prices have slumped on world commodity markets, and the impact of IMF-imposed Structural Adjustment Programmes on small farmers. Useful resources for the post-16 teacher available through the DEDU catalogue) include *Balancing the Books: Development Choices in Namibia*; and *Triumph of Hope: Eritrea's Struggle for Development*; and *Shifting Sands,* which looks at the impact of externally supported 'development' projects on the pastoralist people of India's Thar desert.

Birmingham DEC is producing cross-curricular materials to encourage economic understanding at Key Stages 3 and 4. They include *The Global Money Machine*, with a focus on Taiwan. Save the Children Fund have produced an excellent pack, *Dealing with Debt*, which links the debt problems of individuals in the UK to the impact of the debt crisis on Southern countries. Finally, for teachers wanting to use case studies from Southern countries in their teaching, Glanville's *Introduction to Development Economics* (available from the author – see 'Useful addresses') is designed to fit existing economics syllabuses.

Some useful addresses

ActionAid, Hamlyn House, Macdonald Rd., London N19 5PG (tel. 0171 281 4101)

Birmingham DEC, Gillett Centre, Selly Oak Colleges, Bristol Rd., Birmingham B29 6LE (tel. 0121 472 3255)

CAFOD, Romero Close, Stockwell Rd., London SW9 9TY (tel. 0171 733 7900)

Christian Aid, PO Box 100, London SE1 7RT (tel. 0171 620 4444)

Development Education Association, 29–31 Cowper Street, London EC2A 4AP (tel. 0171 490 8108)

Development Education Dispatch Unit, Leeds DEC, 153 Cardigan Rd, Leeds LS6 1LJ (tel. 0113 278 4030)

Alan Glanville, 31 Hobson Rd., Summertown, Oxford.

Oxfam, 274 Banbury Rd, Oxford OX2 7DZ (tel. 01865 311311)

Save the Children Fund, Mary Batchelor House, 17 Grove Lane, Camberwell, London SE5 8RD (tel. 0171 703 5400)

References

Borowski, R. and West, N. (1992). *Hanging by a Thread: Trade, Debt and Cotton in Tanzania*, Leeds Development Education Centre.

Cole, K., Cameron, J. and Edwards, C. (1991). *Why Economists Disagree*, London, Longman.

Dalton, D. (1994). *A Buyer's Market: Global Trade, Southern Poverty and Northern Action*, London, Christian Aid, Oxfam and WDM.

Ferber, M. and Nelson, J. (eds) (1993). *Beyond Economic Man: Feminist Theory and Economics*, Chicago, University of Chicago Press.

Holmes, M. and Marshall, J. (1989). *Economics for Change* (5 units), Leeds Development Education Centre.

Maunder, P., Myers, D., Wall, N. and LeRoy Miller, R. (1987). *Economics Explained*, London, Collins Educational.

Routledge, L. and Harrison, G. (1994). *Triumph of Hope: Eritrea's Struggle for Development*, Leeds Development Education Centre.

West, N. (1995). *Time for Tea?*, Leeds Development Education Centre.

End note

The term 'the South' is used in this chapter to refer to countries in Asia, Africa and Latin America. This is in preference to the term 'Third World' which has been criticized for failing to recognize global interdependence, for implying a 'third class' status to people in those countries, and for failing to recognize the differences between (and within) those countries.Similarly, if 'development' is seen as an ongoing process in which we are all involved, all countries can be seen as 'developing'.

The debate about terminology is important, but cannot be fully covered in this chapter. 'Countries of the South' is a more acceptable term (though not geographically accurate, and glossing over inequalities *within* countries). The author prefers 'the majority countries', but this is not in common useage.

Environmental perspectives

Ken Webster

Whither economics?

Anyone wishing to teach economics or business 'with the environment' – and this must now be inescapable – is faced with a dilemma. Either they accept the environment as just a new element in their teaching, or they sit back in their chair and wonder whether 'environment' is an invitation to think through rather more closely what it is they are teaching, and why. Two witnesses from a whole raft of thinkers will suffice to explain the dilemma. First the radical.

Henderson, in her book *Paradigms in Progress* (1991, pp. 76–7), insists that global environmentalism and what she calls its underlying 'eco-philosophy' will compete with conventional economic philosophies at their core:

'Increasingly, political parties, corporate ethics statements, major magazines, and new journals are espousing environmentalism – only to learn that its inescapable conclusions challenge almost everything they have been taught to believe in: economic growth, technological progress, the Protestant ethic, materialism, individualistic market competition, even scientific theories based in the mechanistic world views of Isaac Newton and René Descartes.

'A case in point is a ... survey of the environment, "Costing the Earth", published by ... The Economist. The intellectual contortions of the editors were evident in the title, as well as in an editorial, "Growth Can Be Green", which made heroic efforts to salvage the now dysfunctional discipline of economics, whose narrow, short-sighted accounting systems have proved clearly culpable in causing many environmental problems. Economic growth could be reformed and "green growth will indeed be somewhat slower than a dash for the dirty variety", The Economist admitted, adding that "at present, most economic activity takes little account of the costs it imposes on its surroundings. Factories pollute rivers as if the rinsing waters flowed past them for free, power stations burn coal without charging customers for the effects of carbon dioxide belched into the atmosphere, loggers destroy forests without a care for the impact on wildlife or climate. These bills are left for others to pick up – neighbors, citizens of other countries and future generations".'

She quotes *The Economist* a little further:

'... conventional statistics of economic growth are ... particularly blind to

the environment, National income accounts (Gross National Product) take no notice of the value of natural resources: a country that cut down all its trees, sold them as wood chips and gambled away the money ... would appear from its national accounts to have got richer in terms of GNP per person. Equally, they show measures to tackle pollution as bonuses, not burdens ... It would be easier for politicians to talk rationally about effects of sensible environmental policies on growth if governments agreed to remove some of these oddities from the way they keep their economic books.' ...

'Yet kissing such a massive turnaround off as a new verity, which economic theory has already embraced, is little more than barefaced intellectual sleight of hand.'

Henderson is clearly very angry with economists who seek to defend existing models and spend their time 'monetizing' environmental 'externalities' as a way of salvaging a philosophy. She goes further to note that 'Herbert Simon, when accepting his Nobel Prize in Economics, stated that he had not used economic models for a decade and had switched to game theory and other decision sciences.'

Closer to home, as it were, for the second of the two witnesses to upheaval is Ormerod (1994) and his book *The Death of Economics*. In it he notes (pp. 36–7) that the basis of conventional economics is flawed and comparable to the outlook of physical science in the Middle Ages. Ormerod partly rejects conventional economics because of its over-emphasis on the mechanistic Newtonian world view and its linear deterministic models, much as Henderson and Simon have done.

'Economists see the world as a machine. A very complicated one perhaps, but nevertheless a machine, whose workings can be understood by putting together carefully and meticulously its component parts. The behaviour of the system as a whole can be deduced from a simple aggregation of these components. A lever pulled in a certain part of the machine with a certain strength will have regular and predictable outcomes elsewhere in the machine. In the basement of the London School of Economics lives a wondrous object. In the 1950s, Bill Phillips, an engineer turned economist, built a machine to teach his students the workings of the economy. Levers are pulled, buttons pressed. Sluice gates open, and liquids of different colours rush round the tubes of the system in a controlled way. This marvellous machine still survives, the very embodiment of the economist's view of the world.

'Environmentalists, by contrast, see the world as a living organism. Prodding the system in a certain way in a certain place may sometimes cause the beast to hop in one direction, sometimes in another, and sometimes it will not move at all. The behaviour of the system may well be quite different from what might be anticipated from extrapolation of the model of the behaviour of individuals. Individual behaviour does not take

place in isolation. On the contrary, there are impacts on the behaviour of other individuals, which in turn cause feedback elsewhere in the system, and so on and so forth. Behaviour is altogether too complex to be captured by a mechanistic approach.'

Ormerod also engages with Rational Economic Man (of late, 'Person') – that mainstay of economics. Using behavioural studies done by Robert Axelrod (1984) and others, he is convinced that people cooperate far more frequently than the postulates of self-interested calculation allow. Ormerod writes (p. 35):

'This is the real challenge which environmental thinking poses to the economic orthodoxy. The benefits of cooperative behaviour are a key proposition of environmentalists, who, in sharp contrast to the individualistic behavioural model of orthodox economics, have stressed from the outset the fundamental interdependence and interconnectedness of human actions.'

The nature of the dilemma appears clearer now. On the one hand there is the well worked out economics of a world that is assumed to be like a machine, in principle predictable, made up of a myriad of tiny actors all operating according to rational and individualistic welfare-maximizing strategies. In this version of economics the environment is something to allow for, something to bring into a form of market *mechanism*. Monetizing assists this process of integration, ideally, allowing rational decision-making in an extended context. Environmental (and social issues) are assumed to accommodate themselves to the economic rationale. The emphasis is on valuing (monetizing) rather than values (normative statements). This economics believes there to be an objective world out there and to be part of the study of the objective world (science).

On the other hand there is the emerging economics of the open system. The world is viewed as a complex, dynamic and fundamentally interconnected system – no longer predictable in the mechanistic sense and no longer made up of a narrowly self-seeking collection of economic actors. In this dynamic system, the environment – or more properly the biosphere – is one of two overarching contexts (the other is social) within which economic activity takes place. Economics therefore describes a subset of activities that operate within ecological (and social) constraints. These constraints are values (normative statements), so the role of monetizing as a guide to decision-making is useful but limited. For these economists the world is as much 'in here' (a function of our perceptions of it) as 'out there', and economics no longer pretends to be value-free.

For the teacher, the dilemma prompted by the need to incorporate 'the environment' in economics lessons can be summarized as whether to value (monetize) or whether values themselves are to be the main topic of discussion.

That there is an issue, let alone a profound dilemma, is not clear from a look at some of the mainstream texts available to teachers of economics and

265

business. It is almost as if the foregoing argument were interesting but not entirely relevant. The writers have gone down the monetarizing route if they have gone very far at all.

The monetarizing route

Since business education's ethos is the equivalent of individualism, part of the credo of a reductionist method – merely replacing the Economic Person by the rational Economic Company – it will come as no surprise to see a diagram like Figure 20.1 in a text for business education. Examine the diagram, which purports to show the inputs and outputs of a firm. This was produced in 1994 for a new, supposedly enlightened, vocationally oriented qualification. What is missing?

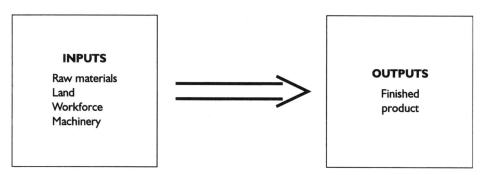

Figure 20.1 The 'inputs' and 'outputs' of a firm

The social and environmental context, that's all! It is almost as though the author considered that the proper remit of business was narrow and the rest could be taken as given.

It is worth a moment to look at some of the 'givens' in this context. The book *Functions of Nature* (deGroot, 1992, p. 20) lists the *regulatory* functions of the natural environment (among a number of other functions):

- *protection against harmful cosmic influences*
- *regulation of the local and global energy balance*
- *regulation of the chemical composition of the atmosphere*
- *regulation of the chemical composition of the oceans*
- *regulation of the local and global climate (incl. water cycle)*
- *regulation of runoff and flood prevention*
- *water catchment and groundwater recharge*
- *prevention of soil erosion and sediment control*
- *formation of topsoil and maintenance of soil fertility*
- *fixation of solar energy and biomass production*
- *storing and recycling of organic matter*
- *storing and recycling of nutrients*

266

- *storing and recycling of human waste*
- *regulation of biological control mechanisms*
- *maintenance of migration and nursery habitats*
- *maintenance of biological and genetic diversity.*

The firm can both influence the degree to which the biosphere is able to provide these services and must utterly depend upon them continuing. How does or should the firm depicted in Figure 20.1 take cognisance of these services? If the firm were suddenly moved to the Moon one imagines that its directors would have more discussion about the functions of a natural environment and its role in their business inputs and outputs.

There is the social side of the firm to consider as well (at least if one agrees that the purpose of economics is to improve the 'quality' of human existence). Customers, people living near to the firm, employees and citizenry generally have a stake in any setup that claims to be a truly responsible business. So the firm's inputs and outputs should include something about its social inputs and outputs.

Henderson uses a diagram (p. 30) – which she calls the 'Three Layer Cake with Icing' – to put the social, environmental and money economies in perspective (see Figure 20.2).

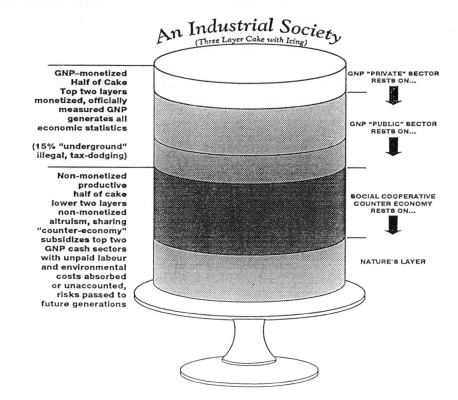

Figure 20.2 An industrial society

While the premise of the 'production process' modelled in Figure 20.1 seems to be that the icing *is* the cake, Henderson attempts to give a leading place to the social and environmental layers of the confection. To the teacher it must be becoming clear that there is a fundamental conflict of values hidden deep within the 'environmental perspective'. Is the icing or the whole cake to be the central concern of economics and business courses?

Not all texts are as naive as our earlier example from which Figure 20.1 is taken, and even that does talk of the physical environment as something the firm must take cognisance of – at least if its market includes appealing to green consumers and if it must take note of government regulation. It is as though 'the environment' is an irritant to business or just another market opportunity. Medieval thinking indeed.

The 'sustainability' route

Many modern businesses, especially the larger firms, are looking towards coming to terms with the environment, through something called 'sustainable development'.

Unhappily, even 'sustainable development' – something of a buzz phrase, with in excess of 65 active definitions according to Jonathan Porritt – does not really heal the gap because it comes in at least two modes. In its *strong* mode it includes the idea that decision-making has to include the social, ethical, environmental and economic for sustainability to have a chance. According to Ekins (1992), such 'green economics' has 'two central objectives in its thinking about allocation and distribution: the elimination of poverty and the mainte-nance of the economy at its *optimal ecological size*' (emphasis added).

In sustainability's *weak* mode there is 'sustainable growth' (e.g. EBEA, 1995). This is, more or less, 'business as usual' but with less impact on the environ-ment; but for cynics it is little more than the 'greening' of business. In support of this approach economists have not been slow to attempt to absorb the debate as being one of market failure (see Figure 20.3 for a summary), and the better textbooks and resource packs have engaged wholeheartedly in this arena.

But Henderson's 'intellectual sleight of hand' is present. For example IUCN, WWF and UNEP, in their publication *Caring for the Earth: A Strategy for Sustainable Living* (IUCN, 1991), contend that there is just no such thing as sustainable growth:

'The confusion has been caused because "sustainable development", "sustainable growth" and "sustainable use" have been used interchangeably, as if their meanings were the same. They are not. "Sustainable growth" is a contradiction in terms: nothing physical can grow indefinitely (p. 10).'

Be this as it may – and it has echoes of Henderson's and Ormerod's criticisms

In the present climate of liberalization and deregulation, neoclassical economics has emerged as an aspiring colonist of this tantalising, but hazardous intellectual territory. Drawing on the concept of social cost introduced by A. C. Pigou, economists have characterized environmental damage as a loss of utility to society as a whole. Monetary value has been proposed as the most appropriate index or yardstick for the measurement of the benefits that are foregone as a consequence of damage to the environment. In the case of those environmental effects that remain unpriced in any market, the problem is to derive monetary values by various analytical means.

Where the economic cost of a reduction in environmental benefits is not included in the price of a commodity, the value of the lost benefits is said to be 'external' to that price. Economists view this as a classic case of market failure: their prescription for countering environmental damage is to incorporate these costs into the market price through taxation or other regulatory mechanisms. In this way, they claim, the allocation of resources is optimized with respect both to economic and environmental factors.

Figure 20.3 Markets and the environment – a summary from Stirling (1993)

of the basis of conventional economics – the weak sustainability approach remains dominant in education circles. So it is that the same textbook that inadequately described the inputs and outputs of the firm (Figure 20.1) without pausing for breath also includes an assignment to promote and sell a green product!

Perhaps this is real life, real business and 'real economy' thinking. Typical examples of 'greening' are reducing energy and raw materials usage, recycling packaging and industrial wastes, reducing wastes, environmental audits, and developing and selling products from sustainable sources. In these ways more businesses *are* greening themselves, while attempting to sell more and more to consumers who can adopt a green veneer by pushing the 'more and more' through a recycling system.

But there are hints of changing values within the system that are hard for teachers of economics to engage with in a neoclassical mindset, because decisions appear to be based on the question 'How *should* we do business?' rather than 'Can I show this in the accounts?'. An example is included in Figure 20.4.

While most people will applaud firms attempting this change of culture, the fact remains that the change is effectively one of preserving the existing regime – based on maximizing production and consumption – while allaying fears that this will crock the ecosystem (and continue to contribute to a global trade system that arguably guarantees poverty for the majority). It is arguable that classroom work on the role of business and the environment or environmental economics must engage in this contrast between, on the one hand, the economics of the promotion of wants and economic growth and, on the other hand, the meeting of needs sustainably with a truly 'humanistic economics' (Lutz and Lux, 1988).

The author, through the offices of WWF (UK), is currently working with B&Q, the DIY retail giant, on materials and stimulus resources for business education. B&Q has a proactive approach to environmental issues using environmental audits within stores and with suppliers, providing training in such matters for staff, and supplying information to customers. B&Q's Environmental Manager, Dr Alan Knight, was interviewed with the intention of gaining access to some of the business thinking and research which prompted the considerable investment of time and money in environmental policy.

There was none. Dr Knight insisted that the policy decision was taken at board level on the basis that it was something a responsible large business should do.

He indicated that there was no demonstrable effect on sales, no clear-cut evidence of cost savings overall, and yet the benefits were real and often non-monetary – in, for example, how staff felt about B&Q, in relationships with suppliers; in terms of working conditions in factories in some developing countries; in terms of how the public at large felt about B&Q: was it 'a good firm'?

Yet he was quick to assert that B&Q would rather sell you three hammers when you needed only one. A recognition of the power of markets and individual firm's competitiveness sits side by side with decisions that are normative – anecdotal evidence perhaps of a transitional period into an economics and business environment which better accommodates the other layers of the Henderson cake (Figure 20.2).

Figure 20.4 How green is a hammer?

In the classroom

How limited the conventional analysis might be when measured against the demands of changing 'world views' can be deduced from a worked classroom example, given here in summary but with sufficient detail for the practitioner to understand the development of the learning situation. What follows is an adaptation (Webster and Ekins, 1995) of the famous production exercise *Trade Game* produced by Christian Aid. This has many similarities to production games used in business education. It points up the general preconceptions of economics or business students and the kinds of questions and reflections necessary to penetrate beyond the conventional wisdom.

Introduction

The game is run a first time to illustrate some of the 'conventional wisdom' of economics:

- that trade, the division of labour, competition, all increase production;
- that money as a medium of exchange and store of value has a role in this process;

- that resource-rich and technologically advanced groups tend to dominate a trading system;

- that organizational and entrepreneurial skills can affect the outcome or success of the individual or group.

In succeeding stages the game is run to reflect the existence of an ecological base, which should encourage students to reflect on the difference between 'needs' and 'wants' as well as aspects of social justice.

Classroom organization

Up to six groups are supplied with resources as in Figure 20.5. Each group represents a trading nation. The intention of such groupings is to suggest a system where resources are unevenly provided, so prompting trading activity. The resources for each group are placed in a large envelope so that the uneven distribution of resources is not apparent when students enter the room.

The rules of the game are read out . The instruction is: 'Make shapes'. The rules indicate that production shapes can be sold to a world bank (representing world-wide demand). A student is usually assigned the job of world bank . The prices for shapes vary according to the shape and to the material from which it is constructed.

The game ends after an allotted time. Students are then asked to rejoin their group and consider:

- whether they thought they were a successful group;

- how they would allocate accumulated cash and resources between themselves;

- how they would improve their performance if the game were rerun.

Two sets of each of the following to make enough for six groups:

A
1 pair of scissors
2 rulers
1 compass
1 set-square
1 protractor
1 sheet of green card
6 'pound notes'
4 pencils

B
8 sheets of red card
2 sheets of green card
2 'pound notes'

C
2 sheets of green card
4 sheets of red card
2 'pound notes'
2 pencils
2 sheets of cardboard

Figure 20.5 Resources for the trading game

Debriefing

The debriefing has two phases:

- Groups first say how they felt. The teacher could use questions such as 'How did you get on?', 'How do you feel about what happened?', 'What did you think about the X group?', 'How did you relate to the world bank?'.

- To draw out some facts and features of the game, on a matrix the teacher asks for starting and finishing positions under the following headings: cardboard, green card, red card, tools, cash, part-finished shapes, and distribution of gains.

It is at this point that the teacher begins to probe students' assumptions, intentions and criteria for success. Considering *criteria for success* first, the teacher asks groups to describe in what ways they felt they were successful and in what ways they felt they failed. Commonly occurring criteria for success are: 'more production', 'more shapes', 'percentage increase in cash', 'getting the upper hand', and (of course) 'Winning!'.

Are there signs of convivial *social criteria*? Do groups, for example, comment: '... we worked well as a group' or '... the jokes we told while working!', or perhaps '... not rushing around all the time' or '... the jokes we told *instead* of working!'. The teacher will be looking for a range of criteria and particularly items that begin to suggest that groups had reflected critically on the game's instruction to 'make shapes'. To what extent had groups asked those most basic of questions: 'Why make shapes?' and 'Why make so many?'.

Were groups subordinating themselves to the 'rules of the economy' (that is 'Make shapes') or were they bending the economy to their needs? ('How many shapes do we *need*?', 'What do the shapes represent?') Did they think about this? Was there a momentum to the game? Did groups get drawn into what was clearly a competitive game? What did the shapes represent anyway? How much production was enough? Did groups behave fairly to each other? Was there more cooperation than competition?

Students are asked to consider the colours and the hitherto concealed meanings of the cards and the returns to different shapes made from each. Did students wonder why there were different colours, or why the cardboard was harder to work and gave fewer returns?

Would knowing that only the red card represented the sustainable product of the land have affected their production systems or trading activities? Would groups have proceeded to use the valuable green card (non-renewable resources) and finally the cardboard (vital environmental functions/ environmental capital) even if they had known what this implied?

Would knowing this beforehand have affected a group's decision on trading and production activity? Would knowing that shapes represented production in different sectors – housing, food and so on – have affected the mix of what they made or how many? Why? Or does the market price matter more? Or is it just 'having more' that matters?

What was the role of *technology* (the scissors and the protractor especially)? Did it speed up resource (card) use? Who benefited – and how? What was the effect on price of not having access to this technology. Was this fair? What did this low price encourage? Cheating? Disregard for card use – whatever the colour?

The discussion, although inherently shaped by student responses and ideas every bit as much as teacher intentions, might move towards a consideration of whether the real world appears rather closer to the game despite our knowledge of environmental, social and technological constraints and pressures than an 'enlightened' position. Attention could also be drawn to the inequitable distribution of wealth within real nations as well as between them which contrasts (in most cases!) with the distribution of income within the group at the end of the game.

Most students tend to allocate rewards within their group at the end of the game reasonably equitably. This may be a most telling contrast. It may be saying in effect: 'The world of business is driven by competitive, selfish rules but within my social group (my team) we don't accept this partial analysis of the motivation of human behaviour and allocate with regard to the quality of social relationships.'

Extension

Students can be asked to run the game again. The rules are the same and the instruction is once more to make shapes, except that a minimum production – for illustration, say, six triangles and one circle shape – is required to maintain the 'health' of the population. Groups have to decide how to trade in the light of what they now know, and recent discussions.

Summary

What has this game to do with a 'green economics' or an economics for sustainability? It should be clear that it mirrors real-life dilemmas. While economic success is measured in terms of production and consumption, and largely mediated in money, the system has a bias towards competitive consumption to the extent that the economy is divorced from the environment and social cohesion that ultimately sustains it.

Conclusion

Galbraith (1977) said that economics always reflects the dominant interest group in society. Schools and colleges appear in the Illich (1972) analysis to be similarly largely conformist, transmitting the dominant cultural values while protesting their commitment to education. It is therefore no disgrace for teachers faced with economics and business syllabuses which treat the

273

functioning and failure of markets as its central concern to feel uncomfortable engaging in environmental issues in this context. In this sense, developments like the teaching materials in *Core Economics* (EBEA, 1995) comprehensively cover environmental economics for the 16–19 age group and the principle of market failure can usefully inform work lower down the school.

However, it might turn out that, given the rapidly changing world of ideas, teachers will wish to keep the radical critique in mind, perhaps using environmental issues to routinely test the limits of the discipline. Stirling (1993, p. 102), in the concluding parts of his examination of environmental valuation, indicates:

'The alternative to valuation lies in acknowledging the fundamentally multi-dimensional character of environmental effects. The complexities of nature and human society are better represented by a number of decision making criteria. Such criteria are far more effectively identified and prioritised through wide political debate, than by small communities of specialists with minority conceptions and interests. Rather than making spurious claims to objectivity, policy-makers should acknowledge that calculation is subordinate to judgement – that the selection and ranking of environmental criteria are inevitably subjective. Although a plural society is unlikely ever to reach consensus over the final choice of criteria, such an admission would at least provide a basis for more accessible political debate.'

As an example of 'values first', Adams (1989) noted, when discussing the impact of car-based transport:

'The direction of the required change is clear. The precise number of motor vehicles to which the third world might be permitted to level-up, or the developed world must be required to level down, will be difficult to specify. But it will depend upon assessments of available energy supplies and the capacities of global environmental sinks. The morality of the wealthy nations "pulling the ladder up behind them" or of the present generation leaving a mess for future generations to clear up are issues best discussed in plain words. Attempting to attach cash values to the variables at issue would be a monumental distraction.'

The tide seems to be running in favour of the radicals. All over the knowledge enterprise, systems thinking, the insights of chaos theory, and the new physics are contributing to re-evaluations of models, processes and assumptions of the conventional world view. Sadly it is upon this world view that much of what is currently in the curriculum depends. Economics and business education will not escape this fundamental process of change. Let us hope that this emerging future will be embraced willingly, for the alternative – to teach the increasingly irrelevant to the increasingly uninterested – is not and never has been an educational activity.

References

Adams, J. (1989). A review in *International Environmental Affairs*.

Axelrod, R. (1984). *The Evolution of Co-operation*, cited in Ormerod, P. (1994). *See below*.

deGroot, R. (1992). *Functions of Nature*, Groningon, Holland, Wolers-Noordhoff.

EBEA (1995). *Core Economics*, Oxford, Heinemann Educational.

Ekins, P. *et al.* (1992). *Wealth Beyond Measure*, London, Gaia Books.

Galbraith, J. K. (1977). *The Age of Uncertainty*, London, BBC/André Deutsch.

Henderson, H. (1991). *Paradigms in Progress*, London, Adamantine Press.

IUCN/UNEP/WWF (1991). *Caring for the Earth*, Switzerland, Earthscan.

Illich, I. (1972). *Deschooling Society*, Harmondsworth, Penguin.

Lutz, D. and Lux, K. (1988). *Humanistic Economics*, New York, Bootstrap Press.

Ormerod, P. (1994). *The Death of Economics*, London, Faber and Faber.

Stirling, A. (1993). *Environmental Valuation: How Much is the Emperor Wearing?*, *Ecologist*, June.

Webster, K. and Ekins, P. (1995). *Real Wealth (Green Economics in the Classroom)*, Aberystwyth, Zeitgeist.

PART 4

TEACHER DEVELOPMENT

21 Teacher development: discussion

Martin Jephcote and Steve Hodkinson

Most professional communities recognize the need for, and the importance of, the professional development of their members. In education there is a highly developed sense of the 'professional', illustrated in the responsibility the profession feels not only for its own development but also for the development of education.

Over the last decade there have been a number of significant changes in the support given to teacher development. In line with a shift away from teacher-led curriculum development to central control over pre- and post-16 curricula, there has been a similar shift in funding to support teacher development in specific targeted areas. For example, the Technical Vocational Education Initiative (TVEI), first introduced in 1983, provided substantial funding for teacher development to meet its limited aims. This was at a time when the Local Education Authorities – hitherto the main providers of courses and/or funding for teachers – were starved of cash. More recently the introduction of the National Curriculum has meant that limited funding has been directed in support of preparing and supporting teachers through its introduction and development, and has had the overall effect of limiting the scope of curriculum and teacher development. The introduction of General National Vocational Qualifications is another example of government-led change (the specifications have been drawn up by a government agency, the National Council for Vocational Qualifications) and brings with it a new system of competency-based assessment. Additionally, transfer of in-service training monies to schools and colleges has had the effect of 'diluting' provision, with priority often given to one-off training events rather than to initiating fundamental long-term change.

Educational change, at all levels and in many countries, is increasingly government-led. As stated in an OECD report (cited by Sikes, 1992, p. 36):

'... contemporary educational and political language is one of 'change', 'reform', and 'improvement'. Scarcely has one set of reforms been formulated, let alone properly implemented, and another is in genesis.'

Typically, change is now imposed on teachers, schools and colleges with the expectation that teachers will adopt given curriculum content and assessment procedures and adapt their styles of teaching and resources. Negotiation, participation and collaboration are, therefore, much less in evidence as aspects of curriculum change and teacher development. As Sikes pointed out

279

(p. 38), teachers' own interpretation of what change means for them influences what they do and how they do it. However, any individual interpretation of, or resistance to, change is well anticipated; in the overall attempt to 'raise standards' the attendant features of testing, inspection and publication of league tables have removed much scope for individual interpretation or local initiative. And to come full circle, funding is again the means by which schools and colleges and the teachers they employ are forced to comply. 'Successful' schools and colleges attract more students and more funding. In further education, through the Quality Assurance System, 'successful' departments are rewarded with additional funding. It appears, therefore, that teacher development has reached a critical stage – professional teachers might need to guard against the culture of compliance and their ultimate deprofessionalization.

But is the picture as bleak as so far portrayed? Clearly, there is some scope for individual and local initiatives. Individual teachers, through personal or career motivation, can choose to undertake short- or long-term courses by taking what is on offer at a University Department of Education (UDE). The Master of Education degree (MEd), and in some cases the Master of Arts degree (MA), are established as the career teachers' qualification(s), providing the mid-point in a variety of qualifications ranging from advanced certificates and diplomas on one side to a doctorate on the other. The relative buoyancy of numbers on such courses indicates a desire by some teachers to have their development and training accredited. Indeed, it is UDEs that have taken on the role as a key provider in what is termed the 'continuing professional development' of teachers. This is defined by Day *et al.* (1995, p.2) as:

'... all those conscious and planned activities which are intended to be of direct or indirect benefit to the individual, group or school, and which contribute, through these, to the quality of education in the classroom. It is the process by which, alone and with others, teachers review, renew and extend their commitment as change agents to the moral purposes of teaching; and by which they acquire and develop critically the knowledge and skills essential to good professional thinking, planning and practice with children, young people and colleagues through each phase of their teaching lives.'

This definition is quoted because it seems to encompass the view of a professional as change agent, not as agent of change – as a person responsible for and committed to the broader purposes of education; and it sees the need for what can be termed 'career-long learning'. The working life of a teacher might typically follow the pattern of trainee teacher, to the early period as a beginning teacher, followed by career progression to either main professional grade or to a position of managerial responsibility. As working life and career patterns change, so too there is a need for support in taking on new roles and responsibilities – such as mentoring students, guiding new teachers and other colleagues.

It is to the professional associations that many teachers turn to fill the vacuum in their professional development. In this respect the Economics and Business Education Association (EBEA), formerly the Economics Association, has done much to support the professional development of teachers. The Economics Education 14–16 Project was an example of curriculum development taking place hand-in-hand with teacher development; and in a rather different way the Economcs 16–19 Project has drawn on and extended the professional expertise of members. The appointment of a Development Officer in the late 1980s to develop Branch activities has provided another source of support for subject specialists, and this has been augmented by both local and national conferences aimed at enhancing the knowledge and skills of teachers.

In Chapters 22 and 23, Keith Wood and Keith Brumfitt each take a rather different approach to initial teacher education and the impact of moves to greater school-focused teacher training. Keith Wood seeks to close the gap between teachers' pedagogical content knowledge and students' understanding of the content. He states (p. 285):

'It is the gap created by the threat of an atomistic, competences view of teaching. It is the gap, the link between means and ends, the closure of which is at the heart of professionalism. And it is the gap ... the bridging of which must be accessed by beginning teachers if they are to develop professional expertise.'

His own research looked at a programme which promoted reflective thinking and action among student teachers with respect to their own content knowledge and their pupils' understanding of the content. Related to the works of Kolb and of Schön, it adds to both by reconceptualizing reflective practice as the development of analytical awareness. Wood suggests that practical teaching experience *per se* will not lead to understanding of teaching; experience needs to be integrated with the learning objectives of teacher education.

Keith Brumfitt draws from his own experiences in initial teacher training and describes a model of school-focused training that employs competency-based assessment. His is a partnership model that places emphasis on the placement as the focus for professional training. In this model, schools and colleges partly control students' professional education, not by providing a place for students to test theory but by providing a new style of training through the development of competence-based assessment strategies. Clearly, Brumfitt has embraced a view of teacher 'training' and of university education where, he asserts, it is not the idea of competence that is controversial but the nature of competence. Moreover, he states that in teacher education the terminology and approaches of competence-based education have been accepted. But is this 'acceptance' embraced wholeheartedly by school teachers (mentors) and university 'trainers', or does it represent an aspect of compliance? We should note, however, that there is little room for divergence. The impact of the Teacher Training Agency (TTA), together with the inspection process in initial teacher education and the need to comply with their requirements and version of what is required, may act as a deterrent to creativity and innovation.

281

The next stage of teacher development – starting out as a teacher – is recorded in Chapter 24 by Richard Dunnill and colleagues. They look at the experiences of three teachers during their first year of teaching. This chapter will provide a source of information to student teachers and their mentors so that they can anticipate and prepare for the variety of issues that will confront them. Two clear messages for newly qualified teachers of economics and business studies are that they need to be *proactive* in their own professional development, and that schools and colleges need to invest in the next generation of experienced teachers and managers.

Mutual support and self-help, through both formal and informal arrangements, are charactersitics of the teaching profession. Recognizing and drawing on the experience and expertise of colleagues, especially subject colleagues, is almost taken for granted. The fact that many teachers of economics and business in schools work in small departments, together with the general nature of school and college in-service programmes and the targeting of LEA provision to National Curriculum subjects, leads Paul Clarke in Chapter 25 to consider examples of local professional development activities that involve teachers working together across schools. The approach taken was to identify a range of common tasks from which each of the teachers could benefit. These tasks were: writing a resource for GNVQ; planning and presenting an in-service programme to other teachers; and taking advantage of a business placement to develop classroom materials. This type of collaborative approach to professional development brings its rewards, but it hinges on the willingness of teachers to join together as learners and as reflective practitioners, and it requires support from those responsible for planning staff development.

Career progression may lead to a position of responsibility such as Head of Department. In Chapter 26, Richard Hughes argues for a collegial approach to leading a team and considers the importance of teamwork – sharing knowledge, sharing skills and sharing responsibility. This, he suggests, is more efficient and more effective than individuals working alone. He values the contribution that staff in his department can make to the team, recognizing their varied teaching, organizational and team skills. He notes, too, the importance of leadership and leadership skills and describes how he has sought to build an 'inclusive team' at his own college. He reveals much about his own style of leadership when he describes his position as a 'privilege', and above all his own concern is for the team member.

In Chapter 27, Ian Chambers and Susan Squires give us some insight into the process of quality assessment, relating changes in the nature and extent of the monitoring and inspection process to business education. They examine the methods employed by the Office for Standards in Education in England (OfSTED) for inspecting schools and the inspection process for post-16 education, undertaken in England by the Further Education Funding Council (FEFC), and make a comparison between the two. They point out that the FEFC has guidelines less detailed than OfSTED, which recognizes the different experiences and traditions in programme delivery. Chambers and Squires conclude their chapter by providing a list of review questions that teachers of economics and business studies can use to prepare for the inspection process.

References

Day, C. *et al.* (1995). 'Quality, achievement, and the continuing professional development of teachers: a UCET discussion paper', a paper circulated at the UCET conference, Nov. 1995.

Sikes, P. J. (1992). 'Imposed change and the experienced teacher', in: Fullan, M. and Hargreaves, A. (eds), *Teacher Development and Educational Change*, London, Falmer Press.

2 The teacher as learner

Keith Wood

Introduction

Marton (1994) has reported that out of over one million words spoken by teachers about teaching – in the course of a study aimed at exploring teachers' views of their work and of the context of their work in as much of an 'open-minded' way as possible – not a single word was spoken about the way the teachers dealt with some particular content in order to help students learn that content.

This issue has been taken up by Marton, who argues for a change of focus in teacher education research from teachers' thinking to a focus on teachers' ways of experiencing, and awareness of, their professional world. In part, he seeks to bridge a gap between teachers' pedagogical content knowledge and students' understanding of the content by relating 'students' ways of being aware of some particular content to the teachers' ways of being aware of the same content'. This is the gap that runs like a thread through the literature on teacher education. It is the gap created by the threat of an atomistic, competences view of teaching (Edwards, 1992). It is the gap, the link between means and ends, the closure of which is at the heart of professionalism. And it is the gap, revealed by research on teachers' thinking (Brown and McIntyre, 1993), the bridging of which must be accessed by beginning teachers if they are to develop professional expertise.

Studies of teachers' awareness (Andersson and Lawenius, 1983; Annerstedt, 1991; Johansson, 1992; Alexandersson, 1994) have revealed that:

- teachers participating in the studies were rarely oriented towards specific learning aims and hence were rarely focusing on the means–ends relation (i.e. there was a relative lack of emphasis on learning and the content of learning);

- teacher educators seem to focus on goals specific for learning the subject to a greater extent than do teachers;

- some teacher educators focus on specific learning goals while others do not.

One implication of the identification of this gap for the development of an initial teacher education curriculum is that, as a central core of that curriculum, teachers should focus on the goals of learning and teaching some specific content in terms of the capabilities that students are supposed to develop. According to Marton (1994, pp. 39–40), these specific goals should be seen in relation to more general goals, and also in relation to the ways in which the teacher could possibly contribute to bringing about these goals:

'Dealing with goals of learning in a specific sense implies ... dealing with relations. Relations between content and learner, relations between specific goals and general goals, relations between goals and means. ... In the case of teachers, relations reflecting a reasonably high degree of analytic awareness are between the intended goals, and the way in which the students are expected to understand a particular content, on the one hand, and the means by which these goals can be reached, on the other hand.'

A further implication is that this should be the focus both of teachers in learning to teach a specific subject matter, *and* of teacher educators in teaching those teachers. There has to be a consistency of approach of teachers and teacher educators.

Johansson has studied the focus of teacher educators' awareness and has argued that in order to be able to discuss specific goals of learning in relation to general goals and in relation to methods for reaching those goals, the teacher educator has to have transcended his or her personal experience of the school as his or her knowledge base. This transcendence is what Marton (1994, p. 39) describes as 'analytic awareness':

'One's own personal experiences do not suffice when it comes to preparing students for a wide range of future situations. There is thus a need to analytically discern comparatively abstract, generative aspects of concrete situations and relate them to each other. This is the way in which means–ends relations or relationships between what is specific and what is general are established.'

Johansson has found that this occurs for a teacher educator when he or she finds a frame of reference outside the concrete situation. Finally, the general implication is clear: teacher educators need to find such a frame of reference in order to transcend their 'taken-for-granted experiential world as a teacher' (Marton, 1994, p. 39). This observation should have a particular resonance at a time when much of the responsibility for teacher education in the UK is being transferred to schools. Similarly, provision of such a frame of reference should be the aim of an initial teacher education programme if it is to focus teachers' awareness on the relationship between means and ends in teaching. This is the relationship that Edwards warns us should not be lost sight of in the attempt to simplify school-based teacher education to a list of atomized competences.

Relating the goals of learning and the means of achieving them

An ITE economics curriculum programme that has been the subject of a research study (Wood, 1995) was intended to promote reflective thinking and action among student teachers in relation to the links between student teachers' content knowledge (and its development into pedagogical content knowledge in the process) and their pupils' understanding of the content. It was to be achieved by relating pupils' ways of being aware of each particular content to the student teachers' ways of being aware of that content.

The programme was designed as a spiral curriculum. This was clearly related to the work of Kolb (1984) on experiential learning and Schön's notion of a reflective practitioner (1983, 1987). It added a new interpretation to both by conceptualizing reflective practice as the development of analytic awareness. With a specific focus on the relationships between means and ends in teaching and learning, student teachers were expected to learn from the experience of working with pupils in classrooms in collaboration with HEI tutors, teachers and fellow students. As part of this experience a specific content was to be operationalized as a process of reflection–action-theory. As an iterative process (see Figure 22.1) applied to new content and contexts for teaching that content, it was intended to develop the analytic awareness of the individual student teacher, thus disposing him or her to theorize – 'to interpret, explain or judge intentions, actions and experience' (Eraut, 1994) – about the

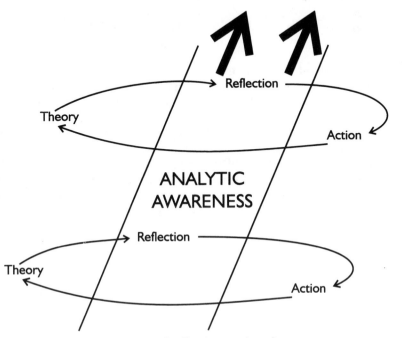

Figure 22.1 An iterative process of reflection–action–theory

relationship between means and ends in teaching. This was the frame of reference provided by the programme.

The spiral curriculum was presented to the student teachers as a plan–teach–review process; that is, collaborative lesson planning, followed by teaching, followed by review drawing on evidence of pupils' learning that would inform replanning and development. The planning stage involves reflection and action, and review involves reflection on the learning outcomes in relation to the plan. This approach to teacher development has its origins in the Economic Awareness Teacher Training (EcATT) Programme through which its relevance to the continuing professional development of teachers has been demonstrated.

It is important to point out that, characteristically, the programme was not prepared in detail at the outset. Rather it was developed organically through the use of a plan–teach–review process by the tutors: a second spiral. Semi-structured interviews were used throughout the programme to identify what student teachers learnt. The interviews were opportunities to explore the meanings held by, or understandings of, or awareness of the student teachers, and so could bring about learning in the student teachers. However, it must be stressed that the intention of the interviews was, in a sense, to hold a mirror to the awareness of the interviewees, and for this reason they were conducted in such a way as to elicit as full and as open a response as possible. The analysis of the interviews at each stage was a major stimulus for the tutors' review process and planning of subsequent interviews.

Student teachers' understandings of teaching economics

The research described above seemed to show that the teaching of economics was conceptualized by beginning teachers in four main, qualitatively different, ways. This section looks at the four conceptions (see Figure 22.2 opposite).

Conception A: Teaching as imparting knowledge to pupils

This sees learning as increasing one's knowledge, which carries all the vagueness identified by other researchers on learning. And in the same way it is, in its vaguest form, superordinate to all the other conceptions. The *meaning* of knowledge is not the focus of this conception; rather the focus is the communication process. Here are some representative comments:

'... pass on knowledge ... as a signpost ...' (Simon, Oct. 91)

'... you've got to transmit information in a clear and logical way ...' (Rehana, Oct. 91)

'... the teacher's job principally is to impart knowledge ...' (John, Nov. 91)

'... imparting information and knowledge ...' (Sarah, Oct. 91)

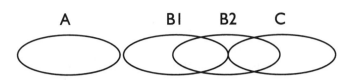

Figure 22.2 The relationship between conceptions of teaching

'... you can just look at it on the surface with the teachers as givers and the pupils as receivers ...' (Gary, Nov. 91)

Conception B1: Teaching as preparing pupils to use knowledge

In this conception the focus remains the communication process as in conception A, but it is a two-way process between teacher and pupil, and not simply from teacher to pupils. However there is a limit placed on the extent to which this communication is two-way, harking back to conception A:

'... at some point you do have to stand back and say, at this point it's not two-way, at this point I'm telling you, you may not like that but ...' (Daniel, Oct. 91)

'... ask or argue, but you know you've got to have some kind of control over it all ...' (Vicky Oct. 92)

Pupils remain an undifferentiated whole – referred to in the third person plural – but 'they' are seen to play a role in the teaching and learning process beyond that of recipients of knowledge.

The process is seen to be complicated by the acceptance that pupils do not enter the classroom as empty vessels that are to be filled with the teacher's knowledge:

'... to adapt the knowledge that you have. In a sense try and extract it through the kids rather than giving it to them ...' (Mark, Oct. 91)

'... Bringing things up from everyday experiences ...' (Kim, Oct. 91)

'... seeing inside a child's mind quickly, being able to identify the signs and use/identify the causes of behaviour and areas of interest of that child and areas of ability and be able to make the most of them ...' (Daniel, Oct. 91)

The outcome of teaching is the development of the capability to apply what is known:

'... trying to apply economics or whatever you're teaching to what they understand, trying to get at their understanding of it so that you're at their level. Not teaching what they won't understand, and putting it into everyday contexts ...' (Daniel, Oct. 91)

'... pupils ... have to see the use of it themselves without the teacher saying this is the use of it ...' (Katerina, Nov. 91)

The approach to teaching is a type of Socratic dialogue with the teacher, through which the learner is encouraged to respond to an issue or problem and, through interaction with the teacher, modify that response in the course of teaching. The dialogue demonstrates the weaknesses in pupils' thinking when applied to problems or issues or an explanation of an economic phenomenon:

'... someone's guiding that thinking. Not in terms of telling you what to think but asking relevant questions ...' (Emma, Oct. 91)

'... you need to look at it how they would look at it and extract from them where they are at that point in knowledge terms – extract where you want them to be ...' (Mark, Oct. 91)

'... They have to go through a process of trying to assimilate information and manipulate it in ways they think appropriate ... the teacher has to facilitate that because most of the theories are fairly logical ... you shouldn't have to do too much to get them there ...' (Salif, Nov. 91)

'... try and turn it back on them and say, "what do you think that?"' (Daniel, Feb. 92)

'... Engage them in conversation ...' (Daniel, Oct. 91)

'... The teacher is not just giving but has to accept different ideas and from that he can organize and structure the delivery of the knowledge ...' (Gary, Nov. 91)

'... You have to find a way of breaking it down. Working with kids, getting them to express their ideas, maybe fumble a little bit, ... that makes them verbalise and express their understanding and that makes them learn better than if they receive it ...' (Daniel, Nov. 91)

'... Get them to understand and question what they're doing and maybe take that understanding and use it all the time, question what they're doing all the time ...' (Tim, Nov. 91)

'... it's an interactive process between the teacher and the pupil ...' (Patrick, Nov. 91)

'... the dynamics of how things are going and how you can influence the course of that ... to steer them to an interest and appreciation of the subject ...' (Salif, Oct. 91)

'... Managing the learning process so that it goes in the direction you want without veering off in directions you don't want ...' (Katerina, Oct. 91)

Conception B2: Teaching as providing opportunities to see the existence of different perspectives on a phenomenon

This conception shares with conception B1 the use of dialogue as stimulus.

The difference is in emphasis on the teacher as a facilitator of dialogue *between* pupils which reveals different perspectives on a phenomenon.

The interaction – sharing of opinions in the process of argument – has thinking as an outcome of teaching. This thinking appears to be stimulated by the need to construct a defence of, or launch an attack on, another's perspective:

'... having arguments in the lesson seems to make a lot of sense ... they were really having to think about it ... they were still arguing as they went out of the door ...' (Katerina, Feb. 92)

'... get them to share ideas and actually make them think a lot more rather than do the thinking for them ...' (Rehana, Feb. 92)

It is possible to suggest that what the pupils think about is the meaning they give to a phenomenon. In this case the outcome of teaching, in the form of pupil learning, is learning as understanding – that is, in the sense of gaining meaning (Marton *et al.*, 1993). The pupil articulates the meaning he or she holds and compares and contrasts it with meanings held by other pupils and the teacher.

The difficulty in describing this conception comes in deciding whether comparing and contrasting is the intention of the teaching process (an end in itself) or whether, through comparing and contrasting, the intention of the teaching process is the gaining of *new* meaning. If it is the former, this conception collapses to conception B1, with the pupils used as an additional source of confutation and individual learners either accepting or rejecting the knowledge implicit in the lesson content designed by the teacher. If it is the latter, the teaching process is seen to be more complex and this conception is encapsulated in conception C. In short, this conception (B2) appears to be a mixture of conceptions B1 and C characterized by confusion over outcome. At one extreme, the approach is an end in itself to organize the classroom so that pupils exchange ideas, argue, discuss:

'... make you aware that other people have different opinions and your one is not necessarily the right one even though you may still stick to it. You would be more flexible and receptive to other people's opinions and evaluate them against yours, seeing the benefits of your own view ...'
(Simon, June 92)

'... listening to each other and arguing points ...' (Melissa, June 92)

'... learning off each other in groups, just bouncing ideas off each other ...'
(Katerina, Nov. 91)

'... the teacher is the catalyst and pupils take it on from there ... The teacher starts something off and hopes the others will pick it up. Then it will evolve from there ... the teacher can learn from the kids. They come up with ideas the teacher hadn't thought of ...' (Rehana, Nov. 91)

'... talking to each other and collaborating with each other; discussing issues ... learning from each other ...' (Dean, Feb. 92)

At the other extreme, the end is changing meaning in the sense of developing a qualitatively different conception of the phenomenon studied. References are made to 'developing ideas', recognizing the 'problems' associated with the existence of different perspectives, and the observation of different frames of reference, all of which can be a powerful cause of change if attention is focused on them:

'... you can bring in different ways of looking at it so that people are learning not just in terms of thinking of different parts of the syllabus but of developing ideas, working collaboratively ...' (David, Oct. 91)

'... to begin to appreciate there's a perspective other than their own – that there are all sorts of value systems and perspectives and frames of reference at work and at play at the same time and these things are sometimes brought together by an incident or set of circumstances and they have an influence on this thing, this outcome ...' (Matthew, Feb. 92)

'... what that information means and where it comes from ...' (Katerina, Feb. 92)

'... they had to debate it ... some did change their viewpoints ...' (Nico, Feb. 92)

'... to realize the different perspectives and the possible problems that arise because people come from different viewpoints with a topic ...' (Mark, Feb. 92)

What is distinctive about conception B2 is that the approach to, or process of, teaching is conflated with the outcome of teaching, because a relationship between approach and outcome is not clearly articulated. From this it could be argued that it is not a conception of teaching at all – but that would be to deny its importance as a kind of bridging conception between B1 and C held by teachers as they develop.

Conception C: Teaching as preparing pupils to be reflective

By 'reflection' is meant the learner's awareness of his or her own learning – or awareness of awareness – as in 'metacognition' (see the end note). For example:

'... I've been thinking about how I've learnt about learning so I can kind of learn about learning on two levels: one by observing other people; one by just thinking about how I'm doing it ...' (Emma, Nov. 91)

'... I can stand back from how I am learning ... and think, oh yes, I know what's going on in my mind now ...' (Rod, June 92)

The outcome of teaching in this conception is learning as seeing something in a different way. This conception involves changing meanings held by those involved in the teaching and learning process:

'... *it was an attempt to change the way the kids were looking at things ...*'
(Matthew, Nov. 91)

'... *must appreciate that difference has occurred and why it has occurred ...*' *(Rod, June 92)*

'... *really brought home to me how difficult it is to change people's conceptions ...*' *(Emma, Nov. 91)*

'... *giving you the power to think beyond that framework ... criticise the whole set of things and look outside that ... a critical thinking thing ...* *(Mark, June 92)*

'... *to be able to take a critical stance ... to be able to stand back and examine it and think, who said that and why have they said that and what does it mean? ...*' *(Matthew, June 92)*

The approach to teaching is to work with content metacognitively, through the teacher focusing on the learner's reflection about that content. In other words, to organize the classroom experiences of the pupils so that the thinking of the pupils about the content of the lesson is made an object of the pupils' thinking. This conception involves a more powerful thinker, and an autonomous learner, able to think about his or her learning:

'... *establish a dialogue or a background to interpreting those experiences ... a dialogue in your mind ...*' *(Emma, Oct. 91)*

'... *pupils are given the opportunity of interpreting their understanding rather than just relating it to very structured knowledge ...*' *(Gary, Feb. 92)*

'... *it's good to teach a group to be introspective ...*' *(Emma, Nov. 91)*

Teacher learning

The economics curriculum programme set out to challenge student teachers' views about teaching economics. There is some evidence that for some student teachers the programme may have been successful in doing this. They changed their conception in the direction from A to C.

From this study it has emerged that the development of teaching competence as it is described here goes hand-in-hand with the development of teachers' subject matter knowledge for teaching. This knowledge develops through teachers working closely with their own and their pupils' responses to subject matter described in terms of what has, and what can be, learnt. This is a way of bridging the gap between teachers' intentions and pupils' meaningful learning. It is achieved through collaborative planning, teaching and review of classroom activities. This approach to teacher learning is as relevant to the continuing professional development of teachers (derived as it is from action-research methods) as it is to initial teacher education.

Bridging the gap between teachers' pedagogical content knowledge, or subject matter knowledge, and pupils' understanding of the content involves a shift of focus from self-as-teacher to pupil learning. The results of this study show that for some student teachers it is possible to achieve such a shift of focus. The study illuminated what is relevant to bringing about this shift of focus. Some examples follow.

The relationship between approach and outcome

It is relevant to create awareness that the approach to teaching and the outcome of teaching are dialectically related.

For example, by the time of the third interview Daniel was reviewing lessons for the sense pupils were making and for the factors in creating activities that might cause pupils to reflect on that sense they were making. He described a collaborative lesson which involved pupils in a business simulation. He wanted pupils to:

'... pick things out and look at them from their own point of view ... it was our [job as teachers] ... to try to turn it back on them and say why do you think that and give some examples ... that didn't just look for profit maximization/cost minimization ...'.

Daniel had identified a narrow conception of business motivation as profit-maximization as one that he wanted pupils to reflect on, and in so doing to become aware of other motivational factors. It proved difficult. Daniel put this down to the effect of the simulation or game on the expectations of the students. The game format gave them an opportunity to behave according to their preconceptions and the format provided little that would challenge those preconceptions:

'... the whole thing was from the perspective of 'your business' ... Knowing it was a game, they would have set in their minds the rules of the game and the rules of the game were: they thought they knew how businesses had acted. That set the tone for the whole thing ...'.

Or, put another way, the pupils could only see this business in the way that they had experienced business – they could not get 'inside' *this* business with a changed awareness. How would he have planned this differently to take account of these problems?

'... I'd probably try to start coming from their own experience ... something we could view from their point of view, starting from their own situation as near as possible and turning it so they'd already seen the other perspective first ... prior to being asked to view the business from inside. Have some other stimulus which would show them another business working in a way that would surprise them – taking into account social costs and all the rest of it ...'.

Whether this would achieve his intention or not, Daniel was clearly attempting to work metacognitively with the pupils' understanding of the content. The review provided an opportunity for the tutors to work with Daniel to develop his understanding.

Communication and the reproduction of knowledge

It is relevant to create awareness that communication in the classroom can be based on reproduction of knowledge unless pupils' meanings are consciously made the object of the teaching.

For example, interviewing pupils before and after lessons had created some cognitive dissonance for Mark because he had seen that what pupils say to the teacher may not have meaning for them. It could be a kind of lip-service, giving the teacher what the pupil perceives is wanted. This was a learning opportunity for Mark because, clearly, he could not work in the way that he described at the outset of the course if he created situations where pupils simply 're-peated after the teacher'. That observation alone could put emphasis on the importance of the tasks set by the teacher if meaningful learning is to occur. Mark said:

'I find interviewing pupils before and after lessons a little confusing because seeing through what they were saying and interpreting that as something that was intrinsically theirs and something that had been fed to them was confusing to me.'

Using evidence of pupils' thinking

It is relevant to use evidence (collected by collaboration) of pupils' thinking to develop teachers' awareness of the meanings held by pupils.

For example, a tutor followed up a lesson on migration that had been taught by Patrick and, in so doing, contrasted the meaning of migration held by the pupils (migration occurred for personal reasons) and the meaning of migration that might be the goal of an economics lesson (migration describes people functioning within the economic system). To change the pupils' conceptions, or initial way of experiencing the phenomena migration, to a new way of experiencing it required an intervention on the part of the teacher. It was Patrick's task, then, in collaboration with the tutor and his teaching partner, to design teaching activities that might produce that change. It was seeing the goal of teaching in such a way that was the readjustment that Patrick had to make. The tutor explained that she had begun to see migration in the way she described as a result of being involved in, and seeking meaning from, the lesson that she had reviewed with Patrick. This exemplified the adjustment that Patrick had to make in order to review lessons by seeking meaning for what the pupils said and the sense they made of the content of the lesson.

Meaningful activities

Relating the activities of teaching to the opportunities for the generation of meaning by pupils is relevant to learning to teach.

For example, Emma reviewed her lesson on the motivation of a business in the following manner with the interviewer (INT):

E   *'I was looking at the law and employment. The lesson was an adaptation of something I did with the fourth years ... What I'd basically done was handed out something on cases of racism. Then basically asked the question, what was going on? ... And they started to tell me and then I said "does the government ever have the right to tell a business what to do? Or to tell a business person what to do?" They went "no, no, no." And then what I tried to do from that was I tried to get them to see the implications of what they said they believed – that the government could never do it. And all that we did was investigate the implications of that view – what it would mean in practice.*

        'By doing that I think they came to see more clearly what that view actually entailed. I think there was a knee-jerk reaction first of all. Then they all moved away from it because they didn't want to be associated with that kind of thing because they had come to see the implications. Then that caused them to shift their view as to what the government was entitled to do.

        Generally, I think learning is to do with getting someone to see their viewpoint more fully for what it is. Getting them to see the implications of something or getting them to see the assumptions upon which something is based. I think once they see that they may learn to stay with that viewpoint. I think they come to understand that viewpoint in a fuller sense so in that sense I think they've learnt.'

INT   *'Right. I understand. Just to go back for a minute, and say where they were and where you think they got to. Give me the context.'*

E   *'In the context?'*

INT   *'Yes, just contrast them – where they were and where they got to.'*

E   *'Where they were is I think they thought profit/business ruled absolutely. And I think also they thought that was the answer they should give in their Economics lesson. I don't know how true it is to say that's necessarily what they really always believed. That was certainly the answer they thought would sound really good, and I'd say "well done" and give them a pat on the head – it's all to do with profit.*

        And I think that the way they changed their minds so they came to see there were certain implications to thinking that, that meant you couldn't interfere with things that we might think were morally unacceptable, you know racism, etc. So I think they came to see all these implications of that. I can't then say for sure.'

INT   *'For example?'*

E   *'For example, they were unhappy with the idea that an employer could choose not to employ someone simply because of their race. They were unhappy with saying that the government should sit back and not do anything about that. How they then balanced those two things up, I think in that lesson they balanced them up and said that the government is entitled to interfere, but* I don't think that conclusion is necessarily where the learning took place. I think learning took place in seeing that there was more than one aspect to that and there were things that had to be weighed up and balanced against each other.' *(my emphasis)*

Comparing meanings

Comparing pupils' and teachers' meanings with the structure of meanings and approaches provided by the discipline of economics is relevant to learning to teach.

For example, one interview provided an example of Tim reviewing a lesson. The interviewing tutor had been involved in collaboration with Tim and his partner in the planning, teaching and review of the lesson. In the brief extract that follows, Tim was reviewing the lesson in question:

T   *'As soon as we started giving out the statements, we realized that the language of them was way out of line. We thought they were their words but what we'd done was take their words and change it into our language. So when we came to the summing up I could see what you said was a professional criticism, not a personal criticism. So ... I thought it through again and I could see that the second task was too difficult for them ... see the limitations in it ... .*

'I still think the starting point ... with the map ... was relevant to their starting point. I still don't think they had a grasp of what you [both] said they had ... For the rest, as we were [teaching] it ... I could see ... they didn't understand ... in the second half of the lesson when we introduced ... the poll tax and income tax I could see ... they were coming out with things that they already thought and weren't doing anything to challenge their thinking ... I can see better ways of doing it now ... the pupils could have got a lot more out of the lesson.'

INT   *'What did he think the pupils got out of the lesson?'*

T   *'I thought they'd been able critically to look at taxation but, when I looked at it, I don't think they did. We might have introduced some new words like 'regressive' as some sort of criteria for looking at taxes, but I don't think we gave them the opportunity to challenge the preconceptions they had originally about taxation ... they might have learnt about regressive taxes and how to use the word*

> *'regression' for taxation – I think there's a chance for that lesson to take it somewhere else ...'.*

Assessment

Interpreting school assessment as the assessment of meaningful learning is important for teacher learning.

For example, Matthew felt the course had 'empowered' him to develop his teaching, but said:

'I'm having trouble with things like assessment ... and I think it would be useful to look at things like that: issues and aspects of teaching, and try and deconstruct them and try, given the tools we've been empowered with on the course, to build our own ideas up.'

The problem over assessment was a problem identified by Matthew early in the course; that is, the constraint exercised by assessment on the curriculum:

'I'm not sure what kids are at the end of an education now. A fistful of qualifications, but what do they mean? I think I would like to see some kind of meaning for the kids ... at the end of their education. Rather than a certificate, to have some kind of skill/ability and as well some knowledge and some proclivity to action ... other than something which enables them just to take another step up ... the educational ladder ...'.

Class management and pupil learning

There is evidence from the study that the separation of classroom management and the object of teaching subject matter content interferes with this shift of focus, this bridging of the gap.

In some cases the classroom experiences provided by the practicum differed so markedly in this respect from what was intended by the programme that student teachers felt able to distinguish between 'real' teaching in school and teaching as it is seen to be perceived by the HEI tutors.

For Mark and Matthew, describing their classroom work in terms of involvement, motivation and learning outcomes allowed the tutor to probe the meanings they held. But for Simon, social roles dominated his thinking and this was reinforced by his experiences in school. In Melissa's case she admitted to taking the 'easy' way which she described in terms of standing at the front using the blackboard – that was the real teaching!

Only where opportunities exist for continuous review of such lessons, concentrating on evidence of outcomes in terms of pupil learning, is it likely that student teachers will be able to reflect on the relationship between managing classroom activities and pupil learning. Continuous review is only possible if school tutors working in classrooms with the student teachers actively support that review process.

Collaboration during teaching practice

The challenges that result from a process of close collaborative review of pupil learning as the outcome of lessons generates reflection, or a process of meta-cognition. This allows teachers to transcend their experience of teaching and subject it to critical review. However, schools cannot always provide opportunities for such a reflective process because that transcendence has not been achieved by the teachers in school.

For example, by the third interview Rehana was questioning whether there was a distinction between learning and understanding. This interview came after the period of her practicum so it was possible that experience of teaching in school may have led to this review of her original position on the existence of a distinction between learning and understanding.

In her second interview, Rehana had appeared to equate learning with remembering. And by now, after the practicum, she said she had a problem about what learning was. She gave an example:

'This thing about still dictating. Do you learn from that? I don't know. I'm not convinced you don't. ... We were talking this morning about a couple of theories – cobweb theory. And I can remember learning how to do it – just demand and supply going round in circles. So I obviously learnt that and I understand it. I was taught in that way, so whether I actually – I'm not sure at all ...'.

It is not clear how Rehana intended to finish that sentence '... so whether I actually – ...'. Perhaps she was beginning to question whether *she* understood it herself when she learnt how to do it as 'just demand and supply going round in circles'. Clearly the cobweb-model is not simply about this.

Rehana was having problems with her teaching because she found she could only transmit to what she described as 'the best able kids'.

Dictation may have been seen as an acceptable part of the teaching and learning process in the TP school. Given this status by colleagues in school, it could – in the view of this student teacher – be contrasted with other acts of teaching. Asked how she was going to work on this problem, Rehana replied that she was going to do 'a lot more group work' because 'you can get them to share ideas and actually make them think a lot more rather than do the thinking for them.' So Rehana had begun to consider alternative ways to *organize* activities.

It may be that Rehana had not begun to think about the meaning of what she intended to teach and how pupil learning could be meaningful. The practicum may not have created opportunities for this development. The following extract from the transcript illustrates this:

R   *'I found costs very difficult to do group work with. And I found myself telling them what they should know ...'.*

INT   'Well, why do you want anyone to study fixed costs?'

R   'Why did I want to do it? Well, I was told to do it, wasn't I?'

INT   'Is that it? Is that the extent of the rationale for doing it? Or do you have another rationale for that?'

R   'At the time, no I didn't'.

INT   'What about now?'

R   'I'm not sure it was actually valid, what I was teaching, at all.'

INT   'So you might not understand the importance of fixed costs then?'

R   'No'.

While Rehana may have come to this conclusion, she could only have done so by beginning to question her own view of fixed costs. For this reason, it appeared to be incorrect to say that she was not focusing on meaning; but, certainly, it appeared to be the case that she had some way to go in creating for herself subject matter that she could teach.

Rehana had found it impossible to collaborate with her partner. She felt that he had been critical only and had not provided evidence of pupils' responses that would allow her to develop. Rehana appeared to have noted the value of this kind of evidence in her comments in the second interview, but her partner had not been willing or able to provide this information. This may have set Rehana back in her development as a teacher because she was working 'in the dark' – as any teacher would be who was transmitting without setting up feedback mechanisms.

The description of the development of teaching competence as it emerged from this study emphasizes the following: being reflective; collaborative relationships; self-knowledge and self-evaluation; and judgement involving interpretation (Winter, 1991). In general, the study shows that where these elements are absent teaching competence (viewed as conception C) is not achieved. Indeed, teaching competence *is* the continued practising of these elements.

The individual student cases provide evidence and discussion of both the value of, and the difficulty of achieving, effective collaboration. It is an aspect of the professional development of teachers that is difficult to organize and which warrants further attention. As many student teachers point out, teaching is still seen as a solitary pursuit – just one teacher and the class.

A relational view of learning

Learning is relational. From this it follows that the ability of a student to show understanding of, in this case, teaching depends on the nature of the phenomenon under study (Bowden *et al.*, 1992). Clearly, the phenomenon of teaching may be apprehended differently in different contexts. The implication of this for teacher educators is that, in seeking to have student teachers develop understanding, they must specify the type of phenomenon (i.e. teaching) of which that understanding is desired.

Circular 9/92 (DFE, 1992) can been examined for its adequacy in specifying the phenomenon of teaching. However, even with a detailed and unambiguous statement, the provision of contexts in which teaching can be apprehended, so that the desired understanding develops, is by no means easy to accomplish under the current arrangements for teacher education in the UK. This has implications for the design of learning experiences for teacher education because, put at its crudest, where knowledge transmission is equated with teaching, a student teacher cannot be expected to show understanding of teaching. Ensuring a range of contexts and experiences, or problem siuations, that require qualitatively different conceptions of teaching from students is an essential prerequisite for effective teacher education. It cannot be assumed that such contexts, and qualitiatively different understandings, will be found wherever teaching occurs. Thus practical teaching experience *per se* will not lead to understanding of teaching. The experience has to be integrated with the learning objectives of teacher education, for example by the creation of professional development schools, or some other means of linking teaching practice with the model of teacher education.

A further implication for teaching is that teacher educators will be in a better position to help student teachers learn if they know what conceptions students hold and in which direction they intend student understanding to develop. This knowledge can be used to design appropriate teaching interventions.

The data from this study and the questions and activities that elicited the data are available to teacher educators to use in making professional judgements about the development of understanding through the teaching and learning process.

Finally, assessment of teaching and the expectations placed on teachers by pupils, parents, school governors and government will have to match the understanding of teaching that is sought. If teaching is seen by society at large as, for example, the transmission of knowledge, then student teachers will not believe that a qualitatively different conception of teaching is an appropriate goal of teacher education. Instead, they will seek to reproduce and employ teaching routines and not value the development of analytic awareness.

References

Alexandersson, M. (1994). *Method and Consciousness*, Gothenburg University.

Andersson, E. and Lawenius, M. (1983). *Teachers' Conceptions of Teaching*, Gothenburg University.

Annerstedt, C. (1991). *Physical Education and Teachers in Physical Education*, Gothenburg University.

Bowden, J., Dall'Alba, G., Laurillard, D.,Martin, E., Marton, F., Masters, G., Ramsden, P., Stephanou, A. and Walsh, E. (1992). 'Displacement, velocity and frames of reference: phenomenographic studies of students' understanding and some implications for teaching', *American Journal of Physics*, vol. 60, pp. 262–9.

Brown, S. and McIntyre, D. (1993). *Making Sense of Teaching*, Milton Keynes, Open University Press.

DFE (1992). *Initial Teacher Training: Secondary Phase, Circular 9/92.*

Edwards, T. (1992). *Change and Reform in Initial Teacher Education* (Briefing no. 9), London, National Commission for Education.

Eraut, M. (1994). *Developing Professional Knowledge and Competence*, Brighton, Falmer Press.

Johansson, J.-E. (1992). *Preschool Methods in Preschool Education*, Gothenburg University

Kolb, D. (1984). *Experiential Learning: Experience as the Source of Learning and Development*, Englewood Cliffs, NJ, Prentice-Hall.

Marton, F. (1994). 'On the structure of teachers' awareness', in: Carlgren, I., Handal, G. and Vaage, S. (eds), *Teachers' Minds and Actions: Research on Teachers' Thinking and Practice*, Brighton, Falmer Press.

Marton, F., Dall'Alba, G., and Beaty, E. (1993). 'Conceptions of Learning', *International Journal of Educational Research*, vol. 19, no. 3, pp. 277–9.

Pramling, I. (1988). 'Developing Children's Thinking About Their Own Learning', *British Journal of Educational Psychology*, 58, pp. 266–78.

Schön, D. (1983). *The Reflective Practitioner: How Professionals Think in Action*, New York, Basic Books.

Schön, D. (1987). *Educating the Reflective Practitioner*, New York, Basic Books.

Winter, R. (1991). 'Outline of a general theory of professional competences', in: Maisch, M. and Winter, R. (eds), *The Development and Assessment of Professional Competences*, Chelmsford, Social Services Department and Anglia Polytechnic.

Wood, K. (1995). 'Learning to teach: a phenomenographic perspective', PhD thesis submitted to the University of London.

End note

This is metacognition viewed from a phenomenographical standpoint, which must be contrasted with a cognitive skills approach to metacognition. According to Pramling (1988) metacognition can be seen in three steps, with the third being the metacognitive level:

- Step 1 is a focus on *what* the learner is thinking about a content.

- Step 2 is a focus on *how* the learner is thinking about that content.

- Step 3 is a focus on the learner's thinking *about her own thinking* about the content.

23 Competency and teacher education

Keith Brumfitt

This chapter considers recent developments in school-focused teacher training. It outlines the changing role of school teachers in the training of new teachers of business/economics, including competence-based assessment, designing school-focused training, and working with students who may be failing. The examples are taken from experience at the University of Brighton and are based on the model of partnership that we have developed with 200 secondary schools and colleges (UoB, 1993).

A changing system

Considerable changes have taken place in Initial Teacher Training (ITT) in England and Wales, affecting schools, colleges and the university sector. The main change has been that the balance of responsibility for training new teachers has shifted away from the higher-education (HE) institutions towards schools and colleges. Wilkin (1992) argues that this change has occurred for two reasons:

- the 'theory–practice' gap, though continually diminishing, still separates what happens in HE institutions from the reality of school life; and

- there has been an increasing awareness that teachers as professionals can, and should, contribute to the training of new recruits.

The move towards school-focused training was first suggested in 1984 in *Circular 3/84* from the DES. This document called for teachers to be involved in the planning of courses and the assessment of students during school experience. This suggestion is fully incorporated within *Circular 9/92* from the DFE, and consequently schools are training students for a much greater percentage of their courses. In addition, *Circular 9/92* placed other responsibilities on teachers. Schools will now need to be involved in the planning of courses, in the interviewing of potential students, in the assessment of students on their school experience, and in playing a significant part in the professional training of subject specialists as full partners of HE institutions. The training institution continues to award the qualification and to ensure that academic standards are maintained. In return for their increased role in student training, schools expect to be recompensed financially by the training institutions.

There is no evidence to suggest that the trend towards school-focused teacher training is likely to be reversed, and so school teachers can expect to continue to be fully involved in preparing recruits to the profession.

In adjusting to the role of a trainer of students (rather than a supporter of students), schools have had to become more familiar with many aspects of ITT. The specialist business studies/economics teacher, often referred to as a subject mentor, is at the heart of the new arrangement. The subject specialist often prepares and delivers the training programme for each student and then has the task of assessing the same student in line with the required competences. Thus the same person has to be a supporter, an advisor, a trainer and an assessor.

The mentor is often assigned a variety of tasks that help to train and support the student. For a mentor under the University of Brighton scheme, these tasks would typically include the following:

- monitor lesson planning;
- analyse the trainee's teaching;
- identify the trainee's strengths and weaknesses in relation to competence statements;
- record competences and suggest ways of improving;
- provide a structured, individualized programme for the student.

As well as a subject mentor, most schools and colleges appoint a professional tutor, whose role is to facilitate the study of whole-school issues. This role often involves responsibility for newly qualified teachers, as well as students, and a subject mentor can expect advice and support from the professional tutor.

The development of partnerships between schools/colleges and HE institutions is a feature of a post-technocratic model of professional education (Bines and Watson, 1992). In such a model the placement becomes the focus for professional training. Associated with this model – where schools and colleges have some control over professional education rather than providing a place for students to 'test' their theory – is the development of competence-based assessment strategies. If this new style of training or education is to succeed, schools and colleges will need to be in genuine partnership with HE institutions, with an equal say in course design, course delivery, assessment and so on.

Competence-based assessment

In some institutions the move to models of competence-based assessment has led to the need for students to provide evidence that they have met all the required competences. *Circular 9/92* does not distinguish between what must be achieved as the student progresses on a course, it refers only to the level of competence required at the end of the course. There are no guidelines as to what can be expected after the first placement, nor how a school or college decides that a student has met each competence statement.

Most ITT providers have a system for recognizing when a student has met the necessary competence. One example of a guideline is:

'Where a student has the opportunity to demonstrate the competence, they should be able to do this three times in three different contexts.'

This means that evidence could be gathered from Year 7, 9 and 12 classes or three different Year 11 groups. Alternatively the evidence could arise from tutor group periods, interaction in the corridors, parent evenings or departmental meetings. If a student can demonstrate meeting a competence three times, this can be recorded on the relevant assessment sheet.

Where a student meets all the necessary competences on the first placement, there may be a case for saying this person is a qualified teacher. However, few ITT providers would accept this view. Students need to demonstrate their competence in two situations as it is the transferability as well as the demonstration of the competences that is important in granting QTS. This implies that there is no carry-forward of competences from one placement to the next. Although there may be differences between individual ITT providers, in most situations a student unable to demonstrate the competence in the second placement (unless there are exceptional circumstances) will fail the teacher training course.

Deciding when a student is competent is easier if a school or ITT provider is using an evidence-based system. Using this sort of system, a student is not assessed as having failed, merely that he or she has not demonstrated the necessary competences by the end of the placement. Each teacher training institution will have its own assessment system, devised with their partner schools. The system used at the University of Brighton is: NE = no evidence; SE = some evidence; C = competent; CC = consistently competent. Examples of the competences used:

- Students need to demonstrate appropriate levels of expectations when organizing pupils' learning.

- Students need to manage the learning environment by providing smooth continuity, starts and finishes to their lessons.

It is the school or college's responsibility to ensure the student has the opportunity to demonstrate each of the competences. A recording of 'NE' against a competence is therefore as much an issue for the school or college to resolve as it is for the student and the higher-education institution. A recording of 'SE' indicates that the mentor has observed the student demonstrating the required competence only once or twice, rather than the required three times. Obviously most students will be able to demonstrate the required competence on many occasions. A problem occurs when the student is weak and is struggling to meet the required standards.

When students are failing to demonstrate the appropriate levels of competence, the task for the school mentor becomes more difficult. It is often difficult to fail a student with whom you have been working for the past few weeks. Most, if not all, ITT providers have a system for students at risk of failing. It is important that this is followed, not just to ensure the student receives a fair deal and has adequate warning of the level of their competence, but also to ensure the school and ITT provider are operating within the regulations set up by the HE institutions. Problems are always created if the student appeals against the decision of failure because the proper procedures were not followed.

The idea of competence as part of any university-based course is not particularly controversial; what *is* often contested is the nature of the competence. Barnett (1994) identifies both *operational* and *academic* competences and raises questions as to the nature of university education when the operational competences become the sole means of measuring the success of students. Barnett argues that university education has changed dramatically in recent years – words such as 'insight', 'understanding', 'reflection' and 'wisdom' have been replaced with 'skill', 'competence', 'outcome', 'information', 'technique' and 'flexibility'. These changes can be seen in the field of teacher education which has accepted the terminology and approaches of competence-based education. We all want our newly qualified teachers to be competent, flexible and reflective, but we also want teachers to demonstrate that they can develop their own ideas and strategies for teaching.

Designing a programme for a student

At the University of Brighton we have taken the view that a training programme for a student should include the following:

- purposeful, structured, individualized and progressive professional development;

- opportunities to consult, negotiate, take initiative (as appropriate);

- access to and appreciation of the teacher's craft knowledge through observing different classes and through collaborative teaching;

- continued observation and collaborative teaching throughout the school experience;

- regular meetings with staff responsible for training, to place issues raised through events in the classroom in the broader professional context and to monitor progress.

In addition, students should take individual responsibility for classes at some point in their school experience. This type of programme, built upon students' self-evaluation, can work for any student, whether a first-year undergraduate or a postgraduate on the final placement. In all cases the emphasis is on collaborative work, rather than the student taking over the teacher's classes.

As schools become more aware of their role as trainers, rather than acting as a place for students to try out their ideas, teachers can expect to share classes and work with students as part of their subject team. This particular approach has been successful in the teaching of GNVQ courses as teachers/lecturers are obliged to form teams for the delivery of the subject content and core skills.

If school-focused training is to be more than a modern-day apprenticeship (to use Bines's and Watson's terminology), this collaborative teaching will need to introduce students to the whole range of skills required by a teacher. The school-focused training will need to be designed to develop the reflective and evaluative skills of the student as well as the practical skills needed in the classroom.

One of the main concerns of mentors is the amount of time it takes to work with a student in school. Each HE institution will have its own requirements, though it is likely that at least a formal commitment of 30 minutes each week will be required. This is the minimum time needed to debrief a student after a lesson has finished. It is not the total amount of time the mentor will be involved with a student. Feedback from mentors to the HE institutions on issues such as the time allocated to mentors, student performance, students causing concern, and so on, form an important link in the partnership arrangements.

Support from the higher-education institution

Before teachers undertake the training of students it is important that they be 'appropriately qualified and prepared' (*Circular 9/92*). Teachers can expect the HE institution to provide good-quality training as well as regular meetings to discuss the progress of mentoring. The ITT provider may set up a mentor group within a group of schools to allow teachers to support and advise each other. There are many examples of good practice in schools in supporting trainee teachers, and one of the main advantages of establishing such a mentor group is the peer support it provides. A mentor support group can be particularly important in business studies and economics because often there is only one specialist teacher in each school and little support for subject-specific problems.

Partnership means joint responsibility for the progress of students. Schools should seek advice when a student is in difficulty or is not performing to the required standard. Waiting until someone from the ITT provider decides to visit the school to discuss student progress can be too late. Some ITT providers are observing and assessing students on their school experience, but increasingly these visits take the form of ensuring that the students are receiving their entitlement in terms of school-focused training, monitoring whether the school has any problems with the students, advising mentors on training strategies and tactics as well as discussing with students their progress in the school placement. In these circumstances, if a teacher needs a second opinion it is often another member of the school staff who provides the advice, though there are some situations where the university tutor and the school mentor will jointly observe a student. This will then lead to a discussion on the student's teaching as a means of sharing a common understanding on the level at which the student is operating.

Designing a school-focused programme

Many of the skills needed to be a successful mentor are generic and are applicable in all subject areas. *Circular 9/92* does not include specific competences or criteria for different subject areas of the secondary curriculum, but states areas of competence for all subjects:

- subject knowledge;

- subject application;

- class management;

- assessment and recording of pupils' progress;

- further professional development.

It is for partnerships to decide specific subject-based criteria, if any. Many teachers of business studies and economics are familiar with the idea of competence-based assessment through GNVQs. However, where the business/economics teacher is often at a disadvantage is in the choice of courses that can be given to the trainee. The main problems can be summarized as follows:

- only examination-based courses available to trainees;

- very little Key Stage 3 work;

- one person departments;

- considerable curriculum development (GNVQ, new A levels);

- students with a variety of backgrounds (Law, Accountancy, Economics, Management and so on).

These five issues can be addressed by a variety of approaches. By considering each problem in turn, it is possible to build up a purposeful, structured, individualized and progressive programme for a trainee.

Examination-based courses

Some schools are facing considerable pressure from parents and governors not to accept too many trainee teachers because of the potential effect on examination classes. As all students have to demonstrate their competence in assessing pupils' work, there are particular problems if all the students' classes are externally examined. As it may be very difficult, if not impossible, to have a student within a business /economics department who does not take responsibility for some examination classes, an ideal arrangement is for a student to have full responsibility only for a Year 10 group. Other groups should be shared.

Even with the group for which the student has full responsibility, there is no need to allow the student to do all the teaching all the time. Collaborative work, team teaching and supporting the student while he or she is in the classroom are all valuable ways of experiencing teaching and learning

Key Stage 3

There are few courses that students can teach at Key Stage 3, but this does not mean they should have no exposure to this age range. Many students taking business studies courses can contribute to Information Technology at Key Stage 3, even if it is a support role with another teacher who lacks experience or confidence with computers. This can be a way for the student to contribute to a subject area without taking responsibility for the whole class.

Similarly, business studies students can contribute to Technology at Key Stage 3. If the school operates a carousel-based programme, then there are many opportunities for the student to become an extra 'pair of hands' in the classroom working alongside a Technology teacher. In addition, as part of the student's wider professional development there will be opportunities to observe other classes outside the business/economics department.

Small departments

In many schools the business/economics department consists of only one teacher. In this situation the mentor may find it difficult to allocate classes to any student teacher. This is where it is particularly important to ensure the student is involved in a variety of activities, not all of which will be in the business/economics department.

One possibility is link work with a local sixth-form college or FE establishment. This allows the student to gain experience of the whole 11–19 age range, as well as bringing back valuable knowledge into the 11–16 institution.

A final suggestion for a small department is the possibility of getting the student involved in the school's work experience programme, either helping the organiser or actually visiting some of the pupils while they undertake their work placement.

Curriculum development

The rapid development of GNVQ courses (and NVQs in some colleges) has created problems with the D32/D33 assessors award. Some students may be following an assessors' award as part of their study at the ITT provider and would welcome an opportunity to be involved across the whole of the GNVQ process, including action planning, delivery and feedback. In these situations the student is of immense value to a business studies team. If students are not familiar with the GNVQ specifications then this will create an opportunity for their school-focused training.

In other subject areas students can be confident that they will have to teach the National Curriculum, and so they will all have a copy of the latest proposals from the Dearing Report. In our subject area the requirements that face a student are much more varied. It is difficult to predict what the students will have to teach. It is unlikely that the ITT provider can prepare students for the diversity, and so there is a need to ensure that a student receives some induction into the department and its courses. Even when the student is not on his or her first placement, it is not safe to assume an awareness of the syllabus, the assessment pattern and the overall design of the courses within the department. The student teacher is also likely to need time to gain familiarity with the department's computers and software.

Variety of backgrounds

As ITT providers have widened the number of courses they offer, partly in response to government initiatives and partly to respond to the shortage of specialist business studies teachers, the background of students has continued to broaden. Increasingly students are entering teaching with work experience as well as a relevant degree and postgraduate training. The range of degree qualifications acceptable to ITT providers has led to considerable diversity in the student population and schools cannot always expect to receive a graduate in Economics or Business Studies.

This variety of background explains the need to create a purposeful, structured, individualized and progressive programme for each student. If the partnership arrangements with the ITT provider are well-developed, the mentor can expect to receive a short curriculum vitae about the student *before* the student arrives in the school. This will help the planning of the student's teaching commitments as well as the training programme the school can provide. It is important to provide a student with a programme that meets his or her needs as well as satisfying the school's requirements of only allowing a student to take full responsibility when the time is right.

Conclusion

There seems to be no doubt that school-focused ITT is here to stay. Students can be an asset to the school. They can bring new ideas, they can provide opportunities for staff to catch up with other duties and tasks, they can also help teachers in researching new curriculum developments. Students should be up-to-date, they should be aware of the new national initiatives, they should be aware of the latest research in the field of business and economics education. The responsibility of the new partnership approach is to ensure that they receive a proper, balanced training programme that does not attempt to exploit their presence in the school or take advantage of their enthusiasm by throwing them 'in the deep end' with all the difficult classes.

References

Barnett R. (1994). *The Limits of Competence: Knowledge, Education and Society*, Milton Keynes, Open University Press.

Bines, H. and Watson, D. (1992). *Developing Professional Education*, Milton Keynes, Open University Press.

DES (1984). *Circular 3/84: Initial Teacher Training – Approval of Courses*, London, DES.

DFE (1992). *Circular 9/92: Initial Teacher Training – Secondary Phase*, London, DFE.

Wilkin, M. (1992). *Mentoring in Schools*, London, Kogan Page.

University of Brighton (1993). *Mentoring in Secondary Schools: Video and Notes*, Brighton, UoB.

4 Starting out as a teacher

Richard Dunnill, Kieron James, Martyn Lucas and Suzanna Nakarada

Introduction

Here are three newly qualified teachers (NQTs) of economics and business commenting on their first year or two in teaching:

'Often it isn't the big things that stump you. I remember how long I used to spend looking for the keys to the reprographics room or staring at my register trying to decide whether a holiday was an authorized absence or not (and) the formal induction programme just doesn't have space for advice on keeping the caretaker happy, but you wish that it did.' (Kieron)

'My first year in teaching certainly taught me that, although the tag of NQT could be applied to me for administrative purposes for the first year, I was learning very quickly that I was in control of my own successes and failures. It was my own belief in my strategies and my style of teaching together with my willingness to experiment, to listen to those people whose opinions I respected, and a readiness to adapt to meet the needs of those around me that got me through my first year.' (Martyn)

'There were fantastic moments such as when my Young Enterprise group won the regional finals and when I almost single-handedly organized a business link with Citroën in Paris. There were disastrous times such as being so tired that I forgot to go to assembly on the one occasion that the Head was taking it! The most pleasing aspect is that the kids become your kids and the department becomes your department to the point where you don't have to check each individual decision that you make with someone else. You survive and you learn from it all.' (Suzanna)

As economics and business specialists, how many times have we read that *labour is a key factor of production,* and that *people are a company's and a country's most precious resource,* and then, as teachers, repeated these sentiments to our classes? It would seem that we all accept those aspects of our subjects which emphasize the central importance of people in economic and business activity, but what about our own profession and our own experiences? Just what are the key learning issues for economics and business NQTs?

This chapter examines these questions by setting some of the issues identified as important by researchers in the field against the experiences of three economics and business NQTs. In the light of this, practical advice is provided to NQTs, together with suggestions for managers in schools and colleges, in Local Education Authorities and in Initial Teacher Training (ITT) institutions, so that new teachers may be provided with the best possible opportunities to succeed.

What does the literature say?

Our early experiences of teaching play a key role in shaping our development as teachers. Earley (1994, p. 1) makes this clear:

'The experience of the first year is most formative and there is therefore a need to set high expectations and standards when there is greatest receptiveness and willingness to learn and develop. Induction – the process which acts as a bridge between training and employment and enables newcomers in any organization to become effective – can be seen as the first step in a comprehensive programme of professional development available throughout a teacher's career.'

Two strands of work emerge from the literature on NQTs: first, work that reviews the experiences and concerns of NQTs during their first year in teaching; and second, work that attempts to set out the characteristics of a model induction programme. The next section of this chapter explores both these strands before we go on to look at the experiences and thinking of three economics and business studies NQTs.

The Structure and Process of Initial Teacher Education (SPITE) project (Reid, 1985a, b) followed a cohort of over 2000 newly qualified teachers into their first posts. Table 24.1 shows the people from whom the NQTs received help during their first year of teaching. The total percentage is greater than 100 because many received help from more than one person. Perhaps predictably, most support came from heads of department and from other teachers, with deputy heads and pastoral heads some way behind. Only 5.5 per cent said that nobody helped them.

Nobody	132	(5.5)
Headteacher	420	(17.5)
Deputy headteacher(s)	843	(35.4)
Head(s) of department	1750	(73.0)
Head(s) of year	652	(27.2)
Other teacher(s)	1693	(70.6)
LEA adviser(s)	530	(22.1)
HMI	81	(3.4)
Someone else	204	(8.5)

Table 24.1 Distribution (and percentages) of people from whom probationers received help (O'Sullivan *et al.*, 1988, p. 133)

The SPITE project also asked NQTs to indicate, from a list of ten items, which issues had caused occasional or frequent problems during their first year of teaching (Table 24.2). Classroom management concerns emerged as the most troublesome issues, followed by the pressures of marking, inadequate textbooks and lesson preparation.

Problem	None	Some	Major	N/A
Teaching subjects for which your training has not equipped you	33.0	36.4	4.2	26.4
Amount of marking time required	34.7	53.7	9.3	2.3
Lack of non-teaching time	47.7	40.8	8.8	2.7
Lesson preparation	41.8	50.6	7.0	0.6
Difficulty in controlling individual classes	21.8	63.5	14.0	0.6
Difficulty in controlling classes	34.4	57.0	7.6	1.0
The administrative tasks associated with teaching	58.1	35.8	3.7	2.4
Inadequate school textbooks	33.2	42.4	20.2	4.0
Inadequate audio-visual resources	49.3	30.8	13.6	6.4
Lack of clear direction from established staff	46.2	39.2	11.8	2.8

Table 24.2 Distribution (percentages) of beginning teachers' problems (O'Sullivan *et al.*, 1988, p. 135)

In March 1992, Her Majesty's Inspectorate (HMI) reported critically on arrangements found in many schools and LEAs for the induction of new teachers (DES, 1992). It found that induction was highly variable and judged it less than satisfactory or poor in one-third of the 42 LEAs and 112 schools visited between 1988 and 1990.

In 1993, OfSTED published a 1992 HMI survey of the quality of performance of 300 NQTs, their initial training experiences and how well they were supported in their first year of teaching. This enabled HMI to compare the quality of NQT performance in 1992 with that of previous surveys of 1981 and 1987. The report concluded that, for secondary NQTs, the quality of teaching, as observed from the survey, was broadly satisfactory and in line with the previous survey of 1987. Moreover, there was good support from subject departments in secondary schools and a general satisfaction with initial teacher training experiences.

On induction, however, the report stated (p. 8) that the provision and effectiveness of induction programmes was very variable and often not built systematically on ITT experiences:

'Schools were largely unaware of their new teachers' strengths and weaknesses at the completion of their training.'

Most recently, the National Foundation for Educational Research (NFER) published findings from an induction research study (Earley *et al.*, 1992; Earley and Kinder, 1994). A summary of the project's major findings is shown in Figure 24.1.

The NQTs themselves

- Around half the sample had seen induction as an important factor in choosing for which jobs to apply.
- Most of their schools offered some kind of informal or formal summer induction programme prior to them taking up their appointments.
- Most worked at least a 50-hour week.

Schools' induction programmes

- Senior managers usually had overall responsibility.
- All the secondary schools in the sample ran centrally organized programmes.
- Most sessions took place after school and covered issues such as differentiation, teaching and learning strategies, administration, pastoral work, time management and cross-curricular issues.
- Individual sessions were also held linked to lesson observation by senior manager, head of department and, sometimes, LEA Adviser.
- Most NQTs taught reduced timetables and/or were relieved of additional work such as form tutor responsibilities or cover.
- Mentors were almost always senior managers or heads of department.
- LEA induction programmes, where they existed, were generally viewed as useful.
- NQT competence profiles were being increasingly developed and used by schools.

Consistency of support

- Although there was all this positive activity throughout the sample of secondary schools, in contrast to some of the primary schools, there was little evidence of consistency in policy or practice. Individual LEAs and schools were often developing their own approaches, many in collaboration with Higher Education Institutions.

Figure 24.1 Summary of NFER findings on induction (Earley, 1994, pp. 131–40)

In summary, therefore, the literature presents the following picture.

- NQTs see induction as important.

- Induction takes place both pre and post appointment.

- School induction is run by deputy heads and heads of department who also act as mentors and classroom observers.

- In practice, NQTs find help mostly from their heads of department, deputy headteachers and other teachers.

- NQTs' main problems centre on classroom management, resources, preparation and marking.

- Their teaching is rated pretty highly by HMI.

- Both HMI and NFER describe many induction programmes as very variable with little continuity from initial training (e.g. Calderhead and Lambert, 1992).

The experiences of three economics and business NQTS

Sources of support

In terms of sources of support (Table 24.1), one of the three quickly found himself assuming more responsibility:

'My head of department got a new post, which meant that before Christmas I was trying to persuade the head that I could do the job which she was leaving! Even if my own self-assurance was naive, I somehow managed to convince him and was given a chance to prove myself.' (Kieron)

However, although this was by no means easy, aspects of Kieron's subject knowledge and application helped considerably:

'The learning curve is steep and perhaps the heavy workload meant that I never really looked up. I believe that my trump card was a good working knowledge of GNVQ assessment – an extremely saleable commodity and one which business teachers should maximize.'

For Martyn and Suzanna, support from their fellow NQTs was important:

'The other NQTs were an invaluable source of ideas, and provided the real shoulders to be cried on.' (Martyn)

'I had managed to find myself a house with two other newly qualified teachers who had recently moved to the area and we all found great friendship and support with one another. (Suzanna)

Suzanna's head of department featured in her experience:

317

'My mentor in school was, fortunately, my head of department and hence I feel like I really got my money's worth, but others were not so fortunate. As an NQT I feel that your head of department often becomes your surrogate mother or father and you come to rely upon her/him heavily for advice and support. Others within the staff you'll seek out later.'

For Martyn, however, a broader network of teachers provided support:

'I did find that there was a great deal to be gained from developing links with other members of staff, and it became increasingly obvious that certain staff members would always be willing to listen to an idea, or comment on an issue, and the dining room provided the place for these discussions to take place. These colleagues were in the minority, and would have a tendency to agree that the problems that an NQT experienced, especially in behaviour management of classes and individuals, were the same for everyone!'

Overall, therefore, it seems that most support came from heads of department and other teachers, although Kieron's special circumstances perhaps make his a somewhat different case.

'Both deputies were very helpful in the first term and one is still very supportive – he's inspirational because he does what he says he'll do and he always seems to have time for you. Other staff and my peers from the PGCE course have been super, but my other vital source of support has been my family. My wife has been so tolerant of the hours and the stress!'

Beginning teachers' problems

None of the three seemed concerned about the first issue in Table 24.2 – teaching subjects for which their training has not equipped them. Perhaps this was because, as mentioned earlier, all of them had areas of subject knowledge in which they were weaker but which they knew they had to teach properly. It is a matter of working on things rather than seeing them as a problem.

On the amount of time required for marking, Martyn summed up their view that this is not simply a matter of being provided with more time. Marking is something to be learned, especially when a full timetable is being taught:

'You learn to handle marking time – I had to get used to allocating sufficient yet not excessive time for it.'

GNVQ marking and assessment, predictably, caused all three some concern, especially since every other member of staff was learning too. Martyn explains how he and the team of which he was a member coped:

'We all get together for an evening regularly and share and compare our assessment – doing this as a group has made it much easier.'

Kieron added:

'I am looking forward to the revised specifications with the new evidence indicators!'

Concerning a lack of non-teaching time, and on preparation issues, all three had comments to make. On preparation prior to starting work in September, Kieron was very realistic about just how prepared anyone can be:

'I suppose it's a bit like the arrival of the first baby. You realize that there has been a conspiracy of silence after all and, although you couldn't have done more, you really are ill-prepared!'

Martyn set himself a target which echoes the point made earlier regarding the breadth of subject knowledge in economics and business:

'I would study my subject areas, and get to know them inside out.'

Suzanna provided an insight into her method of preparing for her new post:

'I did very little preparation work over the summer. I had originally planned to work out a full term of lessons for each subject ... however I found myself surprisingly relaxed and laid back about the whole thing ... even a little unprepared. Looking back this was exactly what I needed to do. The amount of work that I had to cope with in the first few months would not have been as successfully completed if I had not had a complete break before I had begun. I had heard of some teachers devoting the majority of their summer to preparation and then having to scrap the whole lot after the first week and I certainly wasn't prepared to do all of that.'

On starting work, all three found themselves on full teaching timetables. Suzanna, for instance, said:

'My timetable consisted of nine periods of GNVQ Foundation Business, four periods of GNVQ Intermediate Business, six periods of lower sixth A level Business Studies, six periods of GCSE Business Studies plus one period with my Year 12 tutor group. Unlike the other NQT's joining the school that year I had been given a 100 per cent teaching timetable because of the extra pressures of GNVQ.'

These workloads created considerable issues of lesson planning and resource preparation, as Suzanna explained:

'The first few weeks of preparation were horrendous. Every night you're working until about midnight either marking, reading or in my case learning a new subject. I had graduated in 1993 with a degree in Economics and had limited business experience ... I felt guilty in my first few weeks as my teaching style was extremely unimaginative, textbook-based and quite structured ... Looking back this is exactly what I needed. I needed time to get to grips with the subject, to get to know my pupils and what they were capable of. If you're producing all singing, all dancing lessons this task becomes almost impossible! ... There was plenty of time for that.'

No one seems to have found any particular course or topic especially difficult allowing for the newness of GNVQ and the subject knowledge issue mentioned earlier. However, both Martyn and Kieron echoed Suzanna's commitment to personal organization and to sheer hard work:

'I got into the habit of sitting down on a Sunday morning and asking myself what I had to do for the coming week. I used the lesson planning model I had developed in my PGCE year at first and gradually modified and relaxed it as I went on. The GNVQ was difficult at first – it was hard to get away from chalk and talk lessons because I was so concerned about them getting the knowledge.' (Martyn)

'I really missed the time I'd had on the PGCE, but by Christmas I had accepted that I couldn't plan lessons that way and also do everything else. Anyway, I don't think my lessons have suffered in the long term – I've just learned to plan more efficiently. I now plan highlight sessions every so often alongside everyday lessons.' (Kieron)

Regarding matters of classroom management and control, naturally enough, all three experienced some problems although these tended to be with groups or individuals who were just as problematic for other, more experienced teachers. Talking about his Year 10 GCSE Business Studies group, Martyn explained his approach thus:

'I decided that, whatever happened, they were not going to see that they could wind me up so I maintained my friendly, open and positive approach despite everything! Also, I always avoided confrontations with the whole class. This was especially important when, on a Wednesday afternoon, they would come from a maths teacher who ruled them with an iron fist. I just wouldn't imitate him and they took time to cope with this – but they did in the end!'

Kieron explained how he worked to motivate and enthuse his classes:

'Involve them in things they're interested in and bring these things into the lesson. Listen to them and their ideas and take any opportunity that comes up. One day, there was this girl reading Smash Hits under the desk during a lesson on advertising. I quickly brought her and the magazine into the lesson and it went brilliantly.'

A key feature of Martyn's classroom work was his use of genuine negotiation early on in his first year, especially with his GNVQ Intermediate class:

'The bottom line is you've got to give them all a fair opportunity to pass. My key to this is to say to them "look, we've got to do this, how can we do it as well as possible?" And when they come up with some ideas I say "OK, we'll try that but I need something in return." That way, we decided on things like five-minute rests and doing notes on certain days and not on others while I could then insist on deadlines and on getting through the syllabus.'

Martyn also felt it important to gain some impression of his own progress and for this he went straight to the students:

'By asking for students' comments on my teaching style I was able to learn a lot during my first year. After all they saw me in action all the time. It was something that I had asked for from the beginning, and developed into real debriefings with the sixth-form classes.

'At first there was real apprehension on the part of the students to comment upon my teaching, but by the end of the spring term they had accepted it as normal practice. I would invite their ideas on approaches to certain topics, and we would spend dedicated time discussing the course, and how I could best help them reach their targets.

'I found that the danger with this approach was that students would make direct comparisons between my style and that of other teachers, and I had to be quick to point out that these discussions were to be about the time that we spent together as a teaching/learning unit, and that it was not the opportunity to take potshots at other members of staff. This was hard to control at first, but the outcome was first-hand feedback on me as a teacher. It also provided some of the pats on the back, even if I did give them to myself!'

Kieron also tried this but provides a note of caution:

'Don't give students a rope to hang you with, especially in GNVQ with its constant changes. Keep a professional distance and a balance between what's your responsibility and what's theirs.'

Suzanna also talked about her classroom management and relationships with students, in this case with those following GNVQ Foundation Business:

'I was responsible for students who throughout their school lives had been ignored by the system and hence were not the success stories of the school. They lacked confidence, were immature and often quite rude. My first task was to gain their trust and respect. My solution was to show them some attention!

'We talked through every single decision we were going to make. I gave them increasing responsibility and showed them they were capable and could succeed if they tried. It eventually began to work. All the students began to increase their confidence, they worked much harder and often were my favourite class. The downside of this was that they often adopted me as some sort of mother figure. One of my students constantly asked me what he should wear to school, what time he should get up and what his next lesson was – at least I felt wanted! ...

'This turned out to be one of the largest learning experiences so far. Taking responsibility for devising a scheme of work doesn't often come until your second or third years in teaching. However by doing this task so soon it made me face the realities of differentiation, the use of resources and teaching styles. It kept me in the teacher training frame of mind. Coming to *the end of this course now I have a group of confident individuals who will all leave the school with a GNVQ – what a feeling!'*

The issue of administrative tasks generated a common response from all three NQTs. In effect, they found GNVQ administration laborious, but then so did everyone else! It was the work associated with general school matters which sometimes became burdensome. All three had tutor groups and Suzanna's comment was typical:

'I insisted that I was assigned a tutor group as I personally felt that the pastoral side of teaching is extremely important not only to facilitate my relationships with the pupils but also to establish myself as a full member of staff.'

However, as Martyn said, even the most routine tasks take on added significance when part of a new job:

'The students arrived on the following day, and I suddenly became aware of my pastoral role as a form teacher. I had a rough idea of how to run a register but the first several weeks' entries left a lot to be desired in terms of neatness and legibility!'

Kieron added:

'It's really hard when you're charging around working flat out and then someone asks you to check a boy's uniform!'

There was a positive side to all this, however, as Suzanna outlined:

'My tutor group were excellent – they were even quite a support to me in the first few days. They showed me around, assisted me with staff codes and helped with administration enquiries. Often bits of paper would appear in my register with little explanation of what they entailed and the office wanted the reply by tomorrow morning first thing! My motto became "don't panic". After about a week I felt like I'd been there all my life! ... in the nicest possible way.'

On school texts and other resources, all three felt that their schools were fairly well resourced but that is not to say that there were no problems. Martyn would have liked more of a formal introduction to the departmental resources, while Suzanna explained her initial experience thus:

'I had trained in a department where worksheets and IT had been quite a major focus and hence I started my new post with the same habits. The department I had joined relied quite heavily on written texts and student research and hence I felt often guilty in using so much of the department's photocopying budget – I managed to increase it six-fold in my first three months there!'

Finally, with regard to the quality of direction from established staff, Martyn's comment serves to sum-up all three NQT's experience:

'Members of the department and the school provided support to a greater or lesser extent, although in the main, it had to be requested. ...

'My perception of the school's approach to NQTs was to let you get on with it and to be there if you needed a shoulder to cry on. Other members of staff would occasionally pass through my lessons to reach other classes. Feedback was available – from the students. By asking for comments on my teaching style I was able to learn a lot during my first year. After all these people saw me in action all the time and they were the ones in the front line. Although there was a lack of any informal first year programme for NQTs within the school.' (Martyn)

Induction and school programmes for NQTs

In line with the literature, two of the three commented on spending time at their new school during the summer term prior to starting in September:

'I would recommend to any NQT starting their first job that they get into the school as soon as possible as it takes away some of the initial anxiety that we all go through at the beginning of the new term.' (Suzanna)

'Spending a day in the school during the previous summer term definitely helped. It allowed me to be seen around the school, and offered me the opportunity to get lost in the corridors, and find a way out without having a timetable to meet! This day had been originally organized to give me my timetable, and some of the set texts for the courses that I would be taking.' (Martyn)

Their experience of school induction programmes in practice was rather mixed, mirroring the research. Suzanna described her experience as follows:

'All in all, the mentoring system did not produce the required goods. We only had two meetings throughout the whole year ... What we really needed was to share our experiences, let off some steam and seek advice. However at least we were shown some interest.' (Suzanna)

'The school's induction programme involved the newly qualified members of staff meeting once per half term to discuss common issues. ... There were three of these meetings in all, the last at the start of the spring term. My perception of the school's approach to the NQTs was to let you get on with it and to be there if you needed a shoulder to cry on.' (Martyn)

Martyn, alone of the three, mentioned being observed:

'During a year that included an OfSTED visit, there was no formal observation of my teaching. The nature of teaching in the Business Centre, however, meant that other members of staff would occasionally pass through my lessons to reach other classes, and this was deemed to be sufficient. Even this "low key" level of observation did not exist in the area of form teacher.'

'During the whole of my first year, no one saw me in action. Despite this Heads of both the Department and the Year were able to give me very complimentary comments on my teaching! Self assessment became a well developed skill during my first year of teaching!'

There was only one mention of any LEA involvement:

'... most NQTs seemed to agree that the content had been a re-run of the PGCE, and that we had not learnt anything new.' (Martyn)

Conclusions and recommendations

On the basis of the research and the experiences of these three NQTs, there seem to be two clear conclusions to be drawn and some positive suggestions for action to be made.

The first conclusion must be that relying on institutional induction programmes is a risky business for most NQTs, especially for those of us who teach the broad range of courses in economics and business. That should certainly not discourage school and college managers from establishing and operating such programmes since, where they work well, they are most valuable. To this end, therefore, some recommendations are made below for those responsible for NQT induction.

The second conclusion follows naturally from the first. NQTs themselves need to be proactive in their own professional development, and so the chapter ends with some practical advice to NQTs on how to go about this, both in day-to-day matters and in a more strategic sense.

- *Recommendation 1: LEAs and ITT institutions should support school/ college induction programmes*

If you work in one of these organizations, how do you see your role in NQT induction? We recommend that you accept responsibility for supporting schools and colleges as they develop their own programmes – through help with planning, by having staff who can contribute to these school or college-focused programmes, and by accrediting the professional development that occurs.

- *Recommendation 2: Schools and colleges must value their NQTs*

If you are a head of department or senior manager charged with the task of developing and running the induction programme in your school or college, what do you make of the issues raised so far? We recommend that you review your induction programme with your newer teachers, and with ITT institutions, in order to resolve the issues raised here.

In addition, you must take account of the initiative, ambition and commitment of many economics and business NQTs now entering teaching. As Suzanna explained:

'I hated accepting that I was at the bottom of the pile, that I was the naive

*one and that I would be the one to make the most mistakes. If I had
accepted this from the beginning my life would have been a lot easier and
those close to me would have had a lot less ear-ache in the meantime.'*

Suzanna has turned coping with this into a lesson for herself. Such professional realism is a key learning issue for all new teachers, but initiative,
ambition and commitment are the very qualities which will take NQTs from
their initial experiences through to becoming the next generation of heads of
department and headteachers. In order for this to happen, school and college
managers must accept the responsibility for creating the conditions in which
experienced teachers at all levels in an institution are prepared to listen, to
advise and to support NQTs.

- *Recommendation 3: NQTs must take on the responsibility for their own
  professional development*

A summary of the three NQTs' advice is provided in Figure 24.2, but if you are
in training or your first year or two of teaching this chapter has a clear
message. In short, be proactive in your own professional development and
don't give up!

School and college induction programmes are variable and there is only
patchy support from LEAs and ITT institutions. In order to grow as a teacher

Sources of support	Use senior managers, other staff and other NQTs, whoever seems best but use someone! Don't rely on an induction programme. Ask to be observed and for practical feedback.
Preparation	Be prepared but be realistic about what that means.
Marking	Learn to mark and to allocate sufficient but not excessive time to it, and collaborate with the department.
Subject knowledge	Don't be too concerned if you don't know everything immediately but expect to have to learn it sooner rather than later.
Classroom management	Rely on careful planning and organization not simply on personal relationships. Involve the students in their own learning and be yourself. Remember to listen and learn from the students.
Keys to success	Personal organization and sheer hard work. Keep learning as well as teaching.

Figure 24.2 Summary of the three NQTs' advice

of economics and business, you must ensure that you gain opportunities for professional development. As Martyn put it:

'My first year in teaching certainly taught me that, although the tag of NQT could be applied to me for administrative purposes for the first year, I was learning very quickly that I was in control of my own successes and failures. It was my own belief in my strategies and my style of teaching together with my willingness to experiment, to listen to those people whose opinion I respected, and a readiness to adapt to meet the needs of those around me that got me through my first year.'

Checklists from research and statements from NQTs are, of course, all very well. Indeed, they can help us to identify the issues involved in establishing and running effective induction programmes. However, what is really needed is a mechanism for turning these ideas into reality and Kieron provided a clear description of that used by all three NQTs:

'Target-setting is something which we instil in our students, but it is often the very discipline which we overlook ourselves. Nowadays, my goals tend to be fairly short-term and I am careful to ensure that they are both identifiable and achievable. ... But the nature of the job means that sometimes it is easy to lose sight of the everyday triumphs. This is where specific targets can spur us on.'

Martyn described how he has developed his medium- and longer-term targets:

'By adopting a proactive approach to developing my own profile around the school, and to opening the discussions on certain issues with other colleagues, I found that, at the very least, I was getting some confirmation that my own concerns were widely held by others, and that some of my decisions were in keeping with those made by teachers of several years' standing. This helped a great deal to allay fears that I might have been going off at a complete tangent!'

On the issue of coping day-to-day he added:

'There's a mountain of work to do – how am I going to get through it all? Get a big diary or planner and, every night, write a quick TO DO list. Don't worry, you'll never do everything so just list the most important things and asterisk the most important thing of all. Next morning, make sure you at least do that one thing. That way, you'll really feel a confidence boost ...

'The biggest problem each day is the additional things that crop up and which you feel obliged to handle, such as students asking you for some time to discuss their work. Don't just say yes – give them a time to come back to see you ...

'Get into the habit of managing your time, not reacting to everything as it happens. That's the key!'

Of course, the first few weeks are particularly stressful, and school and college managers would do well to note Suzanna's comments:

'I cannot really begin to describe my first few days at school. No matter how hard the school prepares you and supports you, you still feel like you've landed in the middle of a large minefield and one step out of place and there could be a potential disaster! The school seems to forget how important the tiniest little details are ... who the caretakers are ... a very important piece of information – get on the right side of them and you're made! ... Timings of the school day ... were etched onto the back of my hand for the first week.'

Final thoughts

Starting off as a teacher of economics and business requires many qualities and a substantial quantity of hard work. However, as we of all subject specialists should know, proper investment pays real and long-term dividends – in this case, in terms of the quality of our teaching and of our students' learning.

If you are a newly qualified teacher you are beginning one of the most important and stimulating jobs it is possible to have. Remember, it is you who will determine the quality of young peoples' learning in economics and business for years to come! Don't stop learning about it and don't fail to enjoy it!

'I quickly realized that a normal day in education is like that famous free lunch. There's no such thing. One of my principal reasons for joining the profession was a need for less predictability in my working week – I was not disappointed!' (Kieron)

'All in all my first few months were really exhausting yet bucket-loads of fun. Your social life suffers, you're tired and irritable and you feel like you'll never get to know the routines ... however it does get better. Eventually your planning gets easier, the timetable becomes familiar and the kids even begin to recognize you in the corridor!' (Suzanna)

'Remember how important and responsible a job teaching is and how enjoyable it can be – keep smiling!' (Martyn)

References

Calderhead, J. and Lambert, J. (1992). *The Induction of Newly Appointed Teachers,* General Teaching Council Initiative/NFER.

DES (1992). *HMI Report 62/92: The Induction and Probation of New Teachers*, London, HMI/DES.

Earley, P. (1992). *Beyond Initial Teacher Training: Induction and the Role of the LEA,* London, NFER.

Earley, P. and Kinder, K. (1994). *Initiation Rights – Effective Induction Practices for New Teachers,* London, NFER.

HMI (1992). *The Induction and Probation of New Teachers*, HMI report 69/92, London, DES.

OfSTED (1993). *The New Teacher in School: A Survey by HM Inspectors in England and Wales 1992*, London, HMSO.

O'Sullivan, F., Jones, K. and Reid, K. (1988). *Staff Development in Secondary Schools,* Sevenoaks, Hodder & Stoughton.

Reid, K. (1985a). 'The PGCE, teaching practice and the probationary year', in: Hopkins, D. and Reid, K. (eds), *Rethinking Teacher Education*, London, Croom Helm.

Reid, K. (1985b). 'Recent research and developments in teacher education in England and Wales', in: Hopkins, D. and Reid, K. (eds), *Rethinking Teacher Education*, London, Croom Helm.

25 Working together across schools

Paul Clarke

Many teachers of economics and business in schools work in small departments to provide specialist courses. The incorporation of business into some technology courses and the introduction of new vocational courses in some schools have encouraged teamwork, but the onus of professional updating and renewal is still often seen as the responsibility of the individual teacher. This chapter uses examples of local professional development activities to illustrate the benefits for economics and business teachers of working together across schools.

New situations

There have been times in the past when professional development for teachers referred to an initial training year, a probationary year in school and the occasional update meeting linked to an exam syllabus. The new demands of the National Curriculum, of national interest in school and department exam results, of OfSTED inspections and annual appraisal, and of new vocational developments, require a different kind of professional support for teachers. School in-service programmes provide a degree of support but are often of a general nature rather than tailored to the specific needs of any one department. Local Education Authorities have been able to offer fewer specialist courses and those have been targeted mainly at National Curriculum core subjects.

There has also been increasing attention paid to how students learn as much as to how teachers teach. New curriculum developments in economics and business, such as the EBEA's Economics 16–19 Project (EBEA, 1994), the Nuffield A level Economics and Business course (Wales *et al.*, 1995) and GNVQ Business courses (NCVQ, 1995a), put more emphasis on students thinking and investigating for themselves. Teachers need to think of their economics and business as much in terms of outcomes for students as in the form of content lists and key concepts. Thomas (1991) and others argue the case for teachers to pay close attention to the real understanding of ideas that students bring to and take from the classroom. In effect, teachers have to see themselves as learners in their own schools and classrooms.

The statutory requirement in the National Curriculum for schools to prepare students for an adult working life, and non-statutory guidance recommending the provision of 'Economic and Industrial Understanding (EIU)' (NCC, 1991), have also provided an opportunity for business and economics teachers to work together with other colleagues across the curriculum. English teachers and economics specialists have been able to work together to enhance students' understanding using an English assignment on marketing (Wood, 1993). Maths and business teachers have been able to work in tandem to help students to handle numerical data on business costs and estimates (Wood, 1993). This often requires a reinterpretation of the form in which economic ideas are handled in order to recognize the contribution of different subject teachers. Much has been written on the benefits of sharing the planning, teaching, and reviewing of classroom activities (Wood, 1993) in order to develop meaningful and coherent experiences for students. Teachers have welcomed the opportunity to look again at their own subject work with the help of colleagues from other departments.

A similar approach has been used to develop EIU in Personal and Social Education programmes (Clarke and Mackie, 1995). Economics and business teachers have contributed directly or as part of teams to PSE lessons and modules based on themes such as inequality, rights and safety at work, and unemployment. Teachers working together can generate different kinds of information about student learning through the use of careful observation, of interviewing and of video-recording.

The new Technology curriculum has, at various stages of its drafting, implementation and revision, provided business teachers with the opportunity to contribute to the planning and evaluation of design tasks. The experience of planning schemes of work together has given all technology specialists a chance to reappraise their curriculum contribution and their teaching strategies.

The need to work together has become paramount. While some schools have developed or are in the process of creating 'collaborative learning cultures' (Fullan and Hargreaves, 1992), others are less supportive. Moreover, the real and perceived increase in competition between schools for finance and for students has slowed, if not stopped, the momentum for shared development fostered by TVEI and other initiatives. In such circumstances, economics and business teachers could turn to their subject association or other local networks for the opportunity to work across schools.

Working across schools

The attractions of working together across schools may seem obvious. Different institutions and different teachers can offer a range of ideas for managing change and for finding new solutions to problems. But it is not always easy to find common tasks from which everyone can benefit.

The author and others met through a local branch of the EBEA and through a local LEA network where meetings were shared by teachers working in very different situations: for example, in a commercial college providing individual tuition to adults, in a state school providing GNVQ courses for 14–18 students, in an LEA centre supporting an education-business partnership and in a university offering initial and continuing training to PGCE students and experienced teachers. As with teams of teachers in schools, we had our own ideas of 'good resources', and of 'effective' classroom activities, and different time schedules within which we worked with students. We were all interested, however, in developing new materials to meet the needs of GNVQ students and in making better use of contacts developed through education–business partnerships. Together we set out to write a teaching/learning resource which could be published by the EBEA branch and which could form the basis of an in-service day for ourselves and other branch colleagues.

Writing a GNVQ resource

New courses generate a variety of resources of many kinds, but we could find little of immediate appeal to our GNVQ Business students to investigate ways in which businesses provide customer services. A brainstorming session led us to a number of possible sources, one of which was a collection of promotional materials from Royal Mail. We had different ideas about the way forward and very different experiences of working with business contexts in vocational courses.

One suggestion was for a limited task that allowed students to describe Royal Mail customer services accurately. This seemed to be supported by course criteria that expected students to 'identify and describe customer service in an organization' (NCVQ, 1995b).

Another more ambitious idea tied customer services in this context to the whole issue of privatization as a means of improving business efficiency. A third suggestion was to engage students in a simulation using a variety of data and perspectives to represent something of the experience of an industrial visit. We each had a different set of priorities. For example:

- 'I needed a workable resource for my next teaching unit, help with interpreting GNVQ criteria, and ideas to make sure this vocational course didn't become just more textbook work.'

- 'I had not worked with anyone outside my school and it was only my second year of teaching. Could I do anything worthwhile for other people?'

- 'I wanted to produce something for the GNVQ course that carried on the same investigative ideas which were used in new A level curriculum materials.'

We met three times over a couple of months. The first meeting laid down broad parameters. We debated the meaning of the GNVQ specifications ('explain customer services'). Could this be developed to include critical thinking about Royal Mail's provision of customer service? Should students take on a current debate about privatizing the mail service? What background knowledge would be necessary to do this? Could this be written into an activity?

We were able to use another resource developed by a group of teachers as a stimulus to our thinking about learning. (EcATT, 1993)) This began with a photograph that led students to reveal their thinking about business activities and which had enough ambiguity to reveal different interpretations. Different data items were made available to help students pursue some of their own questions and to bring economic/business theories to their attention. This was different from the approach common to many classrooms, which puts theory first followed by the application of data.

A phone call to organizations representing mail customers and workers had generated a considerable quantity of source material. Many GNVQ students are expected to collect such data for themselves as part of an investigation, but this places unrealisitc demands on the organizations involved. It seemed appropriate for us to write some invetigative tasks for students based on a selection of the data and then expect teachers or school libraries to have a fuller set of resource materials for further study.

Each of us took materials from an organization (Royal Mail, customer user organizations, and trade unions) to prepare a selection of data and tasks which might best represent that organization's view on the provision of customer services. We each put our interpretation of the business ideas and of good learning on the table at the next meeting. This required considerable trust but we felt by now that we were working towards a common purpose. We all had chosen tasks which went beyond the descriptive to the analytical and expected students to see the issue from different perspectives. The tasks had become more focused and we were clearer about some of the content. But there were new questions to discuss about the learning and teaching tasks. Should we include data in their original form and expect students to select from quite difficult texts? Would students be able to empathize with a business as well as a customer perspective? How much guidance should be included for teachers unused to role-play as a teaching technique?

We worked on this, tried out one or two ideas on students, agreed a format and wrote various sections of the resource – the introduction for teachers, the tasks for students, and selected data. We were able to draw on one another's strengths: good contacts, the availability of students who could try out materials and ideas, some wordprocessing and page-design skills, and some overall ideas for the resource. Extracts of the final product are shown in Figure 25.1.

The student tasks start with their own experiences of the mail service but move them into data used by the Royal Mail to measure the quality of the service provided. Finally, they are asked to present ideas based on different perspectives of people invited to a travelling radio roadshow. The data were chosen to represent authentic extracts of a business's own documents, including mission statements and statistical tables, as well as the more difficult extracts of a customer charter produced by the government.

Role-briefing sheets allowed students to prepare for the radio roadshow

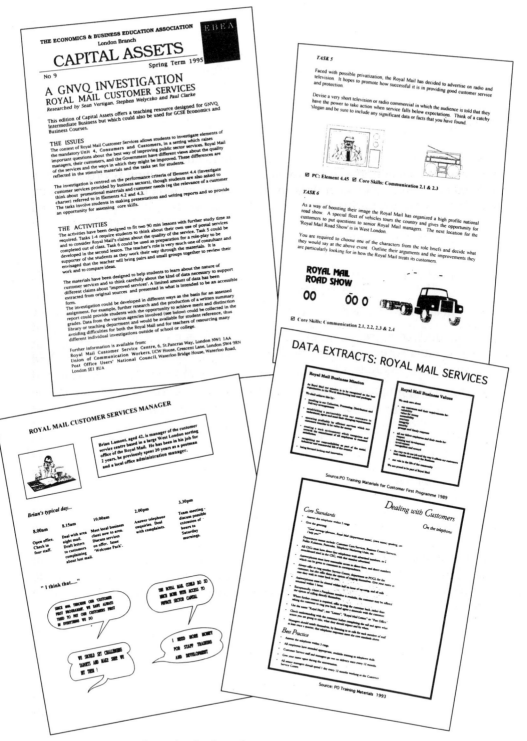

Figure 25.1 Extracts from the final product

interview with the help of a picture of three peoples' typical lifestyles, their experiences of mail services, and their views on how customer services might be improved. The recognition of any similarities and differences between these different perspectives would depend on students' abilities to listen to and question each other. The teacher would need to work more as a facilitator than as a provider of information.

We had different experience of using materials of this kind in the classroom, and so there were reservations about the way in which the economics and business ideas were presented. Would students recognize an issue when it was an implicit part of a task rather than an explicit direction from a teacher? Would a student who is committed to presenting one point of view be able to stand back and see other perspectives? The work generated by some students helped us to feel confidence in some of the tasks, but EBEA branch deadlines for publishing the material constrained any further discussion. Once the re-source was completed and distributed, we were able to draw on our working groups to generate feedback from PGCE groups, from colleagues in the branch, and from students in school.

On reflection, we valued the experience of working together in several ways:

- One derived a great deal of satisfaction from working on something felt to be useful to other teachers, achieved by bouncing ideas off one another and suggesting tactfully where improvements could be made.

- One found it liberating to be able to work on ideas while away from school politics and the constraints of people who say 'It won't work'.

- One said: 'I think we found a worthwhile outcome in terms of good economics and business education and were able to help students question the best way of improving customer services. The resource has some good ideas which start with students' own ideas and then challenge their thinking with some economics and business theory. I'm not sure the tasks are right yet, but they provide a springboard from which others can work.'

Planning a day of inset activities

The experience of putting together a resource with help from business con-tacts led us to organize a day in which other colleagues could have a similar opportunity. INSET days have been a regular feature of EBEA branch activi-ties, but these have generally catered for A level teachers and students. We wanted a GNVQ day that could bring business experts and teachers together to plan assignments and develop resources.

We found that we had different views of effective INSET days. One view was of expert speakers who would take teachers through good GNVQ resources. Another view was of business partners who would talk about their approach to finance and organization. A third view was of teachers visiting a business together and using data to write materials for students.

A planning meeting raised a number of questions:

- Were we providing teachers with business information that they would otherwise find hard to obtain?

- Were we asking everyone, including business partners, to work together to interpret GNVQ criteria?

- Were we providing INSET for business partners as well as for teachers?

- Should we provide examples of other 'good' materials?

While it was difficult to obtain complete agreement on these issues, we felt unwilling to present anyone as an 'expert' with answers for a course that was still in a rapid state of change. We felt that teachers themselves should take responsibility for, and ownership of, part of the day, and that individually we would be able to contribute something to the planning and organization.

Accordingly, one of us made contact with business partners who had shown willingness at a previous meeting to learn how they could best support GNVQ students. Three businesses were sent briefing letters, and two of these were visited to discuss in detail their contribution to the INSET day. The Royal Mail resource proved a useful example to help business partners identify data of use to teachers and students.

Another of our team designed the programme and planned the workshop tasks for teachers; his experience of a similar INSET activity helped him to prepare a briefing sheet and set time-limits for workshops. Another team member used contacts with several schools to find a business teacher with experience of using published case study materials who could provide a contrasting session to the morning workshops.

Examples of materials used as stimulus for discussion and programmes for the day are shown in Figure 25.2. The extracts from a company's annual report and accounts illustrate the materials made available by business partners.

Come the day, we found our joint planning was useful because we all felt confident to support the various groups with their workshop tasks and to introduce the sessions we had organized. We were able to share out jobs such as note-taking and time-keeping and still find time to enjoy the discussion. Inevitably, we took away a number of different impressions from the day:

- 'This was my first involvement with a training day from the other side of the fence. It wasn't easy deciding on the best balance for the day's programme. I was worried about how good the speakers would be and about how well participants from different schools would work together. It made me think hard about what we would do with all the information generated on the day. I was also surprised at the care needed with sharing ideas across schools. One school was concerned about the copyright and ownership of their suggestions.'

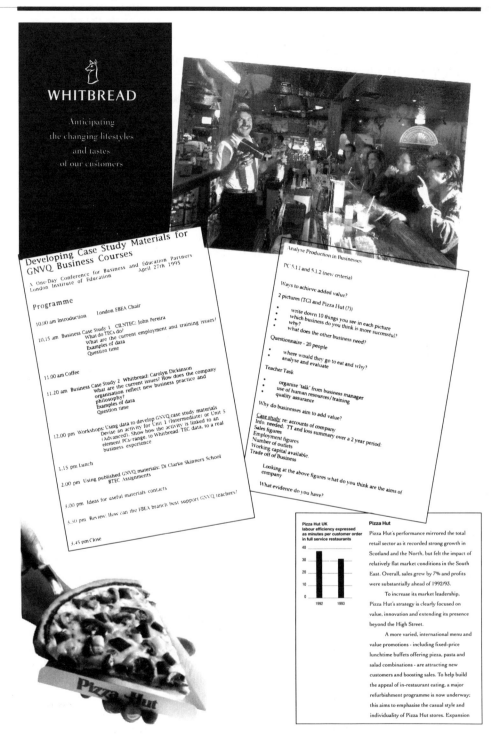

Figure 25.2 Planning INSET

- 'I had no idea how easy it was to contact a business person directly by phone and found myself caught unawares by the need of busy people wanting short answers to their questions. I needed to be very clear about what I wanted from them. In contrast, it proved very difficult to make direct contact with teachers in school and to find the time to have a clear, thoughtful exchange without interruptions. ...

'It was important to write letters confirming arrangements made by phone. It surprised me how many times the original contact person in a particular organization changed during the short time we were organizing this day. ...

'I hadn't anticipated quite how important it was for business contacts to learn more about the educational issues. One contact came to see me in school to discuss the INSET day and she was very interested in, though uninformed about, GNVQ classrooms. Yet this was an organization offering information to support GNVQ courses. It was very useful to look at the students' portfolio work together. ...

'I also learned that while more than one company can be asked to contribute to an INSET day, it is a good idea to give the floor to only one company at a time. There can be a lot of sensitivity about the promotion of company image as well as the sharing of information. Very few contacts were willing to commit themselves for a whole day but found it easier to contribute to a particular session. ...

'Looking back on it from a teacher's perspective, I think they valued the chance to meet and work with business contacts, the package of materials and teaching ideas to take away, and a chance to make contacts in other schools and colleges.'

- 'I was pleased that all three of us were able to take responsibility for the day. It made it easier to move from being organizer to participant at different times of the day, and everyone had a chance to be a leader of a teacher group. It was also good to focus on business case-studies to interpret GNVQ criteria because it took attention away from the day-to-day problems of managing GNVQ and stopped me thinking just about my own students. ...

'We had a lot of good discussion about the nature of business organization and what was reasonable for GNVQ students to explore. I'm not sure whether we shared the same views of a vocational course. I got the feeling that for some people, that meant taking students to visit firms. However, there was a lot of common ground on how students could be helped to investigate the businesses for themselves and what they might do with such data from companies. There was less agreement about the importance of 'business and economic theory'. Some teachers felt you had to teach a few lessons of theory about organization and finance before getting stuck into the data. Others thought you could draw the theory out of the data. Days like this only scratch the surface of such discussion but we might be helping things on their way just a little.'

Business placements

Another source of collaboration has been between teachers and business colleagues based on work placements. Teachers have negotiated placements through education–business partnerships, such as those managed by Norfolk LEA advisory staff. The focus of recent placements has been to develop case study materials to support teaching and learning on GNVQ Business courses. One such placement involved the large supermarket chain, J. Sainsbury plc.

While everyone nowadays is familiar with the experience of shopping at a supermarket, the organization that lies behind the process is less well-known. Companies tend to take for granted that students are familiar with the day-to-day organization. Teachers find it difficult to research the relevant information when they need it. Students find employers less than willing to respond to letters requesting broadly similar kinds of data. A teacher placement has the benefit of placing a business specialist in the heart of an organization with a chance to observe, to interview, and to collect data to support a students' investigations. This collection of data may well be different from what is included in a business' regular information pack.

In this instance, a teacher worked with two Sainsbury personnel to cover the area of 'customer service' and to produce a short case study of how the business deals with the needs of its customers. Over a few days, the teacher was able to identify a number of processes at work such as customer suggestion boxes, queries on the shop-floor, competitor visits, local advertising and group visits. The teacher was able to discuss these examples with a local manager and thus understand their significance as part of the company's strategy.

Sainsbury's specialist managers were able to discuss the company's approach to 'external' services, such as the company's market research, the house magazine, and the use of consumer panels.

Direct contact with training programmes highlighted some of the ways in which the company develops the more subtle forms of service. Trainees are given tips on communication skills and on the use of body language. They are given background updates on company products. Store-based training includes direct contact with customers to understand their differing needs. Customers were also categorized in ways that helped the staff to 'service' particular groups: the 'high-speed shopper' and the 'confused shopper' were two examples of categories.

Procedures dealing with customer complaints and the way in which legal requirements were met were the subject of specific interviews with department managers.

Finally, confidence resulting from the contact of managers and staff with the teacher-researcher led to spin-offs, such as the willingness of the company to allow its training materials to be used as part of a GNVQ resource.

The teacher gained valuable insights in a supportive way but also had to articulate a line of enquiry in order to secure the placement. The process helped the teacher to be clearer about the aims of the GNVQ unit and to think through the kind of data that would support students' own enquiries using the case study material.

Other placements have been used as the basis for a one-day investigation in the context of an INSET day for teachers new to GNVQ Business. It has also been possible to place students at work sites in order to encourage direct investigative skills of a kind difficult to promote in the classroom. Students have had the opportunity to cross-question staff about their organization and their products: they have been able to 'interrogate' data and to see that similar data can be seen differently by those with different perspectives.

A clear message from the experiences of teachers and students on placements is that company information does not always come in tidy parcels, as suggested by conventional textbook chapter headings. It needs organizing and challenging. It needs looking at again and again and the most illuminating data may come from the least likely of sources.

Outcomes of collaborative work

There are some important features of the experiences and opportunties described in this chapter. Working together is often time-consuming and can be difficult when there are different perspectives and different interests involved. But provided there is a common programme of work to which everyone is committed, then those different perspectives can be both creative and productive.

Learning has much to do with social interaction. We are used, as teachers, to putting students in a situation where they have to work with others to explore each other's views and we expect them to learn from each other. The same expectations should apply to us as adult learners.

In choosing to work together on writing a GNVQ resource, on planning an INSET day and on drawing on a business placement, we found ourselves asking tough questions about how students best learn economics and business ideas, how we move from being instructors to facilitators, how we interpreted completely new course criteria, and how we thought about in-service activities. It was important to create the right conditions in which such questions could be asked. As one of us described it afterwards:

'This type of collaborative working can only be recommended. It makes you start to think about issues beyond your own educational institution and exposes you to new ideas and possibilities. It does need to be done in the

right spirit with everyone pulling in the same direction. Each member of the team must be allowed to participate fully and feel they have left their mark on the finished product.'

The opportunities for professional development of this kind depend to an extent on external resourcing, and there is no doubting the reduction in certain support for in-service provision following the recent changes in LEA budgets. But teachers, schools and professional groups can also make more of existing in-service opportunities, if they are willing to see resource writing, INSET planning, shared classroom-reviews, moderation of examination work etc. as serious professional development for those involved.

Much depends on the extent to which teachers are prepared to see themselves as learners and reflective practitioners in their own and others' classrooms; on the willingness of those responsible for staff development planning in school to generate time for team activities within and across curriculum areas; and on the further development of structures for teacher collaboration across schools, such as partnership clusters for initial teacher training, examination group meetings, and local and national meetings organized by professional associations.

References

Clarke, P. and Mackie, K. (1995). 'Making EIU count in PSE courses', *Economic Awareness*, vol 7, no. 2, pp. 8–17.

EBEA (1994). Thomas, L. (ed.), *Teaching and Learning the New Economics*, Oxford, Heinemann Educational.

EcATT (1993). *Young's Brewery: A Case Study of Business Success*, London, University of London, Institute of Education.

Fullan, M. and Hargreaves, A. (1992). *What's Worth Fighting for in Your School?*, Open University Press.

NCC (1991). *Economic and Industrial Understanding: Non-Statutory Guidance*, York, National Curriculum Council.

NCVQ (1995a). *Mandatory Units for Intermediate and Advanced GNVQ Business* (revised editions), London, NCVQ.

NCVQ (1995b). *Intermediate GNVQ Business: Unit 3 – Providing Customer Services*, London, NCVQ.

Thomas, L. (1991). 'A new perspective on learning: what does it mean for economics?', *Economics*, vol. 27, part 2, no. 114, pp. 79–83.

Wales, J., Barnes, S., Wall, N. and Lines, D. (1995). 'The Nuffield way', *Economics and Business Education*, vol. 3, part 1, no. 9, pp. 25–8.

Wood, K. (ed.) (1993). *A Guide to Economic Awareness as a Cross-Curricular Theme*, Harlow, Longman.

End note

The contributions of Sean Vertigan, Stephen Welyczko, Steven Lepper and Mike Hodkinson to the work on which this chapter is based are gratefully acknowledged.

26 Leading a team

Richard Hughes

Teams and teamwork

When I was seeking my first job in teaching, I remember being very concerned that, as an economist, I would very likely end up as a one-person department. This prospect struck me as both professionally and socially undesirable and one of the attractions of my first job was that I would be part of a three teacher team.

Now it is my privilege to lead a department: a team which itself is part of a larger team – the college staff – and which is, in turn, made up of smaller course teams. At the same time, I am both a leader of my department and a member of other teams. I am Head of Social Science, but I am also a member, for example, of the GNVQ Advanced Business course team and of a team of thirteen tutors. Many others in our department also lead teams within the college, as Assistant Principals or Senior Tutors, for example. I am, therefore, amused when I read in management texts of the 'new' concept of matrix organizations, where individuals report to different team leaders for different aspects of their work; it is an idea of a rather older vintage in education.

This complexity highlights two important features of schools and colleges. The first is that leadership in education – far more, I believe, than in other contexts – must support the traditional collegial approach to working. Second, team members will usually have contemporaneous loyalties to a number of teams. These features strengthen the case for the team as the building block of the school or college organization.

As teachers of business studies and economics we are very used to talking about teams in industry and of the trend towards cooperative and participative models of working. Yet, probably, very few of us stop to consider whether the concepts we teach have any relevance to us as teachers. It is therefore worthwhile to consider some of the practical suggestions that have been made about how to lead and participate in effective teams. It is also worthwhile reflecting on the particular applications of these ideas to education generally, and business studies and economics specifically.

Bell (1992) describes teamwork as 'a group of individuals working together towards some common purpose and, in so doing, achieving more than they could alone'. This makes sense: a team is both more efficient and more effective than individuals, and teamwork must be about sharing knowledge, skills and responsibility.

In this chapter I set out some thoughts on the subject. Some ideas are own-grown; some are unashamedly borrowed from others. In discussing and commending ideas, the particular demands on teachers of business studies and economics have been borne in mind, even if references to the subjects are few, for the reason that subject-specific literature in this area is virtually non-existent. General comments about the nature of teams in education have also been considered. Examples quoted are from my own experience of working in a very large department, but are intended to illustrate general principles.

Making teams work

Within a team, staff will have a variety of skills. These may be centred on teaching, on organizational matters or on aspects of team working.

Teaching skills

We can all acknowledge that colleagues have particular strengths to their teaching which we may lack, whilst they will point to aspects of our teaching that they admire. Far too often, however, because we are content to plough our own individual furrow, this knowledge is partial and certainly not being turned to sufficient advantage for us or our students. This is shortsighted. Acknowledging this suggests two approaches: either to allow students to see more than one teacher during their course, particularly on advanced courses; or for the team members to support each other through the sharing of expertise.

Within our department the first is achieved by a modular approach. Although, at any one time, students are taught by one teacher, they will, wherever possible, be taught by different teachers for different modules. Two, or maybe three, teachers in two years is seen as a desirable number. We are also trying to encourage staff to share knowledge and skills through more practical meetings focusing on strategies for teaching and learning. Such task-orientated team meetings should provide a natural opportunity for us to learn from each other. Realistically, however, we know that the opportunities for this may be limited, especially as staff may already be suffering from a surfeit of meetings. This means that other ways of sharing must be found.

Schemes of work can incorporate ideas for teaching approaches or resources, as well as listing the knowledge and skills the students should be acquiring, making them a means of informing staff of good ideas. They could be written collaboratively, or, at the very least, be a way of collecting ideas from all team members. In business and economics teaching this is a particularly relevant approach, as scope for different teaching styles and contexts is so great: the use of IT, the employment of simulations and role-play, group work and field trips, are all readily possible, for example, and it would be a rare teacher indeed who was expert in all.

The different skills and knowledge available are also considerations when choosing syllabuses and organizing courses. A key choice to be made, for example, is whether to choose courses that have an IT component to the assessment. Common sense dictates that, whatever the desirability of so doing, the decision should depend primarily on the skills and interests of the staff within the teaching team. It would make for very bad courses if the teachers were not enthusiastic for, and competent in, the approach adopted. If such enthusiasts exist they can provide the lead that is required and give their support to staff less experienced in the area. Within our department, we have found it invaluable to have an IT enthusiast who has been prepared to organize and encourage those of us who have had more difficulty, for a variety of reasons, in exploiting the opportunities IT provides.

Equally, as more modular courses become available staff knowledge and interest may well be a major influence in determining choices. Many A level syllabuses, notably so far the Cambridge Economics modular scheme, offer a considerable range of options. Staff teaching these options can find a new enthusiasm in developing particular specialisms based on their specific interests or knowledge. Indeed it may, in larger centres, be possible thereby to offer students a limited choice of options.

Team teaching takes the process of sharing one step further, but is not always practicable; talking, however, is always possible. The role of the team leader is to ensure that there are both formal and informal opportunities for talk. Making the sharing of ideas a natural part of teaching the same subject fosters the cooperative approach that enables all team members to employ the best practice employed within the team.

Team organization

The key to employing the organizational skills of staff is *delegation*. There is no reason why the traditional organizational and administrative role of the Head of Department should be done by one person. A division of that role by function is often a sensible approach, even where there is no designated second in the department. Team members could manage the delegated budget, or chair a team meeting. Such roles might be taken on for a period of time, or simply on an *ad hoc* basis. It is also possible to organize the department by course, an approach that is increasingly appealing as the range and level of courses offered by business and economics departments continues to grow.

At Shrewsbury Sixth Form College we have adopted a system whereby each course has a team leader, whose role is practical and task-orientated (see Figure 26.1). Course leaders are responsible for the delivery and assessment of the course, whereas the Head of Social Science has responsibility for timetabling and staffing resourcing, inspection and major development and policy

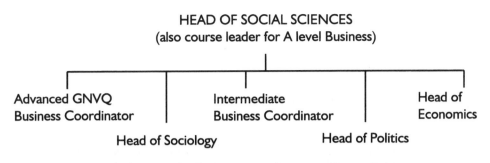

HEAD OF SOCIAL SCIENCES
(also course leader for A level Business)

Advanced GNVQ
Business Coordinator

Intermediate
Business Coordinator

Head of
Economics

Head of Sociology

Head of Politics

Figure 26.1 Structure of the Social Sciences Department at Shrewsbury SFC

issues. This has enabled us to designate course leaders without losing the benefits of an overview of provision. The college's intention is to adopt a model of team organization very similar to this for all subject teams.

Team skills

Since Belbin (1981, 1993) developed the concept of specific team skills, there has been a greater awareness of the roles that individuals play within teams. These roles are based not on a subject or discipline skill, but on personal characteristics. For example, Belbin identifies a role called the 'monitor-evaluator', who will be sober, strategically-minded and discerning, with the ability to see all options and to judge critically. These abilities would be important to a team's success, but would not be sufficient in themselves. Indeed, the monitor-evaluator, Belbin argues, is also likely to be lacking in drive and the ability to inspire others and may be overly critical and thus indecisive. It is possible that we recognize something of ourselves in this pen-portrait; certainly we will recognize the type of person described. This person would be an invaluable team member if complemented by others with different personalities and team skills. Effective teams, Belbin argues, consist of people with a variety of skills. The team roles he identifies are shown in Figure 26.2.

As discussion and decision-making takes place, the various team skills are deployed by the different members. Some play more than one role, but a spread of the skills is necessary for effective decision-making. The team leader's role is to ensure that the team skills available are harnessed effectively and, perhaps, to recruit or develop any that are missing.

In educational institutions it could be that the leader's role is particularly important in these regards. When Belbin carried out his original studies into team effectiveness, he discovered that the teams packed with members of high intelligence rarely did very well in the tasks assigned to them. There was a likelihood for them to be discussion-orientated, rather than task-orientated, as they could too easily see the flaws in any plans of action and always wanted to criticize and discuss further. West-Burnham (1992), in his analysis of the weakness of teams in schools, noted the same tendency. Perhaps this bias towards discussion might be even more marked in social scientists! Certainly,

Roles and descriptions – team-role contribution	Allowable weaknesses
Plant: Creative imaginative, unorthodox. Solves difficult problems.	Ignores details. Too pre-occupied to communicate effectively.
Resource investigators: Extrovert, enthusiastic. Explores opportunities. Develops contacts	Overoptimistic. Loses interest once initial enthusiasm has passed.
Coordinator: Mature, confident, a good chair-person. Clarifies goals, promotes decision-making, delegates well.	Can be seen as manipulative. Delegates personal work.
Shaper: Challenging, dynamic, thrives on pressure. Has the drive and courage to overcome obstacles.	Can provoke others. Hurts people's feelings.
Monitor – evaluator: Sober, strategic and discerning. Sees all options. Judges accurately.	Lacks drive and ability to inspire others. Overly critical.
Teamworker: Co-operative, mild, perceptive and diplomatic. Listens, builds, averts friction, calms the waters.	Indecisive in crunch situations. Can be easily influenced.
Implementer: Disciplined, reliable, conservative and efficient. Turns ideas into practical actions.	Somewhat inflexible. Slow to respond to new possibilities.
Completer: Painstaking, conscientious, anxious. Searches out errors and omissions. Delivers on time.	Inclined to worry unduly. Reluctant to delegate. Can be a nit-picker.
Specialist: Single-minded, self-starting, dedicated. Provides knowledge and skills in rare supply.	Contributes on only a narrow front. Dwells on technicalities. Overlooks the 'big picture'.

Strength of contribution in any one of the roles is commonly associated with particular weaknesses. These are called allowable weaknesses. Executives are seldom strong in all nine team roles.

Figure 26.2 Team roles as summarized by Belbin (1993, p. 23)

it is important for the team leader, whilst acknowledging the intelligence and subject expertise of team members, to look also for the relevant team skills and to use and develop them as necessary.

Specialism and sharing are clearly linked. Within a team it is difficult to have one without the other. An advantage of teamwork is that, in increasingly pressurized times, we don't have to try and do everything. Providing quality courses is likely to depend increasingly on the effectiveness of the team. This will make the role of team leader ever more critical.

Leading the team

Leadership functions

Adair (1988) identifies three, overlapping leadership functions (see Figure 26.3).

According to their own interests and personalities, leaders will tend to emphasize a particular function, helping to produce, perhaps, the leadership 'style' that so often features in interview questions. Ideally, a balance will be struck, whereby all three are considered important and are given due weight. I know that my temptation is to concentrate on building and maintaining the team, so it is important that I should remind myself of the need to plan for, and achieve, specific objectives, as well as considering team members as individuals with their own needs and aspirations. It is certainly invaluable as a team leader to take time out to reflect on whether these elements are considered sufficiently when making decisions.

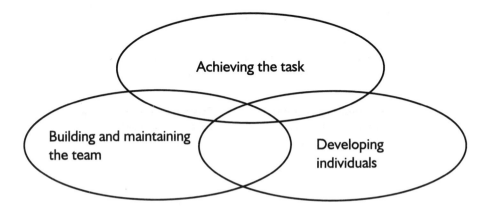

Figure 26.3 Overlapping leadership functions (Adair, 1988)

Leadership styles

Management texts are replete with descriptions of leadership styles. A useful distinction is made by Ball (1987), who bases his taxonomy on specific observation of schools. He identifies four styles: the interpersonal, the managerial, the adversarial–political, and the authoritarian–political.

- *The interpersonal leader* uses informal methods of management, especially individual meetings, and relies heavily on her or his own personality. Whilst this can be very effective at minimizing objection and bringing colleagues along, it can raise individual expectations too high and may also produce an atmosphere of 'closed' decision-making.

- *The managerial leader* uses formal structures a great deal, operating through precise channels and procedures. The danger here is unnecessary bureaucracy, which can create remoteness of relationships and breed resentment of meetings and official jargon.

- *The adversarial–political leader* uses conflict to advance his or her cause, flushing out opposing views and dealing with them. This is not a strategy with which I would feel comfortable, but it is a possible approach in a crisis.

- *The authoritarian–political leader* imposes solutions and strategies on the team. This tends to undermine its cohesiveness and is liable to waste the team talents available, negating much of the purpose of the team.

The style, or mixture of styles, adopted, will tend to reflect the personality and experience of the leader, but should also be appropriate to the particular context.

Leadership tasks

Beyond the foregoing general principles, there are different tasks involved in leading a team which, although varying in detail, are common to the role in whatever form it takes. Interpreting Adair's distinction, there are tasks that involve managing people, whether as a team, or as individuals, and there are tasks that relate to specific team or institution objectives. For my own purposes, I use four general headings for these tasks. The areas thus designated are not equal in scope, but they represent one way of remembering the variety of tasks to be undertaken. Some might claim that they confuse leadership and management, but since a good leader in a school or college should also be a good manager, the distinction does not worry me overduly. The four elements – people, politics, planning and paperwork – are all areas where the team leader in education will need to perform well.

People

Adair makes a useful distinction between building the team and developing individuals. Nevertheless, both can be achieved through the same principal means: building personal relationships. A vital part of leading the team is ensuring that members feel included and valued. This applies to new members, so that, after the process of induction – the provision of necessary information – there will be a process of inclusion, whereby the newcomer is made to feel part of the team. It is also relevant to established staff, who can feel excluded by developments that occur. They may see social circles changing, or new courses taking precedence over their own specialisms. These possibilities must always be considered.

By inclusion, I do not mean the seeking of spurious or superficial agreement, but the conscious involving of team members in the functioning of the department. Everybody should consider that their opinions, skills and knowledge are known and valued and that their contribution is important. This can be achieved both formally, through appropriate structures and well-run meetings, but also informally, through discussions over a pint of beer, or taking time to chat to someone over lunch. Research supports this approach. Hersey and Blanchard (1977) summarize the work of Rensis Likert at the Michigan Institute for Social Research. He placed management styles on a continuum loosely numbered from one to four. In four, management is seen as having complete confidence and trust in subordinates and the informal and formal organizations are often one and the same. All social forces support efforts to achieve stated organizational goals and the team approach is central. Likert's study suggested that such a system produced the highest productivity.

In business and economics departments, the issue of inclusion is particularly important. One reason for this is that the two 'disciplines' are often a marriage of cultures – the A level Economics tradition and the Commerce tradition. A second reason is that they are often complex, with a range of courses being offered. This latter offers an opportunity in that staff can be assigned clear course leadership roles, but it can also lead to situations where people feel that their role, which is time-consuming and energy-sapping, is undervalued and marginalized. The achievement of a team identity is particularly important in this context.

A danger is the creation of vocational ghettos or academic course elites. Using staff according to their strengths is sensible, but the interchange of people and ideas between courses is also desirable, for both course and personal development. As GNVQ courses become more popular, this could be overlooked in the desire to appoint or create specialists. Inclusion will be important if staff are to be fully motivated and able to share best practice.

Simple ideas can work. At Shrewsbury SFC, students opting for Advanced GNVQ Business share induction lessons with their GCE counterparts. This helps to establish parity of esteem for the students, but it also involves all staff in planning and delivering the same induction. This approach is especially relevant as staff find themselves, by necessity, becoming more specialized. If we are all scouring our houses for examples of well-known branded products, then that is positive collaboration!

In broader terms, stressing the importance of things that unite – such as the skills or approaches common across the courses delivered, or the more efficient use of resources produced by a sensible plan for shared use – can produce the cohesive team that produces the sharing advocated above. At the same time, it can create the kind of conditions in which individuals can be developed. Staff will learn more readily from others and will be able to test ideas in a safe, professional environment. This will promote confidence and competence.

Occasionally, of course, the aspirations of an individual will need particular promotion, with courses, say, of especial relevance to the individual rather than the team. But this too benefits all, for it will motivate the individual and increase their contribution to the team.

My contention, and my experience, is that the inclusive, team-building approach advocated above will make conflict unlikely. Leading a team with a concern for including individuals will engender a shared mission and ethos. It would, however, be silly to pretend that differences of opinion or clashes of personality never occur, or that, if they do, they can always be resolved by reasoned discussion. Stewart (1986) quotes Douglas McGregor as pointing out that:

'People often expend more energy in attempting to defeat management's objectives than they would in achieving them. The important question is not how to get people to expend energy, but how to get them to expend it in one direction rather than another.'

The need to direct team members' energies in pursuit of the common goal will occasionally become a source of conflict.

At an interview, I was asked how I would deal with a colleague who would not accept a departmental plan of action. This was a tricky question, for my answer could appear either evasive ('It all depends') or extreme (authoritarian perhaps, or lacking in strength of character). The answer I gave was to say that it does, in fact, 'all depend', but then to go on to quote the following specific example to illustrate how this might be.

A committed and admired colleague had declined to implement a particular change, whilst others wished to proceed. Three possible solutions presented themselves: demand that the colleague comply; abandon the plan; or allow the others to proceed whilst the particular colleague carried on as before.

The first approach risked raising the stakes without, necessarily, solving the problem; this might be justified if a matter of principle were at stake. The second approach would have the advantage of preserving consistency, but would be to allow one person to hold up change. The last option was, therefore, attractive, provided that it was practicable to allow different people to use different systems. In this case it was, and the last approach was adopted. I did not consider this to be a weak approach, but a sensible one, as it had the three virtues of sensitivity, practicability and progression. Change was not prevented, but the team was not fractured. The aim was to show the doubter, over time, that the new system was desirable – and that is, in practice, what happened.

Although flexibility is important, it is possible to frame some principles for dealing with conflict. First, one should keep team aims in proportion. It is rare that proposed change is based on anything other than administrative expediency and remembering this may prevent the leader adopting an unhelpfully authoritarian approach.

Second, awkwardness or intransigence will often be a cover for a real fear of change. This fear is often very specific; discovering the concern and dealing with it may enable the team member to embrace change.

Third, however, it is important that no one is allowed to be bigger than the team and that, if there is a clear consensus for change, it would be wrong to allow one or two members of the team to block the intended course of action. In this case the leader may need to exercise authority explicitly, but must do so with due regard to the individual's pride and to the need to preserve social relationships.

The fourth element, therefore, follows from the previous three: conflict is better avoided in the first place; not by ducking issues, but by building a team ethos and deciding team aims as a team. This returns us to the vital role of the head of department as team leader.

Politics

The team leader is the institutional link between the managers who take a whole-school/college view and those whose role gives them a narrower perspective. As this link , the team leader is often caught in an unenviable position. Subject staff will expect the team leader to fight unashamedly for the team, whilst the management will require an approach that accepts the legitimacy of other, prior claims.

Balancing these competing demands requires briefing the team on the wider issues, whilst ensuring that the department receives a fair apportionment of the available resources: staff time, accommodation and equipment. The achievement of this fair apportionment will require informal politicking as well as the use of formal channels. It requires successful immersion in what Ball (1987, p. 237) describes as the 'micro-politics of the school'. In his book, Ball writes as follows:

'In the contemporary jargon, heads of department are "middle-managers", with all the implications of "line" responsibility that that suggests. It may be that baronial politics and the feudal relationships through which they currently work will be replaced by the bureaucratic procedures and relationships of management theory. On the other hand, the pristine language of management may only serve to obscure the real struggle over policy and budgets – who gets what, when and how?'

Ball, in fact, implicitly answers the question he here poses, for he points out that there is little purpose in distinguishing between formal and informal channels of influence; both will be used. He then goes on (p. 233):

'Careful tending of their patch, positive support from colleagues and positive indicators of department success can put the head of department in a powerful position.'

For me, there are two points here. First, as a team, it is crucial to present a united front; and second, 'tending the patch' requires an intimate knowledge of what senior management priorities are and where decisions take place. In the latter case one asks what is the locus and time of decisions? Does the Principal make decisions alone, or is it the Deputy Principal who is dominant? Which meeting will be crucial?

Leading in the business and economics teaching area may require particular political skills. The subjects may not always be accorded the same treatment as National Curriculum subjects, or as subjects seen as more traditional. At the same time, the teaching of subjects with an IT content may cost more than alternative courses, thus producing an argument for more generous funding. Rapid change in syllabuses, courses and methods also produce funding issues with which the leader must deal.

Formally, the leader represents the team at meetings and in interviews with members of the college or school management team. The aim in these contexts is to express team views and needs with clarity and the necessary forcefulness. The right framework may then be achieved to free the classroom teachers to do their job as well as possible. Often, though, the team leader will fail to meet team expectations and explaining the context for that failure is then important. The team leader's job is to keep the lines of communication open between the team and the senior management, so that debate is informed, and decisions made, in full knowledge of the constraints. In this way conflict will be minimized.

Planning

As Adair clearly points out, nurturing the team must be accompanied by a desire to complete tasks. A leader should have aspirations and ambitions for her or his team. In *Making It Happen*, Sir John Harvey-Jones (1988) tells how at the beginning of each year he takes a few hours to write down on a postcard six hopes and aspirations for that year.

The postcard can stand for whatever method suits the individual, but the principle is a sound one. Setting clear targets provides the opportunity for useful discussion about aims and performance. Increasingly, teams are expected to produce operational plans – the Further Education Funding Council (FEFC), for example, requires such plans as evidence for formula funding claims. These require the setting and review of precise targets and the process can be used to bring the team together. Where explicit planning is not a requirement it is useful to adopt the approach in any case. It is good to have aspirations and even better to have shared aspirations. If the achievement of these aspirations can be measured then better still.

A team leader should anticipate change. This makes team planning more effective and avoids unseemly scrambles to adapt to unanticipated events. Reading, watching and listening are important and time should be made for them. From a curricular perspective, the team leader should be using the resources and support offered by the Economics and Business Education Association (EBEA) and/or the National Association of Business Studies Education (NABSE). The EBEA journal, or the annual conference, in particular are invaluable sources of updating on subject and curriculum change. Busy staff will often be unaware of change and, ultimately, it is the team leader's role to know of likely or actual changes in syllabuses and specifications and to put a framework and timetable in place for meeting the challenge that the change represents.

Equally, it is important to anticipate change within one's own institution. Keeping an eye on changes in structures, policy and curriculum can provide warning of decisions that will soon need to be made. A good leader is rarely surprised!

Once targets are set, ensuring that they are clear and widely known is the next job. The team should be aware of the basis on which review will take place. The review can be both internal and external. Moderators' and verifiers' reports are good checks on processes of assessment and inspection reports will also be increasingly available (the slim, written reports can be augmented by inspectors' comments). The A Level Information System (ALIS) can provide comparative data in a variety of forms, including value-added performance data and attitude surveys. The whole package will often be bought by institutions from the University of Newcastle, but it is also possible to purchase the performance data only through the Secondary Heads' Association (SHA) project.

Internally generated review material will involve student and staff surveys as appropriate. In the past I have surveyed the staff specifically on teamwork, because of my concern to weld together what was a large and diverse department. Reviews can also use examination data: our Social Science results for each student are compared with their other subject results in order to give a comparative guide to our exam performance as a department. This exciting task is given to a student, who is paid at just above the McDonald's rate for the privilege!

Paperwork

This is the bane of most teachers' lives. Increased paperwork is, in part, a function of the attempt to increase accountability; but because it is imposed, it is usually seen as extraneous to the teaching process and, therefore, as a waste of time. Whilst much documentation is now needed for inspection or financial audit, the aim should be to produce the minimum paperwork necessary. Two questions should be asked: 'Is the documentation usefully informative?', and 'Does it communicate more effectively than would have been possible by word of mouth?' Asking the first queston should make for better-quality paperwork; the second should ensure a more appropriate quantity of paperwork. The twin dangers are obscure documents and documents that stop people talking to one another.

Clearly, where a record is needed – say, of the receipt of spending of money, or where key decisions have been made or targets set – then consistent and clear documentation is needed. In many cases the institution should set an appropriate framework, or even produce a standard document. When this is not done, lobbying for it is sensible, but being prepared to produce department documentation may be necessary. If something is liable to be forgotten, or to be confusing, then a document is needed.

Conclusion

Descriptions of the foregoing ideas are intentionally brief, but it is hoped that they are thought-provoking. Team leadership is a privilege, but it is a role that needs clarity of thinking, a concern to see tasks completed, and (above all) a concern for the team members. The complexity of team structures in educational institutions continues to increase and more people will be drawn into the role of leading teams. Remember the competing demands on time, actively seek the contribution of all and make sharing tasks through teamwork a major priority.

References

Adair, J. (1988). *The Action Centred Leader*, London, Kogan Page.

Ball, S. J. (1987). *The Micro-Politics of the School*, London, Methuen.

Belbin, M. (1981). *Management Teams: Why They Succeed or Fail*, London, Heinemann.

Belbin, M. (1993). *Team Roles at Work*, Oxford, Butterworth–Heinemann.

Bell, L. (1992). Managing Teams in Secondary Schools, London, Routledge.

Harvey-Jones, J. (1988). *Making It Happen*, London, Collins.

Hersey, P. and Blanchard, K. H. (1977). *Management of Organizational Behaviour*, 3rd edn, Eaglewood Cliffs, NJ, Prentice-Hall.

Stewart, R. (1986). *The Reality of Management*, London, Pan.

West-Burnham, J. (1992). *Managing Quality in Schools*, Harlow, Longman.

27 Assessing quality

Ian Chambers and Susan Squires

Before OfSTED and FEFC

Prior to the 1990s the majority of teachers of business and economics were not subject to regular external monitoring or inspection. HMI carried out regular inspections in the secondary, tertiary and higher-education sectors, but only a small number of schools and colleges could be covered in any one year, making inspection a 'peculiar' rather than a regular event.

In the late 1980s, LEAs were encouraged by more generous government funding to expand their advisory services and carry out more regular inspection of their schools. However, each LEA was free to develop its own evaluation or self-evaluation criteria and to set its own timetable. External monitoring was also introduced through TVEI, the Department of Employment's Technical and Vocational Education Initiative, during the 1980s, and many teachers of business studies were involved in such monitoring exercises, whose primary function was accountability rather than quality control.

In three important respects, the nature and extent of external monitoring and inspection changed significantly in 1992. In that year the Education (Schools) Act established the Office for Standards in Education (OfSTED) system covering school inspections, and the Further and Higher Education Act established the Further Education Funding Council (FEFC) system covering college inspections.

As a result of these Acts, inspection is to be carried out on a regular four-year cycle for secondary schools and for 16–19 colleges. Thus for teachers, external inspection may become a regular event in their career. Another result of the Acts is that the criteria upon which inspection is based will be published and applied nationally in as uniform a way as possible. Schools and colleges are therefore able to make use of the criteria to prepare for inspection at any time in the cycle. Another change is that inspection reports become public documents and are widely distributed in the local and sometimes national community shortly after inspection is complete. HMI reports were also published in the 1980s, but a considerable time after the event and to a much narrower audience.

The inspection process has become much more systematic and open, and a real challenge to all teachers and tutors of business and economics.

Assessing quality the OfSTED way

'The purpose of inspection is to identify strengths and weaknesses in schools so that they may improve the quality of education offered and raise the standards achieved by their pupils.' (OfSTED Handbook for the Inspection of Schools, 1994a, p. 5)

Thus OfSTED sees the raising of quality and standards as the main outcome from inspection. This is reflected in the main findings of all OfSTED inspection reports which focus upon four main aspects of a school's work:

- the quality of the education provided by the school;

- the educational standards achieved in the school;

- whether the financial resources made available to the school are managed efficiently;

- the spiritual, moral, social and cultural development of pupils at the school.

All other aspects of a school's operation are judged in relation to the impact they have on these four elements.

The criteria used for judging all the significant aspects of a school's work are contained within the 'Framework' for inspection as an 'Inspection Schedule'. All OfSTED inspections and inspection reports are based upon this schedule, to ensure conformity in approach between registered inspectors. The main headings of the Inspection Schedule are shown in Figure 27.1.

The overall schedule relates to judgements made on the performance of the school as a whole. Within Part B of the schedule there will also be judgements made on individual subjects and courses being taught in the school. These judgements will focus upon the central criteria of:

- standards of achievement;

- quality of learning;

- quality of teaching.

In addition, judgements will be made by subject inspectors on the management of various contributory factors – curriculum, assessment, provision for pupils with special educational needs, staffing, resources for learning, accommodation – and how they impact on quality and standards in a particular subject.

Subject inspectors gather evidence in order to make judgements on these aspects from a range of sources prior to and during the week of the inspection:

- analysis of documentary evidence, such as policy statements, planning and schemes of work;

- lesson observation;

THE INSPECTION SCHEDULE AND GUIDANCE ON ITS USE

1   **Main Findings**

2   **Key Issues for Action**

3   **Introduction**

    3.1   Characteristics of the school

    3.2   Key Indicators

PART AASPECTS OF THE SCHOOL

4   **Educational standards achieved by pupils at the school**

    4.1   Attainment and progress

    4.2   Attitudes, behaviour and personal development

    4.3   Attendance

5   **Quality of education provided**

    5.1   Teaching

    5.2   The curriculum and assessment

    5.3   The pupils' spiritual, moral, social and cultural development

    5.4   Support, guidance and pupils' welfare

    5.5   Partnership with parents and the community

6   **The management and efficiency of the school**

    6.1   Leadership and management

    6.2   Staffing, accommodation and learning resources

    6.3   The efficiency of the school

PART BCURRICULUM AREAS AND SUBJECTS

8   **English, mathematics and science**

9   **Other subjects and courses**

PART CINSPECTION DATA

10   **Summary of inspection evidence**

11   **Data and indicators**

Source: Office for Standards in Education, *Handbook for the Inspection of Schools* (1995)

Figure 27.1 OfSTED's Inspection Schedule

- discussions with senior management and staff;

- discussions with pupils;

- analysis of pupils' work;

- analysis of examination and statutory assessment results.

Of these, the most important source of evidence about quality in a subject is lesson observation, with the inspector recording his or her judgements on a form which focuses upon standards of achievement, quality of learning and quality of teaching in the lesson observed. The cumulative evidence derived from lesson observations, from discussions with staff and pupils, and from analysis of documents and data forms the basis for a verbal report on standards and quality in a subject to the Head of Department at the end of the inspection week. A summary paragraph on a subject is then produced and included in the overall OfSTED report on the school.

OfSTED, and business education and economics

Up to December 1995, the appearance of business studies and economics within the OfSTED 'Framework' was limited. Whilst all National Curriculum subjects and religious education were an automatic part of the inspection specifications, business studies, economics and a large number of other subjects were not. A subject's inclusion in an inspection specification was decided by OfSTED centrally, and only a limited number of extra subjects tended to be added to any inspection specification. As Squires (1993) reported, in tenders for the 1993/94 series of inspections, 43 schools requested that business studies/office studies/economics/sociology/politics/law be added to their specification; whilst 157 schools had requested no additional features, 150 had added only a modern foreign language, and 79 had added vocational courses. As she states: 'for business studies and economics teachers there is no automatic right to inspection' (p. 198).

Some elements of business studies are inspected automatically under the existing framework. Contributions to design/technology and information technology at Key Stages 3 and 4 will come within the OfSTED Framework. However, other elements will not be inspected – GCSE business studies/office studies/economics; a level business studies/economics; GNVQ business – if the subjects are not included in the specifications. Without this inclusion there is no specialist inspector to look at this area, no verbal feedback to the Head of Department, and no written report on the subject for governors and parents. Squires concludes (p. 198):

'Any subject which is not inspected is not likely to be high on a school's list of priorities with regard to funding and staff development . . . How will good practice in economics and business studies receive much deserved commendation if it is marginalized in the inspection process?'

Her recommendation is that teachers should request their governors to include business studies or economics in the school's specification, and indeed there have been examples around the country of 11–18 schools paying extra for business education to be inspected. Actual experience in the last year also suggests that, where a business education specialist is part of an OfSTED team, then business education is sometimes inspected and reported upon, even when not part of the tender specifications. But the coverage has been very patchy.

In Tameside, an authority with fourteen 11–16 schools and one 11–18 school, eight schools were inspected between January 1994 and May 1995. Of these, only one school received a full inspection and report on business and vocational education, and this was the 11–18 institution. This was a constructive and useful summary written by a subject specialist, but it was included despite the fact that business education did not appear in the specifications. In two schools, GCSE business studies was mentioned within design/technology or information technology. Indeed, in the second school the high success rate at GCSE Business Studies was mentioned under 'Standards of achievement' as well as under 'Information technology', but there was no separate report explaining why standards were so high. In the remaining five schools, the inspection report made no mention of business studies, despite its presence in Key Stage 4 in all the schools, either as a full GCSE or as a combined course. A summary table is shown in Figure 27.2.

At the time of writing this chapter, the OfSTED Framework is undergoing its third revision. At Key Stage 4, since the freeing up of provision following the Dearing Report, a more flexible approach to inspecting subjects is to be adopted from April 1996, so that popular courses in business studies, economics and other vocational areas will be included in specifications and are more likely to be inspected. At Key Stage 4 one extra day is to be added to the inspection time to facilitate the inspection of the non compulsory curriculum and the vocational curriculum. One extra day is also being included for the GNVQ Part One Pilot. Schools which only teach business studies or economics in Key Stage 4 receive no extra time beyond the above, but schools teaching business studies/economics may receive up to two extra days if there are in total six or more classes of a reasonable size. Up to four extra days are also to be included in specifications for inspection of vocational courses in the sixth form, depending upon the number of students following such courses. Guidance notes on the inspection of GNVQs at Key Stage 4 and post-16 in schools are being included in the revised OfSTED Framework and there is an intention to produce guidance notes on business studies and economics.

These developments should improve the likelihood of departments being inspected in 11–18 schools, although in 11–16 institutions GCSE Business Studies and Economics may be again overlooked. Guidance documentation should improve the consistency and quality of inspection in business education, although inspection by non-specialists will remain a major issue with this area of the curriculum.

School	Age range	Subjects offered	Separate report?	Mention in D&T/IT	
A	11–18	GCSE BS A level BS C&G DVE	Yes	–	–
B	11–16	GCSE BS/IS	No	No	No
C	11–16	GCSE BS GCSE BS/D&T	No	No	No
D	11–16	GCSE BS	No	No	No
E	11–16	GCSE BS	No	No	No
F	11–16	GCSE BS/D&T	No	No	No
G	11–16	GCSE BS	No	No	Yes
H	11–16	GCSE BS/D&T	No	Yes	No

Figure 27.2 OfSTED inspections of business education in Tameside LEA, January 1994 to May 1995

Inspection the FEFC way

Inspection of post–16 provision by the Further Education Funding Council has several similarities to the OfSTED way, but also some significant differences.

The first similarity is the emphasis on the external assessment of quality. In a circular called *Assessing Achievement*, FEFC (1993, p. 7) saw the purpose of this external quality assessment as being to ensure that:

'. . . *provision must not only be fit for its purpose but should aim for high standards and excellence, should satisfy and involve the customer, should encourage continual improvement, and should enable the government to be assured that the large sums of money devoted to this sector of education are being well spent.*'

Thus, as in OfSTED, there is an emphasis upon improvement through inspection as well as a stronger emphasis than OfSTED on external accountability.

A second similarity is that there is a single inspection framework. Each inspection report will set out the inspection team's judgements of the strengths and weaknesses of a range of aspects of college provision (Figure 27.3).

Whilst there is a single framework for inspecting colleges, the guidelines are much less detailed than for the OfSTED inspection process. This is deliberate because the FEFC recognizes that colleges have different experiences and

- *Responsiveness and range of provision*: how well the college responds to national and local targets and needs, and the range of programmes it offers to meet the needs of all possible learners.

- *Governance and management*: how effectively the governors and management develop, implement and monitor whole-college policies and the efficient management of resources.

- *Students' recruitment, guidance and support*: the appropriateness of arrangements to support and monitor students before entry and on course.

- *Teaching and the promotion of learning*: assessing the quality of planning and delivery of programmes and the quality of student learning and relationships with students.

- *Students' achievements*: assessing student achievements in relation to specific programme targets and a range of core skills.

- *Quality assurance*: how effectively quality is monitored at whole-college and programme level.

- *Resources – staffing; equipment and learning resources; accommodation*: the efficient and effective use of a college's resources and their impact on student learning.

Source: *FEFC Assessing Achievement Circular 93/28*, 1993, p.15

Figure 27.3 FEFC's inspection framework: aspects for inspection

traditions in delivering programmes; thus it wants to keep the framework sufficiently flexible to allow for this. In the same way there are more opportunities for colleges being inspected to be involved in and influence the process than in OfSTED. For example, colleges are asked to provide inspectors with reports on quality arising from their own quality-assurance procedures, and the college's own assessment of its strengths and weaknesses may well influence the final inspection report. A senior member of staff will also participate fully in the team inspection.

A further similarity with OfSTED is in the main sources of evidence that inspectors use as the basis for their judgements – observation of delivery, looking at students' work, discussions with students, staff, governors and members of the community, and looking at college documents. But in the process of the inspection, and in the nature of the judgements that are made, the FEFC way differs considerably from OfSTED's. This means that the inspection experience of business studies and economics teachers in colleges may be quite different from that of their colleagues in schools.

A team of inspectors, led by a full-time inspector employed by the FEFC, will carry out the four-yearly inspection of whole-college provision and report on strengths and weaknesses against the headings shown in Figure 27.3. At the same time, specialist inspectors will look at different programme areas – including those for Business, which in 1994 was the second largest programme area in the FE sector with 17 per cent of enrolments (FEFC, 1994a). Whilst their findings will contribute to the overall judgements about the college, they will also produce a written note on the programme area and an assessment grade, based primarily on two aspects of the FEFC framework (teaching and the promotion of learning, and the students' achievements in that curriculum area) but also on other aspects.

The assessment grades are a particular feature of the FEFC process. They are used to summarize judgements on the balance between strengths and weaknesses:

- *Grade 1* is provision that has many strengths and very few weaknesses.

- *Grade 2* is provision in which the strengths clearly outweigh the weaknesses.

- *Grade 3* is provision with a balance of strengths and weaknesses.

- *Grade 4* is provision in which the weaknesses clearly outweigh the strengths.

- *Grade 5* is provision that has many weaknesses and very few strengths.

The grade that a programme receives is likely to be an important public measure of its success, just as the grades that a college receives across the seven aspects in Figure 27.3 are important public indicators of whole-college

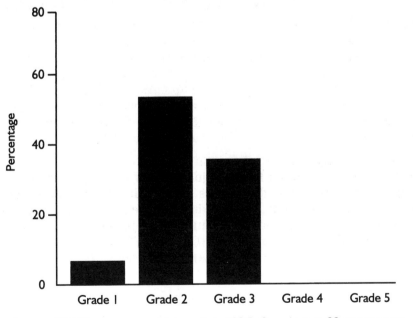

Source: FEFC Inspectorate database (July 1994). Sample size: 88 assessments

Figure 27.4 Business inspection grades 1993/4

363

strengths and weaknesses. In the 1993–94 inspection cycle no Business programme received a grade below 3 out of 88 inspections, and over 60 per cent received a grade one or 2 (see figure 27.4).

Clearly, in the FEFC system, business education programmes are inspected and reported upon, and up to now have been given a high rating. This is a clear contrast to experience under OfSTED inspections. Teachers of A level Business Studies/Economics and GNVQ Business in sixth-form colleges or FE colleges are able to compare their own internal assessments of their department with the views of specialist external assessors on a regular basis. Teachers of GCSE and A level Business Studies/Economics and GNVQ Business in 11–16 or 11–18 schools do not get the same level of quality assessment from OfSTED.

What is less clear in the FEFC system is the weighting that is given to the various aspects that are inspected in a programme when it comes to the final judgement. In the OfSTED system, standards of achievement and quality of learning are the central features of inspecting a subject, with other factors only important if they make a significant positive or negative impact on the first two. In the FEFC system the quality of accommodation for business, or the quality of links with the business community, would appear to have equal importance to the quality of planning, the quality of learning or the standards achieved in business. As with OfSTED, published criteria for quality in a business education programme are not yet available, although the FEFC Chief Inspectors' *Annual Reports* do give some pointers to quality provision, as do specific reports on A and AS level GCE qualifications (FEFC, 1994b), and GNVQ provision by the FEFC (1994c) and by OfSTED (1994b).

What is quality in Business and Economics Education?

This and the following section apply the broad criteria of assessment to the delivery of business education, and identify some review questions that might be useful for business education departments preparing for inspection. The focus for this section is quality in terms of three central aspects: standards of achievement; quality of learning; and quality of teaching.

Standards of achievement

For students following GCSE or A level Business Studies/Economics courses, standards should be judged according to the criteria and requirements of the validating body, contained within the subject syllabuses. For GNVQ Business, standards should be judged in relation to the national standard determined by the subject lead body through the National Council for Vocational Qualifications (NCVQ).

During the process of inspection, the standards of two groups of students will be assessed: those on the course during the inspection, and those who completed courses in the previous year(s). For the second group, both OfSTED and

FEFC inspectors will look at the success rates in public examinations and compare them with national averages.

For example, for GCSE Business Studies the national pass rate at Grades A–C in 1994 was 46.8 per cent, and for GCSE Economics it was 52.1 per cent (DFE, 1994). If a department's results from the previous year are below these figures, this would suggest that standards in relation to national expectations are below average. If they are above 47 or 52 per cent, then this would suggest that standards are above average. OfSTED inspectors also receive information about LEA averages for a subject and could therefore comment in relation to other schools in the local authority. A similar analysis can be carried out for A level passes, and national figures for GNVQ passes are becoming available.

The OfSTED and FEFC frameworks also both allow judgements to be refined in relation to the abilities of the pupils embarking on the courses. OfSTED allows a second judgement to be made taking into account pupils' abilities and previous attainments. FEFC talks more briefly about targets for success rates and added-value ratings. Thus it is important that business education departments are able to show clear evidence about the attainment of students embarking on their courses if they wish to demonstrate improving standards in relation to both national norms and the abilities of their students by the completion of their courses.

The judgement of standards for students on courses, largely done through observation of lessons and by reviewing the work of students, is a more complex judgement. Central to both the OfSTED and the FEFC criteria for judging standards is the development of appropriate knowledge, understanding and skills in the subject – the evidence of what pupils know, understand and can do. In relation to business education, appropriate knowledge, understanding and skills are derived from the GCSE criteria, from the A level Cores and from the national vocational standards for Business. In a recent publication, the National Association of Advisers and Inspectors of Business and Economics Education attempted to summarize the criteria for evaluating standards achieved by business and economics education students in schools (NAAIBEE, 1995, p. 2). This is shown in Figure 27.4.

There are weaknesses here both in terms of the breadth of knowledge and understanding (which seem more appropriate for a GCSE than for an A level course) and in the range of skills. The NAAIBEE criteria omit the skills of applying relevant knowledge to a range of situations, of selecting and analysing relevant economic and business information, and of making reasoned judgements. The best guide for knowledge, understanding and skills has to be the syllabus and assessment criteria of the particular course being inspected; just as for National Curriculum subjects the attainment targets and programmes of study are the base upon which standards are judged.

In addition to standards achieved in relation to the subject itself, both OfSTED and FEFC identify broader competencies that should also be evident in the work of students. OfSTED assesses skills within reading, writing, speaking and

- Knowledge and understanding of:
  - the relationship between business and economic activity and the environment in which it takes place;
  - the interdependence and dynamics within business and economic behaviour in both national and international contexts;
  - the structure, organization and control of the main forms of business;
  - the basic economic problem of scarcity and choice and how production and consumption decisions are made.
- The effective use of business and economics terminology, concepts and methods.
- The use of economic theory as a tool to analyse business problems.
- An understanding of the nature and significance of attitudes and values in business and economic decision-making.
- Competence in communication, numeracy and information technology skills together with skills of critical understanding, investigation and problem-solving.

Figure 27.5 Criteria for judging standards of achievement in business and economics education

listening, number and information technology. FEFC assesses the extent to which students enjoy their studies, their enthusiasm for speaking and writing about their subject, their effectiveness as members of a group, their competence and safety in practical work, and their ability to develop study skills, mathematical and information technology skills and other core skills which form a part of their learning programme. Business education provides an excellent vehicle for the development of these broad competencies, and departments need to make this explicit in both their departmental aims and in their schemes of work and everyday classroom practice.

Quality of learning

The FEFC criteria do not look explicitly at quality of learning. Some aspects, especially attitudes to learning, appear under 'Students' achievements' and have been discussed above; some aspects appear under 'Teaching and the promotion of learning' with an emphasis on what teachers should do to ensure good-quality learning. The present OfSTED criteria, however, place quality of learning as one of the main elements to be reported upon following an inspection.

OfSTED judges quality of learning using three main criteria: progress; learning skills; and attitudes to learning. In relation to business education:

- *Quality in progress* is to be judged in terms of the extent to which students are making progress in the knowledge, skills and understanding associated with business and economics. What have students learnt as a result of that activity?

- *Quality in learning skills* relates to a range of attributes:
  - how well students can apply their business/economics knowledge and understanding to different contexts;
  - the ability of students to select the correct tools, models etc. for business/economic analysis;
  - the ability of students to select and organize resources for learning appropriately;
  - students' willingness to ask questions about the business and economic data they are using;
  - students' ability to take decisions using business and economic data;
  - how far students understand the purpose of activities being undertaken;
  - their ability to evaluate their own work, make suggestions for improvement and learn from their mistakes (e.g. how they would change the way they carried out an Enterprise activity).

- *Quality in attitudes* can be seen as more generic across all learning: how well students respond to challenges, keep on task, work with commitment and enjoyment, collaborate and cooperate or work independently where appropriate, persevere, show initiative and take responsibility. In business and economics lessons where learning is active and where a variety of learning styles are employed, there would be plenty of opportunities for students to demonstrate such attributes.

Quality of teaching

The criteria for quality of teaching in the FEFC framework go slightly further than those in the OfSTED framework as they incorporate assessment within 'Teaching and the promotion of learning'. The OfSTED framework separates teaching from assessment, an artificial division which the proposed revised framework for 1996 may well change. Under quality of teaching, taking the two frameworks together there are two broad quality categories: planning; and the delivery and assessment of learning. In relation to business education:

- *Quality in planning* would require that:
  - clearly identified aims and objectives are understood by the students;
  - schemes of work ensure that aims and objectives are achieved and that syllabus, programmes of study, performance criteria and range are adequately covered;
  - the differing abilities of students are planned for, including extension and support material;
  - resources, including IT, are planned for and suitable for the students;
  - opportunities for assessment are built into planning.

- *Quality in the delivery and assessment of learning* would require:
  - good teacher knowledge and understanding of business/economics;
  - appropriate pace and level of delivery which meets the needs and abilities of students;
  - ensuring that the interests of all students are engaged and sustained;

- high expectations of students (high but attainable challenges);
- a variety of appropriate teaching strategies to be employed, including the opportunity for students to learn through direct and practical experiences of the business and economic world;
- efficient use of learning resources, including IT to reinforce learning;
- good relationships which promote learning;
- the use of assessment to give students regular, positive feedback which helps them make progress;
- that work is set and marked regularly, consistently and fairly;
- that assessments are devised at an appropriate standard and clearly aligned to the assessment objectives of GCSE/GCE or the performance criteria and range of GNVQ Business;
- that students are encouraged to assess and review their own performance and strive for improvement.

Reviewing your own provision in business education

Because the OfSTED and FEFC frameworks are public documents, it is possible for departments to review their own practice prior to any external evaluation. The following questions (based on Squires 1993) are likely to form the basis of the oral questioning carried out by subject inspectors during an OfSTED inspection, but they are also a useful set of questions for post-16 departments of business and economics education to consider.

Standards of achievement

1. What is the department's view of the standards achieved in Key Stage 4 and post-16 in relation to national standards and in relation to students' ability?

2. What baseline assessments are carried out so that improvements in standards can be measured?

3. What strategies/targets exist for improvement?

4. How are standards monitored throughout the department?

5. What standards are being achieved in literacy/communication, numeracy, IT and other core skills within the department?

Curriculum quality and range

1. Is there coherence and provision for progression in the courses on offer?

2. How is short-term/long-term planning organized to ensure consistent syllabus coverage?

3. Do schemes of work exist for every syllabus being delivered?

4. Do staff teaching a particular syllabus share the same scheme of work?

5. Do schemes of work show how the syllabus is being delivered (e.g. pupil activities, expected outcomes, differentiation, assessment opportunities, resources required)?

6. How well does the curriculum provision provide for pupils of different abilities, gender, ethnicity and social circumstances?

Assessment, recording and reporting

1. Does the department have an assessment policy?

2. Is the policy consistent with the school's policy?

3. Is there internal consistency in marking?

4. How does the department ensure that assessment judgements are consistent with external standards?

5. Is assessment positive and does it provide constructive feedback for students?

6. Are consistent assessment records kept?

7. Are all statutory reporting requirements adhered to?

8. Are arrangements for the provision of evidence for external validation/ moderation satisfactory?

Special educational needs

1. Does practice in the subject reflect school SEN policy?

2. How are the exceptional needs of pupils met in the delivery of the subject?

3. How is equal access to the curriculum ensured for pupils with special needs?

Management and administration

1. Is there a designated subject coordinator with defined responsibilities?

2. Is the management structure clear in the department?

3. Are regular meetings held and minuted?

4. How are departmental decisions made and communicated?

5. Do staff work cooperatively?

6. Does the department have a policy; and, if so, how is it developed?

7. Does the department have a development plan; and, if so, how is it developed?

8. Are resources matched to the development plan?

9. How is delivery of the subject monitored across the school?

Resources

1. How is staff development organized?

2. What subject-specific INSET has been attended?

3. Do all staff in the department get access to staff development?

4. What level of funding has the department received?

5. Is funding adequate?

6. What system(s) exist to access funding?

7. Are the learning resources in the department adequate in quality and quantity?

8. Is the accommodation adequate for delivery of the curriculum?

9. Is there sufficient access to IT resources for students?

Other issues

1. What contribution does the subject make to the spiritual, moral, social and cultural development of students?

2. What links with the local community and local industry exist and how are they used to raise standards?

3. How is direct experience of the workplace used to enhance learning?

4. How does the subject contribute to the careers education of students?

5. How is good behaviour and discipline maintained within the department?

Conclusion

Ensuring quality in business and economics education requires departments to look at both the quality of what they are providing directly to students through their subject programmes, and the enhanced quality of education they are providing which students may be using in other areas of the curriculum and in their adult lives.

For example, students carrying out market research for a GNVQ Business assignment will also be developing research skills that can be applied in any social science. Students drawing up a theoretical business plan for an A level project will go through the same processes as a college leaver applying for a small-business grant from a bank. Students calculating the retail price index learn to apply important numerate skills.

Whilst inspection is a stressful process for any department, it does provide good departments with an opportunity to demonstrate the quality of their provision and the value they add across the institution to the quality of students' education. And it provides poorer departments with an agenda for improvement so that they may become good departments. External inspections should be seen as developmental, and should also help departments develop their own methodology towards self-monitoring and review so that regular evaluation becomes built into the working cycle of a department.

It is to be hoped that changes to be brought in to the OfSTED process from 1996 will give all school Business Education departments access to the same quality inspection process that is available to departments in the FE sector.

References

Department for Education (1994). *Statistics for Education: Public Examinations GCSE and GCE,* London, HMSO.

Further Education Funding Council (1993). *Circular 28/93: Assessing Achievement,* September 1993.

Further Education Funding Council (1994a). Chief Inspectors' Annual Report 1994.

Further Education Funding Council (1994b). GCE A Level and AS Level Qualifications, December 1994.

Further Education Funding Council (1994c). *GNVQ in Colleges,* 1994.

National Association of Advisers and Inspectors of Business and Economics Education (NAAIBEE) (1995). *Inspection of Business Studies and Economics in Schools.*

Office for Standards in Education (1994a). *Handbook for the Inspection of Schools,* London, HMSO, 1994.

Office for Standards in Education (1994b). *GNVQ in Schools,* London, HMSO, 1994.

Office for Standards in Education (1995). *Handbook for the Inspection of Schools*, London, HMSO, 1995.

Squires, S. (1993). 'The new inspection framework and its implications for business and economics education', in *Economics and Business Education,* vol. 1, part 1, no. 1, pp 198–200.

End note

As mentioned, this chapter was written during the third revision of the OfSTED Framework. However, the new Inspection Schedule has been included as Figure 27.1.

Index

Entries in this index are restricted to substantial references in the text.

References to authors of academic works are not included in this index. Details of authors referred to in the text are given at the end of the chapter(s) in which they feature.